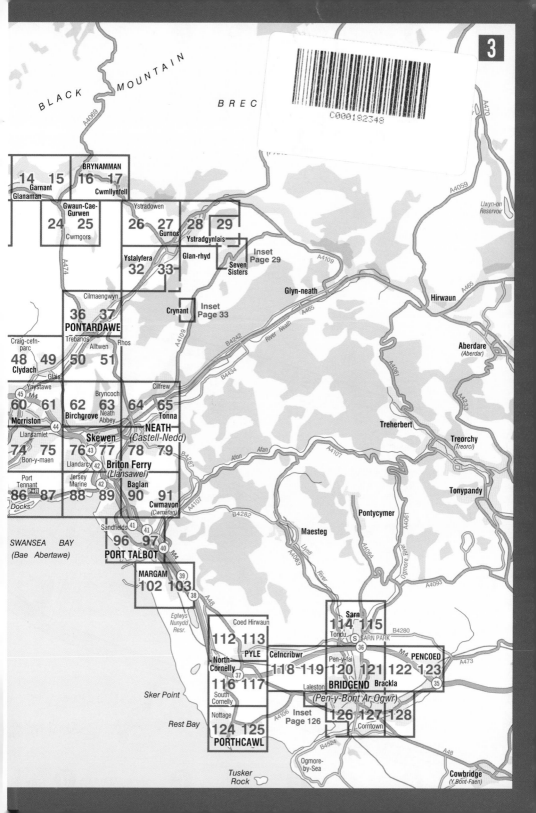

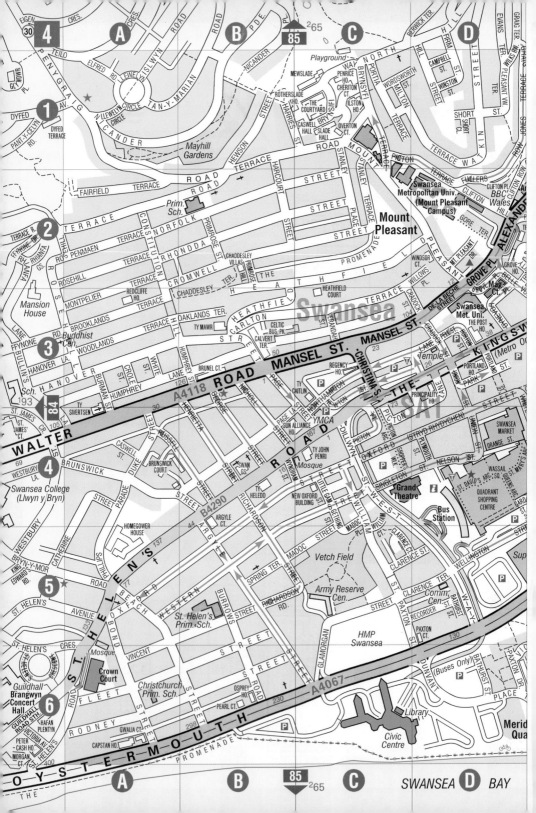

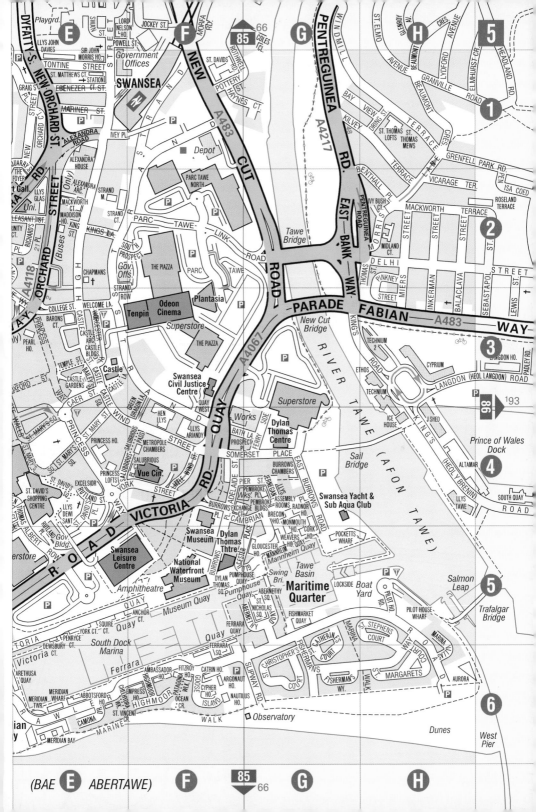

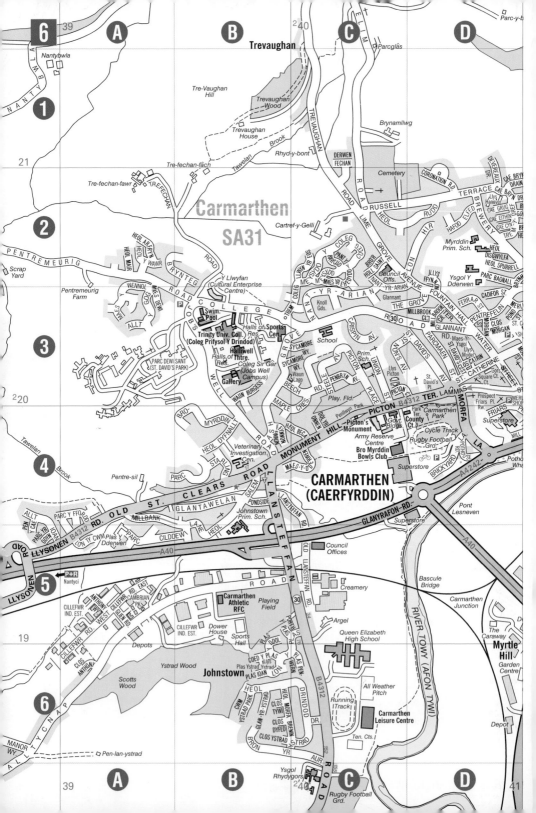

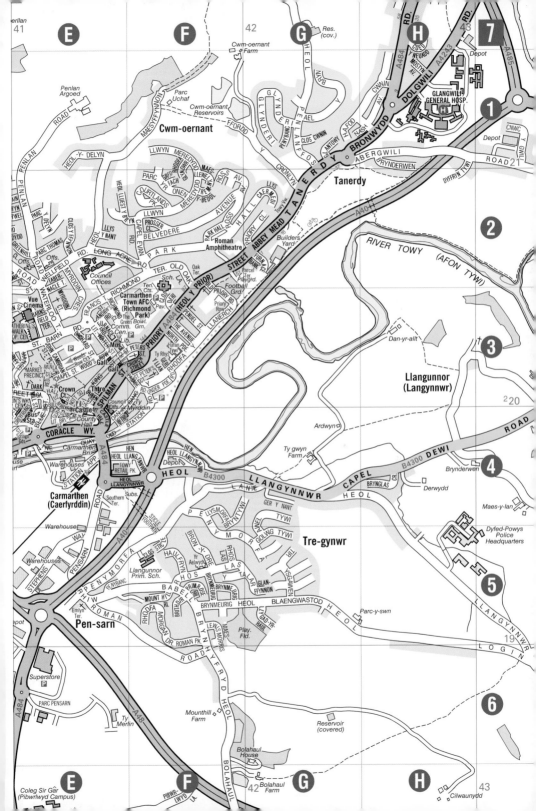

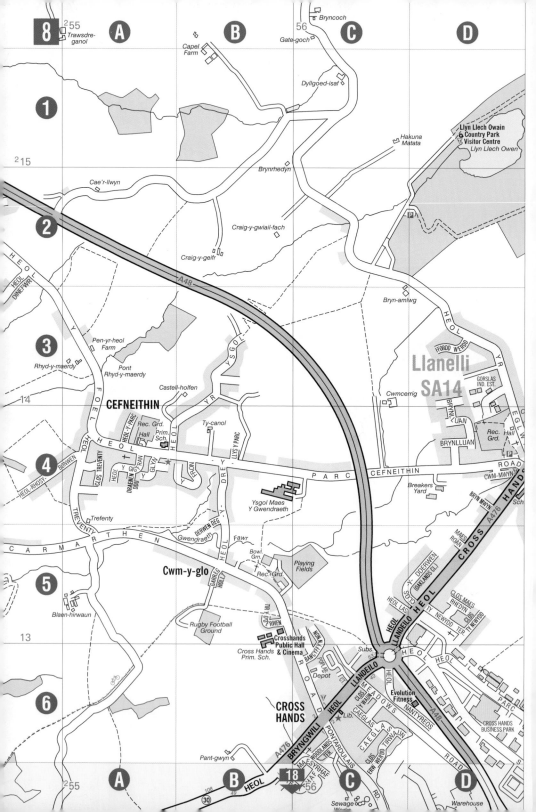

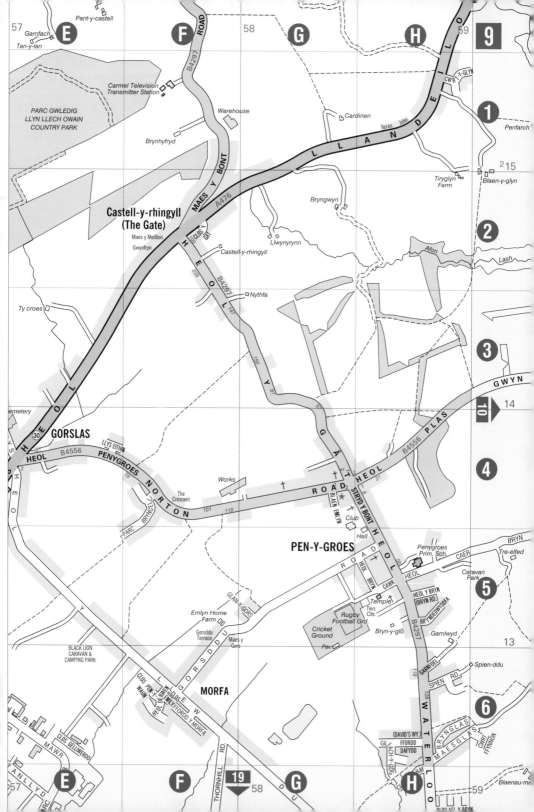

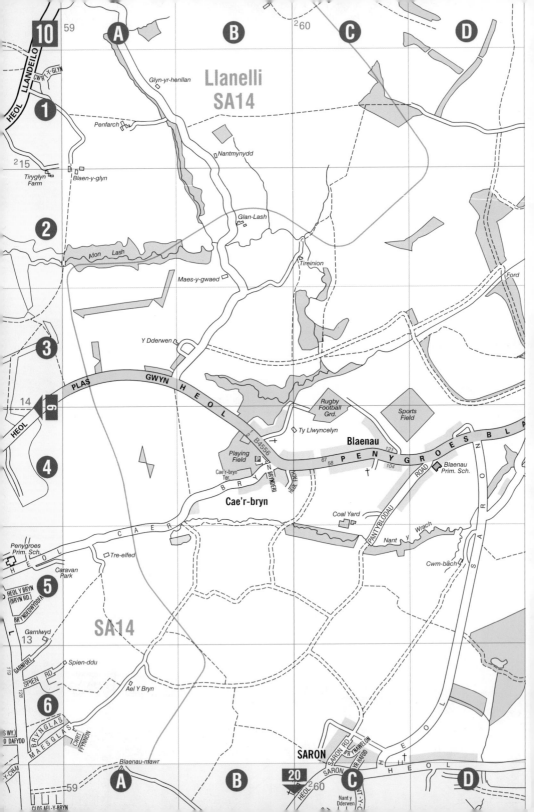

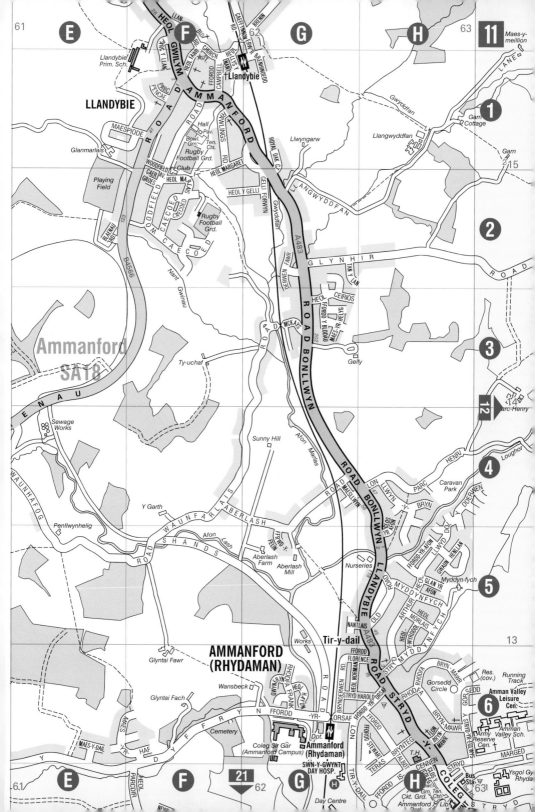

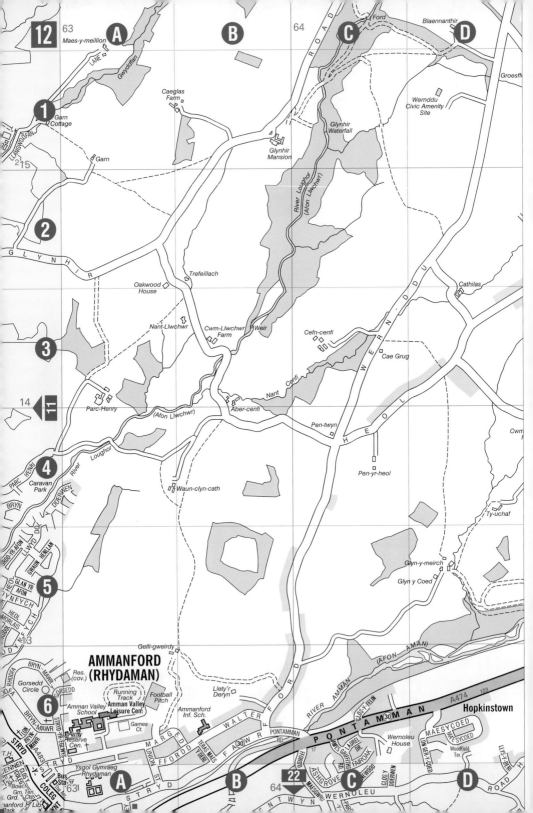

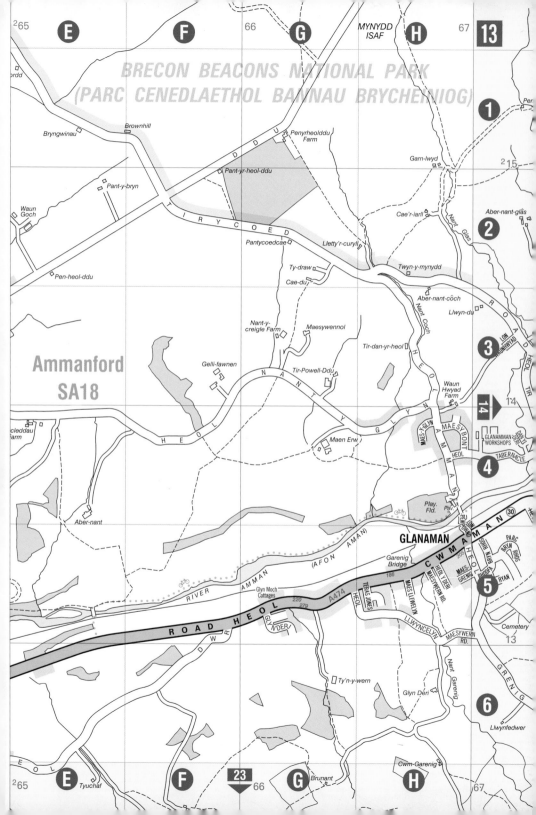

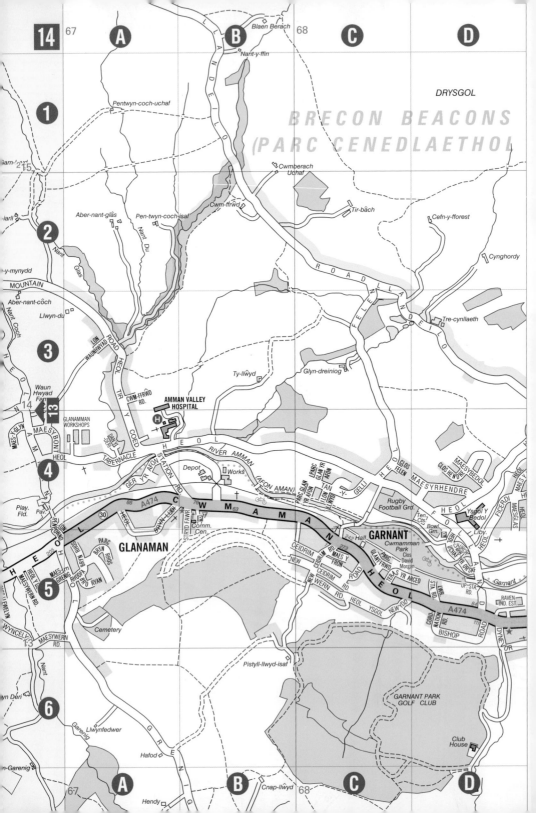

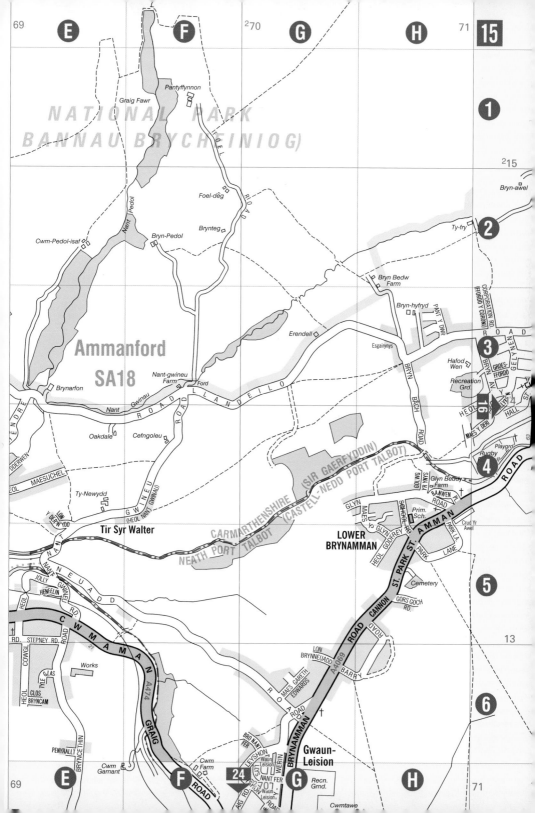

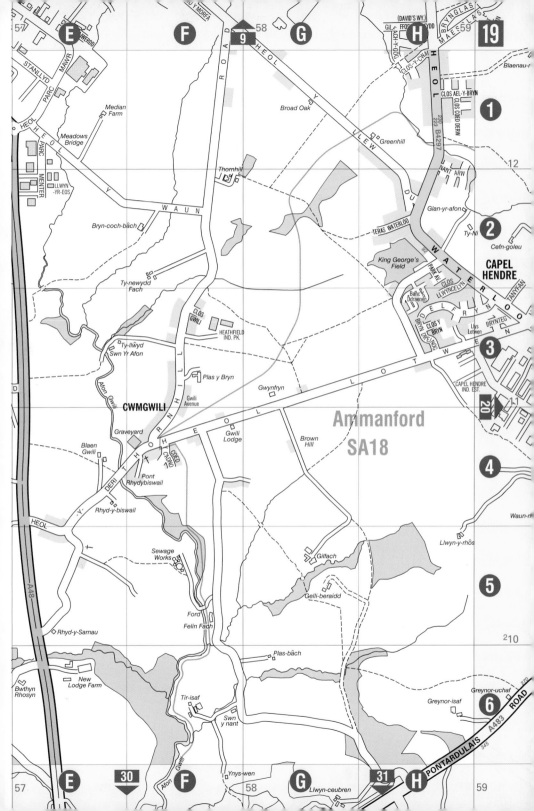

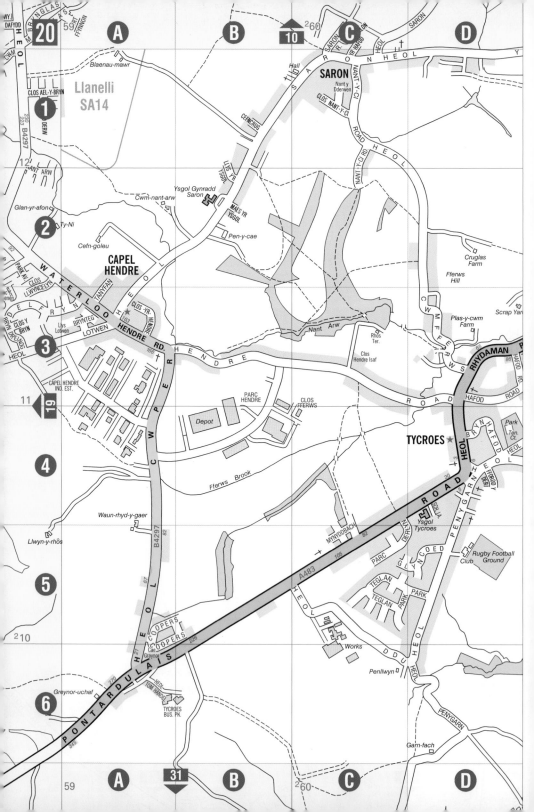

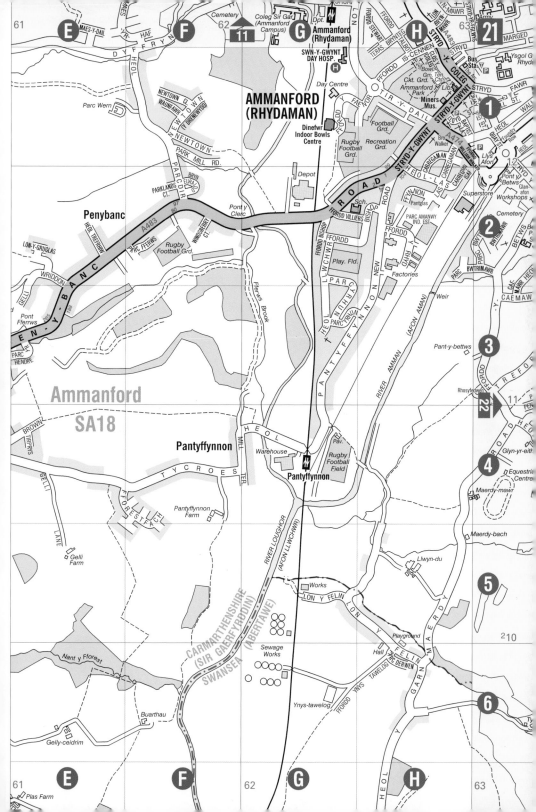

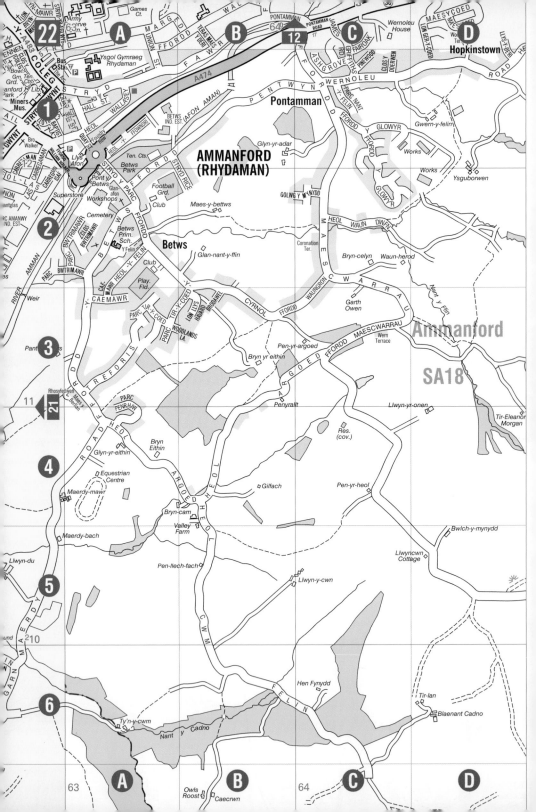

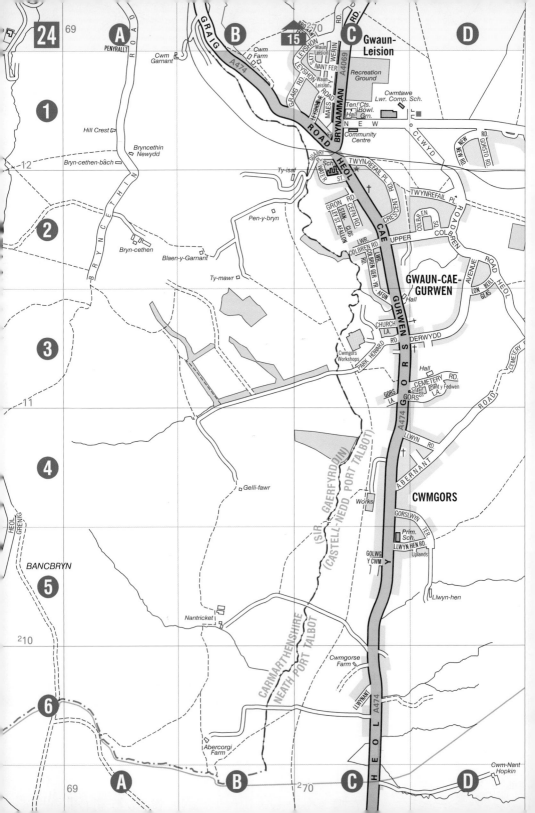

**1**

Cwmnanthir Ter.

ST. DAVIDS RD.
ROAD
BROOK
LAUDERDALE TER.

**TAIRGWAITH**
Hall
HARLECH TER.
KING STREET
12

MORRISTON PL.
LLWYNCELYN
Prim. Sch.
GARTH RD.
RD.

Trotting Track

EDWARD ROAD

**2**

Playing Fields

**Ammanford**
**SA18**

Cemetery

Penlle rfedwen

**3**

H.B.

11

**4**

**Swansea**

**5**

**SA9**

²10

**SA8**

**6**

Fforch Egel Farm

Blaen-egel-fawr

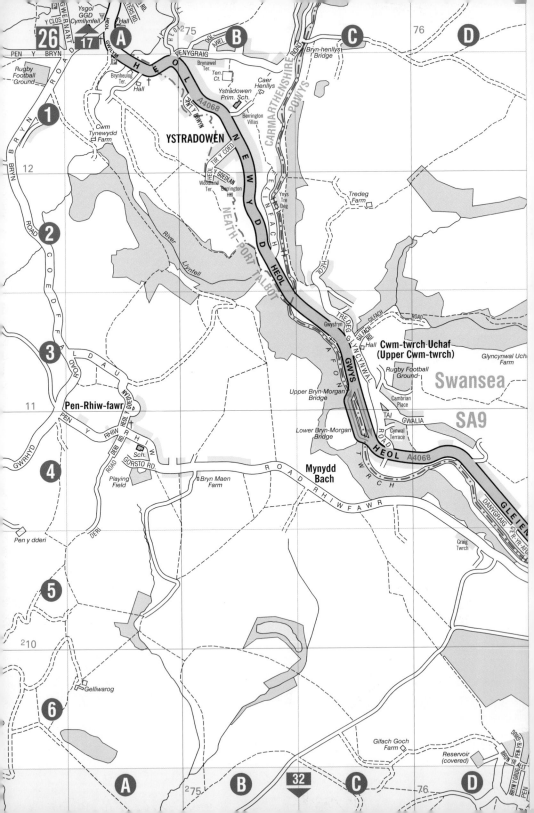

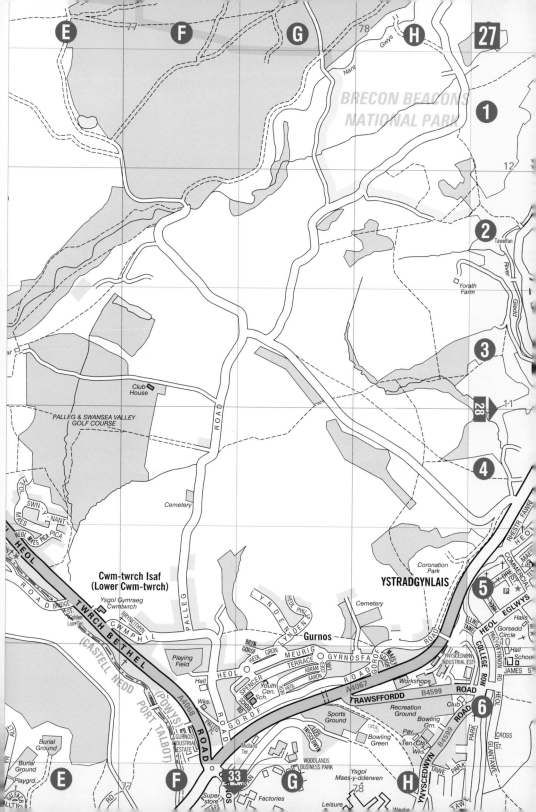

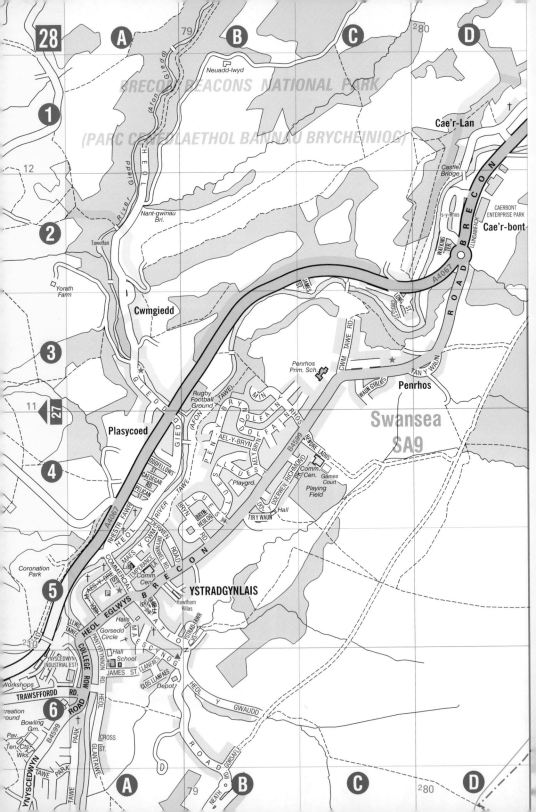

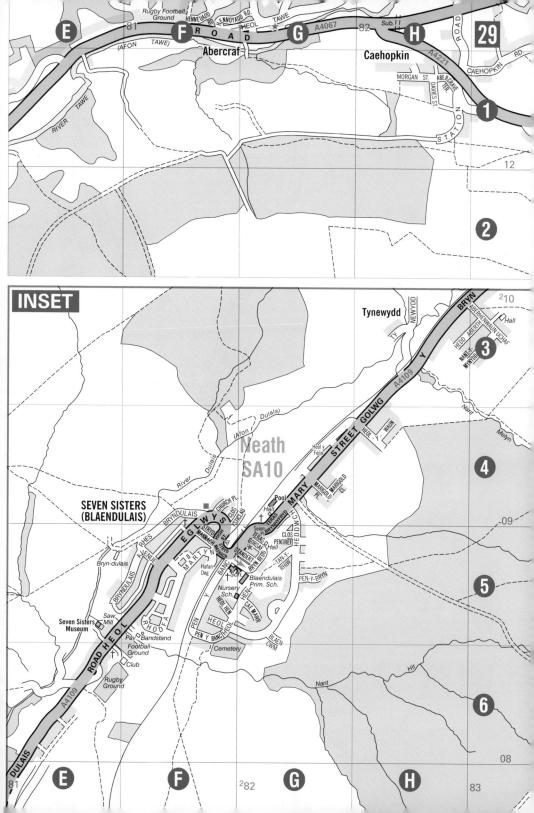

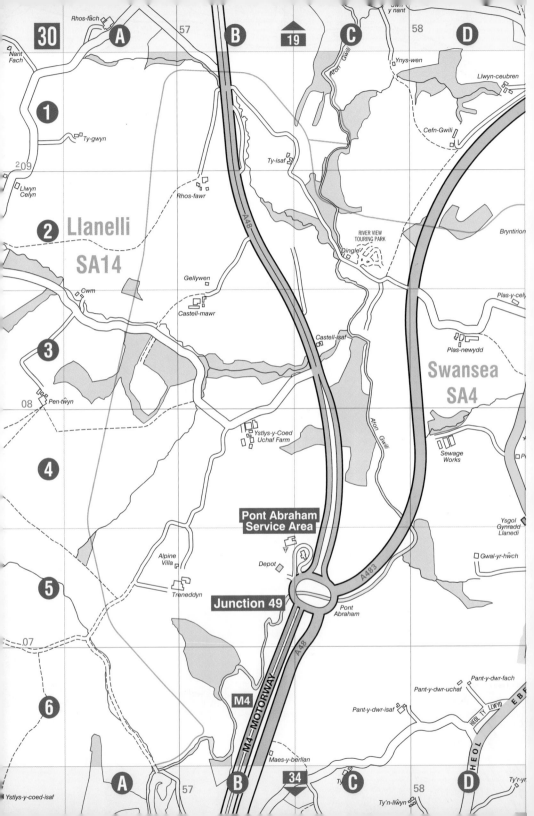

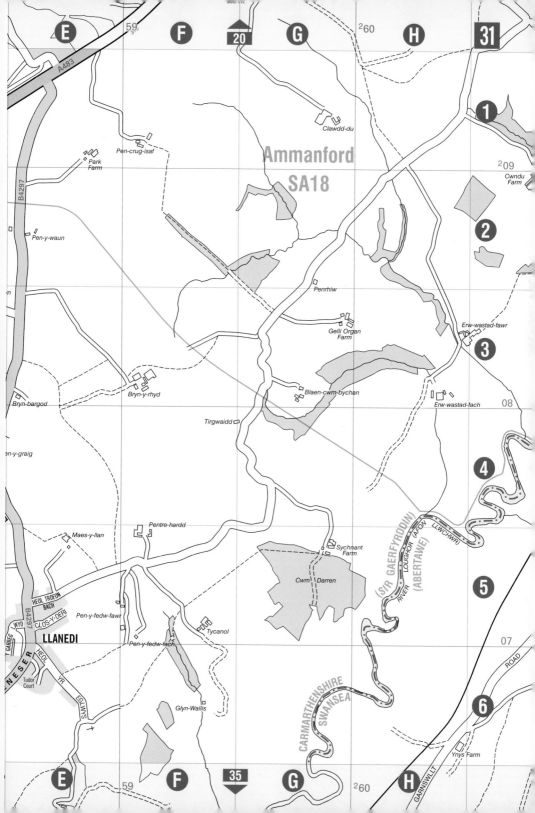

**Ammanford**
**SA18**

Clawdd-du

Pen-crug-isaf

Park Farm

Pen-y-waun

Penrhiw

Gelli Organ Farm

Erw-wastad-fawr

Blaen-cwm-bychan

Erw-wastad-fach

Bryn-y-rhyd

Bryn-bargod

Tirgwaidd

...en-y-graig

Maes-y-llan

Pentre-hardd

Sychnant Farm

RIVER LOUGHOR (AFON LLWCHWR)
(SŶR GAERFYRDDIN)
(ABERTAWE)

Cwm Darren

Pen-y-fedw-fawr

Tycanol

HEOL TROEON BACH

CLOS-Y-DERI

LLANEDI

Pen-y-fedw-fach

Tudor Court

Glyn-Wallis

CARMARTHENSHIRE
SWANSEA

ROAD

Ynys Farm

GARNSWLLT

Cwndu Farm

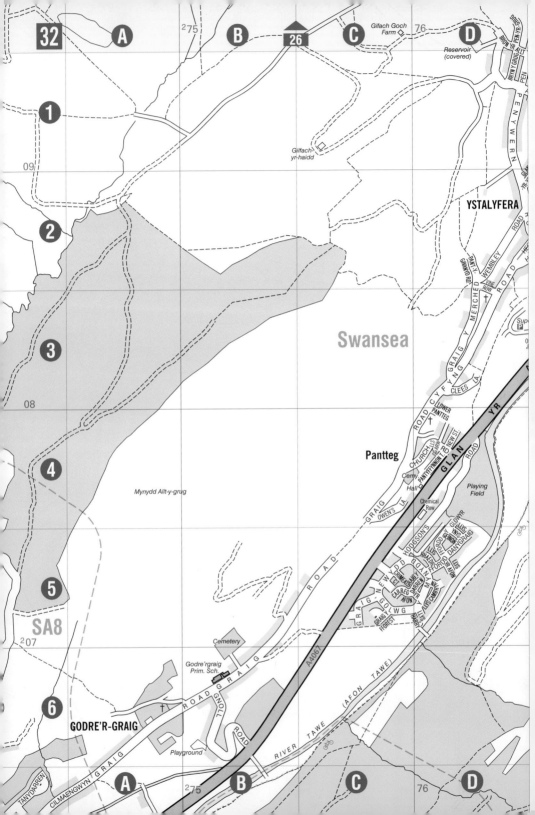

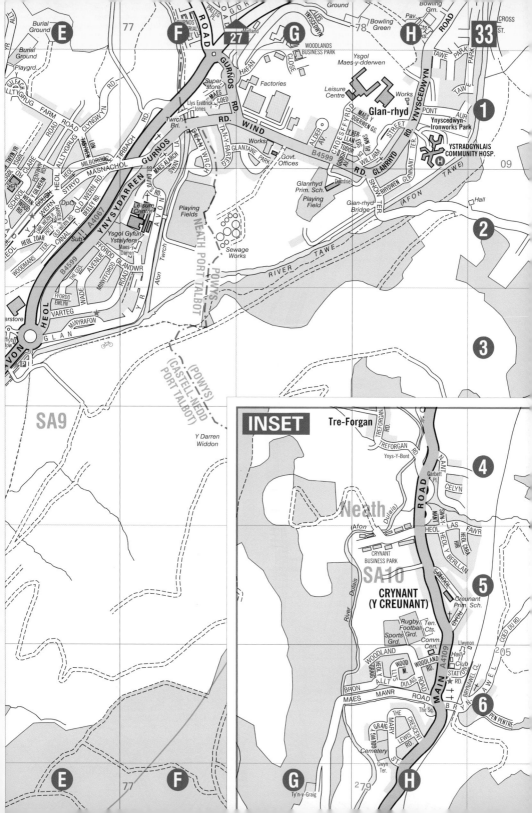

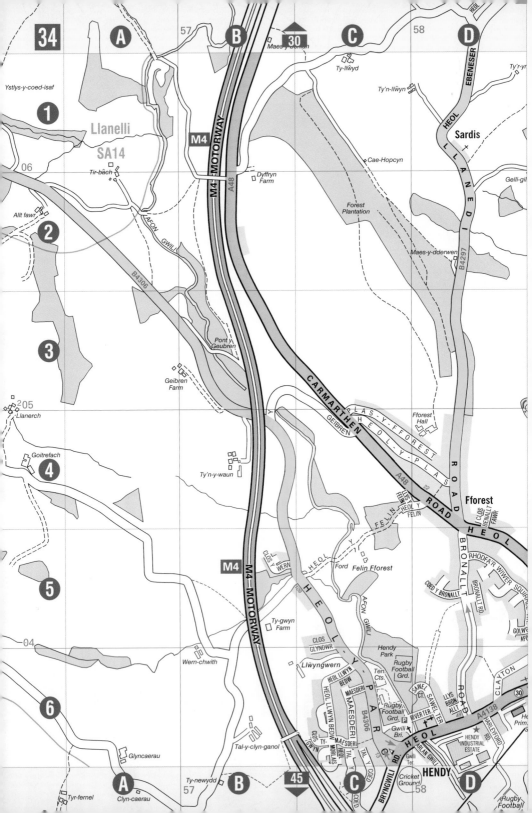

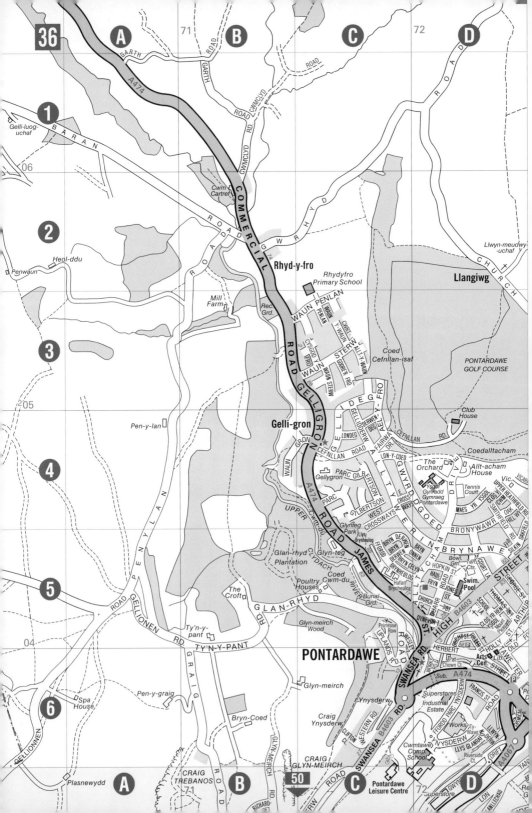

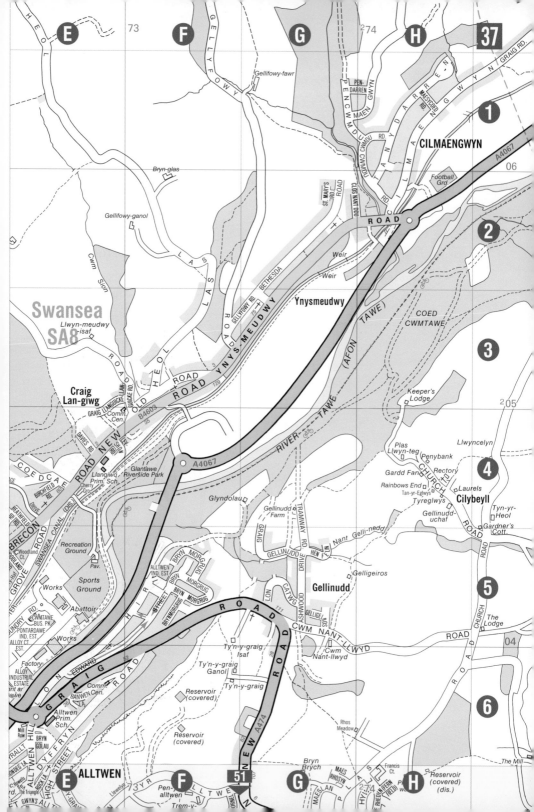

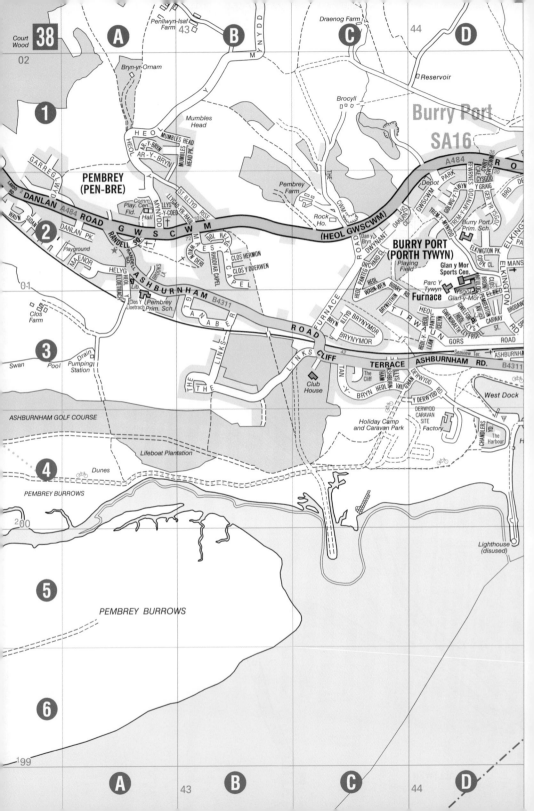

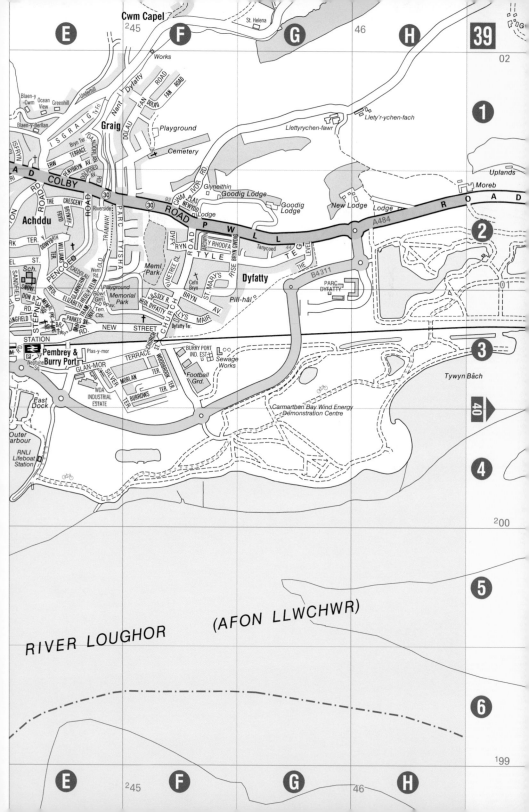

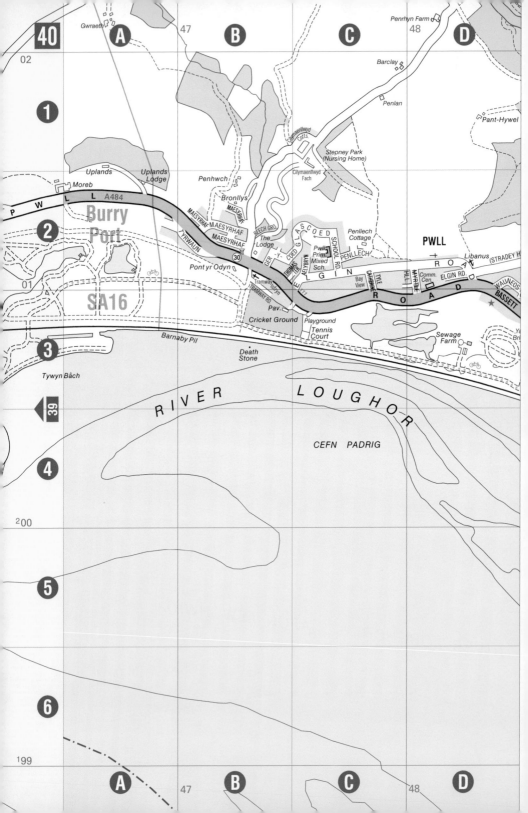

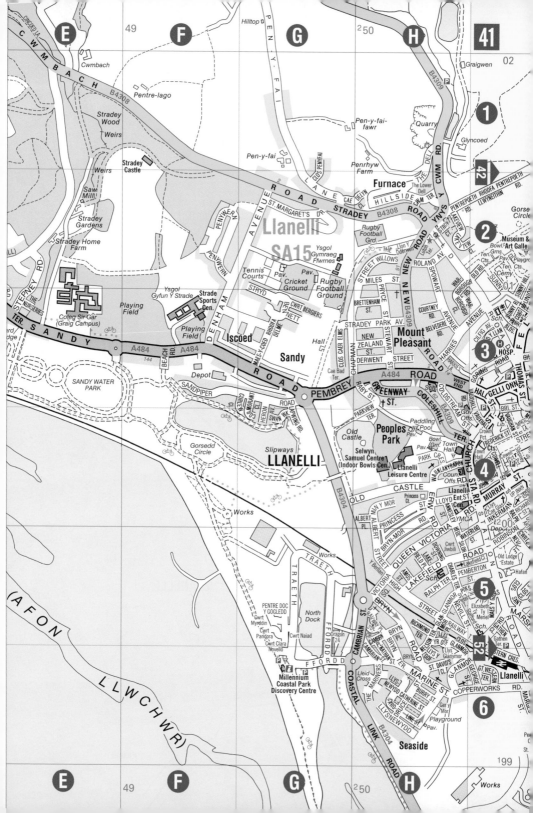

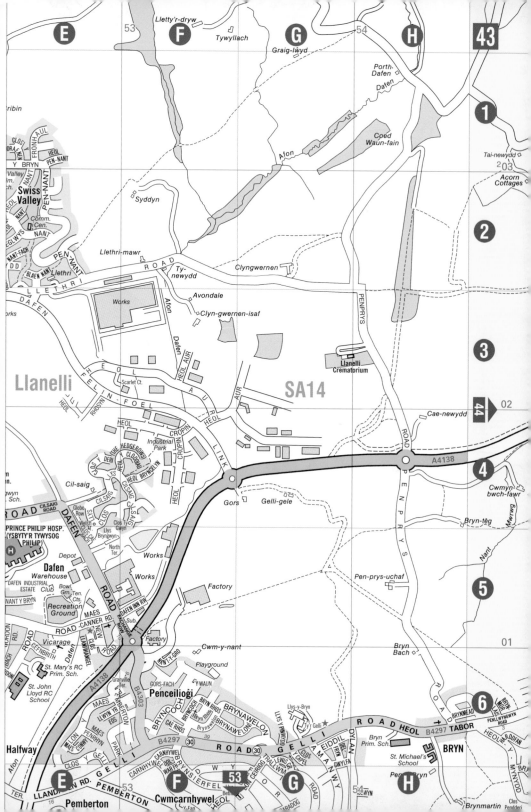

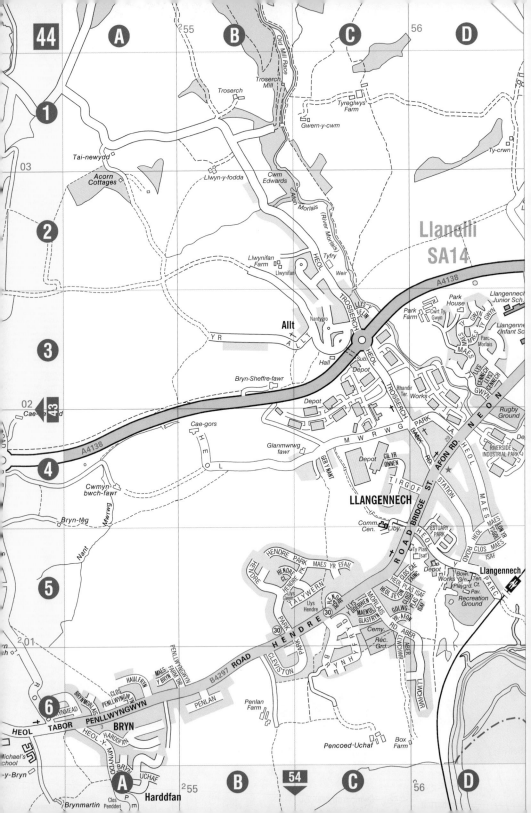

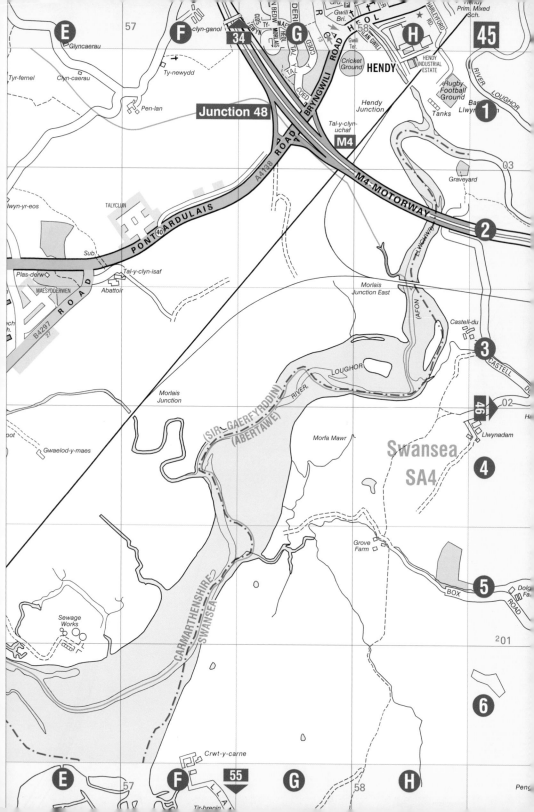

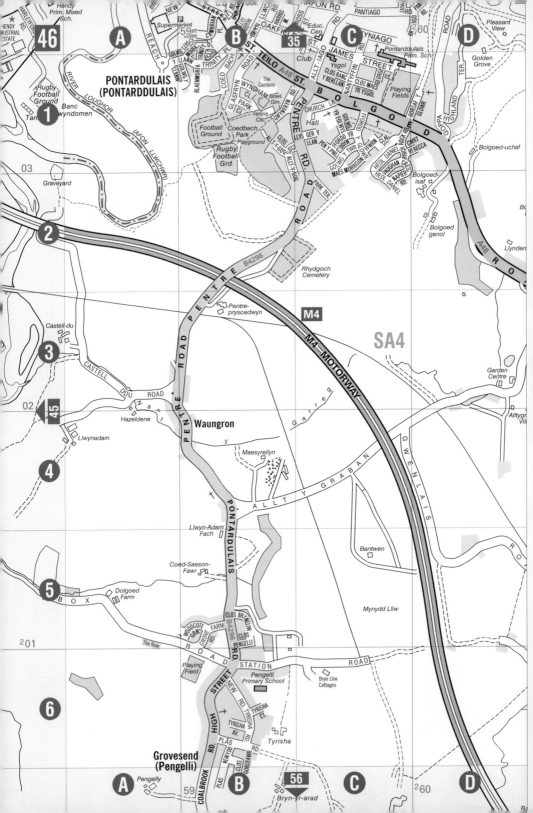

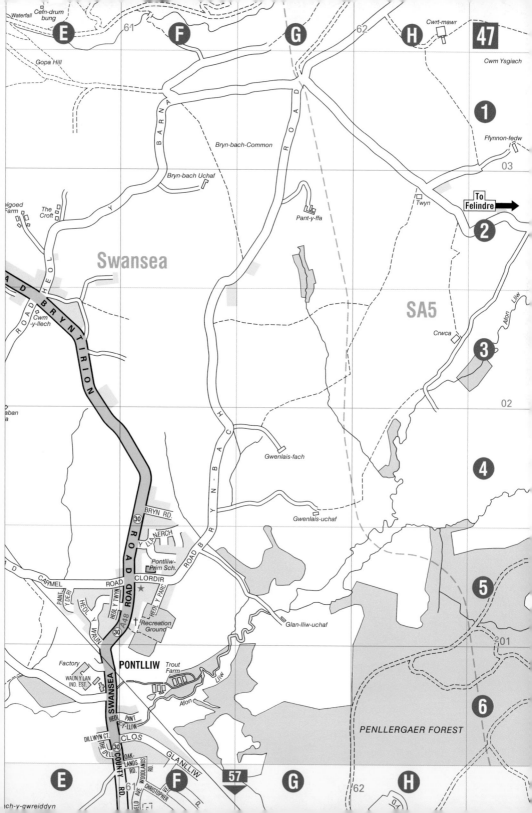

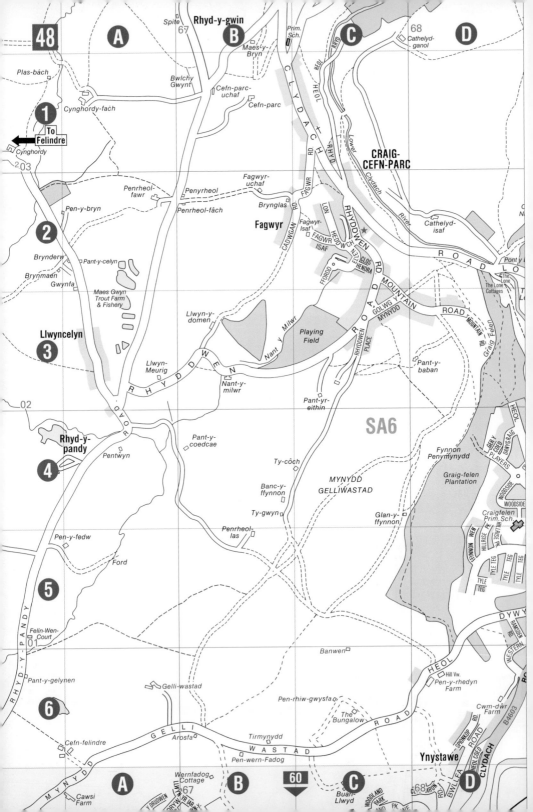

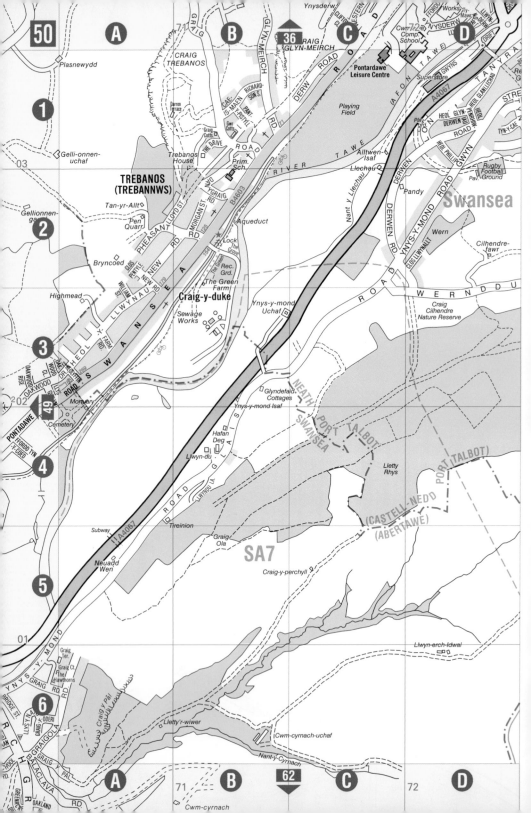

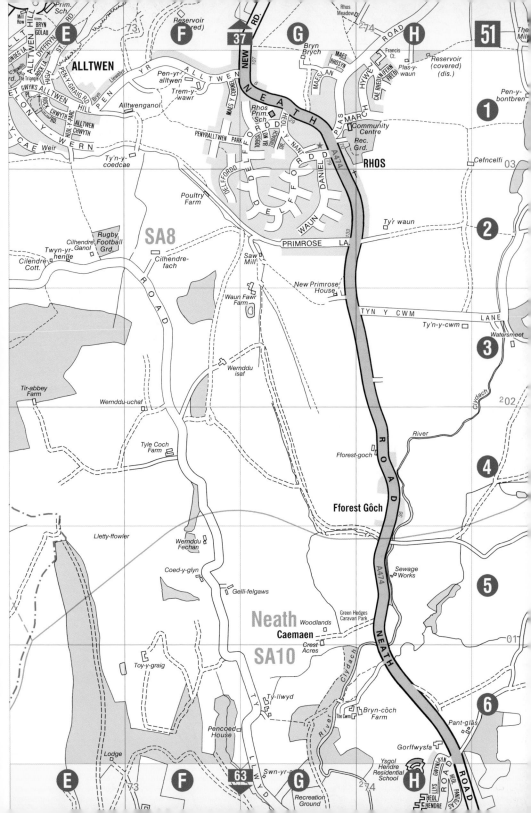

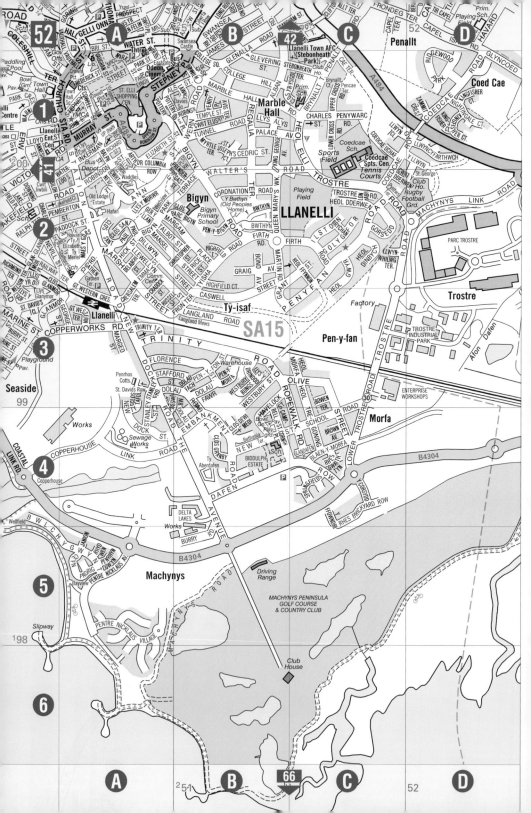

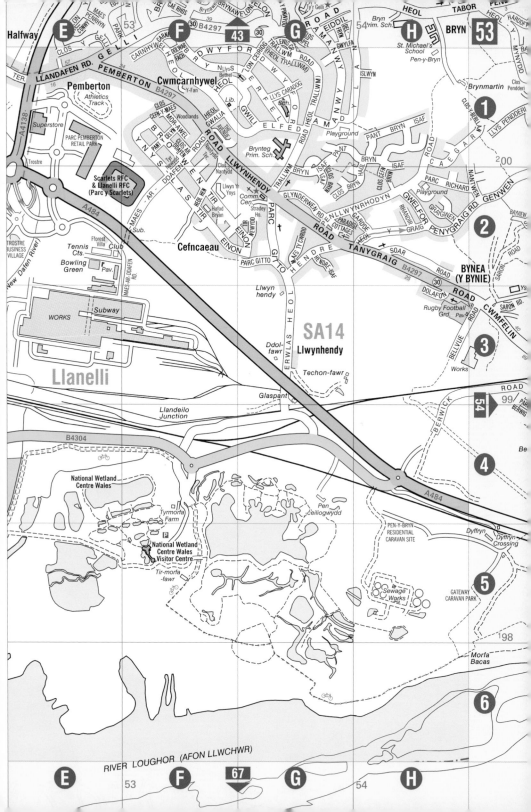

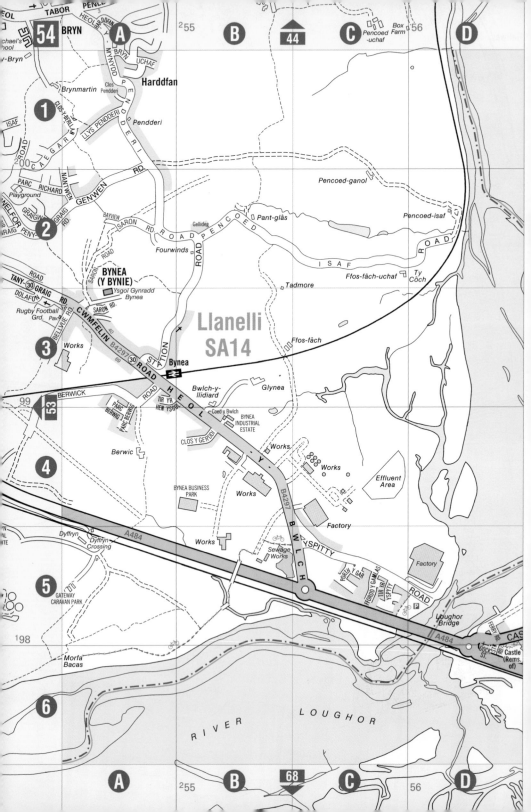

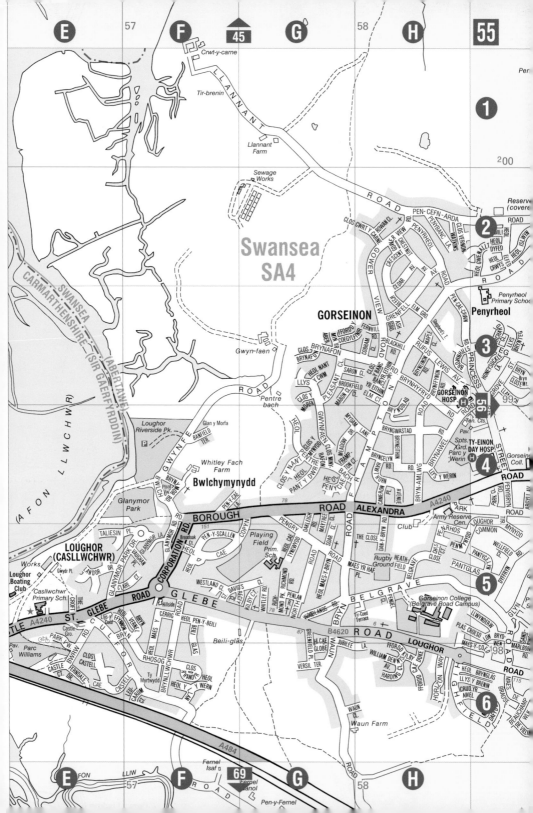

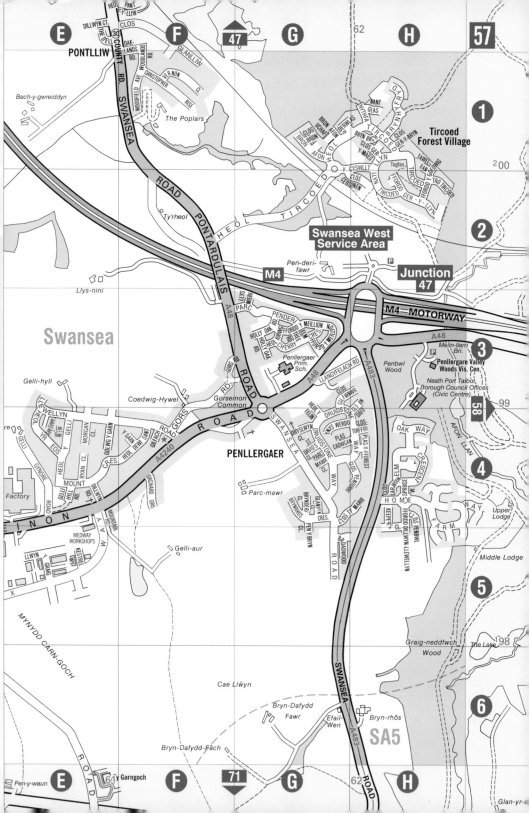

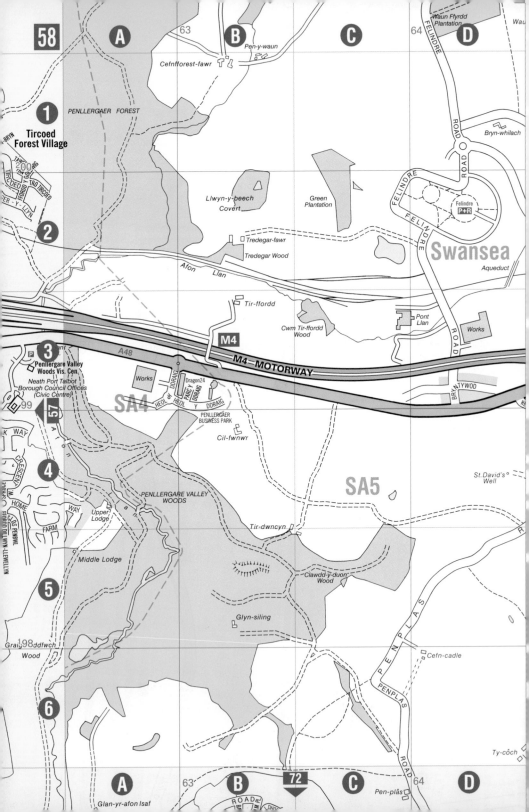

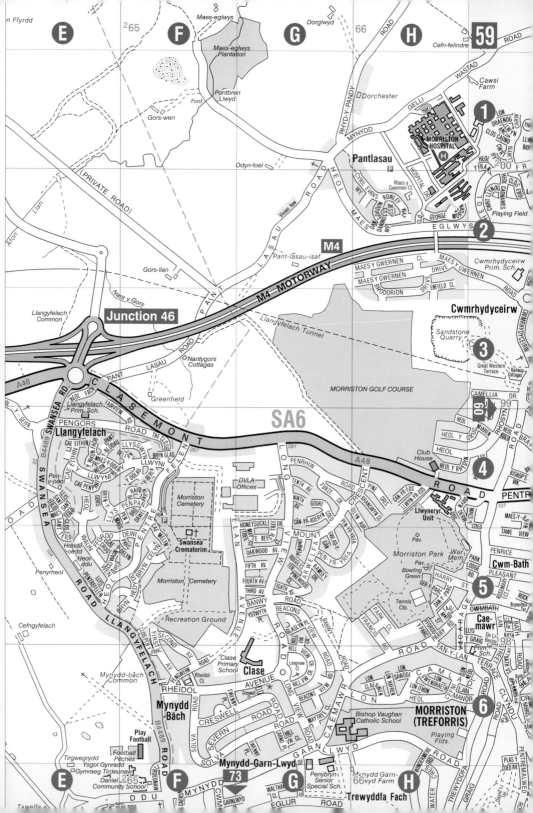

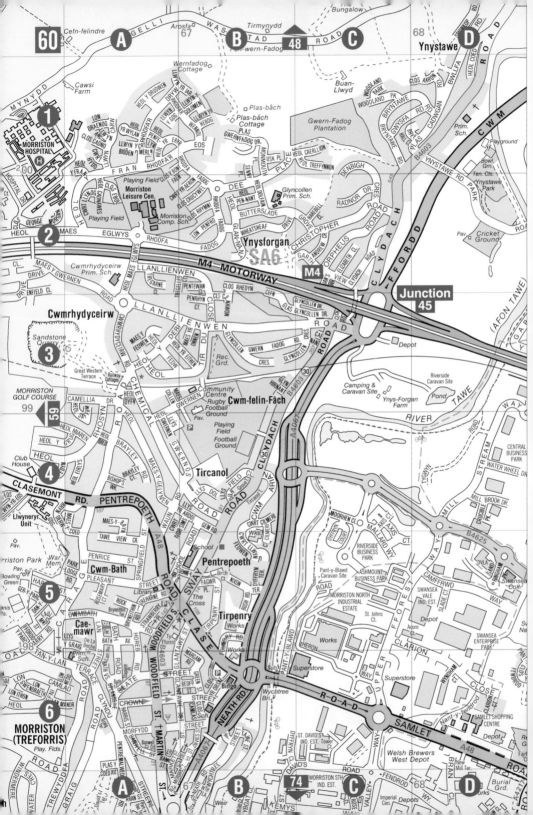

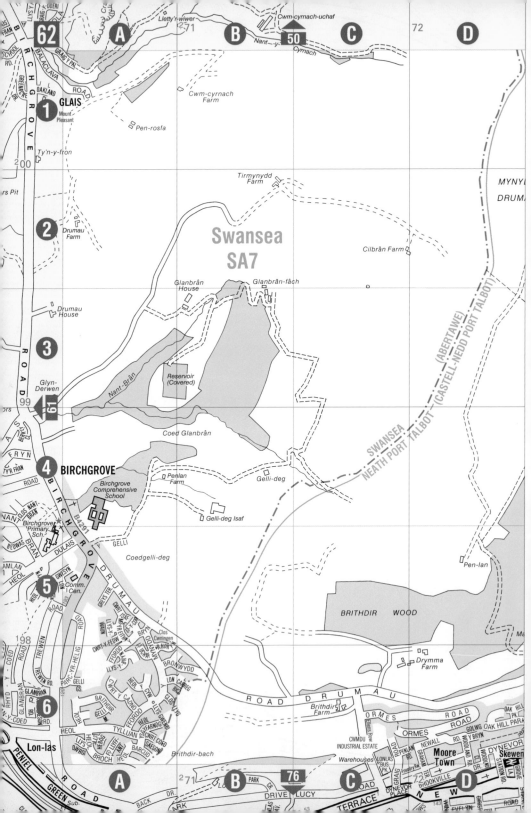

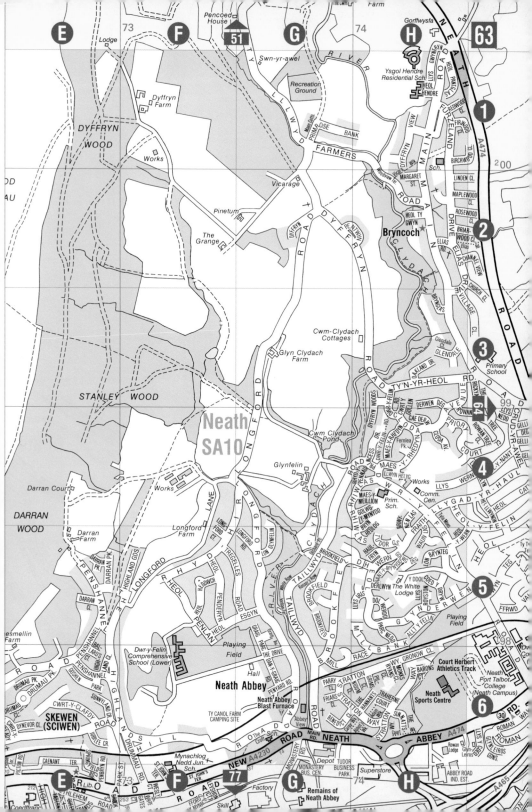

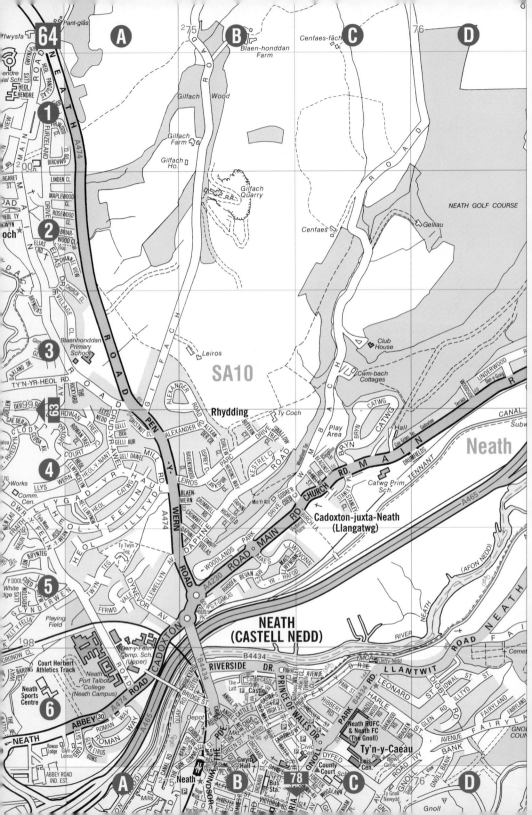

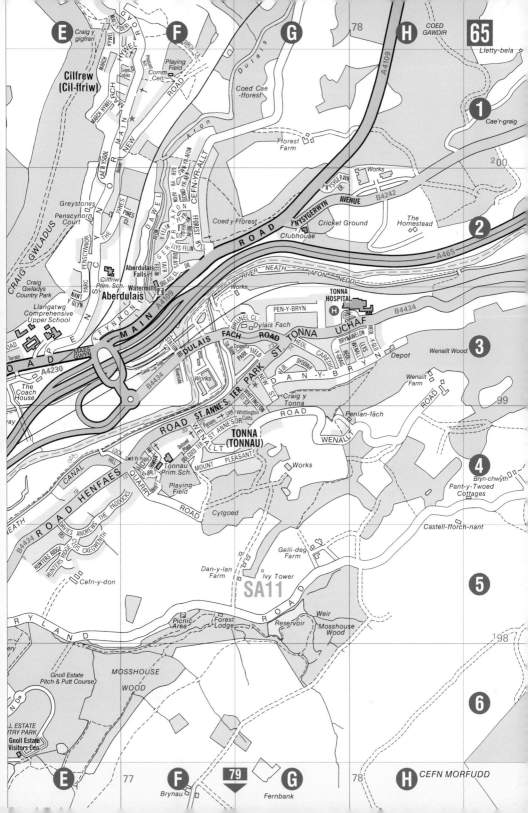

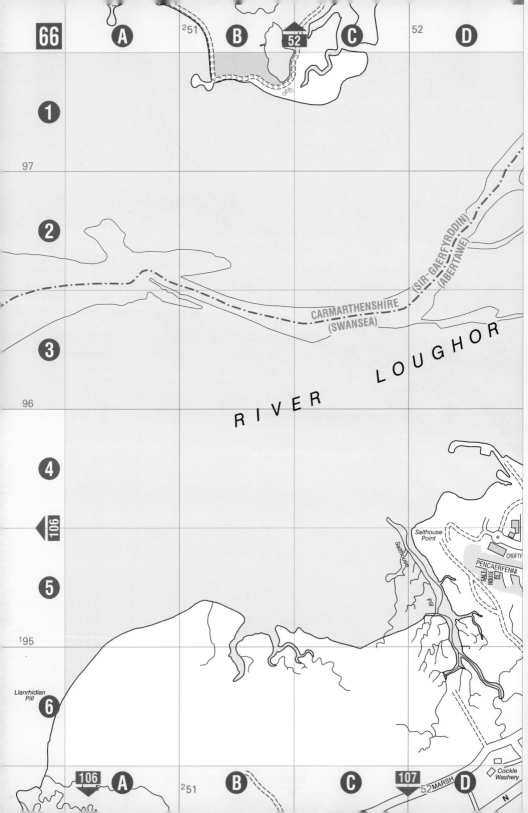

**A** ²51 **B** 52 **C** 52 **D**

**1**

97

**2**

CARMARTHENSHIRE
(SWANSEA)

(SIR- GAERFYRDDIN)
(ABERTAWE)

**3**

96

R I V E R   L O U G H O R

**4**

106

Salthouse
Point

CROFTY

**5**

Salthouse
Pill

PENCAERFENNI

SALT
HOUSE
CL

195

Llanrhidian
Pill

**6**

106 **A** ²51 **B** **C** 107 52 MARSH **D**

◇ Cockle
Washery

N

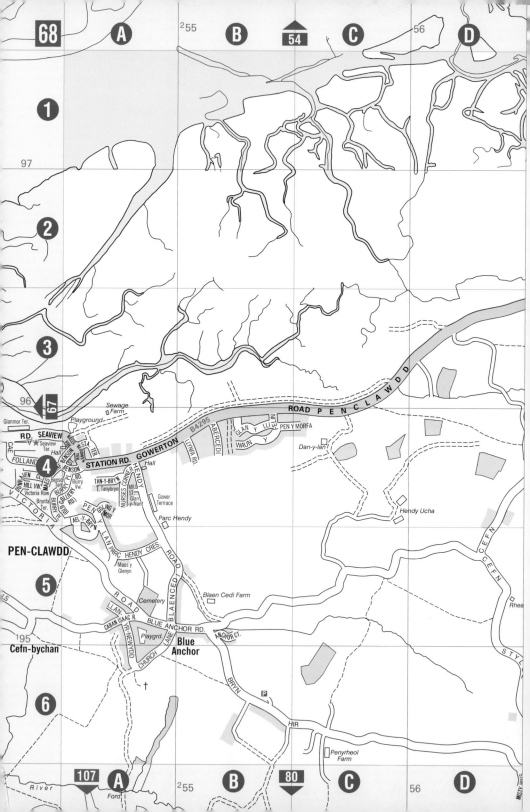

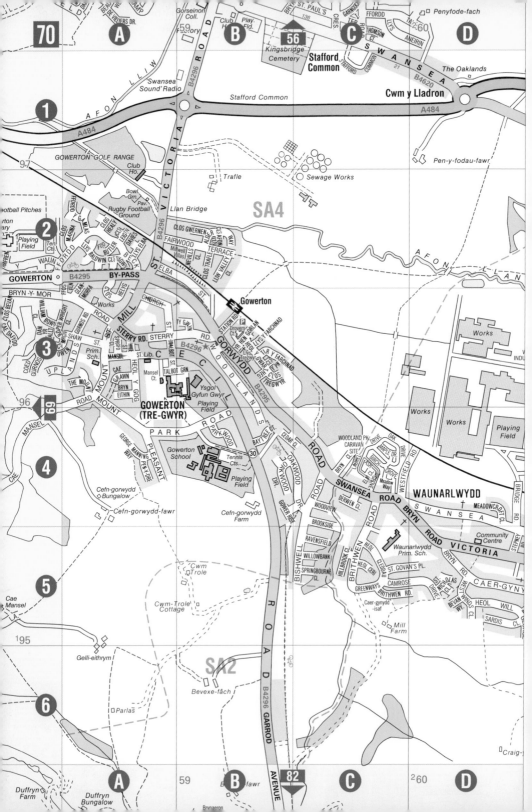

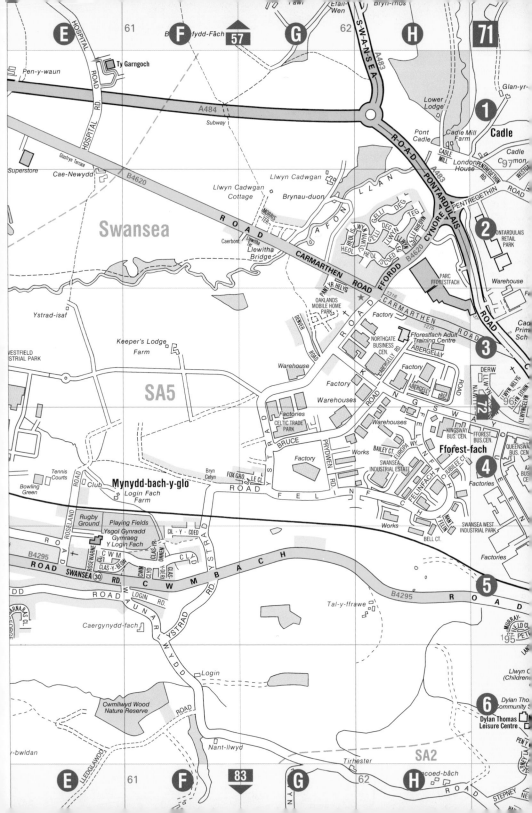

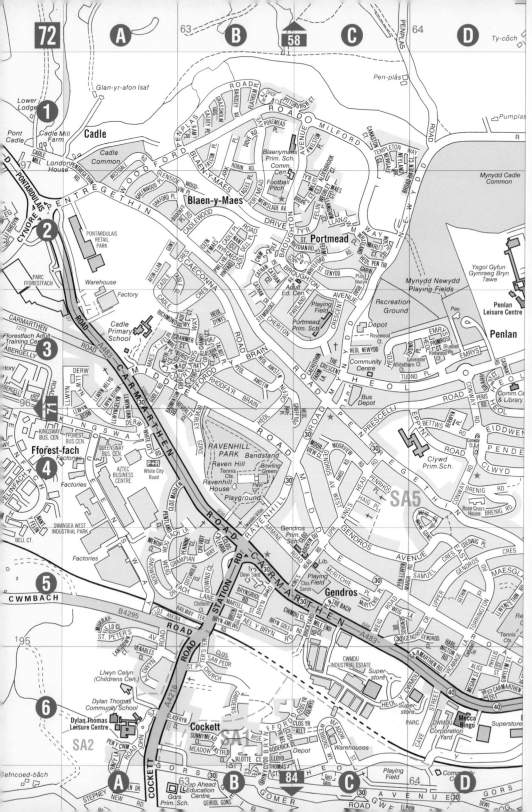

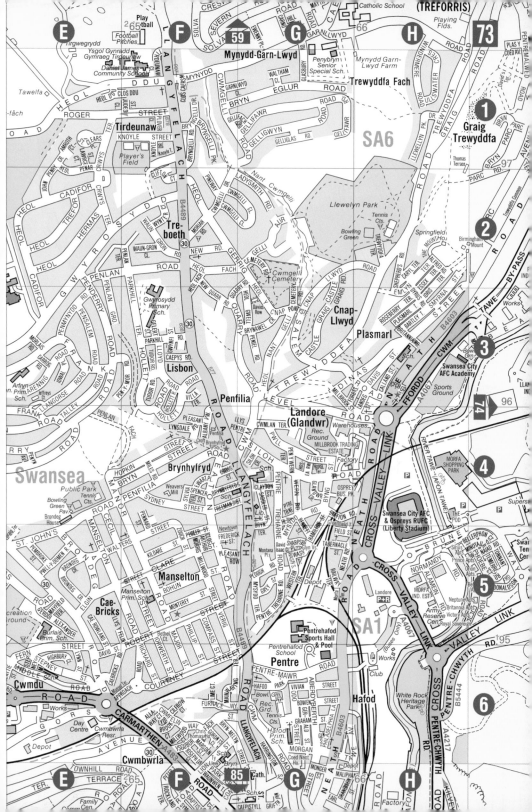

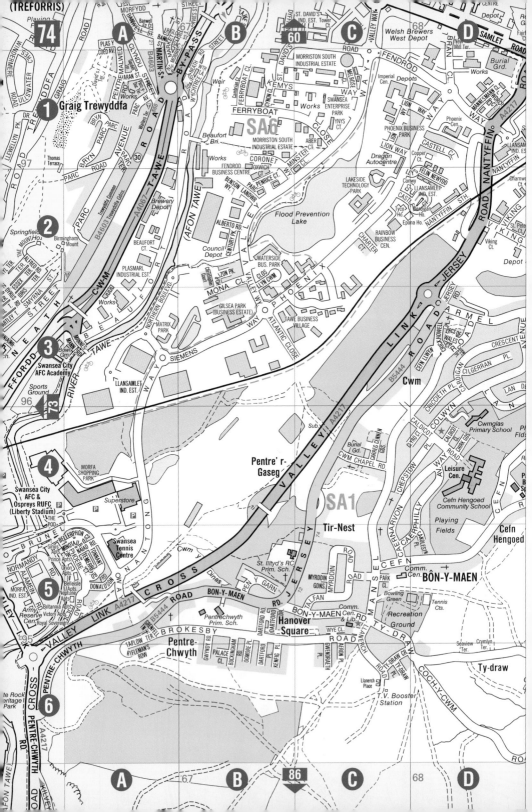

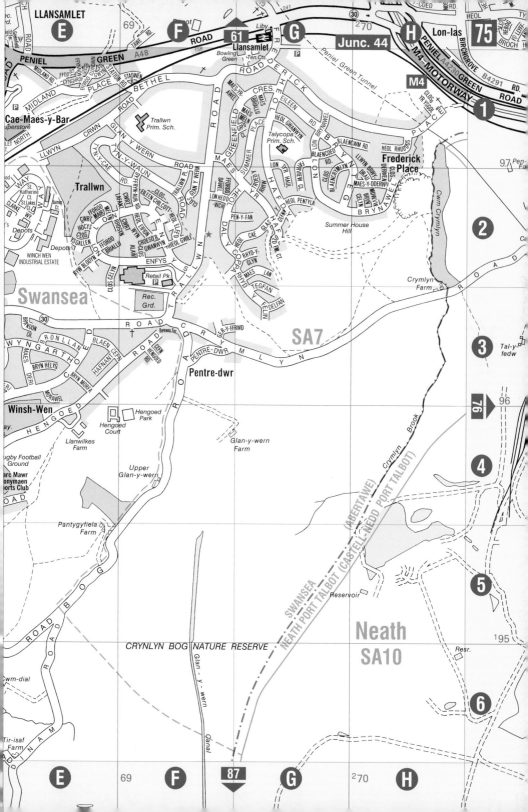

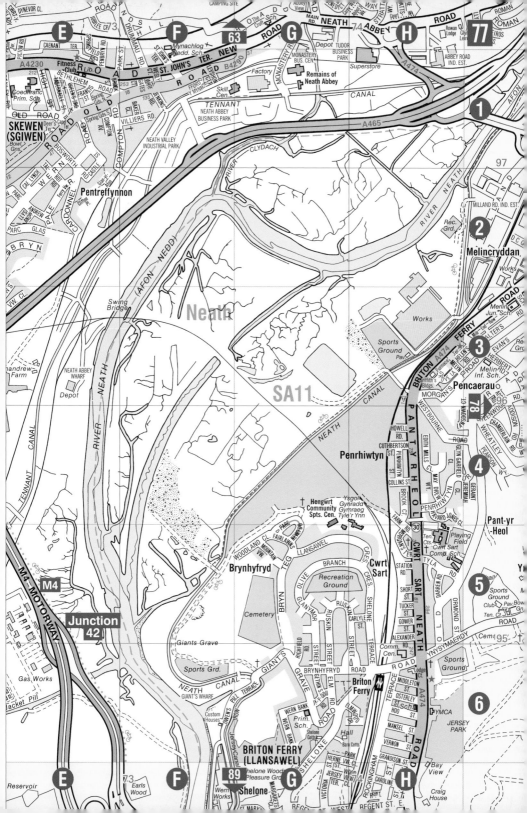

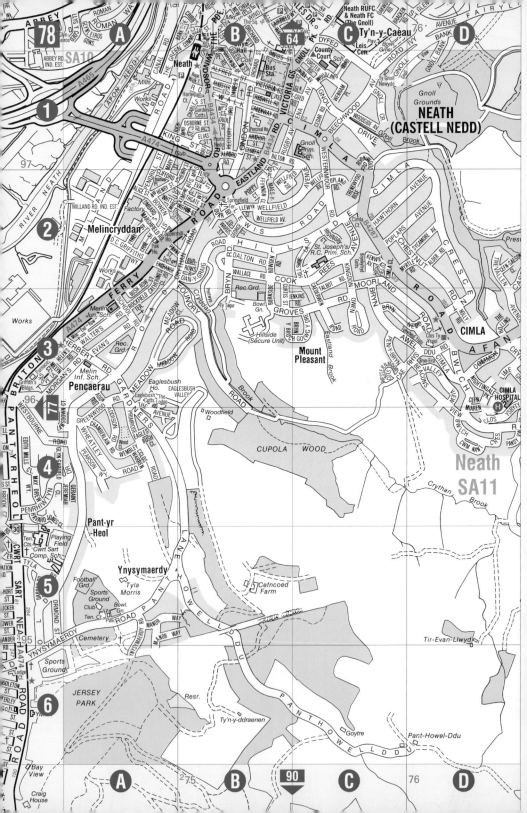

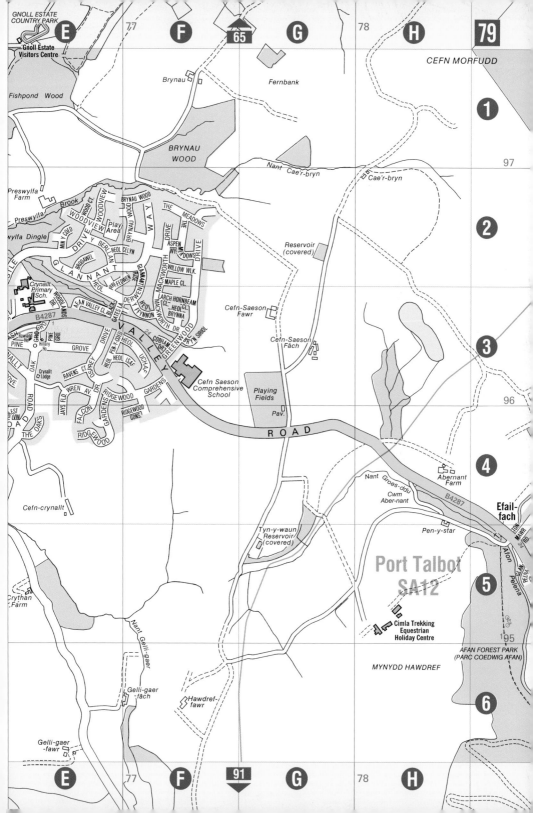

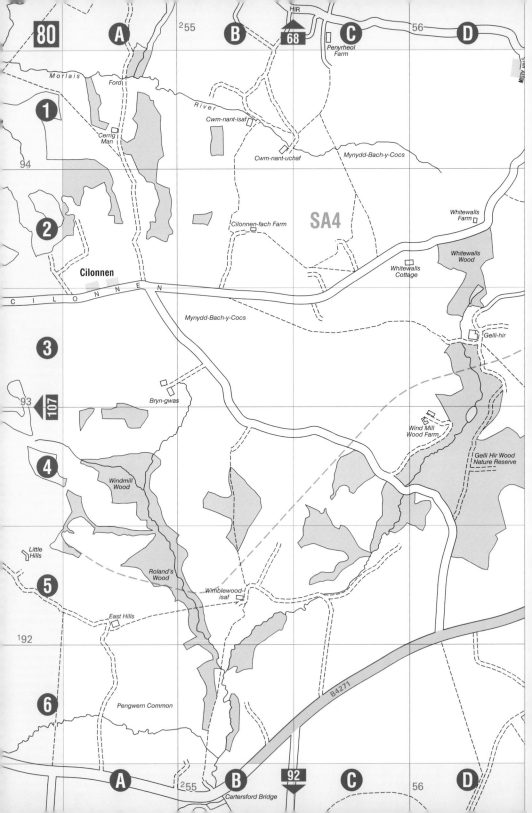

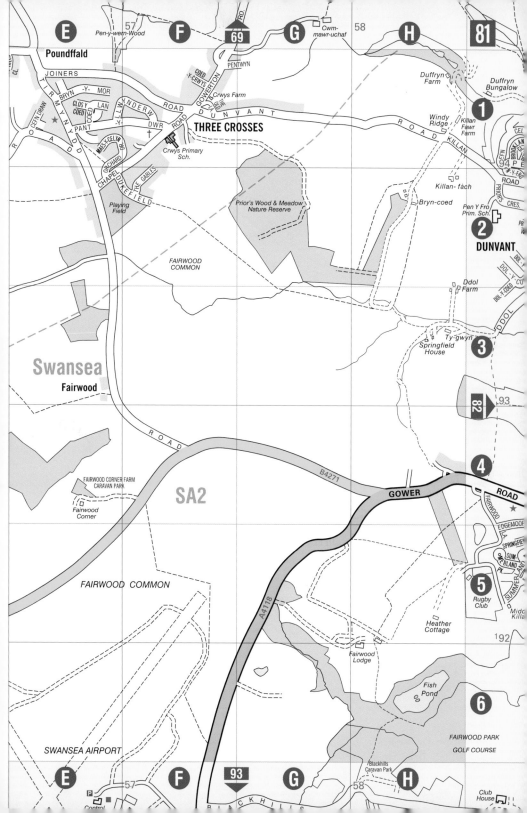

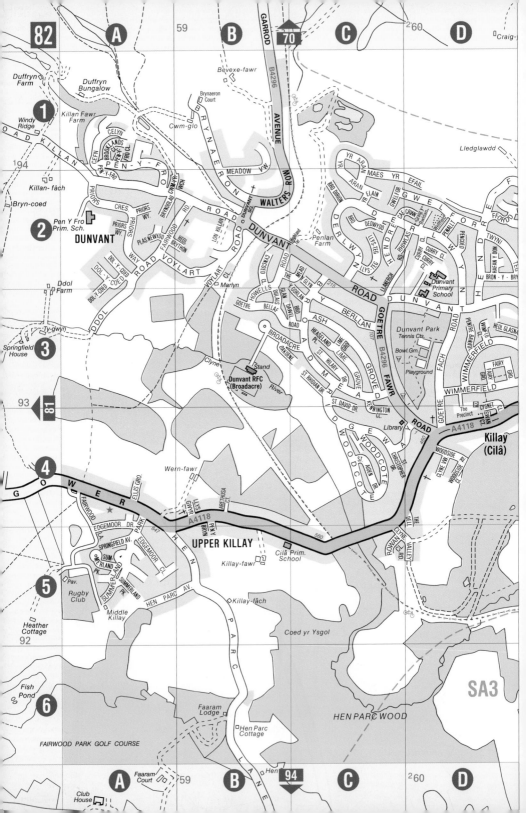

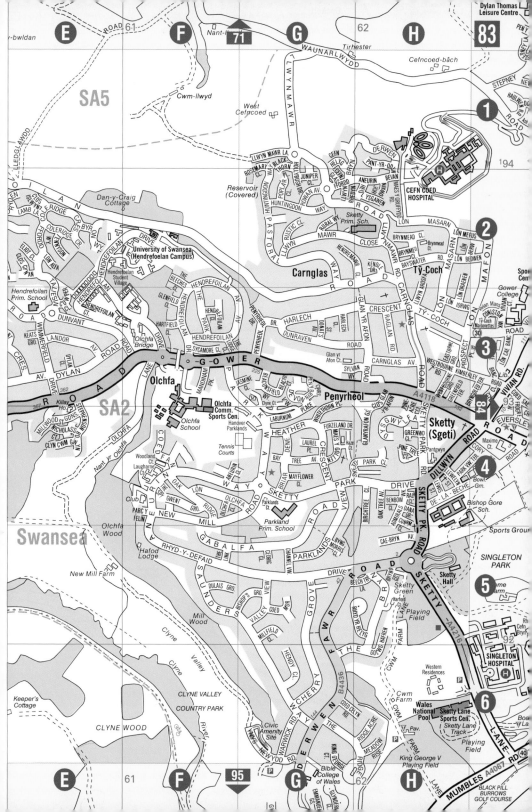

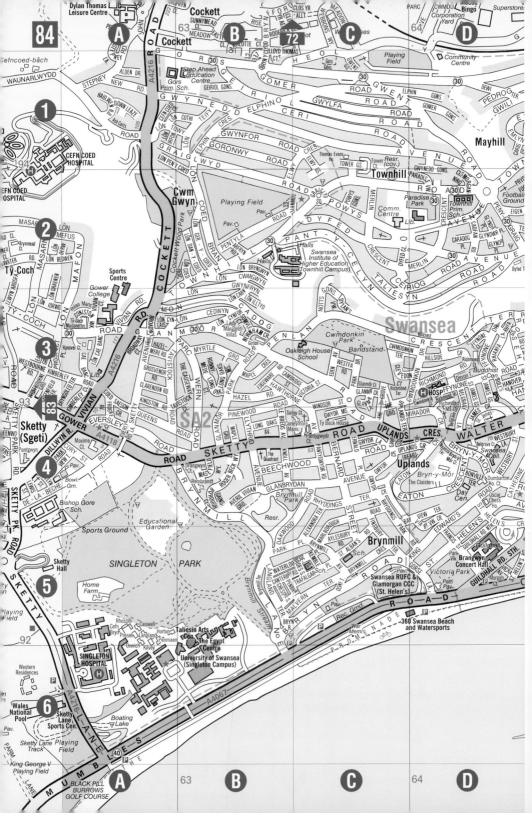

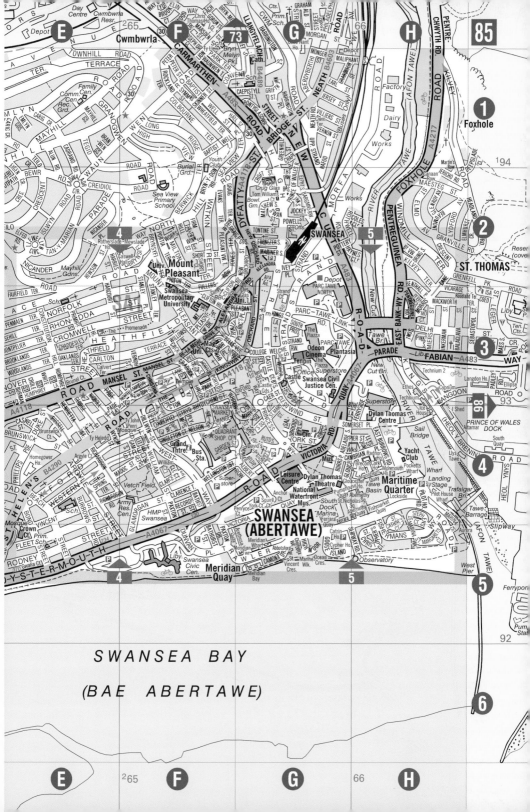

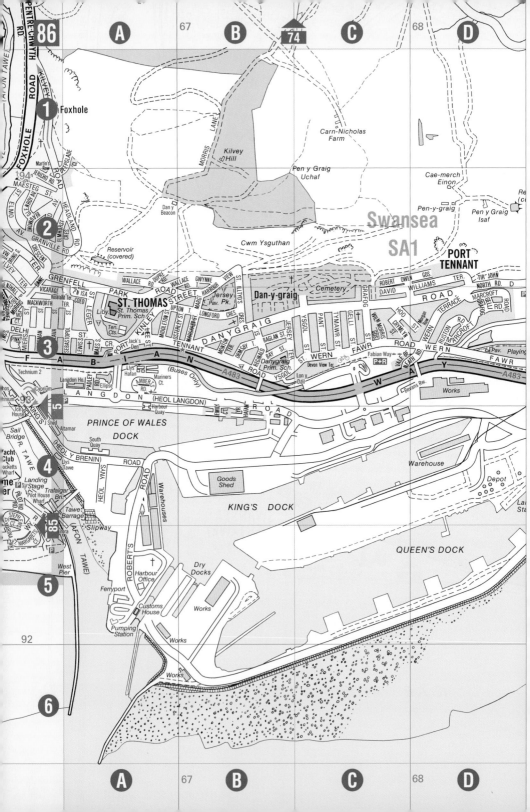

**E** 69 **F** ▲ **75** **G** ²70 **H** **87**

Neath
SA10

Penisa'r-Coed **1**

194
Craig Dan

**2**

A M A Z

CANAL

Glan-y-wern Canal

SWANSEA (ABERTAWE)
NEATH PORT TALBOT
(CASTELL-NEDD PORT TALBOT)

Gellir-allor

P

servoir
overed)

T E N N A N T

Playing
Field

Waste
Incinerator

Works

SWANSEA GATE
BUSINESS PARK

**3**

CRESCENT

W A Y

Crymlyn
Burrows
Works

ROAD

Field

F A B I A N

BALDWIN'S

H F O R D D

Depot

Sewage
Works

CRESCENT ELBA
A483

W A Y

CRYMLYN

**88** ➤ 93

AFAN

SEVERN

Tennant
Pl.

CRYMLYN

W A Y

Margain
Sq.

Oil
Depot

Depot

WAY

Gower Sq.

MARIAN

**4**

PARC

Dunes

Swansea University
Science & Innovation
Campus

Black Rock
Point

nding
ge

*S W A N S E A   B A Y*

*(B A E   A B E R T A W E)*

**5**

92

**6**

**E** 69 **F** **G** ²70 **H**

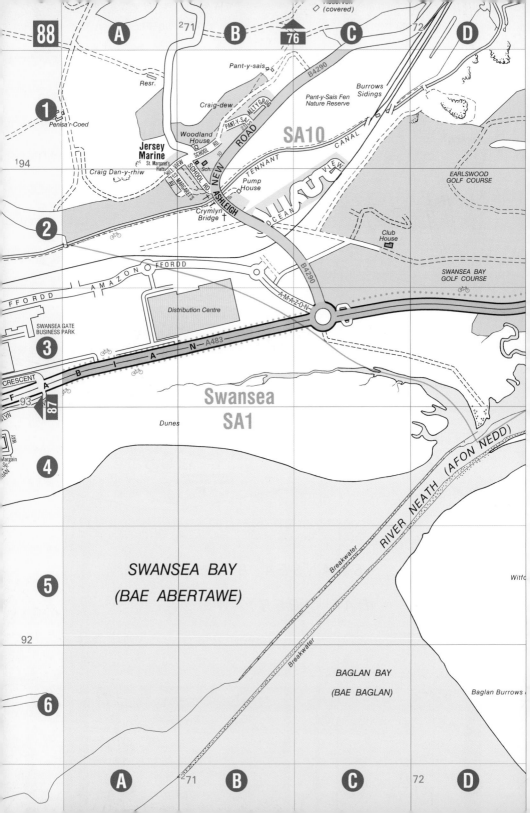

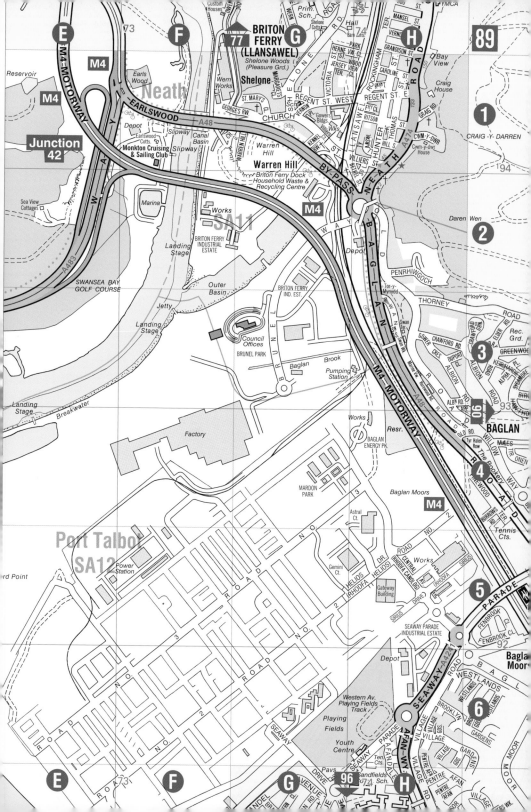

SWANSEA AIRPORT

FAIRWOOD PARK
GOLF COURSE

Club
House

**1**

Control
Tower

BLACKHILLS

LANE

Blackhills
Caravan Park

Brynmoel
Farm

Blackhills

**Blackhills**

SA2

91

Worganrous
Farm

**2**

Uppe
Wernlle

Moorlakes Wood

Fairwood
Common

Lowe
Wernlle

**3**

Hams
Wood

**94** ▶ 190

Kittle Hill
Dairy Farm

**4**

Kittle Hill
Poultry Farm

Ryeground
Farm

A4118

ROAD NORTHWAY

VENNAWAY

Kittle

Kittle
Hill
Dairy Farm

Bishopston
Prim. Sch.

Murton
Green

Man
Gree

**5**

THE GLEBE

PORTWAY

NORTHWAY CT

NORTHLANDS PK

Hall

**Kittle**

BEAUFORT

DRIVE HILL LA

OLD KITTLE RD

CHURCH LA.

MIDDLETON

BISHOPSTON

Bishopston
Sports
Centre

Bishopston
Comprehensive
School

MANSFIELD

Hall

89

**Murton**

B4436

BELVEDERE

KITTLE GREEN

EASTLANDS PK.

EASTLANDS PK.

EASTLANDS PK.

LONG ACRE

TUDOR

Riding
School

PENNARD

B4436

PROVIDENCE
LA.

LONG
ACRE
CT.

**6**

**Pennard**

Hall

WELLFIELD

SOUTH CT

KILN LA.

KILN LA.

HOLLAND DR.

**BISHOPSTON**
**(LLANDEILO FERWALLT)**

ST. TEILO'S
CT.

VENSLAND

HOMEAD

Oldwa

ROAD

WITHY PARK

RIDLEY WY.

WOODSIDE CL.

KILFIELD

OCHR-Y
WOOD

WHITE KNIGHT

**PYLE**

**99** ▼ 58'

PYLE CL.

GERRETTS CL.

CASWELL

BISHOPSTON
VALLEY

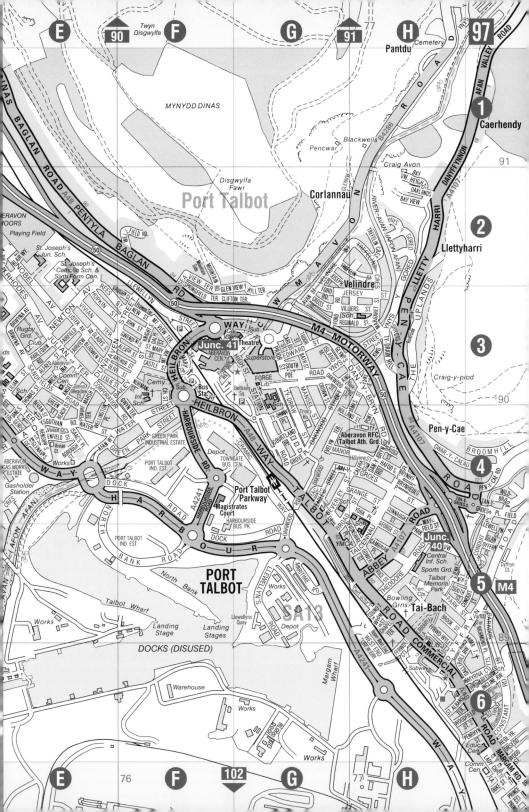

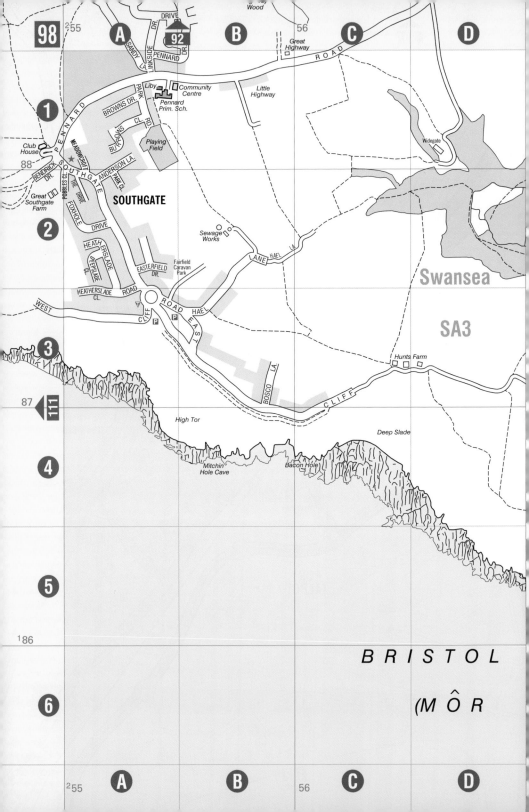

A

SANDY DR.
LINKSIDE DR.
DRIVE
**92**
PENNARD DR.

B

56

Great Highway

C

ROAD

D

Wood

**1**

Club House

88·

PENNARD
PARK RD.
BROWNS DR.
BURROWS CL.
MEADOWCROFT
SOUTHGATE
ANDERSON LA.
THE DRIVE
PARK CL.
POBBLES CL.
FOXHOLE

Liby
Community Centre
Pennard Prim. Sch.

Little Highway

Playing Field

Widegate

Bendrick Dr.
Great Southgate Farm

**SOUTHGATE**

**2**

HEATHERSLADE
PEBSLADE CL.

EASTERFIELD DR.
Fairfield Caravan Park

Sewage Works

LANE
HAEL LA.

Swansea

SA3

HEATHERSLADE CL.
HEATHERSLADE ROAD

WEST

CLIFF

ROAD
HAEL
EAST

P
P
P

Hunts Farm

**3**

87 ◄ **111**

High Tor

BOSCO LA.

CLIFF

Deep Slade

**4**

Mitchin Hole Cave

Bacon Hole

**5**

¹86

*B R I S T O L*

**6**

*(M Ô R*

A

B

56

C

D

**102**

A    <sup>2</sup>76    B    97    C    77    D

**1**

Works

Works

Works

1.88

**2**

Works

Jetty

Travelling
Crane

Pipe

Lines

PORT TALBOT STEEL WORKS

**3**

Sewage
Works

Breakwater

Pipe Lines

Port Talbot
SA13

87

**4**

Reservoir

**5**

*SWANSEA BAY*

*(BAE ABERTAWE)*

Outfall

86

**6**

Ind.
Est.

Margam
Moors

A    <sup>2</sup>76    B    C    77    D

HARBOUR WAY

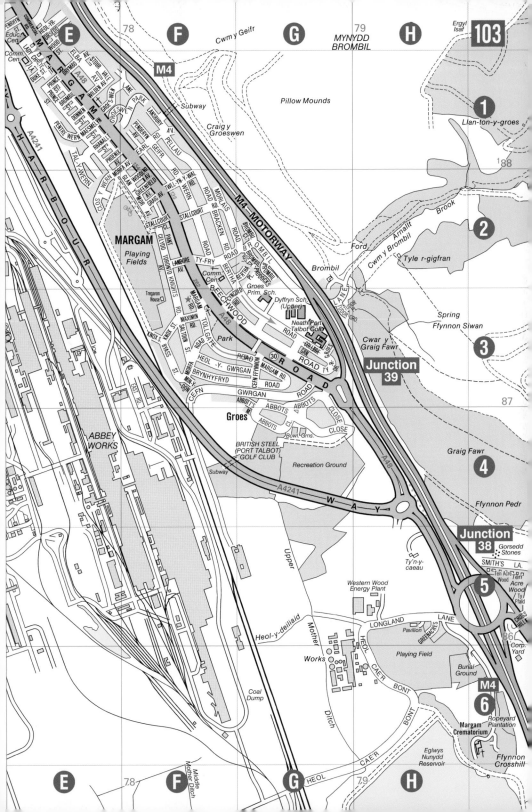

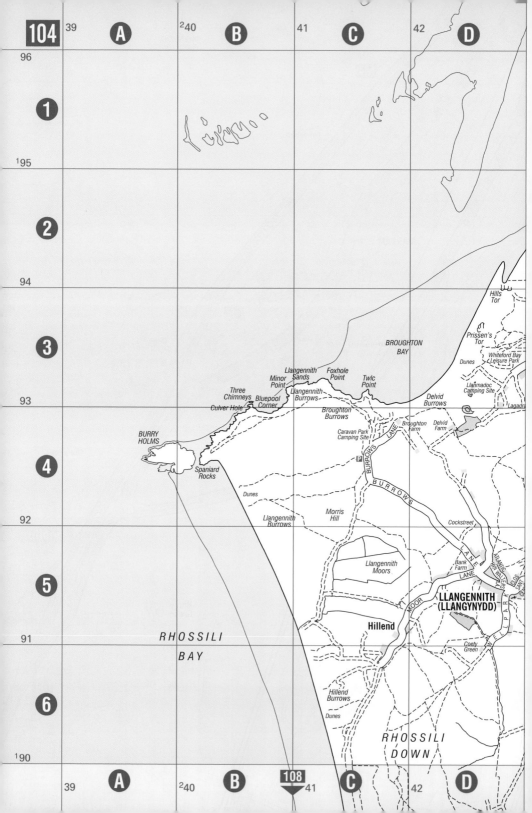

96

**1**

195

**2**

94

**3**

93

BURRY
HOLMS

**4**

92

**5**

91

**6**

190

BROUGHTON
BAY

Hills
Tor

Prissen's
Tor

Whiteford Bay
Leisure Park

Dunes

Llanmadoc
Camping Site

Lagadra

Llangennith
Sands

Minor
Point

Foxhole
Point

Twlc
Point

Delvid
Burrows

Three
Chimneys

Bluepool
Corner

Llangennith
Burrows

Culver Hole

Broughton
Burrows

Broughton
Farm

Delvid
Farm

Caravan Park
Camping Site

Spaniard
Rocks

Dunes

BURROWS LANE

BURROWS

Cockstreet

Llangennith
Burrows

Morris
Hill

Bank
Farm

ATLANTIC
WATERS

LANE

Llangennith
Moors

**LLANGENNITH
(LLANGYNYDD)**

MOOR

**Hillend**

WELLPARK LANE

Coety
Green

*RHOSSILI*

*BAY*

Hillend
Burrows

Dunes

*RHOSSILI*

*DOWN*

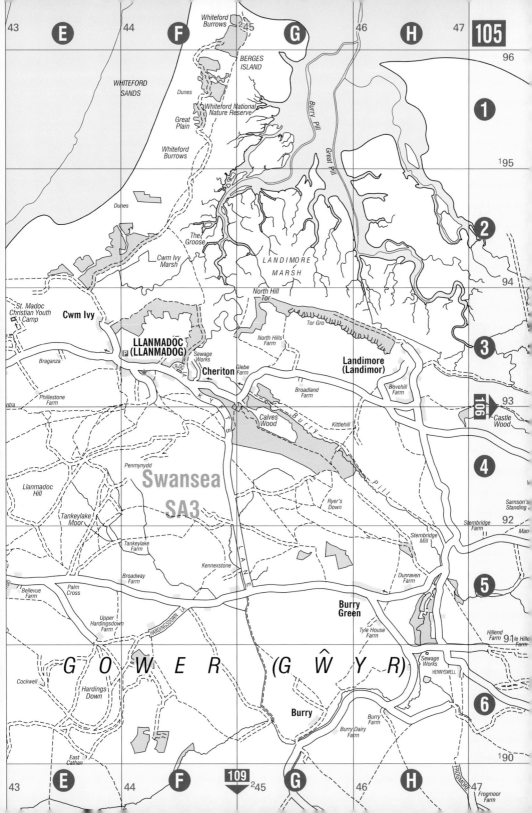

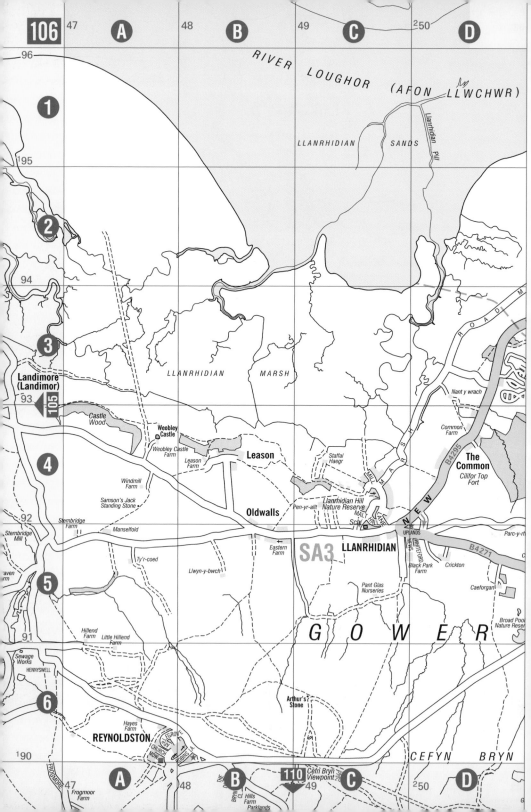

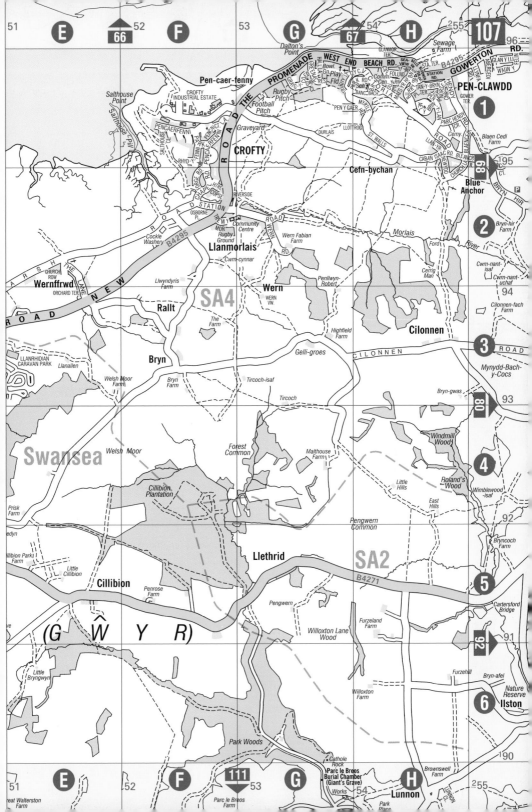

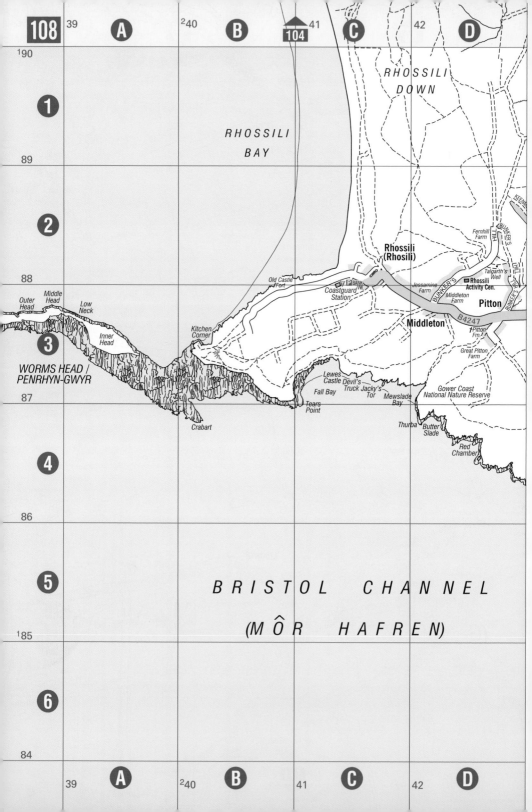

39 **A** ²40 **B** 41 **C** 42 **D**

104

190

**1**

*RHOSSILI
BAY*

*RHOSSILI
DOWN*

89

**2**

KEEN

88

Old Castle
Fort

BANK

Coastguard
Station

Fernhill
Farm

BUNKER'S

Talgarth's
Well

**Rhossili
(Rhosili)**

Jessamine
Farm

Rhossili
**Activity Cen.**

Middleton
Farm

**Pitton**

Middle
Head

Outer
Head

Low
Neck

Kitchen
Corner

BUNKER'S

Inner
Head

B4247

**Middleton**

**3**

*WORMS HEAD /
PENRHYN-GWYR*

Great Pitton
Farm

Pitton
Fm.

87

Lewes
Castle

Devil's
Truck Jacky's
Tor

Fall Bay

Mewslade
Bay

Gower Coast
National Nature Reserve

Tears
Point

Crabart

Thurba

Butter
Slade

Red
Chamber

**4**

86

**5**

*B R I S T O L    C H A N N E L*

*( M Ô R    H A F R E N )*

¹85

**6**

84

39 **A** ²40 **B** 41 **C** 42 **D**

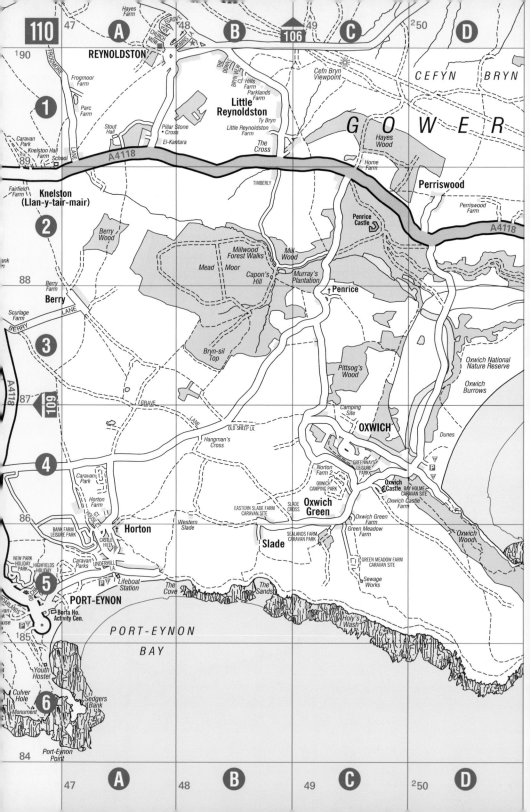

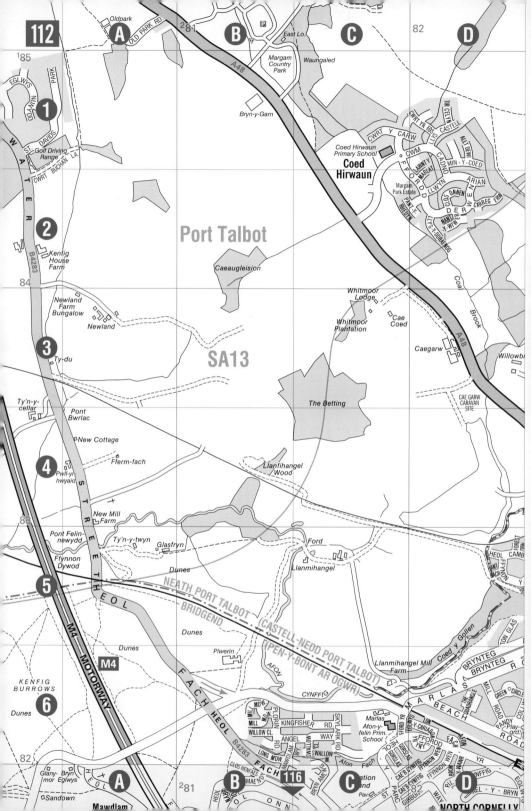

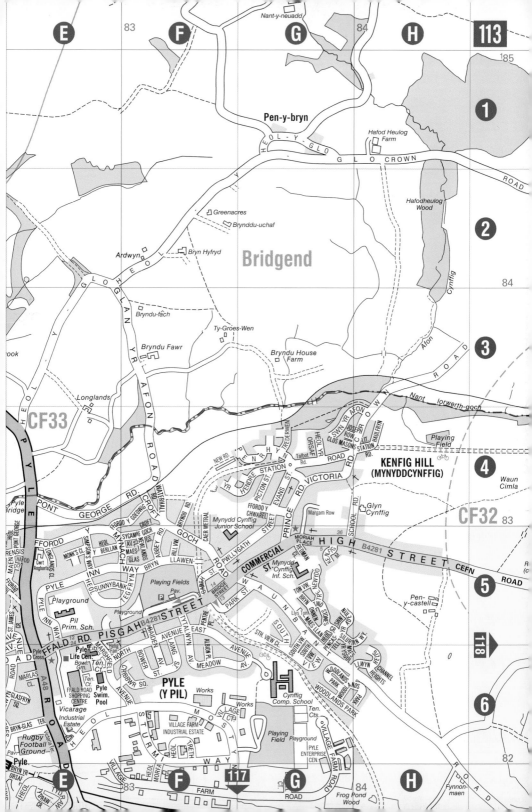

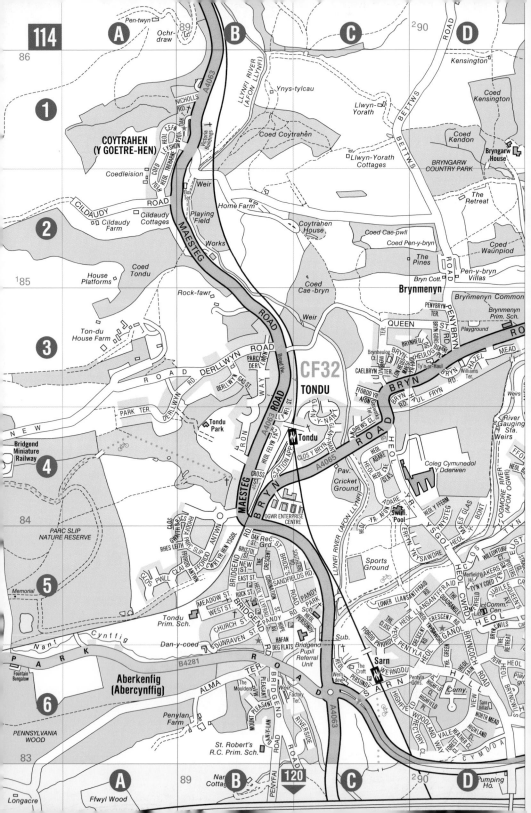

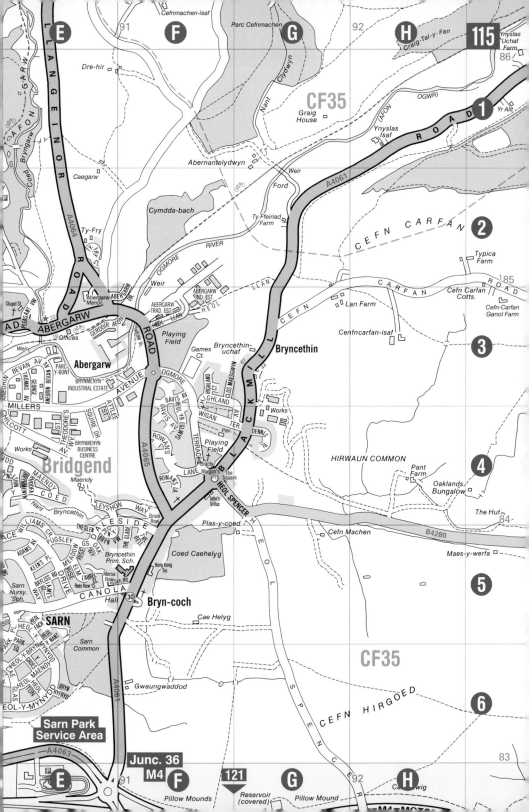

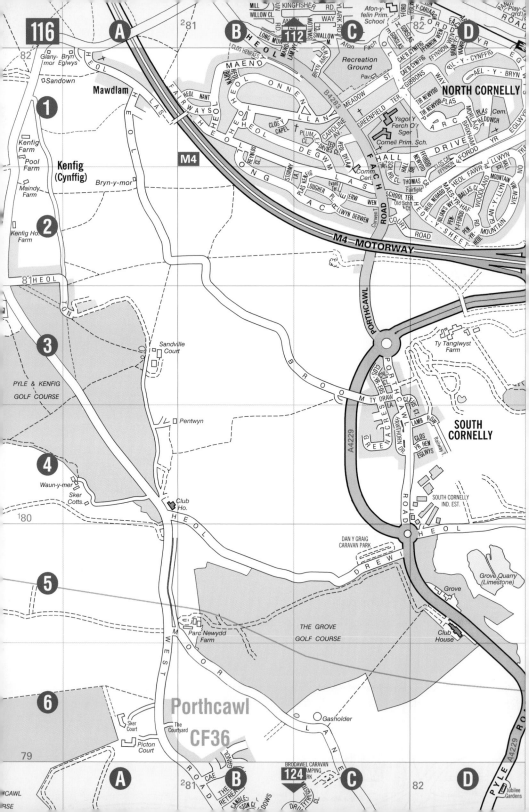

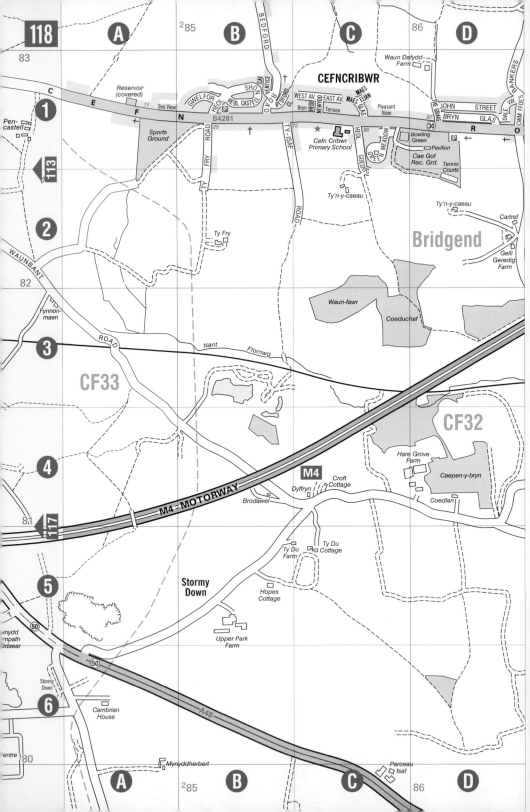

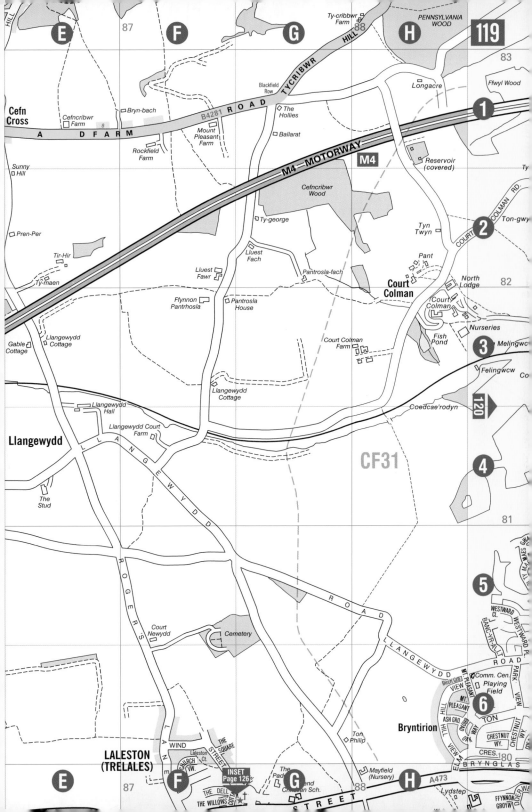

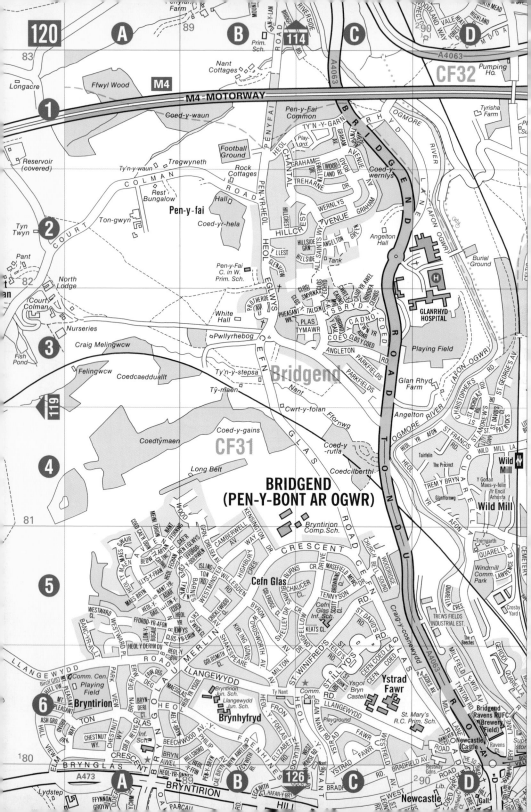

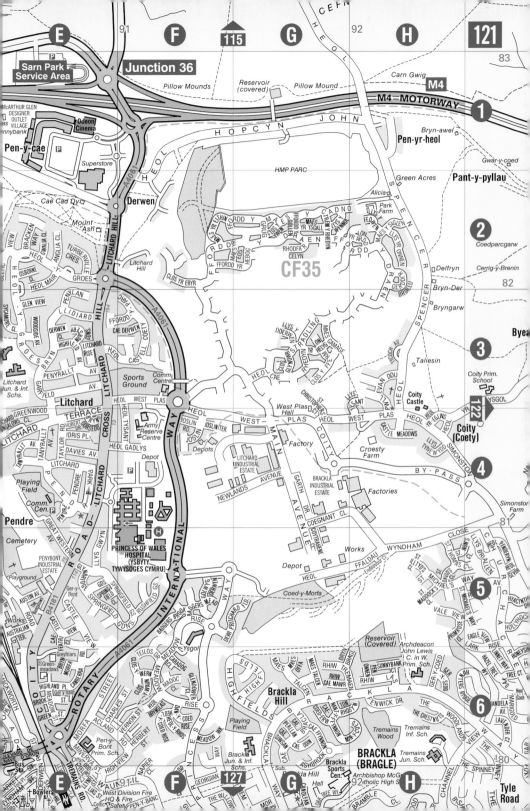

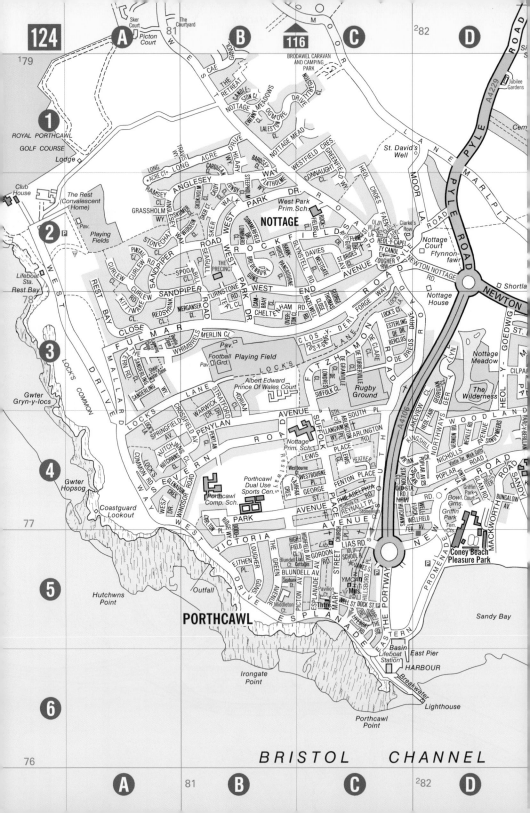

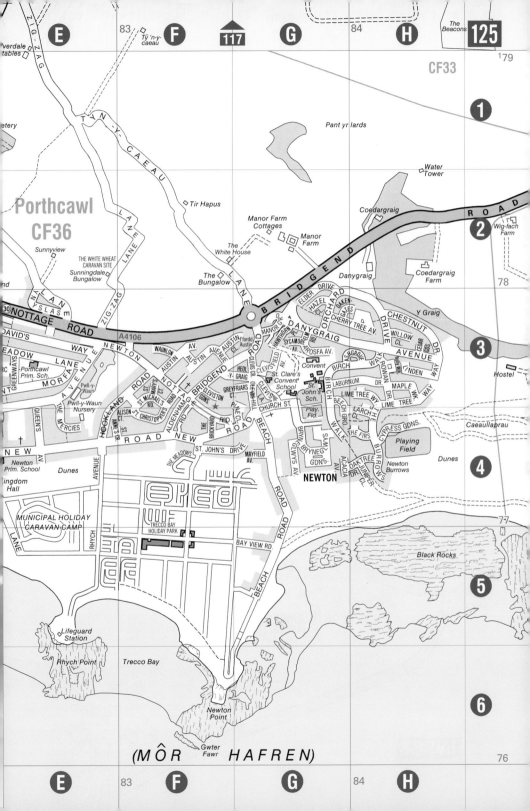

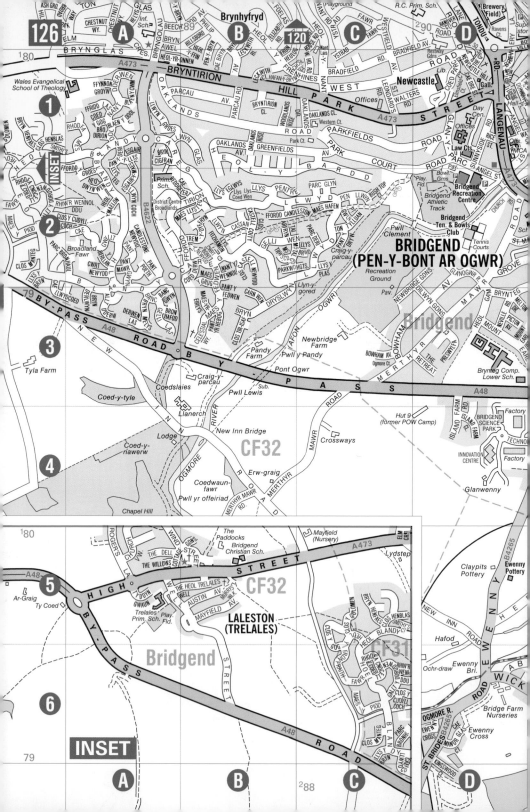

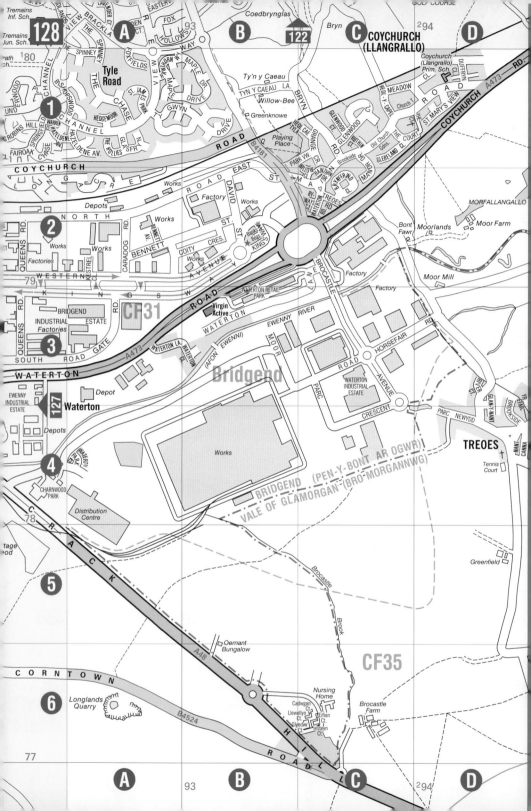

# INDEX

Including Streets, Places & Areas, Hospitals etc., Industrial Estates,
Selected Flats & Walkways, Junction Names & Service Areas, Stations and Selected Places of Interest.

## HOW TO USE THIS INDEX

1. Each street name is followed by its Postcode District, then by its Locality abbreviation(s) and then by its map reference;
   e.g. **Aberavon Rd.** SA12: Bag . . . .2C **96** is in the SA12 Postcode District and the Baglan Locality and is to be found in square 2C on page **96**.
   The page number is shown in bold type.

2. A strict alphabetical order is followed in which Av., Rd., St., etc. (though abbreviated) are read in full and as part of the street name;
   e.g. **Bellevue Rd.** appears after **Belle Vue** but before **Belle Vue Way**

3. Streets and a selection of flats and walkways that cannot be shown on the mapping, appear in the index with the thoroughfare to which they are connected
   shown in brackets; e.g. **Albert Pl.** SA3: T Mum . . . .1E **101** (off Gloucester Pl.)

4. Addresses that are in more than one part are referred to as not continuous.

5. Places and areas are shown in the index in BLUE TYPE and the map reference is to the actual map square in which the town centre or area is located
   and not to the place name shown on the map; e.g. ABERAVON . . . .4D 96

6. An example of a selected place of interest is Ammanford Miners Mus. . . . .1H 21

7. Examples of stations are:
   Ammanford (Rhydaman) Station (Rail) . . . .6G 11;   Bridgend Bus Station . . . .1E 127;   Fabian Way (Park & Ride) . . . . 3C 86

8. Junction names and Service Areas are shown in the index in BOLD CAPITAL TYPE; e.g. PONT ABRAHAM SERVICE AREA . . . .5C 30

9. An example of a Hospital, Hospice or selected Healthcare facility is AMMAN VALLEY HOSPITAL (YSBYTY DYFFRYN AMAN) . . . .4A 14

10. Map references for entries that appear on large scale pages **4** & **5** are shown first, with small scale map references shown in brackets;
    e.g. **Adelaide St.** SA1: Swan . . . .4F **5** (4G **85**)

# MYNEGAI

Yn cynnwys Strydoedd, Lleoedd ac Ardaloedd, Ysbytai ac ati., Stadau Diwydiannol,
Fflatiau a Llwybrau Troed dethol, Enwau Cyffyrdd ac Ardaloedd Gwasaneth,
Gorsafoedd a Detholiad o Fannau Diddorol.

## SUD I DDEFNYDDIO'R MYNEGAI HWN

1. Dilynir pob enw stryd gan ei Ardal Cod Post, wedyn gan fyrfodd(au) ei Leoliad ac wedyn gan ei gyfeirnod map;
   e.e. mae **Aberavon Rd.** SA12: Bag . . . .2C **96** yn Ardal Cod Post SA12 a Lleoliad Baglan a gellir dod o hyd iddi yn sgwâr 2C ar dudalen **96**.
   Dangosir Rhif y Dudalen mewn teip trwm.

2. Glynir yn gaeth wrth drefn y wyddor, gyda Av., Rd., St., ayb (er eu bod wedi eu talfyrru) yn cael eu darllen yn llawn ac fel rhan o enw'r stryd;
   e.e. mae **Bellevue Rd.** yn ymddangos ar ôl **Belle Vue** ond cyn **Belle Vue Way**

3. Mae strydoedd a detholiad o fflatiau a llwybrau na ellir eu dangos ar y mapiau, yn ymddangos yn y mynegai gyda'r dramwyfa y mae'n gysylltiedig
   â hi wedi'i dangos mewn cromfachau; e.e. **Albert Pl.** SA3: T Mum . . . .1E **101** (off Gloucester Pl.)

4. Cyfeirir at gyfeiriadau sydd mewn mwy nag un rhan fel cyfeiriadau nan ydynt yn barhaus.

5. Dangosir ardaloedd a lleoedd yn y mynegai mewn TEIP GLAS ac mae'r cyfeirnod map yn cyfeirio at y sgwâr ar y map lle mae lleoliad canol y dref
   neu'r ardal ac nid at yr enw lle a ddangosir ar y map; e.e. ABERAVON . . . . 4D 96

6. Enghraifft o fan diddorol dethol yw Ammanford Miners Mus. . . . .1H 21

7. Enghreifftiau o gorsafoedd yn:
   Ammanford (Rhydaman) Station (Rail) . . . .6G 11;   Bridgend Bus Station . . . .1E 127;   Fabian Way (Park & Ride) . . . . 3C 86

8. Dangosir enw cyffyrdd a Ardaloedd Gwasaneth yn y mynegai mewn PRIFLYTHYRENNAU TEIP BRAS; e.e. PONT ABRAHAM SERVICE AREA . . . .5C 30

9. Enghraifft o Ysbyty, Hosbis neu gyfleuster gofal iechyd dethol yw AMMAN VALLEY HOSPITAL (YSBYTY DYFFRYN AMAN) . . . .4A 14

10. Mae cyfeirnodau map ar gyfer cofnodion sy'n ymddangos ar dudalennau ar raddfa fawr **4** & **5** yn cael eu dangos gyntaf, gyda chyfeirnodau map ar
    raddfa fechan yn cael eu dangos mewn cromfachau; e.e. **Adelaide St.** SA1: Swan . . . .4F **5** (4G **85**)

## GENERAL ABBREVIATIONS *Talfyriadau Cyffredinol*

| | | | |
|---|---|---|---|
| **App.** : Approach | **Cres.** : Crescent | **Lit.** : Little | **Res.** : Residential |
| **Arc.** : Arcade | **Dr.** : Drive | **Lwr.** : Lower | **Ri.** : Rise |
| **Av.** : Avenue | **E.** : East | **Mnr.** : Manor | **Rd.** : Road |
| **Bk.** : Back | **Ent.** : Enterprise | **Mans.** : Mansions | **Shop.** : Shopping |
| **Blvd.** : Boulevard | **Est.** : Estate | **Mkt.** : Market | **Sth.** : South |
| **Bri.** : Bridge | **Fld.** : Field | **Mdw.** : Meadow | **Sq.** : Square |
| **Bldg.** : Building | **Flds.** : Fields | **Mdws.** : Meadows | **St.** : Street |
| **Bldgs.** : Buildings | **Gdns.** : Gardens | **M.** : Mews | **Ter.** : Terrace |
| **Bungs.** : Bungalows | **Ga.** : Gate | **Mt.** : Mount | **Twr.** : Tower |
| **Bus.** : Business | **Gt.** : Great | **Mus.** : Museum | **Trad.** : Trading |
| **Cvn.** : Caravan | **Grn.** : Green | **Nth.** : North | **Up.** : Upper |
| **Cen.** : Centre | **Gro.** : Grove | **No.** : Number | **Va.** : Vale |
| **Circ.** : Circle | **Hgts.** : Heights | **Pde.** : Parade | **Vw.** : View |
| **Cl.** : Close | **Ho.** : House | **Pk.** : Park | **Vs.** : Villas |
| **Comn.** : Common | **Ho's.** : Houses | **Pas.** : Passage | **Vis.** : Visitors |
| **Cnr.** : Corner | **Ind.** : Industrial | **Pl.** : Place | **Wlk.** : Walk |
| **Cott.** : Cottage | **Info.** : Information | **Pct.** : Precinct | **W.** : West |
| **Cotts.** : Cottages | **Intl.** : International | **Prom.** : Promenade | **Yd.** : Yard |
| **Ct.** : Court | **La.** : Lane | | |

Aberavon: SA12 . . . . . . . . . . . . . .A'von
Abercraf: SA9 . . . . . . . . . . . . . .Aber
Aberdulais: SA10 . . . . . . . . . . . .A'dul
Aberkenfig: CF32 . . . . . . . . . .A'knfig
Alltwen: SA8 . . . . . . . . . . . . . . . . .All
Ammanford: SA18 . . . . . . . . . . .Amm
Baglan: SA12 . . . . . . . . . . . . . . .Bag
Bettws: CF32 . . . . . . . . . . . . . . . .Bet
Birchgrove: SA7 . . . . . . . . . . . . .Birch
Bishopston: SA3 . . . . . . . . . . .Bishop
Blackmill: CF35 . . . . . . . . . . .Blackm
Black Pill: SA3 . . . . . . . . . . . . .Blk P
Blaenau: SA18 . . . . . . . . . . . . . .Blae
Blaen-y-Maes: SA5 . . . . . . . . .Blae M
Blue Anchor: SA4 . . . . . . . . . . .Blu A
Bôn-y-maen: SA1 . . . . . . . . . . . .Bon
Brackla: CF31,CF35 . . . . . . . . .Brack
Bridgend: CF31-32,CF35 . . . . . . . . .Bri
Briton Ferry: SA11-12 . . . . . . . .Brit F
Bryn: SA14 . . . . . . . . . . . . . . . .Bryn
Brynamman: SA18 . . . . . . . . . . .Bry
Bryncethin: CF32 . . . . . . . . . . .Brync
Bryn-coch: CF32 . . . . . . . . . . .Bryn c
Bryncoch: SA10 . . . . . . . . . . . .B'och
Brynmenyn: CF32 . . . . . . . . . .B'myn
Brynmill: SA2 . . . . . . . . . . . . .Brynm
Burry Green: SA3 . . . . . . . . . . .Bury G
Burry Port: SA16 . . . . . . . . . . .Burr P
Bynea: SA14 . . . . . . . . . . . . . . .Byn
Cadle: SA5 . . . . . . . . . . . . . . . . .Cad
Cadoxton-juxta-Neath: SA10 . .C'dxtn
Caehopkin: SA9 . . . . . . . . . . . . .Cae
Cae'r-bont: SA9 . . . . . . . . . . . .C'bont
Cae'r-bryn: SA18 . . . . . . . . . . .C'bryn
Capel Hendre: SA18 . . . . . . . .Cap H
Carmarthen: SA31 . . . . . . . . . .Carm
Carmel: SA14 . . . . . . . . . . . . .C'mel
Caswell: SA3 . . . . . . . . . . . . . .Casw
Cefn Cribwr: CF32 . . . . . . . . . .Cef C
Cefneithin: SA14 . . . . . . . . . . . .Cef
Cheriton: SA3 . . . . . . . . . . . . .Cher
Cilfrew: SA10 . . . . . . . . . . . . . .Cilf
Cilmaengwyn: SA8 . . . . . . . . . .Cilm
Cilonen: SA4 . . . . . . . . . . . . . . . .Cil
Cilybebyll: SA8 . . . . . . . . . . . . .Cily
Cimla: SA11 . . . . . . . . . . . . . . .Cim
Clase: SA6 . . . . . . . . . . . . . . .Clase
Clydach: SA6,SA8 . . . . . . . . . . .Cly
Clyne Common: SA3 . . . . . . . .Cly C
Cockett: SA2 . . . . . . . . . . . . . .C'ett
Coed Hirwaun: SA13 . . . . . . . .Coe H
Coity: CF35 . . . . . . . . . . . . . . .Coity
Corntown: CF35 . . . . . . . . . . . .Corn
Court Colman: CF31 . . . . . . .Ct Col
Coychurch: CF35 . . . . . . . . . . .Coyc
Coytrahen: CF32 . . . . . . . . . . .Coyt

Craig-cefn-parc: SA6 . . . . . . . .Craig-p
Crofty: SA4 . . . . . . . . . . . . . . . .Crof
Cross Hands: SA14 . . . . . . . .Cross H
Crymlyn Burrows: SA1,SA10 . . .Cry B
Crynant: SA10 . . . . . . . . . . . . . .Cry
Cwmavon: SA12-13 . . . . . . . .C'avon
Cwmbwrla: SA5 . . . . . . . . . . .Cwmb
Cwmdu: SA5 . . . . . . . . . . . .Cwmdu
Cwmffrwd: SA31 . . . . . . . . . .Cwmf
Cwmgiedd: SA9 . . . . . . . . . . .C'edd
Cwmgors: SA18 . . . . . . . . . . .C'gors
Cwmgwili: SA14 . . . . . . . . . . . .C'ili
Cwmllynfell: SA9 . . . . . . . . . . .Cwml
Cwmrhydyceirw: SA6 . . . . . .Cwm'crw
Cwm-twrch Isaf: SA9 . . . . . . .Cwm I
Cwm-twrch Uchaf: SA9 . . . . .Cwm U
Dafen: SA14-15 . . . . . . . . . . .Dafen
Dunvant: SA2 . . . . . . . . . . . . .Dunv
Ewenny: CF31,CF35 . . . . . . . . .Ewe
Fairwood: SA2 . . . . . . . . . . . . .Cair
Felindre: SA5 . . . . . . . . . . . . .F'dre
Felinfoel: SA14-15 . . . . . . . . . .F'oel
Fforest: SA4 . . . . . . . . . . . . . . .Ffor
Fforest-fach: SA5 . . . . . . . . . .Ffor F
Ffynnon-ddrain: SA31 . . . . . . . . .Ffy
Foelgastell: SA14 . . . . . . . . . . .Foe
Garnant: SA18 . . . . . . . . . . . .Garn
Garnswllt: SA18 . . . . . . . . . . .G'llt
Gellinudd: SA8 . . . . . . . . . . . . .Gell
Gendros: SA5 . . . . . . . . . . . . .Gen
Glais: SA7 . . . . . . . . . . . . . . .Glais
Glanaman: SA18 . . . . . . . . . . .Glan
Godre'r-graig: SA9 . . . . . . . . .Godr
Gorseinon: SA4 . . . . . . . . . . . .Gor
Gorslas: SA14 . . . . . . . . . . . .Gors
Gowerton: SA2,SA4 . . . . . . . . .Gow
Graig: SA16 . . . . . . . . . . . . . .Graig
Grovesend: SA4 . . . . . . . . . . .Grov
Gwaun-Cae-Gurwen: SA18 . . .Gwaun
Hendre: CF35 . . . . . . . . . . . . . .Hen
Hendy: SA4 . . . . . . . . . . . . . .Hendy
Hernston: CF31 . . . . . . . . . . .Hern
Horton: SA3 . . . . . . . . . . . . . . .Hort
Jersey Marine: SA10 . . . . . . .Jer M
Johnstown: SA31 . . . . . . . . . .John
Kenfig: CF33 . . . . . . . . . . . . . . .Ken
Kenfig Hill: CF33 . . . . . . . . . .Ken H
Killay: SA2,SA5 . . . . . . . . . . . .Kill
Kittle: SA3 . . . . . . . . . . . . . . . .Kit
Knelston: SA3 . . . . . . . . . . . . .Knel
Laleston: CF32 . . . . . . . . . . . .Lale
Landore: SA1 . . . . . . . . . . . . .L'ore
Langland: SA3 . . . . . . . . . . . . .Lan
Llandarcy: SA10 . . . . . . . . . . .L'dcy
Llanddewi: SA3 . . . . . . . . . . .Lland
Llandybie: SA18 . . . . . . . . . . .L'bie

Llanedi: SA4 . . . . . . . . . . . . . .L'edi
Llanelli: SA14-15 . . . . . . . . . .Llane
Llangeinor: CF32 . . . . . . . . . .L'nor
Llangennech: SA14 . . . . . . . . .L'nch
Llangennith: SA3 . . . . . . . . . .Llang
Llangewydd: CF31-32 . . . . . . .L'ydd
Llangunnor: SA31 . . . . . . . . . .Llang
Llangyfelach: SA4-6 . . . . . . . .L'flch
Llanllwch: SA31 . . . . . . . . . . .Llanl
Llanmadoc: SA3 . . . . . . . . . . .L'doc
Llanmorlais: SA4 . . . . . . . . . .Llanm
Llanrhidian: SA3 . . . . . . . . . . .Llanr
Llansamlet: SA6-7,SA10 . . . .L'smlt
Llwynhendy: SA14 . . . . . . . . . .Llwy
Loughor: SA4 . . . . . . . . . . . . . .Lou
Lower Brynamman: SA18 . . . .Lwr B
Maesybont: SA14 . . . . . . . . . .Maes
Manselton: SA5 . . . . . . . . . . . .Man
Margam: SA13 . . . . . . . . . . . .Marg
Mawdlam: CF33 . . . . . . . . . . .Maw
Mayals: SA3 . . . . . . . . . . . . . .May
Mayhill: SA1 . . . . . . . . . . . . .M'hill
Merthyr Mawr: CF32 . . . . . .M Mawr
Middleton: SA3 . . . . . . . . . . .Midd
Morriston: SA6 . . . . . . . . . . . .Morr
The Mumbles: SA3 . . . . . . . .T Mum
Murton: SA3 . . . . . . . . . . . . . .Mur
Neath: SA10-11 . . . . . . . . . . . .Nea
Neath Abbey: SA10 . . . . . . . .Nea A
Newton: CF36,SA3 . . . . . . . . .Newt
Nicholaston: SA3 . . . . . . . . . .Nich
North Cornelly: CF33 . . . . . . .N Cor
Nottage: CF36 . . . . . . . . . . . .Not
Oxwich: SA3 . . . . . . . . . . . . .Oxw
Pantlasau: SA6 . . . . . . . . . . .Pantl
Parkmill: SA3 . . . . . . . . . . . . .Park
Pembrey: SA16 . . . . . . . . . . . .Pem
Penclawdd: SA4 . . . . . . . . . . .Penc
Pencoed: CF35 . . . . . . . . . . .P'coed
Penlan: SA5 . . . . . . . . . . . . .P'lan
Penllergaer: SA4 . . . . . . . . . .Penl
Penmaen: SA3 . . . . . . . . . . .Penm
Pen-Rhiw-fawr: SA9 . . . . . . .P fawr
Penrhos: SA9 . . . . . . . . . . . .P'hos
Pen-y-bryn: CF33 . . . . . . . . .Pen b
Pen-y-cae: CF32 . . . . . . . . .Pen-ca
Pen-y-fai: CF31-32 . . . . . . . .Pen F
Pen-y-groes: SA14 . . . . . . . .Pen g
Pitton: SA3 . . . . . . . . . . . . . . .P'tn
Plasmarl: SA6 . . . . . . . . . . . .Plas
Pontardawe: SA8 . . . . . . . . .P'dwe
Pontardulais: SA4 . . . . . . . . .P'dul
Pontlliw: SA4 . . . . . . . . . . . .P'liw
Pontrhydyfen: SA12 . . . . . . . .Pontr
Port-Eynon: SA3 . . . . . . . . . .Port

Porthcawl: CF36 . . . . . . . . . . .P'cwl
Portmead: SA5 . . . . . . . . . . . .Por
Port Talbot: SA12-13 . . . . . . .P Tal
Port Tennant: SA1 . . . . . . . . .Por T
Pwll: SA15 . . . . . . . . . . . . . . .Pwll
Pyle: CF33 . . . . . . . . . . . . . . .Pyle
Ravenhill: SA5 . . . . . . . . . . . .Rav
Reynoldston: SA3 . . . . . . . . . .Rey
Rhiwceiliog: CF35 . . . . . . . . .Rhiwc
Rhos: SA8 . . . . . . . . . . . . . . .Rhos
Rhosaman: SA18 . . . . . . . . . .Rhosa
Rhossili: SA3 . . . . . . . . . . . . .Rhoss
Rhyd-y-fro: SA8 . . . . . . . . . . .Phyd f
Rhyd-y-pandy: SA6 . . . . . . . .Rhyd p
St Thomas: SA1 . . . . . . . . . . .St T
Sandfields: SA12 . . . . . . . . . .Sand
Sardis: SA4 . . . . . . . . . . . . . .Sard
Sarn: CF32 . . . . . . . . . . . . . . .Sarn
Saron: SA18 . . . . . . . . . . . . .Saron
Scurlage: SA3 . . . . . . . . . . . . .Scur
Seven Sisters: SA10 . . . . . . . .Sev S
Sketty: SA2,SA5 . . . . . . . . . . .Sket
Skewen: SA10 . . . . . . . . . . . .Skew
Slade: SA3 . . . . . . . . . . . . . .Slade
South Cornelly: CF33 . . . . . . .Sth C
Southgate: SA3 . . . . . . . . . . .S'gate
Swansea: SA1,SA5 . . . . . . . . .Swan
Swansea Enterprise Park: SA1,SA6-7
. . . . . . . . . . . . . . . . . . . .Swan Ent
Tairgwaith: SA18 . . . . . . . . . . .Tair
Three Crosses: SA4 . . . . . . . .Thr X
Tircoed Forest Village: SA4 . . . .Tir V
Tirdeunaw: SA5 . . . . . . . . . . .Tird
Tondu: CF32 . . . . . . . . . . . . . .Ton
Tonmawr: SA12 . . . . . . . . . . .Tonm
Tonna: SA11 . . . . . . . . . . . . .Tonna
Townhill: SA1 . . . . . . . . . . . .Town
Trebanos: SA8 . . . . . . . . . . .T'nos
Tre-boeth: SA5 . . . . . . . . . . .Tre b
Treoes: CF35 . . . . . . . . . . . .Treoes
Trevaughan: SA31 . . . . . . . . .Treva
Tumble: SA14 . . . . . . . . . . . .Tum
Tycroes: SA18 . . . . . . . . . . . .Tyc
Uplands: SA2 . . . . . . . . . . . . .Upl
Upper Killay: SA2 . . . . . . . . . .Up K
Waunarlwydd: SA5 . . . . . . . .Wauna
Waungron: SA4 . . . . . . . . . . .Waun
Wernffrwd: SA4 . . . . . . . . . . .Wern
West Cross: SA3 . . . . . . . . .W Cro
Winsh-wen: SA1 . . . . . . . . . .Wins
Ynysforgan: SA6 . . . . . . . . . .Yfgn
Ynysmeudwy: SA8 . . . . . . . . .Ynys
Ynystawe: SA6-7 . . . . . . . . .Ystwe
Ystalyfera: SA9 . . . . . . . . . . .Ysta
Ystradgynlais: SA9 . . . . . . . .Ystra

---

360 Beach & Watersports . . . .5C 84

## A

Abbey Mead SA31: Carm . . . . . .2G 7
Abbey Rd. CF33: Ken H . . . . . .5F 113
  CF35: Ewe . . . . . . . . . . . . .6D 126
  SA13: P Tal . . . . . . . . . . . . .5H 97
Abbey Rd. Ind. Est.
  SA10: Nea . . . . . . . . . . . . . .1H 77
Abbey Vw. SA10: Nea A . . . . . .6G 63
Abbeyville Av. SA12: Sand . . . .4C 96
  (not continuous)
Abbeyville Ct. SA12: Sand . . . .3C 96
Abbots Cl. SA13: Marg . . . . . .3G 103
Abbotsford Ho.
  SA1: Swan . . . . . . .6E 5 (5G 85)
Abbot's Wlk. SA10: Nea A . . . .6H 63
Abbott's M. SA13: Marg . . . . .3G 103
Abbottsmoor SA12: Bag . . . . .2D 96
ABERAFAN . . . . . . . . . . . . . . .4D 96
Aberafan Cen. *SA13: P Tal* . . .3F 97
  (shown as Aberavon Cen.)
ABERAVON . . . . . . . . . . . . . .4D 96
Aberavon Cen. SA13: P Tal . . .3F 97
Aberavon Ct. SA12: A'von . . . .3E 97
Aberavon Gas Works Est.
  SA12: A'von . . . . . . . . . . . .4E 97
Aberavon RFC . . . . . . . . . . . . .4G 97
Aberavon Rd. SA12: Bag . . . . .2C 96
Abercedi SA4: Penc . . . . . . . . .4B 68

Aberclydach Pl. SA6: Cly . . . . .5E 49
Aber Ct. SA6: Swan Ent . . . . . .1C 74
ABERCRAF . . . . . . . . . . . . . . .1F 29
Abercrave Ter. SA9: Cae . . . . . .1H 29
ABERCYNFFIG . . . . . . . . . . . .6A 114
ABERDULAIS . . . . . . . . . . . . . .2F 65
*Aberdulais Falls (NT)* . . . . . . . .2F 65
*Aberdulais Falls Watermills* . . . .2F 65
Aberdyberthi St. SA1: Swan . . .6G 73
ABERGARW . . . . . . . . . . . . . .3E 115
Abergarw Dr. CF32: B'myn . . .3E 115
Abergarw Ind. Est.
  CF32: B'myn . . . . . . . . . . .3F 115
Abergarw Rd. CF32: B'myn . . .3E 115
Abergarw Trad. Est.
  CF32: B'myn . . . . . . . . . . .3F 115
Abergelly Rd. SA5: Ffor F . . . . .3H 71
Abergwili Rd. SA31: Carm . . . . .1H 7
Aberhenwaun Uchaf
  SA10: Sev S . . . . . . . . . . . .3H 29
ABERKENFIG . . . . . . . . . . . . .6A 114
Aberlash Rd. SA18: Amm . . . . .4F 11
Aber Llwchwr SA14: L'nch . . . .5C 44
Abernant Rd. SA18: C'gors . . . .4C 24
Abernethy Quay
  SA1: Swan . . . . . .5G 5 (4H 85)
Abernethy Sq.
  SA1: Swan . . . . . .5G 5 (4H 85)
ABERTAWE . . . . . . . . .4E 5 (4G 85)
Acacia Av. CF36: Newt . . . . . .4G 125
Acacia Cl. SA12: Sand . . . . . . .2B 96
Acacia Rd. SA3: W Cro . . . . . .4F 95
ACHDDU . . . . . . . . . . . . . . . . .2D 38
Acland Rd. CF31: Bri . . . . . . .6E 121

Acorn Ct. SA6: Swan Ent . . . . . .5D 60
Acorn Pl. SA12: Bag . . . . . . . . .3A 90
Adams Av. CF32: Brync . . . . . .5E 115
Adam Wlk. SA10: Nea A . . . . . .6H 63
Adare St. CF31: Bri . . . . . . . . . .1E 127
  SA12: Sand . . . . . . . . . . . .4D 96
Addison Pl. SA12: Sand . . . . . .4D 96
Addison Rd. SA11: Nea . . . . . .3A 78
  SA12: Sand . . . . . . . . . . . .3D 96
Adelaide St.
  SA1: Swan . . . . . . .4F 5 (4G 85)
Admirals Wlk. SA2: Sket . . . . . .4H 83
Adrian Cl. CF36: P'cwl . . . . . . .3B 124
Adulam Row SA15: F'oel . . . . . .3C 42
Aelfryn Ter. SA2: C'avon . . . . . .4G 91
Ael y Bryn SA4: Penc . . . . . . . .4B 68
  SA9: Ystra . . . . . . . . . . . . .4B 28
  SA31: Carm . . . . . . . . . . . . .1G 7
Ael-y-Bryn CF31: Bri . . . . . . . .6A 120
  CF33: N Cor . . . . . . . . . . . .1D 116
  SA3: T Mum . . . . . . . . . . . .3G 101
Aelybryn SA15: Pwll . . . . . . . . .2C 40
Ael y Bryn Cl. SA15: F'oel . . . . .4B 42
Aelybryn Dr. SA15: Llane . . . . .4B 42
Ael y Bryn Rd. SA5: Ffor F . . . . .5B 72
Ael-y-Fro SA8: P'dwe . . . . . . . .4C 36
Aeron Pl. SA1: Bon . . . . . . . . . .6C 74
Afandale SA12: Sand . . . . . . . .6H 89
Afan Valley Cl. SA11: Cim . . . . .3E 79
Afan Valley Rd. SA11: Cim . . . .3D 78
  SA12: C'avon, Pontr . . . . . .1H 97
  SA13: C'avon . . . . . . . . . . .1H 97
Afan Way SA1: Cry B . . . . . . . .4G 87
  SA12: A'von, Sand . . . . . . . .6H 89
Afon Fach CF33: N Cor . . . . . .6D 112

Afon-Llan Gdns. SA5: Por . . . . .2A 72
Afon Rd. SA14: L'nch . . . . . . . .4D 44
Afon-y-Felin SA10: A'dul . . . . . .2F 65
Alamein Rd. SA1: Swan Ent . . .5H 73
Alban Rd. SA15: Llane . . . . . . .6B 42
Albany Cl. SA5: Man . . . . . . . . .4F 73
Alberto Rd. SA6: Swan Ent . . . .2B 74
Albert Pl. *SA3: T Mum* . . . . . .1E 101
  (off Gloucester Pl.)
Albert Row SA1: Swan . . .5E 5 (4G 85)
Albert St. SA15: Llane . . . . . . . .4H 41
Albion Arc. *SA31: Carm* . . . . . .3E 7
  (off Mill St.)
Albion Pl. CF33: Ken H . . . . . . .6F 113
Albion Rd. SA12: Bag . . . . . . . .3H 89
Albion Rd. App. SA12: Bag . . . .3H 89
Alden Dr. SA2: C'ett . . . . . . . . .1A 84
Aldenham CF36: Newt . . . . . . .4F 125
Alder Av. SA9: Ystra . . . . . . . . .1G 33
Alderbrook Cl. SA5: Blae M . . . .2C 72
Aldergrove Cl. SA12: Bag . . . . .6B 90
Alder Rd. SA11: Cim . . . . . . . . .2D 78
Alder Way SA3: W Cro . . . . . . .5D 94
  SA4: Gow . . . . . . . . . . . . . .2B 70
Alderwood Rd. SA3: W Cro . . . .5F 95
Aldwyn Rd. SA1: Swan . . . . . . .6A 72
Alexander Cres. SA10: Nea . . . .4B 64
Alexander Rd. SA10: Nea . . . . . .3A 64
  SA11: Brit F . . . . . . . . . . . .5H 77
Alexandra Arc.
  SA1: Swan . . . . . . .2E 5 (2G 85)
Alexandra Ho. SA1: Swan . . . . .1E 5
Alexandra Rd.
  SA1: Swan . . . . . .2D 4 (3F 85)
  SA4: Gor . . . . . . . . . . . . . . .4H 55

Alexandra St. SA12: A'von ....3F 97
Alexandra Ter. SA2: Brynm ....5C 84
Alford Rd. SA11: Nea ........1B 78
Alfred Rd. SA6: Plas ........2H 73
Alfred St. SA11: Nea ........1B 78
 SA12: A'von ............3E 97
Alice St. SA5: Cwmdu .......6D 72
 SA11: Nea ..............2A 78
Alison Ct. CF36: Newt ....4F 125
Allaway Ct. SA1: Swan .....6F 73
Allister St. SA11: Nea ......1B 78
Alloy Ct. Est. SA8: P'dwe ....5E 37
Alloy Ind. Est. SA8: P'dwe ...6E 37
All Saints Pl. SA12: C'avon ...5H 91
All Saints Way CF31: Pen F ..2C 120
ALLT ..................3C 44
Allt Dderw CF31: Bri .....3A 126
Allt-tago Rd. SA4: P'dul ....1C 46
Allt Ioan SA31: John .......4A 6
ALLTWEN ................1E 51
Alltwen Chwyth SA8: All ....1E 51
Alltwen Hill SA8: All .......1E 51
 (not continuous)
Alltwen Ind. Est. SA8: All ...5F 37
Alltycham Dr. SA8: P'dwe ...5D 36
Alltycnap Rd. SA31: John ...6A 6
Allt y Felin SA10: Nea ......5H 63
Allt y Gog SA31: Carm .....3A 6
Allt y Graban Rd.
 SA4: P'dul, Waun ......4B 46
Allt y Grug SA10: Jer M ....1B 88
Alltygrug Farm Rd. SA9: Ysta ..1E 33
Alltygrug Rd. SA9: Ysta ....2E 33
 (shown as Heol Alltygrug)
Allt-y-Waun SA8: Phyd f ....3C 36
Alltywerin SA8: P'dwe .....4C 36
Alma Ter. CF32: A'knfig ....6B 114
Alpha Pl. SA12: Bag .......3A 90
Als St. SA15: Llane ........1A 52
Altamar SA1: Swan ....4H 5 (4H 85)
Alun Rd. SA1: M'hill .......1E 85
Alyson Way CF35: P'coed ...3F 123
Amanwy SA14: Llwy ......6G 43
Ambassador Ho. SA1: Swan ...6F 5
Amber Cl. SA12: Sand ......2A 96
Amberley Dr. SA3: Lan .....2E 101
Ambleside SA3: W Cro ....4F 95
AMMANFORD ............1A 22
Ammanford Bus Station .....1H 21
Ammanford Miners Mus. .....1H 21
Ammanford (Rhydaman) Station
 (Rail) ................6G 11
Amman Rd. SA18: Lwr B ....4H 15
AMMAN VALLEY HOSPITAL
 (YSBYTY DYFFRYN AMAN) 4A 14
Amman Valley Leisure Cen. ..6A 12
Amos St. SA15: Llane ......5H 41
Amroth Ct. SA5: P'lan .....1E 73
Anchor Ct. SA1: Swan ..5F 5 (4G 85)
 SA4: Blu A .............5B 68
Anderson La. SA3: S'gate ...2A 68
Andrew Cres. SA6: Yfgn ....2C 60
Andrews Cl. CF32: Ton .....4C 114
Andrew St. SA15: Llane ....6B 42
Andrew Ter. SA15: Llane ...6B 42
Aneddfan SA12: C'avon ....4H 91
Aneurin Bevan Av.
 CF32: B'myn ..........3E 115
Aneurin Cl. SA2: Sket .....4F 83
Aneurin Way SA2: Sket ....4F 83
Angel Pl. SA11: Nea .......6B 64
Angel St. CF31: Bri ......1D 126
 SA11: Nea .............6B 64
 SA12: A'von ...........3E 97
Angelton Grn. CF31: Pen F ..2C 120
Angel Way CF32: N Cor ....6B 112
Anglesey Way
 CF36: Not, P'cwl ......2B 124
Angleton Rd. CF31: Pen F ..3C 120
Annesley St. SA15: Llane ...4H 41
Ann St. SA15: Llane .......2A 52
Anton Ct. SA4: P'dul ......6F 35
Apollo 6 Cinema .........4C 96
Appledore Pl. SA3: Newt ...6D 94
Applegrove SA3: Rey ......6A 106
Approach Rd. SA5: Man ....6E 73
Aran St. SA6: Morr ........1A 74
Arcade, The SA15: Llane ....1A 52
 (off Stepney St)
SA18: Amm ...........1H 21
Arcade Ter. SA18: Garn .....5C 14
 (shown as Teras yr Arced)

Ardwyn SA16: Burr P ......2F 39
Ardwyn Rd. SA18: Bry .....3B 16
Ardwyn Va. CF35: P'coed ...3F 123
Arennig Rd. SA5: P'lan ....3E 73
Arethusa Ct. SA2: Up K ....4B 82
Arethusa Quay
 SA1: Swan ......6E 5 (5G 85)
Arfryn SA18: Bry ........2B 16
Arfryn Av. SA15: Llane .....6A 42
Arfryn Rd. SA2: C'ett ......2B 84
Argoed Rd. SA18: Amm ....4A 22
 (shown as Heol Argoed)
Argonaut Ho. SA1: Swan ....6F 5
Argyle Ct. SA1: Swan ..4B 4 (4E 85)
Argyle St. SA1: Swan ..5B 4 (4E 85)
Argyll Av. SA4: Gor .......4A 56
Argyll Ct. SA4: Gor .......4A 56
 (off Lime St.)
Arhosfa CF31: Bri ........4D 120
Arlan Gwili SA4: Hendy ....6D 34
Arlington Pl. CF36: P'cwl ...4C 124
Arlington Rd. CF36: P'cwl ..4C 124
Armine Rd. SA5: Gen ......5B 72
Arosfa Av. CF36: Newt .....3G 125
Arthur's Stone ..........6C 106
Arthur St. SA11: Nea ......1B 78
 SA12: A'von ...........3F 97
 SA15: Llane ...........1A 52
 SA18: Amm ............6H 11
 (shown as Stryd Arthur)
Arthur Ter. SA8: P'dwe .....5D 36
Arwelfa SA6: Morr ........5G 59
Ar-y-Bryn SA16: Pem ......1A 38
Ascot Dr. SA12: Bag .......3A 90
Ashbrook CF31: Brack .....6G 121
Ashburnham Dr. SA3: May ...2D 94
Ashburnham Golf Course ...3C 38
Ashburnham Rd.
 SA16: Burr P ..........3D 38
 SA16: Burr P, Pem .....2A 38
Ash Cotts. SA2: C'ett .....1A 84
Ash Gro. CF31: Bri .......6H 119
 SA2: Kill .............3C 82
 SA4: Gor .............3H 55
 SA5: Wauna ..........4C 70
 SA11: Cim ............3E 79
 SA12: Bag ............3A 90
 SA31: Carm ...........4B 6
Ashgrove CF36: Newt .....3G 125
 SA18: Amm ............1C 22
Ashleigh Cl. SA2: Sket ....1H 95
Ashleigh Ct. SA2: Sket ....1G 95
Ashleigh Ter. SA10: Jer M ..2B 88
Ashmawr Ct. SA4: Crof ....5E 67
Ashmount Bus. Pk.
 SA6: Swan Ent .........5C 60
Ash St. SA6: Morr ........1B 74
Ashwood Dr. SA8: Gell .....5G 37
Aspen Way SA11: Cim ......2F 79
Assembly Rooms SA1: Swan ..4G 5
Aster Vw. SA12: Sand .....1B 96
Astral Ct. SA12: Bag ......4H 89
Atlantic Cl. SA7: Swan Ent ..3B 74
Atlantic Haven SA3: Llang ...5D 104
Attlee Av. SA12: Sand .....4D 96
Attlee St. CF32: B'myn ....3B 115
Auburn Av. SA12: Sand ....2A 96
Aurora SA1: Swan ....6H 5 (5H 85)
Austin Av. CF31: Bri ......5E 121
 CF32: Lale ............5B 126
 CF36: Newt ...........3F 125
Austin Cl. CF36: Newt .....3F 125
Australian Ter. CF31: Bri ...5E 121
Avan St. SA13: P Tal ......3G 97
Avenue, The SA11: Nea ....3A 78
 SA12: C'avon ..........4G 91
 SA14: Llwy ............1F 53
 SA15: Llane ...........4B 52
 SA31: Carm ...........3F 7
Averil Vivian Gro. SA2: Sket ..4B 84
Avis Ter. SA15: Llane ......1B 52
Awel Deg SA7: Birch ......3F 61
Awel Tywi SA31: Carm .....4G 7
Axis St. SA7: Swan Ent ....4C 60
Aylesbury Rd. SA2: Brynm ..5C 84
Aztec Bus. Cen. SA5: Ffor F ..4A 72

## B

Babell Rd. SA31: Carm .........5E 7
 (shown as Rhiw Babell)
Bach Rd. SA12: Sand .......1A 96
Back Dr. SA10: Skew .......1A 76
Badgers Brook CF31: Brack ..5F 121

Badgers Mead CF31: Brack ..5F 121
Badminton Gdns. SA5: Rav ...3A 72
BAGLAN .................5B 90
Baglan Bay Retail Pk.
 SA12: Bag ............1C 96
Baglan Bay Shop. Cen.
 SA12: Bag ............1C 96
Baglan Energy Pk. SA12: Bag ..4H 89
Baglan Hgts. SA12: Bag ....3C 90
BAGLAN MOORS ...........6A 90
Baglan Moors Ind. Pk.
 SA12: Bag ............2D 96
Baglan Rd. SA12: Bag .....2H 89
Baglan Station (Rail) ......5A 90
Baglan St. SA1: Por T .....3B 86
Baglan Way SA12: Bag .....6A 90
Bagle Ct. SA12: Bag .......5B 90
 (off Fernley Dr.)
Baiden Av. CF33: Ken H ....5F 113
Bailey Ct. SA5: Ffor F .....4H 71
Bailey St. SA12: A'von .....3F 97
Bakers Way CF32: Brync ...5D 114
Balaclava Rd. SA7: Glais ...1H 61
Balaclava St.
 SA1: St T .......3H 5 (3H 85)
Bala Pl. SA5: Rav .........4B 72
Baldwin's Cres. SA1: Cry B ..3F 87
Ballarat CF35: P'coed ......1H 123
Ballard's Ct. SA10: Nea A ..6E 63
Ballas Cl. CF33: N Cor .....2D 116
Banc Bach SA4: Penc ......4H 67
Banc Gelli Las CF31: Bri ...3A 126
Banc Gwyn CF31: Bri ......3A 126
Banc y Daraenen
 SA8: Cap H ...........3H 19
Bancyffynnon SA14: Cross H ..6C 8
Banc-yr-Allt CF31: Bri .....5A 120
Banc yr Eithin SA4: Gor ....3H 55
Banfield Ter. SA4: Lou .....4F 55
Bankers Hill CF32: Cef C ...1D 118
Bank Farm Leisure Pk.
 SA3: Hort ............5H 109
Bank Rd. SA14: L'nch ......4D 44
Banks Bldgs. CF31: Bri ....2B 128
Bank Side SA11: Nea ......6B 64
Bank Vw. SA3: Rhoss .....2C 108
Banwell Rd. SA6: Morr .....6A 60
Banwell St. SA6: Morr .....6A 60
Banwen La. SA8: All .......6E 37
Banwen Pl. SA18: Lwr B ....4H 15
Banwy Rd. SA6: Clase .....5G 59
 (not continuous)
Baptist La. SA18: Amm .....1H 21
Baptist Well Pl. SA1: Swan ..1F 85
Baptist Well St. SA1: Swan ..1F 85
Bardsey Av. SA5: Blae M ...1B 72
Bardsey Cl. CF36: Not .....1B 124
Bargemans Row SA1: Swan ..2G 85
Barnabas Cl. SA5: Wauna ...5E 71
Barn Cotts. SA11: Brit F ...6G 77
Barnes Av. CF31: Bri ......5A 120
Barn Rd. SA31: Carm ......3E 7
Barnsfield Ter. SA31: Carm ..3E 7
Barons Ct. SA1: Swan .....3E 5
 SA10: Nea A ...........6H 63
Barry Rd. SA18: Lwr B .....6G 15
Bartley Ter. SA6: Plas .....3H 73
Bassett Ter. SA1: Pwll .....3D 40
Bath Av. SA6: Morr ........5A 60
Bath La. SA1: Swan ...4F 5 (4G 85)
Bath Rd. SA6: Morr ........5A 60
Bath St. SA13: P Tal ......3G 97
Bath Ter. SA6: Morr .......6A 60
Bathurst St.
 SA1: Swan ......5D 4 (4F 85)
 (not continuous)
Bath Vs. SA6: Morr ........6A 60
Bay Holme Cvn. Site
 SA3: Oxw .............4D 110
Bayliss Rd. CF32: Brync ...5E 115
Bay St. SA1: Por T ........3B 86
Bayswater Rd. SA2: Sket ...4G 83
Bay Tree Av. SA2: Sket ....4G 83
Baytree Ct. SA4: Gow .....4B 70
Bay Vw. SA1: St T ....1G 5 (2H 85)
 SA4: Penc ............2H 67
 SA13: P Tal ...........2H 97
 SA15: Pwll ............2C 40
Bayview SA14: Byn ........2A 54
 SA15: Llane ...........5A 52
Bay Vw. Cl. SA1: Swan ....4D 84
Bay Vw. Cres. SA1: Swan ...4D 84
Bay Vw. Gdns. SA10: Skew ..3D 76
Bay Vw. Hgts. SA13: P Tal ..2H 97

Bay Vw. Rd. CF36: Newt ....5G 125
 SA14: Dafen ..........6D 42
Bay Vw. Ter. SA1: Swan ....4C 84
Baywood Av. SA3: W Cro ...4F 95
BBC Wales .............3F 85
Beach Cl. CF33: Pyle ......6D 112
 CF36: Newt ...........4G 125
 SA4: Penc ............4H 67
 SA15: Llane ...........4D 52
Beach St. SA1: Swan ...5A 4 (4E 85)
 SA12: A'von ...........4E 97
Beaconsfield Ct. SA2: Sket ..3G 83
Beaconsfield Rd.
 SA10: C'dxtn ..........4C 64
Beaconsfield Way SA2: Sket ..3G 83
Beacons Vw. SA11: Cim ....3D 78
Beacons Vw. Rd. SA6: Clase ..5G 59
Beattie St. SA5: Cwmdu ....6E 73
Beauchamp Wlk. SA4: Gor ..6A 56
Beaufort Av. SA3: Lan .....3E 101
Beaufort Cl. SA3: Lan .....3E 101
Beaufort Ct. SA5: Rav .....3B 72
 SA6: Swan Ent ........2A 74
Beaufort Dr. SA3: Kit ......5F 93
Beaufort Gdns. SA3: Kit ....5F 93
Beaufort Rd. SA6: Swan Ent ..3A 74
Beaumont Cres.
 SA1: St T .......1H 5 (2H 85)
Beddgelert Fld. CF31: Bri ...2B 126
Bedford Rd. CF32: Cef C ...1B 118
Bedford Rd. CF32: Cef C ...1B 118
Bedford St. SA6: Morr .....6B 60
Bedw Arian CF31: Bri ......5A 120
Beech Cres. SA4: Gor ......3H 55
Beeches, The CF31: Bri ....5D 120
Beeches Cl., The SA3: Sket ..2F 83
Beech Gro. CF36: Newt ....3G 125
Beech Rd. SA31: Carm .....3B 6
Beech Tree Cl. SA6: Clase ..5G 59
Beech Tree La. SA2: Sket ..5H 83
Beechwood Av. CF31: Bri ..6A 120
 SA11: Nea ............1C 78
Beechwood Gro.
 CF35: P'coed ..........2G 123
Beechwood Rd. SA2: Upl ...4B 84
 SA3: Marg ............3F 103
Beili Glas SA4: Lou .......5F 55
Belgrave Cl. SA4: Gor .....5H 55
Belgrave Cl. SA1: Swan ....4D 84
Belgrave Gdns. SA1: Swan ..4D 84
Belgrave La. SA1: Swan ....3D 84
Belgrave Rd. SA4: Gor .....5H 55
Belleisle Apartments
 SA1: Swan Ent ........5A 74
Bellerphon Ct. SA1: Swan Ent ..5A 74
Belle Vue Ct. SA4: Penc ...4A 68
Bellevue Rd. SA3: W Cro ...6E 95
Belle Vue Way
 SA1: Swan .......2D 4 (3F 85)
Bellvue Rd. SA14: Byn .....3H 53
Belvedere Av. SA31: Carm ..2F 7
Belvedere Cl. SA3: Kit .....5F 93
Belvedere Rd. SA15: Llane ..3H 41
Benbow Cl. SA2: Sket .....4H 83
Bendrick Dr. SA3: S'gate ...3H 111
Benedict Cl. SA10: Nea A ..6G 63
Bennett Av. CF31: Bri .....2A 128
Bennett St. CF31: Bri .....2A 128
 SA1: L'ore ............4G 73
Benson Rd. SA4: Penc .....4A 68
Benson St. SA4: Penc .....4A 68
Benson Way SA6: Swan Ent ..2B 74
Benthall Pl. SA1: St T ..2H 5 (2H 85)
Berkeley Cl. SA7: Birch ....4H 61
Berllan Deg SA15: Dafen ...6D 42
Berma Cl. SA3: T Mum .....3G 101
Bernard St. SA2: Brynm, Upl ..4C 84
Berrington Hill SA9: Cwml ..2B 26
Berrington Vs. SA9: Cwml ..1B 26
BERRY .................3A 110
Berrylands SA12: Sand ....4C 96
Berry La. SA3: Scur .......3H 109
Bertha Pl. SA13: Marg .....2G 103
Bertha Rd. SA14: Byn .....4H 53
Berwick Rd. SA14: Byn ....4H 53
Berwick Ter.
 SA1: Swan, Town ...1D 4 (2F 85)
Berw Rd. SA1: M'hill .......2E 85
 (not continuous)
Berwyn Pl. SA5: P'lan .....4D 72
Beryl Rd. SA5: Cly ........4F 49

Bethania Rd.—Brunner Dr.


**Bethania Rd.** SA6: Cly . . . 5E 49
SA14: Tum . . . 2A 18
**Bethania Ter.** *SA12: C'avon . . . 4H 91*
*(off Cattybrook Ter.)*
SA15: Llane . . . 4B 52
**Bethany La.** SA3: W Cro . . . 5F 95
**Bethany Sq.** SA13: P Tal . . . 3G 97
**Bethel Cl.** SA5: Man . . . 5F 73
**Bethel La.** SA4: Penc . . . 4H 67
**Bethel Rd.** SA4: Penc . . . 4H 67
SA7: L'smlt . . . 1F 75
SA9: Cwm I . . . 6F 27
**Bethel St.** SA11: Brit F . . . 1H 89
**Bethesda Ct.** *SA1: Swan . . . 2G 85*
*(off Prince of Wales Rd.)*
**Bethesda Rd.** SA8: Ynys . . . 2G 37
**Bethesda St.** SA1: Swan . . . 2G 85
**Bethlehem Rd.** SA10: Skew . . . 1E 77
**Bettsland** SA3: W Cro . . . 4E 95
**Bettws Rd.** CF32: Bet, B'myn . . . 1C 114
SA5: P'lan . . . 4D 72
BETWS . . . 2A 22
**Betws Ind. Est.** SA18: Amm . . . 1A 22
**Betws Rd.** *SA18: Amm . . . 4A 22*
*(shown as Ffordd-y-Betws)*
**Bevans Row** SA1: Por T . . . 3C 86
**Bevans Ter.** SA7: L'smlt . . . 3F 75
**Bevan St.** SA12: A'von . . . 4E 97
**Bevan Way** SA5: Wauna . . . 5D 70
**Beverley Cl.** SA5: Rav . . . 3B 72
**Beverley Gdns.** SA5: Rav . . . 4B 72
**Beverley St.** SA13: P Tal . . . 4G 97
**Bevin Av.** SA12: Sand . . . 4C 96
**Biddulph Est.** SA15: Llane . . . 4B 52
BIGYN . . . 2B 52
**Bigyn La.** SA15: Llane . . . 2A 52
**Bigyn Pk. Ter.** SA15: Llane . . . 2A 52
**Bigyn Rd.** SA15: Llane . . . 1B 52
**Bilton Rd.** SA11: Nea . . . 1B 78
**Birch Ct.** SA6: Morr . . . 5B 60
BIRCHDALE . . . 5G 61
**Birches, The** SA6: Cly . . . 4G 49
**Birchfield Rd.** SA3: W Cro . . . 4E 95
SA8: P'dwe . . . 4E 37
BIRCHGROVE . . . 4H 61
**Birch Gro.** CF31: Bri . . . 6H 119
SA5: Wauna . . . 4C 70
**Birchgrove Rd.** SA7: Birch . . . 4H 61
SA7: Birch, Glais . . . 6H 49
**Birch La.** SA10: C'dxtn . . . 4C 64
SA10: Cilf . . . 1F 65
**Birch Rd.** SA12: Bag . . . 3A 90
**Birch Rock Rd.** SA4: P'dul . . . 1C 46
**Birchtree Cl.** SA2: Sket . . . 4H 83
**Birch Wlk.** CF36: Newt . . . 3G 125
**Birchwood Cl.** SA10: B'och . . . 1H 63
SA12: Bag . . . 5B 90
**Birkdale Cl.** SA3: May . . . 2E 95
**Birmingham Mt.** SA6: Plas . . . 2H 73
**Bishop Rd.** SA18: Garn . . . 5D 14
**Bishop's Gro.** SA2: Sket . . . 5G 83
**Bishops Mead** SA12: Bag . . . 1C 96
BISHOPSTON . . . 6G 93
**Bishopston Rd.** SA3: Bishop . . . 5G 93
Bishopston Sports Cen. . . . 5H 93
**Bishop's Wlk.** SA6: Morr . . . 4A 60
**Bishopswood** CF31: Brack . . . 1H 127
Bishop's Wood Nature Reserve
. . . 1A 100
**Bishwell Rd.** SA4: Gow . . . 5C 70
**Bittern Ct.** SA10: Nea . . . 4B 64
**Blackfield Row** CF32: Cef C . . . 1G 119
**Blackgates La.** SA11: Cim . . . 3E 79
**Blackhill Rd.** SA4: Gor . . . 3H 55
BLACKHILLS . . . 1A 94
**Blackhills Cvn. Pk.** SA2: Cair . . . 1H 93
**Blackhills La.** SA2: Cair . . . 1F 93
**Black Lion Cvn. & Camping Pk.**
SA14: Gors . . . 6E 9
**Black Lion Rd.** *SA14: Gors . . . 4E 9*
*(shown as Heol y Llew Du)*
**Blackmill Rd.** CF32: Brync . . . 4F 115
CF35: Blackm . . . 4F 115
BLACK PILL . . . 2G 95
Blackpill Burrows Golf Course
. . . 1H 95
Blackpill Lido . . . 2G 95
**Blackthorn Pl.** SA2: Sket . . . 1G 83
BLAENAU . . . 4C 10
**Blaenau Rd.**
SA18: Amm, Blae, L'bie . . . 4D 10
**Blaencedi** SA4: Blu A . . . 5A 68
**Blaen Cefn** SA1: Wins . . . 3E 75
**Blaencoed Rd.** SA7: L'smlt . . . 1G 75
**Blaen Cwm** SA10: Sev S . . . 5G 29
**Blaencwm Rd.** SA7: L'smlt . . . 1G 75
BLAENDULAIS . . . 5F 29
**Blaen Emlyn** SA14: Pen g . . . 4G 9
**Blaenmorfa** SA4: P'dul . . . 1B 46
**Blaen Nant** SA14: F'oel . . . 2E 43
**Blaenwern** SA10: Nea . . . 4B 64
**Blaen-y-Berllan** SA16: Graig . . . 1E 39
**Blaen y Cwm** CF31: Bri . . . 1A 126
**Blaen-y-Cwm** SA16: Graig . . . 1E 39
**Blaen y Ddol** CF31: Bri . . . 1A 126
**Blaen-y-Fro** CF35: P'coed . . . 2H 123
BLAEN-Y-MAES . . . 2B 72
**Blaen-y-Maes Dr.** SA5: Blae M . . . 1B 72
**Blaen-y-Morfa** SA15: Llane . . . 4C 52
**Blair Way** SA12: A'von . . . 2E 97
**Blandy Hill** CF31: Bri . . . 1A 126
**Blandy Rd.** *CF31: Bri . . . 6C 126*
*(shown as Heol Blandy)*
**Blodwen St.** SA12: A'von . . . 3E 97
**Blodwen Ter.** SA4: Penc . . . 4A 68
BLUE ANCHOR . . . 5A 68
**Blue Anchor Rd.** SA4: Blu A . . . 5A 68
**Bluebell Way** SA5: P'lan . . . 3D 72
**Blue St.** SA31: Carm . . . 4E 7
**Blundell Av.** CF36: P'cwl . . . 5B 124
**Blundell Ct.** CF36: P'cwl . . . 5B 124
**Boarlands, The** SA3: Port . . . 5H 109
**Boat House, The**
SA3: T Mum . . . 2G 101
**Bog Rd.** SA7: L'smlt . . . 5E 75
**Bohun St.** SA5: Man . . . 5F 73
**Bolgoed Rd.** SA4: P'dul . . . 1C 46
**Bond Av.** SA15: Llane . . . 2B 52
**Bond St.** SA1: Swan . . . 5A 4 (4E 85)
**Bonllwyn** SA18: Amm . . . 4H 11
**Bonllwyn Rd.**
SA18: Amm, L'bie . . . 3G 11
**Bonville Ter.** SA1: Swan . . . 4D 84
BON-Y-MAEN . . . 5D 74
**Bon-y-Maen Rd.** SA1: Bon . . . 5B 74
**Border Rd.** SA12: Sand . . . 1B 96
Borfa House Activity Cen. . . . 5H 109
**Borough Rd.** SA4: Lou . . . 4F 55
**Borough St.** SA12: A'von . . . 4E 97
**Bosco La.** SA3: Penn . . . 3B 98
**Bosworth Rd.** SA10: Skew . . . 1E 77
**Boulevard de Villenave D'Oron**
CF31: Bri . . . 6D 120
**Bowden Rd.** SA11: Nea . . . 2B 78
**Bowen St.** SA1: Swan . . . 6G 73
SA11: Nea . . . 2A 78
**Bowen Ter.** SA15: Llane . . . 3C 52
**Bower St.** CF33: Ken H . . . 6F 113
**Bowham Av.** CF31: Bri . . . 3C 126
Bowlers . . . 1E 127
Bowling & Bingo Hall . . . 4B 96
BOX . . . 6B 42
**Box Rd.** SA4: Grov . . . 5H 45
**Box Ter.** CF32: Coyt . . . 2B 114
SA15: Llane . . . 6C 42
**Bracken Rd.** SA11: Nea . . . 6C 64
SA13: Marg . . . 2F 103
**Bracken Way** CF31: Bri . . . 2E 121
BRACKLA . . . 1G 127
BRACKLA HILL . . . 6G 121
**Brackla Ind. Est.**
CF31: Brack . . . 4G 121
Brackla Sports Cen. . . . 1G 127
**Brackla St.** CF31: Bri . . . 1E 127
**Brackla St. Cen.** CF31: Bri . . . 1E 127
**Brackla Way** CF31: Brack . . . 6G 121
**Bradfield Av.** CF31: Bri . . . 1C 126
**Bradfield Rd.** CF31: Bri . . . 1C 126
**Bradford St.** SA15: Llane . . . 6C 42
**Bragdu** CF35: P'coed . . . 3E 123
BRAGDY . . . 3A 122
BRAGLE . . . 1G 127
**Brahms Av.** SA12: Sand . . . 1A 96
**Bramble Cl.** CF31: Brack . . . 1H 127
**Bramblewood Cl.** SA12: Bag . . . 5B 90
**Bramley Dr.** SA3: Newt . . . 6E 95
**Bran Cl.** SA7: Swan Ent . . . 6D 60
**Brandon Cres.** SA1: Wins . . . 3E 75
**Brandy Cove Cl.** SA3: Lan . . . 2F 101
**Brandy Cove Rd.** SA3: Bishop . . . 1G 99
**Brangwyn Cl.** SA6: Morr . . . 4H 59
Brangwyn Concert Hall
. . . 6A 4 (5D 84)
**Brangwyn Ct.** SA2: Sket . . . 4B 84
**Branwen Gdns.** SA1: M'hill . . . 1E 85
**Brayley Rd.** SA6: Morr . . . 4A 60
**Brecon Ho.**
SA1: Swan . . . 4G 5 (4H 85)
*SA12: Sand . . . 4C 96*
*(off Moorland Rd.)*
**Brecon Rd.** SA8: P'dwe . . . 5E 37
SA9: C'bont, P'hos, Ystra
. . . 5A 28
**Bredenbury Gdns.**
CF36: Not . . . 2B 124
**Brenig Rd.** SA5: P'lan . . . 4D 72
**Bres Rd.** SA15: Llane . . . 1A 52
**Brettenham St.** SA15: Llane . . . 3H 41
Brewery Field . . . 6D 120
**Brewery La.** CF31: Bri . . . 1D 126
**Brewery Rd.** SA31: Carm . . . 2D 6
**Brian Cres.** CF36: P'cwl . . . 4C 124
**Briar Dene** SA2: Sket . . . 4G 83
**Briar Rd.** SA12: Sand . . . 3B 96
**Briars Ct.** SA5: Blae M . . . 2C 72
**Briarwood Cl.** SA10: B'och . . . 2H 63
**Briarwood Gdns.** SA3: Newt . . . 1B 100
**Briary Way** CF31: Brack . . . 1H 127
**Brick Row** *SA10: Sev S . . . 5F 29*
*(off High St.)*
**Brickyard, The** CF36: Newt . . . 4F 125
**Brickyard Cotts.** SA11: Nea . . . 6B 64
**Brickyard La.** SA31: Carm . . . 4D 6
**Brickyard Rd.** SA5: Ffor F . . . 5C 72
BRIDGEND . . . 1E 127
Bridgend Athletic Track . . . 2D 126
Bridgend Bus Station . . . 1E 127
**Brighton Ind. Est.** CF31: Bri . . . 3H 127
Bridgend Miniature Railway
. . . 4A 114
Bridgend Recreation Cen. . . . 2D 126
**Bridgend Retail Pk.**
CF31: Bri . . . 3F 127
**Bridgend Rd.** CF31: Pen F . . . 1C 120
CF32: A'knfig . . . 5B 114
(not continuous)
CF36: Newt . . . 3F 125
Bridgend RUFC . . . 6D 120
**Bridgend Science Pk.**
CF31: Bri . . . 4D 126
Bridgend Station (Rail) . . . 1E 127
Bridgend Tennis & Bowls Club
. . . 2D 126
**Bridge Rd.** SA5: Wauna . . . 4D 70
**Bridge St.** CF33: Ken H . . . 5F 113
SA1: Swan . . . 1G 85
SA6: Cly . . . 5E 49
SA7: Glais . . . 6H 49
SA9: Cwm I . . . 5E 27
SA11: Nea . . . 6B 64
SA13: P Tal . . . 4H 97
SA14: L'nch . . . 4D 44
SA15: Llane . . . 6A 42
SA16: Burr P . . . 3E 39
SA31: Carm . . . 4E 7
**Bridge Ter.** SA13: P Tal . . . 4H 97
**Bridle M.** SA3: T Mum . . . 3G 101
**Brierley La.** CF31: Bri . . . 3E 127
**Brighton Rd.** SA4: Gor . . . 4B 56
**Bristol St.** CF32: A'knfig . . . 5B 114
**Britannia Apartments**
SA1: Swan Ent . . . 5H 73
**Britannia Rd.** SA6: Plas . . . 3H 73
**Brithdir** SA31: Carm . . . 5F 7
**Brithwen Rd.** SA5: Wauna . . . 5C 70
(not continuous)
British Steel (Port Talbot) Golf Club
. . . 4G 103
BRITON FERRY . . . 6H 77
**Briton Ferry Ind. Est.**
SA11: Brit F . . . 2F 89
(not continuous)
**Briton Ferry Rd.** SA11: Nea . . . 3H 77
Briton Ferry Station (Rail) . . . 6H 77
**Brixham** CF33: N Cor . . . 1D 116
Broadacre . . . 3B 82
**Broadacre** SA2: Kill . . . 3B 82
**Broad Haven Cl.** SA5: P'lan . . . 2C 72
**Broadmead** SA2: Dunv, Kill . . . 3C 82
**Broadmead Cres.**
SA3: Bishop . . . 6A 94
**Broadoak Ct.** SA4: Lou . . . 5F 55
**Broad Oak Way** CF31: Bri . . . 6H 119
**Broad Parks** SA3: W Cro . . . 4E 95
Broad Pool Nature Reserve . . . 5D 106
**Broad St.** SA13: P Tal . . . 5G 97
**Broad Vw.** CF32: Ton . . . 3B 114
**Broadview Cl.** SA3: T Mum . . . 2E 101
**Broadview La.** SA3: T Mum . . . 2F 101
**Broadway** SA2: Sket . . . 3A 84
**Broadway Ct.** SA2: Sket . . . 3A 84
**Broadwood** SA4: Penl . . . 5G 57
**Brocastle Av.** CF31: Bri . . . 2C 128
**Bro Dawel** SA2: Dunv . . . 3C 82
SA6: L'flch . . . 4F 59
**Brodawel** SA11: Cim . . . 2E 79
SA16: Burr P . . . 3D 38
SA18: Amm . . . 3B 22
**Brodawel Cvn. & Camping Pk.**
CF36: Not . . . 1B 124
**Bro Dedwydd** SA2: Dunv . . . 2C 82
**Bro-Deg** CF35: P'coed . . . 3G 123
**Bro Deri** SA16: Burr P . . . 2D 38
**Bro Dirion** CF31: Bri . . . 1A 126
SA2: Dunv . . . 2C 82
**Brodorion Dr.** SA6: Cwm'crw . . . 3H 59
**Brohawddgar** SA14: F'oel . . . 3C 42
**Bro Hedydd** SA31: Carm . . . 2D 6
**Brokesby Rd.** SA1: Bon . . . 5A 74
**Brombil Ct.** SA13: Marg . . . 2G 103
**Brombil Gdns.** SA13: Marg . . . 2G 103
**Brombil La.** SA13: Marg . . . 2G 103
**Brombil Paddocks**
SA13: Marg . . . 2G 103
**Brombil St.** SA13: Marg . . . 1E 103
**Bro-Myrddin** SA31: Carm . . . 4B 6
Bro Myrddin Bowls Club . . . 4C 6
**Bron Afon** SA4: Tir V . . . 1G 57
**Bron Afon Uchaf** SA4: Tir V . . . 1G 57
**Bron Allt** SA10: Cry . . . 6G 33
**Bronallt Rd.** SA4: Ffor, Hendy . . . 5D 34
**Bronant Fer** SA18: Gwaun . . . 6G 15
**Brondeg** SA5: Man . . . 5E 73
**Brondeg Cres.** SA5: Man . . . 5E 73
**Brondeg Ho.** SA5: Man . . . 4E 73
**Brondeg La.** SA8: All . . . 1E 51
**Bron Hafod** CF31: Bri . . . 3A 126
**Bronllan** SA1: Wins . . . 3E 75
**Bronwydd** SA7: Birch . . . 6A 62
**Bronwydd Rd.** SA31: Carm . . . 1H 7
**Bron-y-Bryn** SA2: Kill . . . 2D 82
**Bron-y-Dae** SA31: Carm . . . 5F 7
**Bron yr Allt** SA9: Ysta . . . 6D 26
**Bron yr Aur** SA31: John . . . 6B 6
**Bron-y-Wawr** CF33: N Cor . . . 1D 116
**Bronywawr** SA8: P'dwe . . . 5D 36
**Brook Ct.** *CF31: Bri . . . 6E 121*
*(off Brook St.)*
SA11: Brit F . . . 4H 77
**Brookdale St.** SA11: Nea . . . 1B 78
(Elias St.)
SA11: Nea . . . 2B 78
(Eva St.)
**Brookfield** SA10: Nea A . . . 5G 63
**Brookfield Cl.** SA4: Gor . . . 3G 55
**Brookfield Pl.** SA5: Por . . . 2A 72
**Brooklands** SA12: C'avon . . . 6H 91
**Brooklands Cl.** SA2: Dunv . . . 1A 82
**Brooklands Ter.**
SA1: Swan . . . 3A 4 (3E 85)
**Brooklyn Gdns.** SA3: W Cro . . . 6F 95
SA12: Bag . . . 6H 89
**Brooklyn Ter.** SA3: Newt . . . 1D 100
**Brook Row** CF32: Brync . . . 4F 115
**Brookside** CF35: Coyc . . . 1C 128
CF35: Treoes . . . 4D 128
SA4: Gow . . . 4C 70
**Brookside Cl.** SA12: Bag . . . 5B 90
**Brooks La.** SA16: Pem . . . 2A 38
**Brook St.** CF31: Bri . . . 6E 121
SA10: Skew . . . 1E 77
SA13: P Tal . . . 5H 97
**Brook Ter.** SA18: Tair . . . 1F 25
**Brook Va.** CF35: P'coed . . . 3F 123
**Brookvale Rd.** SA3: W Cro . . . 5E 95
**Brookville Dr.** SA10: Skew . . . 1D 76
**Brookville Gdns.** SA10: Skew . . . 1D 76
**Brookway Cl.** SA12: Bag . . . 5B 90
**Broomhill** SA13: P Tal . . . 4H 97
**Bro'r Holl Saint** SA31: Carm . . . 2C 6
**Bro Ryan** SA18: Glan . . . 5A 14
**Broughton Av.**
SA5: Blae M, Por . . . 2B 72
**Bro Walker** SA18: Amm . . . 1H 21
**Bro-Wen** SA14: Llwy . . . 1F 53
**Brown Av.** SA15: Llane . . . 4C 52
**Brownhills** SA4: Gor . . . 3H 55
**Browning Cl.** CF31: Bri . . . 5C 120
**Browns Dr.** SA3: S'gate . . . 1A 98
**Bruce Rd.** SA5: Ffor F . . . 4G 71
**Brunant Rd.** SA4: Gor . . . 4A 56
**Brunel Cl.** SA11: Tonna . . . 3G 65
**Brunel Ct.** CF33: Pyle . . . 1G 117
SA1: Swan . . . 3B 4 (3E 85)
**Brunel Ind. Est.** SA12: C'avon . . . 6G 91
**Brunel Pk.** SA11: Brit F . . . 3G 89
**Brunel Way**
SA1: Swan, Swan Ent . . . 5H 73
SA11: Brit F . . . 3G 89
**Brunner Dr.** SA6: Cly . . . 3F 49

**Brunswick Ct.**
SA1: Swan . . . . . . . .4A **4** (4E **85**)
**Brunswick St.**
SA1: Swan . . . . . . . .4A **4** (4E **85**)
**Brwyna Av.** SA12: A'von . . . . . .3E **97**
**Brwynen Las** SA10: Nea . . . . . .4H **63**
**Brychan** SA15: Llane . . . . . . . .2C **52**
**Brymbo Av.** SA13: Marg . . . . . .1E **103**
**BRYN**
SA4 . . . . . . . . . . . . . . . .3F **107**
SA14 . . . . . . . . . . . . . . . .6A **44**
**Bryn, The** SA2: Sket . . . . . . . .6G **83**
**Brynaeron** SA2: Dunv . . . . . . . .1B **82**
**Brynaeron Ct.** SA2: Dunv . . . . . .1B **82**
**Brynafan Ter.** SA12: C'avon . . . .6H **91**
**Brynafon Rd.** SA4: Gor . . . . . . .3G **55**
**Brynallt Ct.** SA15: Llane . . . . . .1C **52**
**Brynallt Ter.** SA15: Llane . . . . . .1C **52**
**Bryn Amlwg** CF33: N Cor . . . .1C **116**
**Brynamlwg** SA6: Cly . . . . . . . .3G **49**
SA15: Llane . . . . . . . . . . . .6C **42**
**Bryn-Amlwg Rd.** SA4: Gor . . . .4H **55**
SA5: Ffor F . . . . . . . . . . . . .5B **72**
**BRYNAMMAN** . . . . . . . . . . . . .3B **16**
**Brynamman Hall Cinema** . . . .3A **16**
**Brynamman Ind. Est.**
SA18: Bry . . . . . . . . . . . . . .3C **16**
**Brynamman Rd.**
SA18: Gwaun, Lwr B . . . . . .1C **24**
**Brynau Dr.** SA3: May . . . . . . . .2E **95**
**Brynau Wood** SA11: Cim . . . . . .2F **79**
**Bryn Av.** SA16: Burr P . . . . . . .3F **39**
SA18: Bry . . . . . . . . . . . . . .3A **16**
**Bryn Awel** CF31: Bri . . . . . . . .6A **120**
SA11: Cim, Nea . . . . . . . . . .3C **78**
**Brynawel** SA8: P'dwe . . . . . . . .5D **36**
SA10: Cry . . . . . . . . . . . . . .6H **33**
**Brynawel Cl.** SA10: Cry . . . . . .6H **33**
**Brynawel Cres.** SA5: Tre b . . . . .3G **73**
**Bryn Awelon** CF31: Bri . . . . . .6B **120**
**Brynawelon** SA9: Cwml . . . . . . .4G **17**
SA11: Tonna . . . . . . . . . . . .3D **65**
SA14: Llane . . . . . . . . . . . . .6F **43**
SA18: Saron . . . . . . . . . . . .6C **10**
**Brynawel Rd.** SA4: Gor . . . . . .4H **55**
SA9: Ystra . . . . . . . . . . . . . .5A **28**
**Brynawel Ter.** SA9: Cwml . . . . . .1B **26**
**Bryn Bach** SA4: Tir V . . . . . . . .1H **57**
**Bryn Bâch Rd.** SA18: Bry . . . . . .3H **15**
**Bryn-Bach Rd.** SA4: P'liw . . . . .4F **47**
**Bryn Bedd** SA10: Sev S . . . . . .5G **29**
**Bryn Bragl** CF31: Brack . . . . . .6G **121**
**Brynbrain** SA9: Cwml . . . . . . . .4G **17**
**Brynbrain Rd.** SA9: Cwml . . . . . .5G **17**
*(shown as Heol Brynbrain)*
**BRYNBRYDDAN** . . . . . . . . . . . . .5F **91**
**Brynbryddan** SA12: C'avon . . . .5G **91**
**Brynbryddan Cotts.**
SA12: C'avon . . . . . . . . . . . .5F **91**
**Bryncanol** SA14: Dafen . . . . . .6D **42**
**Bryn Catwg** SA10: C'dxtn . . . . .4C **64**
**Bryn Celyn** SA5: Wauna . . . . . .4F **71**
SA7: L'smlt . . . . . . . . . . . . .2H **75**
SA8: P'dwe . . . . . . . . . . . . .5C **36**
**Bryncelyn** SA15: L'flch . . . . . . .5F **59**
**Bryncelyn Rd.** SA4: Gor . . . . . .4H **55**
**Bryncerdin Rd.** SA3: Newt . . . .1C **100**
**BRYNCETHIN** . . . . . . . . . . . . . .3G **115**
**Bryncethin Rd.** SA18: Garn . . . .2A **24**
**Brynceunant** SA18: Bry . . . . . . .3B **16**
**Bryn Cigfran** CF31: Bri . . . . . . .1A **126**
**Bryn Cl.** SA4: Gor . . . . . . . . . .3A **56**
SA4: Gow . . . . . . . . . . . . . .4C **70**
**BRYN-COCH** . . . . . . . . . . . . . .4F **115**
**BRYNCOCH** . . . . . . . . . . . . . . . .2H **63**
**Bryncoch** SA14: Llane . . . . . . .6F **43**
**Bryncoch Rd.** CF32: Sarn . . . . .5D **114**
**Bryncwar Rd.** SA14: Pen g . . . . .5H **9**
*(shown as Heol Bryn Cawr)*
**Bryncwils** CF32: Sarn . . . . . . .5D **114**
**Bryndedwyddfa** SA14: Pen g . . . .5H **9**
**Bryn Deri** CF31: Bri . . . . . . . . .6A **120**
**Brynderi** SA18: C'bryn . . . . . . .4B **10**
**Brynderi Cl.** SA4: Penl . . . . . . .4G **57**
**Brynderi Ct.** CF31: Bri . . . . . . .6A **120**
**Bryn Derlwyn** CF31: Bri . . . . . .3A **126**
**Bryn Derwen** SA2: Sket . . . . . .1G **83**
SA8: P'dwe . . . . . . . . . . . . .5C **36**
**Brynderwen** SA31: Carm . . . . . .1H **7**
**Brynderwen Rd.**
SA18: Amm . . . . . . . . . . . . .6G **11**
**Bryn Derw Gdns.** SA6: Morr . . .4H **59**
**Bryndolau** SA2: Dunv . . . . . . . .2A **82**
**Bryn Dreinog** SA18: Cap H . . . .3H **19**
**Bryn Dryslwyn** CF31: Bri . . . . . .3B **126**

**Bryndulais Av.** SA10: Sev S . . . .5E **29**
SA14: Llane . . . . . . . . . . . . .6C **42**
**Bryndulais Row** *SA10: Sev S* . . . .5F **29**
*(shown as Rhes Bryndulais)*
**Bryndu Rd.** CF33: Ken H . . . . .4F **113**
**Bryn Eglur Rd.** SA6: Morr . . . . .1G **73**
**Bryneglwys Av.** CF36: Newt . .4G **125**
**Bryneglwys Gdns.** CF36: Newt .4G **125**
**Bryneinon Rd.** SA4: Gor . . . . . .3H **55**
**Bryn-Eira** SA11: Cim . . . . . . . .3D **78**
**Bryn Eithin** SA4: Gow . . . . . . .3A **70**
**Bryneithin** SA16: Burr P . . . . . .3C **38**
**Bryneithin Rd.** SA4: Gor . . . . . .4H **55**
SA6: Morr . . . . . . . . . . . . . .5A **60**
**Bryneithin Ter.** SA6: Morr . . . . .5A **60**
**Brynhyn** SA9: Cwm I . . . . . . . .5F **27**
**Bryn Elli** SA4: Dafen . . . . . . . .5D **42**
**Bryn Euraidd** SA18: Amm . . . . .2F **21**
**Brynfa Ter.** SA4: Penc . . . . . . .4H **67**
**Brynffordd** SA1: Town . . . . . . .6B **72**
**Brynffrwd Cl.** CF35: Coyc . . . .2C **128**
**Brynffynon Rd.** SA4: Gor . . . . . .3H **55**
**Brynfield Ct.** SA3: Lan . . . . . .2D **100**
**Brynfield Rd.** SA3: Lan . . . . . .2C **100**
**Bryngarn Rd.** CF35: Rhiwc . . . .1H **123**
**Bryngarw Country Pk.** . . . . . .1D **114**
**Bryngarw House** . . . . . . . . . .1D **114**
**Bryngelli Dr.** SA5: Tre b . . . . . .1F **73**
**Bryngelli Pk.** SA5: Tre b . . . . . .1F **73**
**Bryngelli Rd.** SA5: Tre b . . . . . .1F **73**
**Bryn Glas** CF32: Cef C . . . . . .1D **118**
SA6: L'flch . . . . . . . . . . . . . .4F **59**
**Brynglas** CF31: Bri . . . . . . . . .1A **126**
SA10: B'och . . . . . . . . . . . . .3H **63**
SA14: Pen g . . . . . . . . . . . . .6H **9**
**Brynglas Av.** SA12: C'avon . . . .5F **91**
**Brynglas Cres.** SA31: Llang . . . .4H **7**
**Brynglas Rd.** SA5: Ffor F . . . . .5B **72**
**Bryn-Glas Ter.** CF33: Pyle . . . .6E **113**
**Bryn Golau** SA8: All . . . . . . . . .6E **37**
**Bryngolau** CF31: Bri . . . . . . . .6A **120**
SA4: Gor . . . . . . . . . . . . . . .4H **55**
SA14: Dafen . . . . . . . . . . . . .5D **42**
**Bryngoleu Rd.** SA5: Ffor F . . . .5B **72**
**Bryngoleu Ter.** SA2: Sket . . . . .3A **84**
**Bryn Gorof** SA9: Cwm I . . . . . .6G **27**
**Bryn Gors** CF32: B'myn . . . . . .3D **114**
**Bryn Gorsedd** CF31: Bri . . . . .4E **121**
**Bryn Gorwel** SA31: Carm . . . . . .2D **6**
**Bryngwastad Rd.** SA4: Gor . . . .4H **55**
**Bryn Gwdig** SA16: Burr P . . . . .2F **39**
**Bryngwili Rd.** SA4: Hendy . . . . .1G **45**
**Bryngwyn** SA10: Skew . . . . . . .2B **76**
**Bryngwyn Av.** SA4: Gor . . . . . .6B **56**
**Bryngwyn Bach** SA14: Dafen . . .5D **42**
**Bryngwyn Rd.** SA14: Dafen . . . .5D **42**
**Bryngwyn Sports Cen.** . . . . . .4D **42**
**Brynhafod** SA18: Tyc . . . . . . . .4D **20**
**Brynhaul St.** SA31: Carm . . . . . .2D **6**
**Bryn Hawddgar** SA6: Cly . . . . .4F **49**
**Bryn Hedydd** SA6: L'flch . . . . . .5F **59**
**Bryn Helyg** SA1: Wins . . . . . . .3E **75**
**Bryn Henfaes** CF31: Bri . . . . .5C **126**
**Bryn Heulog** SA10: Nea . . . . . .4H **63**
**Brynheulog** CF32: B'myn . . . . .3C **114**
SA9: Ystra . . . . . . . . . . . . . .4B **28**
SA12: C'avon . . . . . . . . . . . .5G **91**
SA14: Dafen . . . . . . . . . . . . .4C **42**
**Brynheulog Bungs.**
SA12: C'avon . . . . . . . . . . . .5G **91**
**Brynheulog Ct.** CF32: B'myn . . .3C **114**
**Brynheulog Pl.** SA13: P Tal . . . .4H **97**
**Brynheulog St.** SA13: P Tal . . . .4H **97**
**Brynheulog Ter.** SA9: Cwml . . . .1A **26**
SA12: C'avon . . . . . . . . . . . .5G **91**
**Bryn Hir** SA4: Blu A . . . . . . . . .6B **68**
**BRYNHYFRYD**
CF31 . . . . . . . . . . . . . . . . .6B **120**
SA5 . . . . . . . . . . . . . . . . . .4F **73**
SA11 . . . . . . . . . . . . . . . . .5G **77**
**Bryn Hyfryd** CF32: Sarn . . . . . .6E **115**
**Brynhyfryd** SA4: Tir V . . . . . . .1H **57**
SA14: L'nch . . . . . . . . . . . . .6C **44**
SA16: Burr P . . . . . . . . . . . .2E **39**
SA31: Carm . . . . . . . . . . . . .5F **7**
**Brynhyfryd Cotts.** SA31: Cim . . .2C **78**
**Brynhyfryd Rd.** SA4: Gor . . . . . .3H **55**
SA11: Brit F . . . . . . . . . . . . .6G **77**
SA13: Marg . . . . . . . . . . . . .3F **103**
SA15: Llane . . . . . . . . . . . . .6A **42**
**Brynhyfryd Sq.** SA5: Man . . . . .4F **73**
**Brynhyfryd St.** SA5: Man . . . . . .4F **73**
**Brynhyfryd Ter.** *SA10: Sev S* . . . .4G **29**
*(shown as Teras Brynhyfryd)*

**Bryniago** SA4: P'dul . . . . . . . . .6H **35**
**Bryn Illtyd** SA16: Burr P . . . . . .3C **38**
**Bryn Isaf** SA14: Llwy . . . . . . . .2G **53**
**Bryn Llawen** CF33: Ken H . . . .5F **113**
**Bryn Llewelyn** SA8: All . . . . . . .1E **51**
**Bryn Lliidiard** CF31: Bri . . . . . .3E **121**
**Bryn Lliw Cotts.** SA4: Grov . . . .6C **46**
**Bryn-Lloi Rd.** *SA18: Glan* . . . . .4A **14**
*(shown as Heol Bryn-Lloi)*
**Brynlluan** SA14: Gors . . . . . . . .3D **8**
**Brynllwchwr Rd.** SA4: Lou . . . . .6F **55**
**BRYNMAIR CLINIC DAY HOSPITAL**
. . . . . . . . . . . . . . . . . . . . .6A **42**
**Brynmawr Av.** SA4: Gor . . . . . .6H **55**
*(shown as Rhodfa Bryn-Mawr)*
**Brynmawr La.** *SA18: Amm* . . . . .6H **11**
*(shown as Lon Bryn-Mawr)*
**Brynmawr Rd.** SA2: Brynm . . . .6H **43**
**Brynmead Cl.** SA2: Sket . . . . . .2H **83**
**Brynmead Ct.** SA2: Sket . . . . . .2H **83**
**Brynmelyn Av.** SA15: Llane . . . .6B **42**
**Bryn-Melyn St.** SA1: Swan . . . . .6F **73**
**Bryn Melys** CF31: Bri . . . . . . .3A **126**
**BRYNMENYN** . . . . . . . . . . . . . .3D **114**
**Brynmenyn Bus. Cen.**
CF32: B'myn . . . . . . . . . . . .4E **115**
**Brynmenyn Ind. Est.**
CF32: B'myn . . . . . . . . . . . .3E **115**
**Brynmeurig** SA31: Carm . . . . . . .5F **7**
**BRYNMILL** . . . . . . . . . . . . . . . .5C **84**
**Brynmill Av.** SA2: Brynm . . . . . .5C **84**
**Brynmill Cres.** SA2: Brynm . . . .5C **84**
**Brynmill La.**
SA2: Brynm, Sket . . . . . . . . .4B **84**
**Brynmill Ter.** SA2: Brynm . . . . .5B **84**
**Bryn Morfa** CF31: Bri . . . . . . . . .6E **121**
**Bryn Morgrug** SA8: All . . . . . . .5F **37**
**Brynmorlais** SA14: Brynm . . . . .6A **44**
**Bryn-Mor Rd.** SA15: Llane . . . .5H **41**
**Bryn Mwyn** SA14: Gors . . . . . . .4D **8**
**Brynna Rd.** SA12: C'avon . . . . .5F **91**
**Bryn Nedd** SA11: Cim . . . . . . . .5C **78**
**Brynnewydd Gdns.** SA2: Sket . .5H **83**
**Bryn Onnen** CF33: Ken H . . . . .5G **113**
SA8: P'dwe . . . . . . . . . . . . .5D **36**
**Bryn Parc** SA6: Morr . . . . . . . . .1A **74**
**Bryn Pl.** SA15: Llane . . . . . . . . .5H **41**
**Bryn Pobydd** CF35: P'coed . . . .3G **123**
**Bryn Rhedyn** CF35: P'coed . . . .3F **123**
**Bryn Rhos** SA14: Llane . . . . . . .6F **43**
**Brynrhos Cres.** SA4: Penl . . . . .4G **57**
**Bryn Rhosog** SA4: Lou . . . . . . .5E **55**
**Bryn Rhosyn** SA6: L'flch . . . . . .4F **59**
**Bryn Rd.** CF32: A'knfig, B'myn, fon
. . . . . . . . . . . . . . . . . . . . .4B **114**
CF35: Coyc . . . . . . . . . . . . .1C **128**
SA2: Brynm . . . . . . . . . . . . .5B **84**
SA4: Lou . . . . . . . . . . . . . . .5G **55**
SA4: P'dul . . . . . . . . . . . . . .6E **35**
SA4: P'liw . . . . . . . . . . . . . .4F **47**
SA5: Ffor F . . . . . . . . . . . . .5B **72**
SA5: Wauna . . . . . . . . . . . . .4C **70**
SA6: Cly . . . . . . . . . . . . . . .4E **49**
SA9: Cwml, P fawr . . . . . . . . .1A **26**
SA9: Ystra . . . . . . . . . . . . . .4B **28**
SA11: Nea . . . . . . . . . . . . . .2B **78**
SA14: Pen g . . . . . . . . . . . . .5H **9**
SA15: Llane . . . . . . . . . . . . .5H **41**
SA18: Bry . . . . . . . . . . . . . .3A **16**
**Brynsierfel** SA14: Llwy . . . . . . .1F **53**
**Brynsifi Way**
SA1: Swan . . . . . . . . .1C **4** (2F **85**)
**Bryn Siriol** SA11: Cim . . . . . . . .3F **79**
SA14: Dafen . . . . . . . . . . . . .4C **42**
**Brynsiriol** *SA18: Gwaun* . . . . . .1C **24**
*(off Leyshon Rd.)*
**Brynsiriol Rd.** SA5: Ffor F . . . . .5B **72**
**Bryn St.** SA5: Man . . . . . . . . . .4F **73**
**Brynsyfi Ter.**
SA1: Swan . . . . . . . .1C **4** (2F **85**)
**Bryntawe Hall Cl.** SA6: Ystwe . .1C **60**
**Bryntawe Rd.** SA6: Ystwe . . . . .1C **60**
**Brynted Ter.** *SA18: Amm* . . . . .1H **21**
*(shown as Teras Brynteg)*
**Bryn Teg** SA11: Brit F . . . . . . .5G **77**
**Brynteg** SA6: Cly . . . . . . . . . . .5E **49**
SA7: L'smlt . . . . . . . . . . . . .1G **75**
SA18: Cap H . . . . . . . . . . . .3A **20**
SA31: Carm . . . . . . . . . . . . .2B **6**
**Brynteg Av.** CF31: Bri . . . . . . . .3D **126**
CF33: Pyle . . . . . . . . . . . . . .6D **112**
**Brynteg Gdns.** CF31: Bri . . . . .2E **127**
**Brynteg Rd.** SA4: Gor . . . . . . . .3A **56**

**Bryn Ter.** CF32: Cef C . . . . . . .1C **118**
SA1: L'ore . . . . . . . . . . . . . .5G **73**
SA3: T Mum . . . . . . . . . . . .2F **101**
SA4: Gor . . . . . . . . . . . . . . .5C **56**
SA15: Llane . . . . . . . . . . . . .5H **41**
*(not continuous)*
SA16: Graig . . . . . . . . . . . . .1E **39**
**BRYNTIRION** . . . . . . . . . . . . . .6A **120**
**Bryn Tirion** SA6: Cly . . . . . . . .4F **49**
**Bryntirion** SA15: Llane . . . . . . .6B **42**
**Bryntirion Cl.** CF31: Bri . . . . . .1B **126**
**Bryntirion Hill** CF31: Bri . . . . . .1A **126**
**Bryntirion Rd.** SA4: P'liw . . . . . .3E **47**
**Bryntirion Ter.** SA15: Llane . . . .6B **42**
**Bryntywi** SA31: Carm . . . . . . . . . .4F **7**
**Bryntywod** SA5: L'flch . . . . . . .3D **58**
**Bryn Uchaf** SA14: Bryn . . . . . .1A **54**
**Bryn Vernel** SA4: Lou . . . . . . . .5F **55**
**Bryn Vw. Cl.** SA3: Rey . . . . . . .1B **110**
**Bryn y Broch** SA11: Nea . . . . . .1D **78**
**Bryn y Clochydd** SA15: Llane . .1B **84**
**Bryn-y-Don Rd.** SA1: Swan . . . .2F **85**
**Bryn y Felin** SA14: Felin . . . . . .3D **42**
**Bryn-y-Gors** SA6: L'flch . . . . . .4E **59**
**Bryn-y-Mor** SA4: Thr X . . . . . . .1E **81**
**Bryn-y-Mor Cres.** SA1: Swan . . .4D **84**
**Bryn-y-Mor Rd.**
SA1: Swan . . . . . . . . .5A **4** (4D **84**)
SA4: Gow . . . . . . . . . . . . . .2F **69**
**Brynymor Rd.** SA4: Lou . . . . . . .4F **55**
**Bryn yr Grug** SA9: Ysta . . . . . . .1D **32**
**Bryn yr Orsaf** CF33: N Cor . . . .1E **117**
**Buckingham Rd.** SA4: Bon . . . . .6B **74**
**Bude Haven Ter.** SA3: W Cro . . .6E **95**
**Bullin's La.**
SA1: Swan . . . . . . . . .3A **4** (3D **84**)
**Bull La.** SA31: Carm . . . . . . . . . .3E **7**
**Bungalow Av.** CF36: P'cwl . . . .4D **124**
**Bungalows, The** CF31: Bri . . . . .5E **121**
**Bunker's Hill**
SA3: Midd, P'tn . . . . . . . . . .3D **108**
**Burgley Cl.** SA5: Rav . . . . . . . . .3B **72**
**Burke Av.** SA12: A'von . . . . . . .5D **96**
**Burman St.** SA1: Swan . . .3A **4** (3E **85**)
**Burnham Dr.** SA3: Newt . . . . . .6D **94**
**Burns Cres.** CF31: Bri . . . . . . .5B **120**
**Burnside** SA11: Nea . . . . . . . . .3B **78**
**Burns Rd.** SA12: A'von . . . . . . .5D **96**
**Burrows, The** CF36: Newt . . . .4H **125**
**Burrows Cl.** SA3: S'gate . . . . . .1A **98**
**Burrows La.** SA3: Llang . . . . . . .4C **94**
**Burrows Pl.**
SA1: Swan . . . . . . . . .4F **5** (4G **85**)
**Burrows Rd.**
SA10: Skew . . . . . . . . .5B **4** (4E **85**)
SA11: Nea . . . . . . . . . . . . . .2D **76**
SA11: Nea . . . . . . . . . . . . . .2B **78**
SA12: Bag . . . . . . . . . . . . . .4A **90**
**Burrows Ter.** SA16: Burr P . . . . .3F **39**
**BURRY** . . . . . . . . . . . . . . . . . .6G **105**
**BURRY GREEN** . . . . . . . . . . . . .5G **105**
**Burry Pl.** SA4: Penc . . . . . . . . .4H **67**
**BURRY PORT** . . . . . . . . . . . . . .3E **39**
**Burry Port Ind. Est.**
SA16: Burr P . . . . . . . . . . . . .3F **39**
**Burry Rd.** SA15: Llane . . . . . . . .5A **52**
**Burry St.** SA15: Llane . . . . . . . .6H **41**
**Burry Vw.** SA4: Penc . . . . . . . . .4A **68**
**Burton Dr.** SA12: Sand . . . . . . .4C **96**
**Bush Rd.** SA6: Morr . . . . . . . . .5B **60**
**Bush Row** SA11: Nea . . . . . . . .3A **78**
**Bush Top Cl.** CF31: Bri . . . . . . .2C **126**
**Buttercup Cl.** SA3: W Cro . . . . .6D **94**
**Butterslade Gro.** SA6: Yfgn . . . .2B **60**
**Bwlch Cres.** SA4: Lou . . . . . . . .4D **78**
**Bwlch Rd.** SA4: Lou . . . . . . . . .4F **55**
SA11: Cim . . . . . . . . . . . . . .3D **78**
SA12: Bag, C'avon . . . . . . . . .4C **90**
SA15: Llane . . . . . . . . . . . . .4A **52**
**Bwlchymynydd** . . . . . . . . . . . . .4F **55**
**Bwllfa Rd.** SA6: Ystwe . . . . . . .1D **60**
**Bwrw Rd.** SA6: Lou . . . . . . . . . .6E **55**
**Byass St.** SA13: Marg . . . . . . . .3F **103**
**BYEASTWOOD** . . . . . . . . . . . . .3A **122**
**BYNEA** . . . . . . . . . . . . . . . . . .3A **54**
**Bynea Bus. Pk.** SA14: Byn . . . . .4B **54**
**Bynea Ind. Est.** SA14: Byn . . . . .4B **54**
**Bynea Station (Rail)** . . . . . . . . .3A **54**
**Byng Morris Cl.** SA2: Sket . . . . .5G **83**
**Byng St.** SA1: L'ore . . . . . . . . .4G **73**
**By-Pass Rd.** CF31: Bri . . . . . . .3B **126**
CF32: Bri, Lale . . . . . . . . . . .5A **126**
**Byron Av.** CF31: Bri . . . . . . . . .5B **120**

Byron Way—Cefncaeau


**Byron Way** SA2: Kill . . . . . . . . . . .2E **83**
**By-Ways Ct.** CF35: Coyc . . . . . .2C **128**

## C

**Caban Isaac Rd.** SA4: Blu A . . . .5A **68**
**Cadfan Rd.** SA1: Town . . . . . . . .2D **84**
**Cadifor St.** SA31: Carm . . . . . . . . .3D **6**
CADLE . . . . . . . . . . . . . . . . . . .1A **72**
**Cadle Cl.** SA5: Por . . . . . . . . . . .2B **72**
**Cadle Cres.** SA5: Por . . . . . . . . .3A **72**
**Cadle Dell Pl.** SA5: Por . . . . . . . .2B **72**
**Cadle Mill** SA5: Cad . . . . . . . . . .1H **71**
**Cadle Pl.** SA5: Por . . . . . . . . . . .2B **72**
**Cadlewood Rd.** SA5: Por . . . . . . .2B **72**
**Cadnant Rd.** SA5: P'lan . . . . . . . .3D **72**
CADOXTON-JUXTA-NEATH . . . . .4C **64**
**Cadoxton Rd.** SA10: Nea . . . . . . .6A **64**
**Cadoxton Ter.** SA10: C'dxtn . . . .4D **64**
**Cadrawd Rd.** SA1: M'hill . . . . . . .1E **85**
**Cadwaladr Circ.** SA1: M'hill . . . .2E **85**
**Cadwgan Rd.** SA6: Craig-p . . . . .2B **48**
**Caeau Duon** CF35: P'coed . . . . .2H **123**
**Caebabell Ter.** SA5: Cwmdu . . . .6D **72**
**Cae Bad Ter.** SA15: Llane . . . . . .3G **41**
**Cae Banc** SA2: Sket . . . . . . . . . . .3A **84**
**Cae Beddgelert** CF31: Bri . . . . .2B **126**
**Cae Bracla** CF31: Brack . . . . . . .6G **121**
CAE-BRICKS . . . . . . . . . . . . . . .5E **73**
**Caebricks Rd.** SA5: Cwmb . . . . .6E **73**
**Cae Brombil** *SA13: Marg . . . . .2G 103*
*(shown as Brombil Paddocks)*
**Cae Bron** CF31: Brack . . . . . . . .1G **127**
**Cae Bryn** CF31: Bri . . . . . . . . . .1B **126**
**Cae-Bryn Av.** SA2: Sket . . . . . . . .5H **83**
**Cae Bryn Drain** SA31: Carm . . . . .2D **6**
**Cae Canol** SA12: Bag . . . . . . . . .3B **90**
(not continuous)
**Cae Castell** SA4: Lou . . . . . . . . . .6E **55**
**Cae Celyn** SA31: Carm . . . . . . . . .2D **6**
**Caecerrig Rd.** SA4: P'dul . . . . . . .6F **35**
**Caecoed** SA18: L'bie . . . . . . . . . .2F **11**
**Cae-Coed-Erw** CF31: Brack . . . .6G **121**
**Caeconna Rd.** SA5: Por . . . . . . . .2B **72**
**Cae Copor** SA12: C'avon . . . . . . .6G **91**
**Cae Cotton** SA14: Llane . . . . . . . .6C **42**
**Cae Crug** SA6: L'flch . . . . . . . . . .5E **59**
**Cae Crwn** SA2: Dunv . . . . . . . . . .2C **82**
**Caedegar Rd.** SA9: Ystra . . . . . . .4A **28**
**Cae Delyn Cl.** SA15: Llane . . . . .2G **41**
**Cae Derw** SA10: B'och . . . . . . . .4H **63**
**Cae Derwen** CF31: Bri . . . . . . . .3F **121**
**Caederwen Rd.** SA11: Nea . . . . .3C **78**
**Caedolau** SA16: Burr P . . . . . . . .2E **39**
**Cae Dre St.** CF31: Bri . . . . . . . .1D **126**
**Cae-du-Bach** SA15: Llane . . . . . .6B **42**
**Caedu Rd.** SA9: Cwml . . . . . . . . .6H **17**
**Cae Eithin** SA6: L'flch . . . . . . . . .4E **59**
SA31: Carm . . . . . . . . . . . . .2D **6**
**Caeffatri Cl.** CF31: Bri . . . . . . . .5E **121**
**Cae Ffwrnes** SA16: Burr P . . . . .1D **38**
**Cae Ffynnon** CF31: Brack . . . . .6G **121**
**Caeffynnon Rd.** SA18: L'bie . . . . .1F **11**
**Cae Folland** SA4: Penc . . . . . . . .4H **67**
**Cae Ganol** CF36: Not . . . . . . . . .1B **124**
**Caegar** SA14: Llwy . . . . . . . . . . .1H **53**
**Cae Garw Cvn. Site**
CF33: Pyle . . . . . . . . . . . . .3D **112**
**Cae Glas** CF35: Ewe . . . . . . . . .6D **126**
CF35: P'coed . . . . . . . . . . .4H **123**
SA4: Gor . . . . . . . . . . . . . . .4B **56**
SA12: C'avon . . . . . . . . . . . .5G **91**
**Caeglas** SA14: Cross H . . . . . . . . .6C **8**
SA14: F'oel . . . . . . . . . . . . .4C **42**
**Cae Grawn** SA4: Gow . . . . . . . . .3A **70**
**Cae Graynor** SA18: Tyc . . . . . . . .6A **20**
**Cae-Groes Ter.** SA10: C'dxtn . . . .4C **64**
**Cae Grug** SA31: Carm . . . . . . . . . .2D **6**
**Cae Gwyllt** CF31: Bri . . . . . . . . .2A **126**
**Cae Gwyn Rd.** SA4: P'dul . . . . . .6G **35**
CAEHOPKIN . . . . . . . . . . . . . . .1H **29**
**Caehopkin Rd.** SA9: Cae . . . . . . .1H **29**
**Caelbryn Ter.** CF32: B'myn . . . .3C **114**
**Cae Llwydcoed** CF31: Bri . . . . .6C **126**
**Cae-Is-Maen** SA8: T'nos . . . . . . .1B **50**
**Cae Lynch** SA10: Skew . . . . . . . .2E **77**
CAEMAEN . . . . . . . . . . . . . . . . .5G **51**
CAE-MAES-Y-BAR . . . . . . . . . . .1D **74**
**Cae Mansel La.** SA4: Gow . . . . .5H **69**
**Cae Mansel Rd.**
SA4: Gow, Thr X . . . . . . . . .5G **69**
CAE-MAWR . . . . . . . . . . . . . . . .5A **60**
**Cae Mawr** SA10: Sev S . . . . . . . .5G **29**
**Caemawr** SA18: Amm . . . . . . . . .3A **22**
**Caemawr Rd.** SA6: Morr . . . . . . .6G **59**
**Cae Melyn** SA6: L'flch . . . . . . . . .5F **59**
**Cae Morfa** SA10: Skew . . . . . . . .2B **76**
**Cae Morfa Rd.** SA12: Sand . . . . .2B **96**
**Cae Nan** SA6: Morr . . . . . . . . . . .3C **60**
**Caenant Ter.** SA10: Skew . . . . . .6E **63**
**Cae Odin** CF31: Brack . . . . . . . .6G **121**
**Cae Penpant** SA6: L'flch . . . . . . .4E **59**
**Cae Pentice** CF32: Cef C . . . . . .1B **118**
**Cae Perllan** CF31: Brack . . . . . .6G **121**
**Caepistyll St.** SA1: Swan . . . . . .1G **85**
**Caepys Rd.** SA5: Tre b . . . . . . . . .3F **73**
**Caer Berllan** CF35: P'coed . . . .2H **123**
**Caerbont** SA5: Ffor F . . . . . . . . .2F **71**
**Caerbont Ent. Pk.**
SA9: C'bont . . . . . . . . . . . . .2D **28**
CAE'R-BRYN . . . . . . . . . . . . . . .4B **10**
**Caer Bryn Rd.** *SA14: Pen g . . . . . .5H 9*
*(shown as Heol Caer Bryn)*
**Cae'r-bryn Ter.** SA18: C'bryn . . .4B **10**
**Caer Castell Ho.** CF31: Bri . . . .2H **127**
**Cae'r Cynffig** CF33: N Cor . . . . .1C **116**
(not continuous)
**Caer Efail** CF35: P'coed . . . . . . .2H **123**
**Caereithin Farm La.**
SA5: Rav . . . . . . . . . . . . . . .3C **72**
CAERFYRDDIN . . . . . . . . . . . . . .3E **7**
Caerfyrddin Gorsaf (Rheilffordd)
. . . . . . . . . . . . . . . . . . . .4E **7**
**Caer Groes** SA18: L'bie . . . . . . . .2F **11**
**Caer-gynydd-isaf** SA5: Wauna . . .5C **70**
**Caer-Gynydd Rd.**
SA5: Wauna . . . . . . . . . . . . .5D **70**
**Cae Rhedyn** CF35: Coity . . . . . .3G **121**
SA8: Rhos . . . . . . . . . . . . . .1H **51**
CAERHENDY . . . . . . . . . . . . . . .1H **97**
**Cae'r Hen Eglwys** CF31: Bri . . .5B **120**
**Cae Rhos** SA14: Llane . . . . . . . . .6F **43**
**Cae Rhys Ddu Rd.** SA11: Cim . . .3C **78**
CAE'R-LAN . . . . . . . . . . . . . . . .1D **28**
**Caerllysi** CF35: P'coed . . . . . . . .3E **123**
**Caernarvon Way** SA1: Bon . . . . .5C **74**
**Caer Newydd** CF31: Brack . . . . .6A **122**
**Cae Rowland St.** SA5: Cwmb . . .5E **73**
**Caerphilly Av.** SA1: Bon . . . . . . .5C **74**
**Caersalem Ter.** SA15: Llane . . . .3A **52**
**Caer St.** SA1: Swan . . . . .3E **5** (3G **85**)
**Caer Wetral** CF33: Ken H . . . . . .5F **113**
**Cae'r Ysgol** SA10: Cilf . . . . . . . .2E **65**
**Cae Siwsan** CF31: Brack . . . . . .6G **121**
**Cae Talcen** CF35: P'coed . . . . . .2H **123**
**Cae Ter.** SA15: Llane . . . . . . . . . .1C **52**
**Caewallis St.** CF31: Bri . . . . . . .2E **127**
**Cae Ysgubor** CF31: Brack . . . . .1G **127**
**Caldey Pl.** SA5: Blae M . . . . . . . .1B **72**
**Caldicot Cl.** SA1: Bon . . . . . . . . .4D **74**
**Caldicot Rd.** SA1: Bon . . . . . . . .4D **74**
**Caldy Cl.** CF36: Not . . . . . . . . . .2B **124**
**Calfaria Cl.** SA13: P Tal . . . . . . .4H **97**
**Calland St.** SA6: Plas . . . . . . . . .3H **73**
**Callencroft Ct.** SA3: Newt . . . . .1D **100**
**Calvert Ter.**
SA1: Swan . . . . . . . .3B **4** (3E **85**)
**Camberwell Av.** CF31: Bri . . . . .5B **120**
**Cambray Cl.** CF36: Not . . . . . . .3B **124**
**Cambrian Ct.** SA6: Swan Ent . . . .1B **74**
*SA31: Carm . . . . . . . . . . . . . .3E 7*
*(off Cambrian Pl.)*
**Cambrian Pk.** SA31: John . . . . . . .5A **6**
**Cambrian Pl.**
SA1: Swan . . . . . . . .4F **5** (4G **85**)
SA4: P'dul . . . . . . . . . . . . . .6F **35**
SA9: Cwm U . . . . . . . . . . . . .3C **26**
SA13: P Tal . . . . . . . . . . . . . .5H **97**
SA15: Llane . . . . . . . . . . . . .5H **41**
SA31: Carm . . . . . . . . . . . . . .3E **7**
**Cambrian St.** SA15: Llane . . . . . .6H **41**
**Cambrian Way** *SA31: Carm . . . . . .3E 7*
*(off John St.)*
**Cambridge Cl.** SA3: Lan . . . . . .2E **101**
**Cambridge Gdns.** SA3: Lan . . . .2F **101**
**Cambridge Rd.** SA3: Lan . . . . . .2E **101**
**Cambridge St.** SA2: Upl . . . . . . .3B **84**
**Camellia Dr.** SA6: Morr . . . . . . .3A **60**
**Cameron Pl.** SA4: Gor . . . . . . . . .4H **55**
**Camffrwd Way**
SA6: L'smlt, Swan Ent . . . . .5D **60**
**Camona Dr.**
SA1: Swan . . . . . . . .6E **5** (5G **85**)
**Campbell Rd.** *SA18: L'bie . . . . . . .1F 11*
*(shown as Ffordd Campbell)*
**Campbell St.**
SA1: Swan . . . . . . . .1D **4** (2F **85**)
SA15: Llane . . . . . . . . . . . . .4B **52**
**Camrose Dr.** SA5: Wauna . . . . . .5C **70**
**Canaan Row** SA1: St T . . . . . . . .2H **85**
**Canal Rd.** SA11: Nea . . . . . . . . . .1A **78**
**Canal Side** SA10: A'dul . . . . . . . .3F **65**
**Canal Ter.** SA9: Ysta . . . . . . . . . .2E **33**
**Canaston Ct.** SA5: P'lan . . . . . . .1C **72**
**Canberra Rd.** CF31: Bri . . . . . . .6E **121**
**Candleston Cl.** CF36: Not . . . . .1B **124**
**Candlestone Newydd**
CF31: Bri . . . . . . . . . . . . . .2A **126**
**Candleston Pl.** SA1: Bon . . . . . . .5D **74**
**Cannisland Pk.** SA3: Park . . . . . .3D **92**
**Cannon St.** SA18: Lwr B . . . . . . .5H **15**
**Canola** CF32: Sarn . . . . . . . . . . .5D **114**
**Canolfan** CF31: Brack . . . . . . . .1G **127**
**Canterbury Rd.** SA2: Brynm . . . .5B **84**
**Cantref Ct.** SA5: Rav . . . . . . . . . .3B **72**
**Can-yr-Aderyn** SA6: Morr . . . . . .4G **59**
**Can-yr-Eos** SA6: Morr . . . . . . . . .4H **59**
CAPEL . . . . . . . . . . . . . . . . . . .6D **42**
**Capel Bldgs.** SA6: Cly . . . . . . . . .5F **49**
**Capel Dewi Rd.** SA31: Llang . . . . .4G **7**
**Capel Evan Rd.** SA31: Carm . . . . .2F **7**
CAPEL HENDRE . . . . . . . . . . . . .3A **20**
**Capel Hendre Ind. Est.**
SA18: Cap H . . . . . . . . . . . .3H **19**
**Capel Isaf Rd.** SA15: Llane . . . . .6D **42**
**Capel-Newydd La.**
SA15: Llane . . . . . . . . . . . . .6A **42**
**Capel Rd.** SA6: Cly . . . . . . . . . . .4F **49**
SA14: Dafen . . . . . . . . . . . . .6D **42**
**Capel Ter.** SA10: Skew . . . . . . . .1E **77**
SA15: Llane . . . . . . . . . . . . .6C **42**
**Capstan Ho.** SA1: Swan . . . . . . . .6A **4**
**Caradog Cl.** CF31: Brack . . . . . .6F **121**
**Caradog Pl.** SA1: Town . . . . . . . .2D **84**
**Caradog Rd.** CF31: Bri . . . . . . . .2A **128**
**Caradog St.** SA13: P Tal . . . . . . .5H **97**
**Cardigan Cl.** CF36: Not . . . . . . .1B **124**
**Cardigan Cres.** SA1: Wins . . . . .3D **74**
**Cardigan Ho.** SA7: Swan Ent . . . .2C **74**
**Cardonnel Rd.** SA10: Skew . . . . .2E **77**
**Careg Llwyd** CF31: Bri . . . . . . . .1A **126**
**Carew Pl.** SA1: Wins . . . . . . . . . .3D **74**
**Carey Wlk.** SA10: Nea A . . . . . . .6G **63**
**Carig Cres.** SA1: M'hill . . . . . . . .1E **85**
(not continuous)
**Carig Gdns.** SA1: M'hill . . . . . . . .1D **84**
**Carlos St.** SA13: P Tal . . . . . . . . .3G **97**
**Carlton Pl.** CF36: P'cwl . . . . . . .4B **124**
**Carlton Rd.** SA6: Cly . . . . . . . . . .4E **49**
**Carlton Ter.**
SA1: Swan . . . . . . . .3B **4** (3E **85**)
**Carlyle St.** SA11: Brit F . . . . . . . .5H **77**
CARMARTHEN . . . . . . . . . . . . . . .3E **7**
Carmarthen Athletic RFC . . . . . .5B **6**
Carmarthen Castle . . . . . . . . . . . .4E **7**
Carmarthen Leisure Cen.
Llansteffan Rd. . . . . . . . . . .6C **6**
**Carmarthen Rd.** SA1: Swan . . . . .6F **73**
SA4: Ffor . . . . . . . . . . . . . . .3C **34**
SA5: Cwmdu . . . . . . . . . . . . .6D **72**
SA5: Ffor F, Gen . . . . . . . . . .2G **71**
SA5: Gen . . . . . . . . . . . . . . .6D **72**
SA14: Cross H . . . . . . . . . . . .5A **8**
Carmarthen Bus Station . . . . . . .4E **7**
Carmarthen Station (Rail) . . . . . .4E **7**
Carmarthen Town AFC
(CPD Tref Caerfyddin) . . . . .3F **7**
Carmarthen Town Mus. & Gallery
. . . . . . . . . . . . . . . . . . . .3E **7**
**Carmel Rd.** SA1: Wins . . . . . . . .3D **74**
SA4: P'liw . . . . . . . . . . . . . .5E **47**
CARNGLAS . . . . . . . . . . . . . . . .2G **83**
**Carnglas Av.** SA2: Sket . . . . . . . .3H **83**
**Carnglas Rd.** SA2: Sket . . . . . . . .3H **83**
**Carnhywel** SA14: Llwy . . . . . . . . .1F **53**
**Carno Pl.** SA6: Clase . . . . . . . . . .6G **59**
**Carn Wen** CF31: Bri . . . . . . . . . .3B **126**
**Caroline Av.** CF33: N Cor . . . . . .1C **116**
**Caroline St.** CF31: Bri . . . . . . . .1E **127**
SA11: Brit F . . . . . . . . . . . . .1H **89**
SA15: Llane . . . . . . . . . . . . .6H **41**
CAR'R-BONT . . . . . . . . . . . . . . .2D **28**
**Carregaman** SA18: Amm . . . . . . .2H **21**
**Carregamman Isaf**
SA18: Amm . . . . . . . . . . . . .2H **21**
**Carreg Cennen Gdns.**
SA1: Bon . . . . . . . . . . . . . . .4C **74**
**Carreg Erw** SA7: Birch . . . . . . . .3G **61**
SA13: Coe H . . . . . . . . . . . .2D **112**
**Carreglwyd Camping & Cvn. Pk.**
*SA3: Port . . . . . . . . . . . . . .5H 109*
*(off Overton La.)*
**Carreg yr Afon** SA9: Godr . . . . . .5C **32**
**Carrick Av.** SA15: Llane . . . . . . . .5A **42**
**Carrog Rd.** SA5: P'lan . . . . . . . . .3E **73**
**Cartersford Pl.** SA3: W Cro . . . . .5F **95**
**Carway St.** SA16: Burr P . . . . . . .3D **38**
**Caryl Ter.** SA6: Plas . . . . . . . . . .2H **73**
CASLLWCHWR . . . . . . . . . . . . .5F **55**
**Castell Cl.** SA7: Swan Ent . . . . . .1D **74**
**Castell Ddu Rd.** SA4: Waun . . . .3A **46**
CASTELL NEDD . . . . . . . . . . . . .6B **64**
CASTELL-Y-RHINGYLL . . . . . . . .2F **9**
**Castle Acre** SA3: T Mum . . . . . . .6F **95**
**Castle Arc.** SA1: Swan . . .3E **5** (3G **85**)
**Castle Av.** SA3: T Mum . . . . . . .1E **101**
**Castle Bailey St.**
SA1: Swan . . . . . . . .3E **5** (3G **85**)
Castle Bingo
Bridgend . . . . . . . . . . . . .1E **127**
Morriston . . . . . . . . . . . . .6B **60**
**Castle Bldgs.** SA1: Swan . . . . . . .3E **5**
**Castle Ct.** SA4: Lou . . . . . . . . . .6E **55**
SA7: Swan Ent . . . . . . . . . . .2C **74**
**Castle Cres.** SA3: T Mum . . . . .1E **101**
**Castle Dr.** SA11: Cim . . . . . . . . .2D **78**
**Castle Gdns.**
SA1: Swan . . . . . . . .3E **5** (3G **85**)
**Castle Graig** SA6: Morr . . . . . . . .3G **73**
**Castle Graig Rd.** SA6: Morr . . . .3G **73**
**Castle Gro.** SA4: Lou . . . . . . . . . .5E **55**
**Castle Hill** SA3: Hort . . . . . . . . .5A **110**
SA31: Carm . . . . . . . . . . . . . .4E **7**
**Castle La.** SA1: Swan . . . .3E **5** (3G **85**)
**Castle Lofts** *SA1: Swan . . . . . . . . .3E 5*
*(off Castle St.)*
**Castle Mdws.** CF35: Coity . . . . .4H **121**
**Castle Quay** SA11: Nea . . . . . . . .6B **64**
**Castle Rd.** SA3: T Mum . . . . . . . .6F **95**
**Castle Sq.** SA1: Swan . . .3E **5** (3G **85**)
SA3: T Mum . . . . . . . . . . . .1E **101**
**Castle St.** CF31: Bri . . . . . . . . .3G **127**
SA1: Swan . . . . . . . .3E **5** (3G **85**)
SA3: T Mum . . . . . . . . . . . .1E **101**
SA4: Lou . . . . . . . . . . . . . . .5D **54**
SA10: Skew . . . . . . . . . . . . .2E **77**
SA11: Nea . . . . . . . . . . . . . .6B **64**
SA12: A'von . . . . . . . . . . . . .3F **97**
**Castle Vw.** CF31: Bri . . . . . . . . .5E **121**
SA3: Blk P . . . . . . . . . . . . . .2F **95**
SA11: Nea . . . . . . . . . . . . . .6B **64**
**Castle Wlk.** SA11: Nea . . . . . . . .6B **64**
CASWELL . . . . . . . . . . . . . . . . .2H **99**
**Caswell** SA2: Sket . . . . . . . . . . . .5A **84**
**Caswell Av.** SA3: Casw . . . . . . .1C **100**
**Caswell Bay Ct.** SA3: Casw . . . .2A **100**
**Caswell Bay Rd.** SA3: Bishop . . .1G **99**
**Caswell Dr.** SA3: Casw . . . . . . .1B **100**
**Caswell Hall**
SA1: Swan . . . . . . . .1C **4** (2F **85**)
**Caswell Rd.**
SA3: Bishop, Casw, Lan . . .1G **99**
**Caswell St.**
SA1: Swan . . . . . . . .4A **4** (4E **85**)
SA15: Llane . . . . . . . . . . . . .3B **52**
**Cathan Cl.** SA5: Por . . . . . . . . . .2B **72**
**Cathan Cres.** SA5: Por . . . . . . . .2B **72**
**Cathedral Way** SA12: Bag . . . . . .1C **96**
**Catherine St.**
SA1: Swan . . . . . . . .5A **4** (4D **84**)
SA12: Sand . . . . . . . . . . . . .3D **96**
SA15: Llane . . . . . . . . . . . . .6H **41**
**Catrin Ho.** SA1: Swan . . . .6F **5** (5G **85**)
**Cattle St.** SA11: Nea . . . . . . . . .6B **64**
**Cattybrook Ter.** SA12: C'avon . . .4H **91**
**Causeway, The** SA2: Sket . . . . . .3B **84**
**Cave St.** SA5: Cwmdu . . . . . . . . .6D **72**
**Cawdor Pl.** SA15: Llane . . . . . . .6A **42**
**Cecil Rd.** SA2: Dunv . . . . . . . . . .3B **70**
SA4: Gor . . . . . . . . . . . . . . .3B **56**
SA4: Gow . . . . . . . . . . . . . . .3B **70**
**Cecil St.** SA5: Man . . . . . . . . . . .4E **73**
SA11: Nea . . . . . . . . . . . . . .2A **78**
**Cedar Av.** SA4: Gor . . . . . . . . . . .2H **55**
**Cedar Cl.** SA4: Gow . . . . . . . . . .4B **70**
**Cedar Ct.** SA7: L'smlt . . . . . . . . .4E **61**
**Cedar Cres.** SA3: W Cro . . . . . . .4E **95**
**Cedar Gdns.** CF36: Newt . . . . . .3H **125**
SA12: Bag . . . . . . . . . . . . . .4A **90**
**Cedar Rd.** SA11: Nea . . . . . . . . .1C **78**
**Cedric Cl.** SA2: Sket . . . . . . . . . .5G **83**
**Cedric St.** SA15: Llane . . . . . . . .1B **52**
**Cefnbrith** SA14: Dafen . . . . . . . .6E **43**
**Cefn Bryn** SA2: Sket . . . . . . . . . .5A **84**
SA16: Burr P . . . . . . . . . . . .2F **39**
CEFN-BRYN-BRAIN . . . . . . . . . .4G **17**
Cefn Bryn Viewpoint . . . . . . . .1C **110**
CEFN-BYCHAN . . . . . . . . . . . . .5H **67**
CEFNCAEAU . . . . . . . . . . . . . . .2E **53**

**Cefn Carfan Rd.**
CF32: Brync . . . . . . . . . . .3G 115
**Cefn Celyn** SA2: Dunv . . . . .1A 82
**Cefn Coed** CF31: Bri . . . . . . .6C 120
**Cefn Coed Cres.** SA2: C'ett . . . .1A 84
**CEFN COED HOSPITAL** . . . . . .1H 83
**Cefn Coed La.** CF31: Bri . . . . .6C 120
**Cefn Coed Rd.** SA12: C'avon . . . .5F 91
**CEFNCRIBWR** . . . . . . . . . . .1C 118
**CEFN CROSS** . . . . . . . . . . .1D 118
**Cefncrug** SA18: Saron . . . . . . .1B 20
**Cefndon Ter.** SA12: C'avon . . . .5G 91
**Cefn Draw** SA4: Thr X . . . . . .1E 81
**CEFN-DRUM** . . . . . . . . . . . .6H 35
**Cefneithin Rd.** SA14: Gors . . . . .4C 8
**Cefn Ffynnon** SA13: Marg . . .3G 103
**CEFN GLAS** . . . . . . . . . . . .5B 120
**Cefn Glas** SA2: Sket . . . . . . . .2G 83
SA6: Yfgn . . . . . . . . . . . . .2B 60
**Cefn Glas Rd.**
CF31: Bri, Pen F . . . . . . .3B 120
**Cefn Gwrgan Rd.** SA13: Marg . . .3F 103
**Cefn Helyg** SA2: Sket . . . . . . .1G 83
**CEFN HENGOED** . . . . . . . . . .4D 74
**Cefn Hengoed Community**
**Leisure Cen.** . . . . . . . . .4D 74
**Cefn Hengoed Rd.** SA1: Wins . . .4D 74
**Cefnllan Rd.** SA8: P'dwe . . . . . .4C 36
(Fairway Dr.)
SA8: P'dwe . . . . . . . . . . .4C 36
(Gellideg)
**Cefn Llwyn** SA1: Bon . . . . . . . .3D 74
**Cefn Miaren** SA11: Cim . . . . . .3D 78
**Cefn Nant** CF35: P'coed . . . . . .2F 123
**Cefn Padrig** SA15: Llane . . . . .5A 52
**Cefn Parc** SA10: Skew . . . . . . .2D 76
**Cefn Rd.** CF32: Cef C . . . . . . .1A 118
SA1: Bon . . . . . . . . . . . . . .5C 74
SA7: Glais . . . . . . . . . . . . . .6G 49
SA18: Gwaun . . . . . . . . . . .2C 24
**Cefn-Saeson Cl.** SA11: Cim . . . .2D 78
**Cefn Saeson Rd.** SA7: Birch . . .6H 61
**Cefn Stylle Rd.** SA4: Gow . . . . .5D 68
**Cefn y Maes** SA5: Por . . . . . . .2B 72
**Cefn-yr-Allt** SA10: A'dul . . . . . .2F 65
**Ceidrim Rd.**
SA18: Glan, Garn . . . . . . . .5C 14
**Ceiriog Rd.** SA1: Town . . . . . . .2C 84
**Celestial Way** CF31: Bri . . . . . .3B 126
**Celtic Bus. Pk.** SA1: Swan . . . .3E 85
(off Carlton Ter.)
**Celtic Cl.** CF31: Bri . . . . . . . .1E 127
**Celtic Trade Pk.** SA5: Ffor F . . .4G 71
**Celtic Vw.** CF31: Bri . . . . . . . .2D 120
**Cemetery Rd.** CF31: Bri . . . . . .5D 120
SA5: Tre b . . . . . . . . . . . . . .2G 73
(not continuous)
SA18: C'gors, Gwaun . . . . . .3D 24
(not continuous)
**Central Av.** SA12: Bag . . . . . . .5H 89
**Central Bus. Pk.**
SA7: Swan Ent . . . . . . . . .4D 60
**Century Pk.** SA6: Swan Ent . . . .2B 74
**Ceri Rd.** SA1: Town . . . . . . . .1C 84
**Cerise Cl.** SA12: Sand . . . . . . .1A 96
**Chaddesley Ter.**
SA1: Swan . . . . . . . . .3B 4 (3E 85)
**Chaddesley Vs.** SA1: Swan . . . . .2B 4
**Chaffinch Cl.** CF31: Brack . . . .1H 127
**Chalice Cl.** SA12: Bag . . . . . . .1B 96
**Challacombe Pl.** SA3: Newt . . . .6D 94
**Chamberlain Rd.** SA11: Nea . . . .4A 78
**Chandlers Yd.** SA16: Burr P . . . .4D 38
**Channel Ct.** SA12: A'von . . . . . .4C 96
(off Channel Vw.)
**Channel Hgts.** CF33: Ken H . . . .6H 113
**Channel Vw.** CF31: Brack . . . . .6A 122
SA2: Sket . . . . . . . . . . . . . .5G 83
SA3: Lan . . . . . . . . . . . . . .2F 101
SA10: B'och . . . . . . . . . . . .2A 64
SA12: A'von . . . . . . . . . . . .4C 96
**Chantal Av.** CF31: Pen F . . . . .1B 120
**Chantry Cl.** SA5: Rav . . . . . . . .3B 72
**Chapel Cl.** SA12: Bag . . . . . . . .1B 96
SA4: Thr X . . . . . . . . . . . . . .2E 81
**Chapel St.** CF31: Bri . . . . . . . .2E 127
CF32: B'myn . . . . . . . . . .3E 115
SA1: Swan . . . . . . . . . . . . .1G 85
SA3: T Mum . . . . . . . . . . .1E 101
SA4: Gor . . . . . . . . . . . . . .4C 56
SA18: Bry . . . . . . . . . . . . .3A 16
SA31: Carm . . . . . . . . . . . .3E 7
**Chapel Ter.** SA13: P Tal . . . . . .5H 97
**Chapmans** SA1: Swan . . . . . . .2E 5

**Chapman St.** SA15: Llane . . . .3H 41
**Charles Av.** CF35: P'coed . . . .2G 123
**Charles Ct.** SA4: Gor . . . . . . . .5H 55
**Charles St.** CF31: Bri . . . . . . .6E 121
SA10: Skew . . . . . . . . . . . .1D 76
SA11: Nea . . . . . . . . . . . . .1B 78
SA15: Llane . . . . . . . . . . . .1C 52
**Charles Ter.** SA15: Llane . . . . .5H 41
**Charlotte Ct.** SA1: Town . . . . . .6B 72
**Charnwood Ct.** SA1: Wins . . . . .2D 74
**Charnwood Pk.** CF31: Bri . . . .4H 127
**Charter Ct.** SA7: Swan Ent . . . .2C 74
**Chase, The** CF31: Brack . . . . .1A 128
**Chaucer Cl.** CF31: Bri . . . . . . .5B 120
**Cheapside** CF31: Bri . . . . . . . .1E 127
(Brackla St.)
CF31: Bri . . . . . . . . . . . . .3G 127
(South Rd.)
**Chelhydra Wlk.**
SA1: Swan . . . . . . . .6E 5 (5G 85)
**Chelsea Av.** CF31: Bri . . . . . . .5B 120
**Cheltenham Rd.** CF36: Not . . . .3B 124
**Cheltenham Ter.** CF31: Bri . . . .2E 127
**Chemical Rd.** SA6: Morr . . . . . .3A 60
SA8: P'dwe . . . . . . . . . . . .6D 36
**Chemical Row** SA9: Godr . . . . .4D 32
**Chepstow Pl.** SA1: Bon . . . . . .1C 84
**CHERITON** . . . . . . . . . . . . .3F 105
**Cheriton Cl.** SA1: Swan . . . . . . .1C 4
**Cheriton Cres.** SA5: Por . . . . . .3B 72
**Cherry Cres.** SA4: Penl . . . . . .3G 57
**Cherry Gro.** SA2: Sket . . . . . . .6G 83
SA8: P'dwe . . . . . . . . . . . .4E 37
SA12: Bag . . . . . . . . . . . . .3B 90
**Cherry Tree Av.** CF36: Newt . . .3G 125
**Chesshyre St.** SA2: Brynm . . . .5A 84
**Chestnut Av.** SA3: W Cro . . . . .5D 94
SA4: Gor . . . . . . . . . . . . . .2H 55
**Chestnut Cl.** SA10: Nea . . . . . .4A 64
**Chestnut Dr.** CF36: Newt . . . .3H 125
**Chestnut Rd.** SA11: Cim . . . . . .2C 78
SA12: Bag . . . . . . . . . . . . .3A 90
**Chestnuts, The** CF31: Brack . . .6H 121
**Chestnut Way** CF31: Bri . . . . .6A 120
**Cheviot Cl.** SA5: Ffor F . . . . . . .5B 72
**Chilcott Av.** CF32: B'myn . . . . .4E 115
**Chiltern Cl.** SA5: Ffor F . . . . . . .5B 72
**Chirk Gdns.** SA1: Bon . . . . . . .4D 74
**Chiswick Cl.** CF31: Bri . . . . . .5B 120
**Chopin Rd.** SA12: Sand . . . . . .1A 96
**Chorleywood Cl.**
CF31: Brack . . . . . . . . . .1F 127
**Christchurch Rd.** SA12: Bag . . . .1C 96
**Chris Thomas Ho.** SA1: Swan . .6F 73
**Christina St.**
SA1: Swan . . . . . . . . .3C 4 (3F 85)
**Christopher Ct.**
SA6: Swan Ent . . . . . . . . . .2B 74
**Christopher Ri.** SA4: P'liw . . . . .1F 57
**Christopher Rd.** SA6: Yfgn . . . . .2C 60
SA10: Skew . . . . . . . . . . . .1D 76
**Christopher St.** SA15: Llane . . . .2A 52
**Chrome Av.** SA12: Sand . . . . . .2A 96
**Church Bank** CF31: Brack . . . . .5A 122
**Church Bell Sound** CF31: Bri . .5C 120
**Church Cl.** SA7: L'smlt . . . . . . .6E 61
SA10: B'och . . . . . . . . . . . .2A 64
**Church Cres.** SA12: Bag . . . . . .5B 90
**Church Gdns.** SA2: C'ett . . . . . .6B 72
**Churchill Cl.** CF31: Bri . . . . . .1C 126
**Church La.** SA3: Bishop . . . . . .5G 93
SA4: Blu A . . . . . . . . . . . . .6A 68
SA4: P'dul . . . . . . . . . . . . .1C 46
SA12: Bag . . . . . . . . . . . . .5B 90
SA18: C'gors . . . . . . . . . . .3C 24
SA31: Carm . . . . . . . . . . . .3E 7
**Church Mdw.** SA3: Rey . . . . . .6A 106
**Church Pk.** SA3: T Mum . . . . .2F 101
**Church Pk. La.** SA3: T Mum . . .2F 101
**Church Pl.** CF36: P'cwl . . . . . .5C 124
SA10: Sev S . . . . . . . . . . . .4F 29
SA11: Nea . . . . . . . . . . . . .6B 64
**Church Row** CF31: Bri . . . . . .2D 126
SA4: L'edi . . . . . . . . . . . . . .6E 31
(shown as Heol yr Eglwys)
SA7: L'smlt . . . . . . . . . . . . .6E 61
SA8: Cily . . . . . . . . . . . . . .4H 37
SA8: Ynys . . . . . . . . . . . . .2D 36
SA9: Godr . . . . . . . . . . . . .4D 32
SA10: C'dxtn . . . . . . . . . . .4C 64
SA12: Bag . . . . . . . . . . . . .4B 90
SA14: Gors . . . . . . . . . . . . .3D 8
(shown as Heol yr Eglwys)
SA16: Burr P . . . . . . . . . . .3F 39

**Church Row** SA4: Wern . . . . . . .2E 107
SA18: Garn . . . . . . . . . . . . .5D 14
**Church Sq.** SA12: C'avon . . . . . .5H 91
(School Ter.)
SA12: C'avon . . . . . . . . . . .5H 91
(Somerset Pl.)
**Church St.** CF32: A'knfig . . . . . .5B 114
CF36: Newt . . . . . . . . . . .3G 125
SA4: Gow . . . . . . . . . . . . . .3A 70
SA8: P'dwe . . . . . . . . . . . .5D 36
SA11: Brit F . . . . . . . . . . . .1F 89
(not continuous)
SA12: A'von . . . . . . . . . . . .3F 97
SA15: Llane . . . . . . . . . . . .1A 52
SA16: Burr P . . . . . . . . . . .3F 39
SA18: L'bie . . . . . . . . . . . . .1F 11
SA31: Carm . . . . . . . . . . . . .3F 7
**Church Ter.** CF35: Coyc . . . . . .1C 128
**Church Vw.** CF32: Lale . . . . . . .5A 126
SA12: Bag . . . . . . . . . . . . .4B 90
**Cifach Glyd** SA6: Plas . . . . . . .3H 73
**CILÁ** . . . . . . . . . . . . . . . . . .3D 82
**Cildaudy Rd.** CF32: Coyt . . . . . .2A 114
**Cilddewi Pk.** SA31: John . . . . . . .5A 6
(shown as Parc Cilddewi)
**CIL-FFRIW** . . . . . . . . . . . . . .1F 65
**Cilfig Av.** SA15: Llane . . . . . . . .6A 42
**CILFREW** . . . . . . . . . . . . . . .1F 65
**Cilfrow Ct.** SA1: Swan . . . . . . .6F 73
**Cilgant y Lein** CF31: N Cor . . . .1E 117
**Cilgerran Pl.** SA1: Swan . . . . . .3D 74
**Cilifor Top Fort** . . . . . . . . . . .4D 106
(not continuous)
**Cillefwr Ind. Est.** SA31: John . . . .5A 6
**Cillefwr Rd. E.** SA31: John . . . . .5A 6
**Cillefwr Rd. W.** SA31: John . . . . .5A 6
**CILLIBION** . . . . . . . . . . . . . . .5E 107
**CILMAENGWYN** . . . . . . . . . . .1H 37
**Cilmaengwyn**
SA8: Cilm . . . . . . . . .2H 37, 6A 32
**CILONNEN** . . . . . . . . . . . . . .3H 80
**Cilonnen Rd.** SA4: Cil, Thr X . .3H 107
**Cilparc** CF36: P'cwl . . . . . . . .3D 124
**Cilsaig Rd.** SA14: Dafen . . . . . .4E 43
**Cilwrfa Row** SA15: Llane . . . . . .6B 42
**CILYBEBYLL** . . . . . . . . . . . . .4H 37
**Cil-y-Coed** SA5: Wauna . . . . . .5F 71
**Cilymaenllwyd Cotts.**
SA15: Pwll . . . . . . . . . . . . .1B 40
**Cilymaenllwyd Fach**
SA15: Pwll . . . . . . . . . . . . .2C 40
**Cil yr Onnen** SA14: L'nch . . . . .4C 44
**Citrine Av.** SA12: Sand . . . . . . .2A 96
**Citrine Cl.** SA12: Sand . . . . . . .2A 96
**Civil Justice Cen.**
Swansea . . . . . . . .3F 5 (3G 85)
**Clare Ct.** SA4: Lou . . . . . . . . . .5E 55
**Clarence Ct.**
SA1: Swan . . . . . . . . .5C 4 (4F 85)
**Clarence St.**
SA1: Swan . . . . . . . . .5C 4 (4F 85)
**Clarence Ter.**
SA1: Swan . . . . . . . . .5D 4 (4F 85)
**Clarendon Rd.** SA2: Sket . . . . . .3A 84
**Clare Rd.** SA9: Ysta . . . . . . . . .1E 33
**Clare St.** SA5: Man . . . . . . . . .5F 73
**Clarice St.** SA12: Sand . . . . . . .3D 96
**Clarion Cl.** SA6: Swan Ent . . . .5C 60
**Clarion Rd.** SA6: Swan Ent . . . .6D 60
**Clarke's Row** CF36: Not . . . . . .2C 124
**Clarke Way** SA1: Wins . . . . . . .2E 5
**CLASE** . . . . . . . . . . . . . . . . . .6G 59
**Clasemont Rd.**
SA6: L'flch, Morr . . . . . . . . .3E 59
**Clase Rd.**
SA6: Morr, Swan Ent . . . . . . .5B 60
**Clas-y-Bedw** SA5: Wauna . . . . .5E 71
**Clas-y-Deri** SA5: Wauna . . . . . .5F 71
**Clas-yr-Onnen** SA5: Wauna . . . .5F 71
**Clayton Dr.** SA4: P'dul . . . . . . .6D 34
**Clayton Rd.** SA4: Ffor, Hendy . .6D 34
SA4: L'ore . . . . . . . . . . . . .4G 73
**Clees La.** SA9: Ysta . . . . . . . . .3D 32
**Cleighton Ter.** SA10: C'dxtn . . . .4C 64
**Clevedon Ct.** SA2: Upl . . . . . . .3C 84

**Cleveland Av.** SA3: T Mum . . . .3G 101
**Clevis Ct.** CF33: Sth C . . . . . .3C 116
**Clevis Cres.** CF36: Newt . . . . .3G 125
**Clevisfield Av.** CF36: Newt . . . .3G 125
**Clevis Hill** CF36: Newt . . . . . .3G 125
**Clevis La.** CF36: Newt . . . . . .3G 125
**Cleviston Gdns.** CF36: Newt . . .3F 125
**Cleviston Pk.** SA14: L'nch . . . . .6B 44
**Clews Ct.** SA1: Swan . . . . . . . .5D 84
(off Francis St.)
**Cliff, The** SA16: Burr P . . . . . . .3C 38
**Clifflands Cl.** SA3: T Mum . . . . .2D 100
**Clifford St.** SA11: Nea . . . . . . .2A 78
**Cliff Ter.** SA16: Burr P . . . . . . .3C 38
**Clifton Cl.** SA5: Tre b . . . . . . . .2F 73
**Clifton Hill** SA1: Swan . . .2D 4 (3F 85)
**Clifton Pl.** SA1: Swan . . .2D 4 (3F 85)
SA10: Skew . . . . . . . . . . . .2E 77
**Clifton Row** SA1: Swan . . .2D 4 (3F 85)
**Clifton Ter.** SA3: T Mum . . . . .2G 101
SA12: A'von . . . . . . . . . . . .3F 97
SA15: Llane . . . . . . . . . . . .6C 42
(not continuous)
**Cloda Av.** SA10: B'och . . . . . . .4H 63
**Cloisters, The** SA1: Swan . . . . .4D 84
**Cloisters Wlk.** SA12: Bag . . . . . .1C 96
**Clordir Rd.** SA4: P'liw . . . . . . . .5F 47
**Clos Aaron** SA6: Ystwe . . . . . . .1D 60
**Clos Aderyn Du** SA5: Gen . . . . .5C 72
**Clos Ael-y-Bryn** SA14: Pen g . . .1H 19
**Clos Afallon** SA18: Gwaun . . . . .2C 24
**Clos Afon Llan** SA4: Gow . . . . .2B 70
**Clos Alaw** SA7: L'smlt . . . . . . . .2F 75
**Clos Allt-y-Gog** SA4: P'dul . . . . .1B 46
**Clos Andreas** SA15: Llane . . . . .6B 42
**Clos Aneira** SA5: Ffor F . . . . . . .5A 72
**Clos Anthony** SA31: John . . . . . .6A 6
**Clos Ar Ddafen** SA14: Llwy . . . .1F 53
**Clos Arthur Morris** SA5: Man . . .5F 73
**Clos Banc y Berllan**
SA4: P'dul . . . . . . . . . . . . .1C 46
**Clos Benallt Fawr** SA4: Ffor . . .4D 34
**Clos Bevan** SA4: Gow . . . . . . . .3H 69
**Clos Blaencrymlyn**
SA7: L'smlt . . . . . . . . . . . .2G 75
**Clos Bronheulog**
SA16: Burr P . . . . . . . . . . .2D 38
**Clos Brynafon** SA4: Gor . . . . . .3G 55
**Clos Bryncam** SA18: Garn . . . . .6E 15
**Clos Bryn Dafydd** SA4: Penl . . . .3H 57
**Clos Bryngwili** SA4: Hendy . . . .1G 45
(off Tal y Coed)
**Clos Bryngwyn** SA4: Gor . . . . . .6C 56
**Clos Bryn Haul** SA14: Llwy . . . .2G 53
**Clos Bryn Isaf** SA14: Llwy . . . . .2G 53
**Clos Brynlliw** SA4: Grov . . . . . .5B 46
**Clos Burlais** SA5: Cwmdu . . . . .6D 72
**Clos Cadno** SA6: Cwm'crw . . . .1A 60
SA7: L'smlt . . . . . . . . . . . . .5E 61
**Clos Cae Bach** SA14: Dafen . . . .5E 43
**Clos Cae Dafydd** SA4: Gow . . . .3H 69
**Clos Cae Fainc** SA14: L'nch . . . .5C 44
**Clos Cae Felin** SA14: F'oel . . . .2C 42
**Clos Cae Ffynnon**
CF33: N Cor . . . . . . . . . . .1D 116
**Clos Caegwenith**
SA11: Tonna . . . . . . . . . . . .5E 65
**Clos Caer Elms** SA15: Llane . . . .3G 41
**Clos Caersalem** SA6: Morr . . . .1F 73
**Clos Calfaria** SA5: Ffor F . . . . . .5B 72
**Clos Camlas** SA6: Morr . . . . . . .6B 60
**Clos Castell Coity** CF31: Bri . . .2B 126
**Clos Castell Newydd**
CF31: Bri . . . . . . . . . . . . .2B 126
**Clos Catrin** SA31: Carm . . . . . . .3D 6
**Clos Cefn Bryn** SA14: Llwy . . . .2H 53
**Clos Cefn-y-Maes** SA14: Llwy . .1F 53
**Clos Celyn** SA7: L'smlt . . . . . . .2E 75
**Clos Cenawon** SA6: Cwm'crw . . .3B 60
**Clos Cerdinen** SA4: Tir V . . . . . .2H 57
**Clos Ceri** SA6: Cly . . . . . . . . . .4F 49
**Clos Cerrig** SA18: C'gors . . . . . .3D 24
**Clos Cilfwnwr** SA4: Penl . . . . . .3G 57
**Clos Cilsaig** SA14: Dafen . . . . . .4E 43
**Clos Coed Arian** SA12: Sand . . .3C 96
**Clos Coed Derw** SA14: Pen g . . .1H 19
**Clos Cribyn** SA14: F'oel . . . . . .1D 42
**Clos Crucywel** SA6: Cwm'crw . . .5A 62
**Clos Cwnin** SA31: Carm . . . . . . .1G 7
**Clos Cwningen** SA7: Birch . . . . .5A 62
**Clos Cwrt y Carne** SA4: Gor . . .2G 55
**Clos Cynan** SA2: Kill . . . . . . . . .2E 83
**Clos Danylan** SA14: F'oel . . . . . .2C 42
**Clos David Morgan**
SA18: Garn . . . . . . . . . . . .5C 14

Clos Ddu SA5: Tird . . . . . . . . . . . .1F 73
Clos Delyth SA4: Gor . . . . . . . .4B 56
Clos Derwen SA7: L'smlt . . . . .2H 75
Clos Dewi Medi SA15: Llane . . . .4B 52
Clos Dickenson SA12: Bag . . . .4H 90
(shown as Dickenson Cl.)
Clos Dyfed SA3: John . . . . . . . .6B 6
Close, The CF32: Sarn . . . . . . .5C 114
SA3: W Cro . . . . . . . . . .6E 95
SA4: Gor . . . . . . . . . . .5H 55
SA5: L'flch . . . . . . . . . .4F 59
Clos Ebol SA4: Cwm'crw . . . . .2A 60
Clos Eileen Chilcott
SA7: L'smlt . . . . . . . . . . . .2F 75
Clos Emily SA14: Cross H . . . . .6F 9
Clos Erw Werdd
SA14: Cross H . . . . . . . . . .1C 18
Clos Felen SA18: Garn . . . . . .4C 14
Clos Fferws SA18: Cap H . . . . .3C 20
Clos Gelliwerdd SA14: Cross H . .6E 9
Clos George Morgan
SA6: Pantl . . . . . . . . . . . . .2H 59
Clos Ger-y-Bryn SA4: Tir V . . . .1H 57
Clos Ger-y-Maes SA4: Tir V . . . .1H 57
Clos Glanlliw SA4: P'liw . . . . . .5F 47
Clos Glanmor SA15: Llane . . . .5H 41
Clos Glan-yr-Afon SA2: Sket . . .3H 83
Clos Glan y Wern SA7: L'smlt . . .2F 75
Clos Glyndwr CF35: Coity . . . .3G 121
SA4: Hendy . . . . . . . . . .6C 34
Clos Gorsfawr SA4: Grov . . . . .1B 56
Clos Granby SA15: Llane . . . . .4B 52
Clos Gwaith Brics CF32: Ton . . .4A 114
Clos Gwenallt SA8: All . . . . . . .6E 37
(off Alltwen Hill)
Clos Gwernen SA4: Gow . . . . . .2B 70
Clos Gwili SA14: C'ili . . . . . . . .3F 19
Clos Havard Jones
SA11: Brit F . . . . . . . . . . . .4H 77
(shown as Havard Jones Cl.)
Clos Healy SA4: Gow . . . . . . . .2A 70
Clos Helyg SA4: Gow . . . . . . . .3A 70
Clos Henblas CF31: Bri . . . . . .5C 126
Clos Hendra SA6: Craig-p . . . . .2C 48
Clos Hendre Isaf SA18: Tyc . . . .3C 20
Clos Henfaes CF33: N Cor . . . . .1B 116
Clos Hermon SA16: Pem . . . . . .2B 38
Clos Islwyn SA2: Kill . . . . . . . .2E 83
Clos Joslin CF35: Brack . . . . . .4F 121
(shown as Joslin Cl.)
Clos Leighton Davies
SA4: Gow . . . . . . . . . . . . .2A 70
Clos Llan-Dy-Fan SA4: Gor . . . .5B 56
Clos Llanfihangel
SA14: Dafen . . . . . . . . . . .5E 43
Clos Llarwydden SA4: Penl . . . .4H 57
Clos Llwynallt SA8: All . . . . . . .2D 50
Clos Llwyn Celyn
SA18: Cap H . . . . . . . . . . .3H 19
Clos Llyg SA7: Birch . . . . . . . .6A 62
Clos Llyn Cwm
SA6: Swan Ent . . . . . . . . . .2B 74
Clos Madlen SA5: Ffor F . . . . . .4A 58
Clos Maesgwyn CF32: Brync . . .3F 115
Clos Maes Isaf SA14: L'nch . . . .5D 44
Clos Maes yr Ysgol SA4: P'dul . . .1C 46
Clos Manteg CF31: Bri . . . . . .6C 126
Clos Marina SA4: Gow . . . . . . .2A 70
Clos Masons CF33: Ken H . . . . .4G 113
Clos Melin Mynach SA4: Gor . . .6B 56
Clos Minyrafon SA4: Gor . . . . .4G 55
Clos Morgan SA31: Carm . . . . .3D 6
Clos Morgannwg SA1: Town . . . .2D 84
Clos Morgan Owen SA4: Gow . . .3H 69
Clos Nant Bran SA7: Birch . . . . .4H 61
Clos Nant Ddu SA8: Ynys . . . . .2G 37
Clos Nant-y-Ci SA18: Saron . . . .1C 20
Clos Nantydd SA14: Llwy . . . . . .1F 53
Clos Onnen SA13: Coe H . . . . .2D 112
Clos Parc Bigyn SA15: Llane . . .2B 52
Clos Penbwl SA4: Penl . . . . . . .4H 57
Clos Pendderi SA14: Bryn . . . . .1A 54
Clos Penderri SA4: Penl . . . . . .4H 57
Clos Pengelli SA4: Gow . . . . . .5B 46
Clos Penglyn CF35: P'coed . . . .1H 123
Clos Penllwyngwyn
SA14: Bryn . . . . . . . . . . . .6A 44
Clos Penpant SA4: P'dul . . . . . .6G 35
Clos Pentref SA10: Sev S . . . . .5G 29
Clos Pentyle SA8: T'nos . . . . . .2A 50
Clos Pen y Banc SA6: Clase . . . .5F 59
Clos Penyfai SA15: Llane . . . . . .2G 41
Clos Pen-y-Waun
SA14: Cross H . . . . . . . . . . .6F 9

Clos Plas Isaf SA14: L'nch . . . . .5D 44
Clos Pwll Clai CF32: Ton . . . . . .5A 114
Clos Ray Powell
CF35: P'coed . . . . . . . . . . .5G 123
Clos Rhandir SA4: Lou . . . . . . .6F 55
Clos Rhedyn SA6: Cwm'crw . . . .2B 60
Clos Rhymni SA6: Cwm'crw . . . .2B 60
Clos San Pedr SA2: C'ett . . . . . .6B 72
Clos Sant Cenydd
SA3: Llang . . . . . . . . . . . .5D 104
Clos Sant Paul SA15: Llane . . . .2A 52
(not continuous)
Clos Sant Pedr SA15: Llane . . . .2A 52
(off Paddock St.)
Clos Sant Teilo SA5: L'flch . . . . .4E 59
Clos Saron SA5: Gen . . . . . . . .5C 72
Clos Smyrna CF31: Pen F . . . . .3C 120
Clos Sticle SA31: Carm . . . . . . .5F 7
Clos Tan-y-Cefn CF31: Bri . . . . .2G 127
Clos Tan-y-Fron CF31: Bri . . . . .2G 127
Clos Tirffordd SA4: Penl . . . . . . .4H 57
Clos Tir-Isaf CF31: Bri . . . . . . .3B 126
Clos Trafle SA4: Gow . . . . . . . .2B 70
Clos Tregwyr SA4: Gow . . . . . . .3B 70
Clos Treventy SA14: Cross H . . . .4A 8
Clos Ty-Gwyn SA4: Hendy . . . . .6C 34
Clos Tygwyn SA4: Gow . . . . . . .2A 70
SA6: Cly . . . . . . . . . . . . .4F 49
Clos ty Gwyn SA14: Dafen . . . . .4E 43
Clos ty Mawr SA4: Penl . . . . . . .4G 57
Clos Tyn y Coed
CF32: Brync, Sarn . . . . . .5D 114
Clos ty Tafol SA15: Llane . . . . . .3A 52
Clos ty Ysgol SA11: Cim . . . . . . .3D 78
Clos Vernon Watkins
SA4: Gor . . . . . . . . . . . . .2H 55
Clos Warren SA11: Nea . . . . . . .4A 78
Clos Waun Wen SA6: L'flch . . . . .5E 59
Clos y Banc yr Eithin
SA4: Gor . . . . . . . . . . . . .3H 55
Clos-y-Berllan SA14: Llwy . . . . . .1A 54
Clos y Bont Faen
SA6: Cwm'crw . . . . . . . . . . .2A 60
Clos y Bryn CF32: Ton . . . . . . .4C 114
Clos y Capel CF33: N Cor . . . . .1B 116
SA14: Llwy . . . . . . . . . . .6G 43
Clos y Coed CF31: Pen F . . . . .3C 120
Clos y Coedwr SA6: Cly . . . . . . .5E 49
Clos y Coleg SA18: Amm . . . . .1H 21
Clos y Cudyll Coch CF31: Bri . . .6C 126
Clos y Cwm SA8: P'dwe . . . . . . .4D 36
Clos-y-Cwm SA14: Pen g . . . . . .1H 19
Clos y Dderwen SA16: Pem . . . .2B 38
SA18: Amm . . . . . . . . . . . .1C 22
Clos-y-Dderwen
SA14: Cross H . . . . . . . . . . .5D 8
Clos y Ddraenen SA14: F'oel . . . .1E 43
Clos y Deri SA4: L'edi . . . . . . . .5E 31
SA14: Dafen . . . . . . . . . . .4E 43
SA31: Carm . . . . . . . . . . .3F 7
Clos-y-Deri CF36: Not . . . . . . . .3C 124
Clos-y-Felin SA18: Amm . . . . . . .6C 12
Clos y Fendrod SA7: L'smlt . . . . .6D 60
Clos y Fferm CF35: Coity . . . . . .3G 121
Clos y Ffynnon SA31: Carm . . . . .2E 7
Clos y Fran SA7: Glais . . . . . . . .6H 49
Clos y Gat SA14: Gors . . . . . . . .2F 9
Clos y Gelli SA14: Llane . . . . . . .1E 53
Clos y Gerddi SA14: Byn . . . . . .4B 54
Clos y Gog CF32: Lale . . . . . . .5C 126
Clos y Golomen CF32: Lale . . . .5C 126
Clos-y-Grug CF36: Not . . . . . . .3C 124
Clos-y-Gweydd SA4: Gow . . . . . .3H 69
Clos y Lloetrach SA16: Pem . . . .3A 38
Clos y Maerdy SA4: Gor . . . . . .6B 56
Clos y Mynydd SA4: Gor . . . . . .6G 55
Clos y Nant SA4: Gor . . . . . . . .4G 55
Clos y Porthmon SA4: Gow . . . . .3B 70
Clos yr Ael SA1: Town . . . . . . .6B 72
Clos yr Afon SA18: Amm . . . . . .4H 11
Clos yr Allt SA1: Town . . . . . . . .6C 72
Clos yr Eglwys SA1: Town . . . . .6C 72
Clos-yr-Eirin CF31: Bri . . . . . . .5A 120
Clos-yr-Eos CF33: Sth C . . . . . .3C 116
Clos yr Eryr CF35: Bri . . . . . . . .2F 121
Clos yr Hendre SA18: Cap H . . . .3A 20
Clos yr Hen Eglwys
CF33: Sth C . . . . . . . . . . .4D 116
Clos yr Hen Ysgol
SA8: P'dwe . . . . . . . . . . . .5D 36
Clos yr Hesg SA7: L'smlt . . . . . . .5E 61

Clos yr Onnen SA7: L'smlt . . . . . .5E 61
Clos yr Orsaf SA6: Morr . . . . . . .6B 60
Clos yr Ysgol SA7: L'smlt . . . . . .1H 75
SA15: Llane . . . . . . . . . . .1B 52
Clos Ysbyty SA11: Cim . . . . . . .4D 78
Clos Ysgallen SA7: L'smlt . . . . . .2E 75
Clos Ysticlau SA10: Sev S . . . . .4F 29
Clos Ystrad SA31: Carm . . . . . . .6B 6
Clos-y-Talcen CF31: Pen F . . . . .3C 120
Clos y Waun SA14: Cross H . . . . .6C 8
Clos-y-Waun CF31: Brack . . . . . .6F 121
Clos y Wern SA4: Hendy . . . . . .5B 34
SA13: Marg . . . . . . . . . . .2E 103
Clos-y-Wern CF31: Brack . . . . . .6F 121
Clos y Ywen CF35: Coity . . . . . .2G 121
Clovelly Pl. SA3: Newt . . . . . . . .6D 94
Club La. SA9: Ystra . . . . . . . . . .5A 28
Clwyd Rd. SA5: P'lan . . . . . . . .4D 72
SA18: Gwaun . . . . . . . . . .1D 24
Clwyd Wen SA4: Gow . . . . . . . .3H 69
Clydach
SA18: Amm . . . . . . . . . . . .6H 11
(shown as Stryd-y-Coleg)
Clydach Rd. SA6: Cly, Craig-p . . .1C 48
SA6: Morr, Yfgn, Ystwe . . .4B 60
(not continuous)
Clydach Wharf SA6: Ystwe . . . . .6E 49
Clyn Cwm Gwyn SA2: Kill . . . . . .4E 83
Clyndu St. SA6: Morr . . . . . . . . .6A 60
Clyne Castle SA3: Blk P . . . . . . .2F 95
Clyne Cl. SA3: May . . . . . . . . . .3D 94
CLYNE COMMON . . . . . . . . . . .5B 94
Clyne Common SA2: Sket . . . . . .3G 83
Clyne Cres. SA3: May . . . . . . . .3D 94
Clyne Dr. SA3: Blk P . . . . . . . . .3F 95
Clyne Golf Course . . . . . . . . . . .2D 94
Clyne Valley Country Pk. . . . . . . .6F 83
Clyne Valley Ind. Est.
SA4: Kill . . . . . . . . . . . . . .5C 82
Clyne Vw. SA2: Kill . . . . . . . . . .4D 82
Clyro Ct. SA1: Bon . . . . . . . . . .4D 74
CNAP-LLWYD . . . . . . . . . . . . .3G 73
Cnap Llwyd Rd. SA6: Morr . . . . .3G 73
Cnwc y Gwili SA31: Carm . . . . . .1H 7
COALBROOK . . . . . . . . . . . . . .2B 56
Coalbrook Rd. SA4: Grov . . . . . .2B 56
Coastal Link Rd.
SA15: Llane . . . . . . .6G 41, 4A 52
Cobblers Ct. SA15: Llane . . . . . .6A 42
Cobham Cl. SA4: Gor . . . . . . . .3H 55
Cobham Dr. SA11: Cim . . . . . . .3F 79
Coch-y-Cwm Rd. SA1: Bon . . . . .6D 74
COCKETT . . . . . . . . . . . . . . . .6A 72
Cockett Rd. SA2: C'ett . . . . . . . .2A 84
Coed Bach CF35: P'coed . . . . . .3F 123
SA4: P'dul . . . . . . . . . . .1B 46
COED CAE . . . . . . . . . . . . . . . .1D 52
Coedcae SA8: P'dwe . . . . . . . . .4E 37
Coedcae Rd. SA15: Llane . . . . . .2C 52
(not continuous)
Coed Cae'r Odin CF31: Bri . . . . .4A 120
Coedcae Uchaf SA15: Llane . . . .1C 52
Coed Ceirios SA7: L'smlt . . . . . . .5E 61
Coed Celyn Rd. SA2: Sket . . . . . .6G 83
Coed Derw CF31: Bri . . . . . . . .2B 126
Coed Du Rd. SA10: Cry . . . . . . . .5H 33
Coedfan SA2: Sket . . . . . . . . . . .4F 83
Coed Fedwen SA7: Birch . . . . . . .3F 61
Coedffaldau SA9: P fawr . . . . . . .2A 26
Coed Gurnos SA4: Gow . . . . . . .3H 69
Coed Helyg CF31: Bri . . . . . . . .6A 120
COED HIRWAUN . . . . . . . . . . . .2D 112
Coed Lan SA4: Thr X . . . . . . . . .1E 81
Coedlan SA9: Cwm I . . . . . . . . .6G 27
Coed Mor SA2: Sket . . . . . . . . .5G 83
Coed Nant No. SA1: Swan . . . . .6G 73
Coed Parc SA3: C'avon . . . . . . .5G 91
Coed Parc Ct. CF31: Bri . . . . . .1D 126
Coed Saeson Cres.
SA2: Sket . . . . . . . . . . . . .3A 84
Coed Tymaen CF31: Bri . . . . . . .5B 120
Coedwig Pl. SA5: Gen . . . . . . . .5D 72
Coed y Bronallt SA4: Hendy . . . .5D 34
Coed y Bwlch SA14: Byn . . . . . .4B 54
Coed y Cadno CF31: Pen F . . . . .3C 120
SA14: C'ili . . . . . . . . . . . .4F 19
Coed-y-Crwys SA4: Thr X . . . . . .1F 81
Coed y Dryw SA10: Nea . . . . . . .5H 63
Coed y Gog CF31: Bri . . . . . . . .1A 120
Coed-y-Graig CF35: P'coed . . . .2G 123
Coed-y-Mwstwr Golf Course
. . . . . . . . . . . . . . . . . . . .6D 122
Coed y Neuadd SA31: Carm . . . .1H 7
Coed y Pals SA31: John . . . . . . .6B 6
Coegnant Cl. CF31: Brack . . . . . .4G 121
COETY . . . . . . . . . . . . . . . . . .4A 122
COITY . . . . . . . . . . . . . . . . . .4A 122

Coity By-pass CF35: Coity . . . . . .4G 121
Coity Castle . . . . . . . . . . . . . . .3H 121
Coity Cres. CF31: Bri . . . . . . . . .2B 128
Coity Rd. CF31: Bri . . . . . . . . . .6E 121
Coity Rd. Sidings CF31: Bri . . . . .5E 121
Colbourne Ter. SA1: Swan . . . . . .1F 85
Colbren Sq. SA18: Gwaun . . . . . .2D 24
Colby Rd. SA16: Burr P . . . . . . . .2E 39
Coldstream St. SA15: Llane . . . . .3H 41
Coleridge Cl. CF31: Bri . . . . . . . .5B 120
Coleridge Cres. SA2: Kill . . . . . . .2E 83
Coles Cl. SA1: Swan . . . . .1G 5 (2H 85)
Coleshill Ter. SA15: Llane . . . . . .3H 41
College Cl. CF31: Bri . . . . . . . . .2F 127
College Grn. SA13: Marg . . . . . . .3G 103
College Hill SA15: Llane . . . . . . .1B 52
College Rd. SA31: Carm . . . . . . .3B 6
College Row SA9: Ystra . . . . . . . .6A 28
College St. SA1: Swan . . . .3E 5 (3G 85)
Collwyn Rd. CF33: Pyle . . . . . . . .6D 112
Colonel Rd. SA18: Amm . . . . . . .2A 22
(shown as Ffordd-y-Cyrnol)
Coltshill Dr. SA3: Newt . . . . . . . .1D 100
Columbia Row SA15: Llane . . . . .1A 52
Colwyn Av. SA1: Wins . . . . . . . . .4D 74
Combined Court
Carmarthen . . . . . . . . . . . . .3E 7
Llanelli . . . . . . . . . . . . . . . .1A 52
Commercial Rd. SA8: Phyd f . . . .2B 36
SA13: P Tal . . . . . . . . . . .6H 97
Commercial St.
CF33: Ken H . . . . . . . . . . .5G 113
SA9: Ystra . . . . . . . . . . . . .5A 28
SA10: Sev S . . . . . . . . . . .5F 29
(shown as Stryd Masnach)
SA11: Nea . . . . . . . . . . . . .6B 64
COMMON, THE . . . . . . . . . . . .4D 106
Compass Row SA8: P'dwe . . . . . .5C 36
(off James St.)
Compton Av. SA10: Skew . . . . . . .1E 77
Compton Rd. SA10: Skew . . . . . . .1E 77
Conduit La. SA31: Carm . . . . . . .3E 7
(off King St.)
Conduit Pl. SA13: P Tal . . . . . . . .5H 97
Conduit St. SA13: P Tal . . . . . . . .5H 97
Coney Beach Pleasure Pk. . . . . . .5D 124
Coniston Wlk. SA2: Sket . . . . . . .3A 84
Connaught Cl. CF36: Not . . . . . . .2C 124
Connaught St. SA13: P Tal . . . . . .4H 97
Constant Rd. SA13: P Tal . . . . . . .6H 97
Constitution Hill
SA1: Swan . . . . . . . . .2A 4 (3E 85)
Convent St. SA1: Swan . . . . . . . .1F 85
Conway Ct. SA5: P'lan . . . . . . . .4D 72
Conway Rd. SA5: P'lan . . . . . . . .4D 72
Conway St. SA7: Swan Ent . . . . .2C 74
Cook Rees Av. SA11: Nea . . . . . .2B 78
Coombes Rd. SA10: Skew . . . . . .1D 76
Coombe-Tennant Av.
SA11: Nea . . . . . . . . . . . . .1C 76
Coopers SA18: Tyc . . . . . . . . . . .6A 20
Coopers Rd. SA18: Tyc . . . . . . . .6A 20
(shown as Heol Cwper)
Copley Cl. SA3: Bishop . . . . . . . .5A 94
Copley Lodge SA3: Bishop . . . . .5A 94
Copper Ct. SA7: Swan Ent . . . . . .1D 74
Copperhouse La. SA15: Llane . . .4A 52
Copperhouse Link Rd.
SA15: Llane . . . . . . . . . . . .4A 52
Coppermill Ho. SA11: Nea . . . . . .2A 78
Copperworks Rd.
SA15: Llane . . . . . . . . . . . .6H 41
Coracle Way SA31: Carm . . . . . . .4E 7
Coral Ct. SA12: Sand . . . . . . . . .2A 96
Cork Ho. SA1: Swan . . . . .5G 5 (4H 85)
CORLANNAU . . . . . . . . . . . . . .2G 97
Cormorant Cl. SA15: Llane . . . . . .4G 41
Cormorant Way
SA3: W Cro . . . . . . . . . . . .6D 94
Cornelius Cl. CF33: Sth C . . . . . .3C 116
Corner Ho. Gallery, The
SA18: Amm . . . . . . . . . . . . .1A 22
(off Heol Wallasey)
Cornish Pl. SA15: Llane . . . . . . .4B 52
Cornish Row SA12: C'avon . . . . . .4H 91
CORNTOWN . . . . . . . . . . . . . . .6G 127
Corntown Rd.
CF35: Corn, Ewe . . . . . . . . .6F 127
CORNTWN . . . . . . . . . . . . . . . .6G 127
Cornwall Pl. SA3: T Mum . . . . . .1F 101

Coronation Rd.—Dafen Rd.


Coronation Rd. SA15: Llane ... 2B 52
SA18: Garn ... 5D 14
SA31: Carm ... 2D 6
Coronation St. CF32: A'knfig ... 5B 114
Coronation Ter. SA18: Amm ... 2C 22
Coronet Way SA6: Swan Ent ... 1B 74
Corporation Av. SA15: Llane ... 4C 42
Corporation Cl. SA15: Llane ... 6B 42
Corporation Rd. SA4: Lou ... 5F 55
SA12: A'von ... 3E 97
SA18: Bry ... 3A 16
Correymore Mans. SA2: Upl ... 4B 84
Cory St. SA2: Sket ... 4A 84
Cotswold Cl. SA5: Ffor F ... 5B 72
Cottage Gdns. CF32: Lale ... 5A 126
Cound Ter. SA13: P Tal ... 5H 97
County Court
Carmarthen ... 4D 6
Neath ... 6C 64
County Rd. SA4: P'liw ... 6E 47
Court, The CF35: Corn ... 6H 127
CF35: Coyc ... 1C 128
COURT COLMAN ... 2H 119
Court Colman Rd.
CF31: Ct Col, Pen F ... 2H 119
Court Herbert Athletics Track
... 6H 63
Courtland Bldgs. *SA13: P Tal ... 4G 97*
*(off Courtland Pl.)*
Courtland Pl. SA13: P Tal ... 4G 97
Courtlands Pk. SA31: Carm ... 2F 7
Courtlands Way SA5: Rav ... 3B 72
Court La. SA8: P'dwe ... 5D 36
Courtney Rd. SA15: Llane ... 3H 41
Courtney St. SA5: Man ... 6F 73
Court Rd. CF31: Bri ... 1E 127
CF33: N Cor ... 2C 116
Court Wlk. SA10: Nea ... 6H 63
Courtyard, The CF36: Not ... 6A 116
SA1: Swan ... 1C 4
Cove Rd. SA12: Sand ... 3C 96
Cowbridge Rd. CF31: Bri ... 2E 127
Cowell Pct. SA15: Llane ... 1A 52
Cowell Rd. *SA18: Garn ... 6E 15*
*(shown as Heol Cowgl)*
Cowell St. SA15: Llane ... 1A 52
Cowper Cl. SA2: Kill ... 3E 83
COYCHURCH ... 1C 128
Coychurch Crematorium
CF35: Coyc ... 6B 122
Coychurch Rd.
CF31: Brack, Bri ... 2E 127
CF35: Coyc, P'coed ... 1D 128
Coychurch Rd. Gdns.
CF31: Bri ... 2E 127
COYTRAHEN ... 1A 114
Coytrahene Cl. CF31: Brack ... 5G 121
Crack Hill CF31: Bri ... 4G 127
CF35: Bri ... 4G 127
Cradock St.
SA1: Swan ... 3C 4 (3F 85)
SA15: Llane ... 3A 52
CRAIG-CEFN-PARC ... 1C 48
Craig Cilhendre Nature Reserve
... 3D 50
CRAIG FAWR ... 4H 35
Craig Gwladys Country Pk. ... 2E 65
CRAIG LAN-GIWG ... 3F 37
CRAIG-Y-DUKE ... 3B 50
Cramic Way SA13: P Tal ... 4G 97
Cranfield Ct. SA5: Rav ... 3B 72
Cranmer Ct. SA5: Rav ... 3B 72
Crawford Grn. SA12: Bag ... 3A 90
Crawford Rd. SA12: Bag ... 3H 89
Crawshay Ct. SA3: Lan ... 2D 100
Creidiol Rd. SA1: M'hill ... 2E 85
Crescent, The CF31: Bri ... 1F 127
CF32: A'knfig ... 5B 114
SA5: P'lan ... 3C 72
SA10: Cry ... 6H 33
SA14: Gors ... 4F 9
SA16: Burr P ... 2E 39
Crescent Rd. CF32: Sarn ... 5D 114
SA18: Gwaun ... 2C 24
Crestacre Cl. SA3: Newt ... 1C 100
Creswell Ct. SA6: Clase ... 6G 59
Creswell Rd. SA6: Clase ... 6F 59
SA11: Nea ... 1B 78
Cribb's Row SA11: Nea ... 6B 64
Cribbwr Sq. CF33: Ken H ... 6F 113
Cribin La. SA14: F'oel ... 2D 42
Criccieth Pl. SA1: Wins ... 4D 74
Crickhowell Pl. SA1: Bon ... 3D 74
Cricklewood Cl. CF31: Bri ... 5B 120
Crimea Ct. SA9: Godr ... 5C 32
Crimson Av. SA12: Sand ... 2A 96
Crimson Cl. SA12: Sand ... 2A 96
Crimson Ct. SA12: Sand ... 2A 96
Crispin Av. SA31: Carm ... 3C 6
Croesffyrdd SA9: Ystra ... 1G 33
Croeso'r Gwanwyn
SA7: L'smlt ... 2F 75
Croft, The CF32: A'knfig ... 6C 114
SA4: Lou ... 5E 55
SA10: Nea A ... 6G 63
Croftfield Cres. SA3: Newt ... 1C 100
Croft Goch Gdns.
CF33: Ken H ... 4F 113
Croft Goch Rd. CF33: Ken H ... 4F 113
Crofton Dr. SA12: Bag ... 4B 90
Croft Rd. SA11: Nea ... 6B 64
Croft St. SA1: Swan ... 2G 85
Croft Ter. SA5: Man ... 4F 73
CROFTY ... 5E 67
Crofty Ind. Est. SA4: Crof ... 5D 66
Crole St. SA1: Swan ... 3A 4 (3E 85)
Cromwell Av. SA10: Nea ... 4B 64
Cromwell Rd. SA10: Nea ... 4B 64
Cromwell St.
SA1: Swan ... 2A 4 (3E 85)
Cronin Av. SA12: A'von ... 5C 96
Crosby Yd. CF31: Bri ... 5D 120
Cross Acre SA3: W Cro ... 4D 94
Crossfield Av. CF36: P'cwl ... 4B 124
CROSS HANDS ... 6C 8
Cross Hands Bus. Pk.
SA14: Cross H ... 6D 8
Cross Hands Food Pk.
SA14: Cross H ... 1D 18
Crosshands Public Hall & Cinema
... 5B 8
Cross Hands Rd. *SA14: Gors ... 5D 8*
*(shown as Heol Cross Hands)*
Cross Hill SA13: Marg ... 5H 103
Cross Rd. SA15: Llane ... 6A 42
Cross St. CF31: Bri ... 1E 127
CF32: Ton ... 4B 114
SA4: Gor ... 4B 56
SA4: P'dul ... 6G 35
SA5: Man ... 4F 73
SA9: Ystra ... 6A 28
(Heol Glantawe)
SA9: Ystra ... 3C 28
(Long St.)
SA13: P Tal ... 3G 97
Cross Valley Link SA1: Bon ... 6H 73
SA1: L'ore ... 5H 73
Crown Court
Swansea ... 6A 4 (5E 85)
Crown Pde. *SA15: Llane ... 6A 42*
*(off Water St.)*
Crown Pct. SA15: Llane ... 1A 52
Crown Rd. CF33: Ken H ... 1H 113
(Heol-y-Glo)
CF33: Ken H ... 4H 113
(Lit. Station Rd.)
Crown St. SA6: Morr ... 6A 60
SA13: P Tal ... 3G 97
Crown Way SA10: L'dcy ... 4C 76
Crucible Pk. SA7: Swan Ent ... 4D 60
Crud yr Awel CF31: Pen F ... 3C 120
SA4: Gor ... 6H 55
SA18: Lwr B ... 4H 15
Crud-yr-Awel SA10: Nea ... 4A 64
Crwys Ter. SA5: P'lan ... 1E 73
CRYMLYN BURROWS ... 3H 87
Crymlyn Gdns. SA10: Skew ... 2A 76
Crymlyn Parc SA10: Skew ... 2A 76
Crymlyn Rd. SA7: L'smlt ... 3F 75
SA10: L'smlt, Skew ... 3F 75
Crymlyn St. SA1: Por T ... 3C 86
(not continuous)
Crymlyn Ter. SA1: Bon ... 5D 74
Crymlyn Way SA1: Cry B ... 4H 87
Crynallt Lodge SA11: Cim ... 3E 79
Crynallt Rd. SA11: Cim ... 3D 78
CRYNANT ... 5H 33
Crynant Bus. Pk. SA10: Cry ... 5H 33
Crynlyn Bog Nature Reserve ... 6F 75
Crythan Rd. SA11: Nea ... 2B 78
Culfor Rd. SA4: Lou ... 5E 55
Cunard Row SA12: C'avon ... 5H 91
Cunard Ter. SA12: C'avon ... 5H 91
Cunningham Cl. SA2: Sket ... 4H 83
Curlew Cl. CF36: Not ... 2A 124
SA3: May ... 3D 94
SA10: Nea ... 4B 64
SA15: Llane ... 3G 41
Curlew Rd. CF36: Not ... 2A 124
Curry Cl. SA2: Dunv ... 2D 82
Curtis St. SA11: Nea ... 3B 78
Curwen Ter. CF33: N Cor ... 2C 116
Custom Ho's. SA11: Brit F ... 6F 77
Customs Ho. *SA13: P Tal ... 4G 97*
*(off Talbot Rd.)*
Cuthbertson St. SA11: Brit F ... 4H 77
CWM ... 3D 74
Cwm, The SA10: B'och ... 6G 51
SA16: Burr P ... 2C 38
CWMAFAN ... 5G 91
Cwmamman Rd. *SA18: Glan ... 5F 13*
*(shown as Heol Cwmaman)*
Cwm Arian SA6: Morr ... 4B 60
CWMAVON ... 5G 91
Cwmavon Rd.
SA12: C'avon, P Tal ... 3G 97
Cwmbach Cotts. SA3: May ... 3E 95
Cwmbach Rd.
SA5: Ffor F, Wauna ... 5F 71
SA10: C'dxtn ... 4C 64
SA15: Llane ... 1E 41
CWM-BATH ... 5A 60
Cwmbath Rd. SA6: Morr ... 5A 60
Cwmberri CF35: Coity ... 1A 122
CWMBWRLA ... 6F 73
Cwmbwrla Workshops
*SA1: Swan ... 6F 73*
*(off Ysgubor Fâch St.)*
Cwm Cadle SA5: Por ... 2B 72
Cwm Cadno SA13: Coe H ... 1D 112
CWM CAPEL ... 1F 39
CWMCARNHYWEL ... 1F 53
Cwm Chapel Rd. SA1: Bon ... 4C 74
Cwmclais Rd. SA12: C'avon ... 5F 91
Cwm Clyd SA5: Wauna ... 5E 71
Cwm Clydach Nature Reserve
... 2E 49
Cwmclyd Rd. SA8: Phyd f ... 1B 36
Cwmdonkin Cl. SA2: Upl ... 3D 84
Cwmdonkin Dr. SA2: Upl ... 3D 84
Cwmdonkin Ter. SA2: Upl ... 3C 84
CWMDU ... 6E 73
Cwmdu Cl. SA5: Ffor F ... 5B 72
Cwmdu Ind. Est.
SA5: Cwmdu ... 6C 72
SA10: Skew ... 6C 62
Cwmdu Rd. SA8: Cilm ... 1H 37
Cwm Farm La. SA2: Sket ... 6H 83
CWM-FELIN-FACH ... 3B 60
Cwm Felin Rd. *SA18: Amm ... 4B 22*
*(shown as Heol Cwm Felin)*
Cwmfelin Rd. SA14: Byn ... 3A 54
Cwmfelin Way SA1: Swan ... 6F 73
Cwmfferws Rd. *SA18: Tyc ... 1C 20*
*(shown as Heol Cwmfferws)*
Cwm Ffoes CF32: Cef C ... 1D 118
Cwm-Ffrwd Rd. SA18: Glan ... 3A 14
Cwmgarw Rd.
SA18: Bry, Rhosa ... 3B 16
Cwmgelli Cl. SA5: Tre b ... 2F 73
Cwmgelli Dr. SA5: Tre b ... 2F 73
Cwmgelli Rd. SA6: Morr ... 1F 73
CWMGIEDD ... 3A 28
CWMGORS ... 4C 24
Cwmgors Workshops
SA18: C'gors ... 3C 24
CWMGWILI ... 4F 19
CWM GWYN ... 2B 84
Cwm Ivor Rd. SA16: Burr P ... 2F 39
CWM IVY ... 3E 105
Cwmlan Ter. SA1: L'ore ... 4G 73
Cwm Level Rd. SA5: Man ... 4G 73
SA6: Plas ... 3G 73
Cwmllwyd Wood Nature Reserve
... 6E 71
CWMLLYNFELL ... 6H 17
Cwm-Mwyn SA14: Gors ... 4D 8
Cwm Nant SA11: Cim ... 4D 78
Cwmnanthir Ter. SA18: Tair ... 1F 25
Cwm Nant-Llwyd Rd.
SA8: Gell ... 5G 37
CWM-OERNANT ... 2F 7
Cwmphil Rd. SA9: Cwm I ... 5F 27
CWMRHYDYCEIRW ... 3A 60
Cwmrhydyceirw Rd.
SA6: Cwm'crw ... 3A 60
Cwm Rd. SA1: Swan ... 6G 73
Cwmtawe Bus. Pk.
SA8: P'dwe ... 5E 37
Cwm Tawe Rd. SA9: Ystra ... 3C 28
Cwm Ter. SA1: Swan ... 1G 85
SA15: Llane ... 2H 41
CWM-TWRCH ISAF ... 5F 27
CWM-TWRCH UCHAF ... 3C 26
Cwm-y-Dwr SA11: Brit F ... 1H 89
Cwm-y-dwr Ho. SA11: Brit F ... 1H 89
CWM-Y-GLO ... 5B 8
CWM Y LLADRON ... 1C 70
Cwm-yr-Wch SA2: Dunv ... 2A 82
Cwm Ystrad Pk. SA31: John ... 6B 6
Cwrt Afon Lliedi *SA15: Llane ... 5G 41*
*(off Pentre Doc y Gogledd)*
Cwrt Anghorfa CF33: Pyle ... 5E 113
Cwrt Beaufort SA3: W Cro ... 6F 95
Cwrt Bergiers SA15: Llane ... 3G 41
Cwrt Bont Newydd CF31: Bri ... 2B 126
Cwrt Buchan La.
SA13: Marg ... 2A 112
Cwrt Cilmeri SA6: Morr ... 4B 60
Cwrt Clara Novello
SA15: Llane ... 5G 41
Cwrt Coed Saeson SA7: Birch ... 6A 62
Cwrt Dewi Sant SA4: Gor ... 4B 56
Cwrt Elusendy SA15: Llane ... 1B 52
Cwrt Emily SA7: Birch ... 5G 61
Cwrt Ffynnon SA14: Pen g ... 6A 10
Cwrt Gwscwm SA16: Burr P ... 1D 38
Cwrt Hocys SA7: L'smlt ... 2E 75
Cwrt Hydd SA6: Cwm'crw ... 1A 60
Cwrt Hywell SA4: Gor ... 4A 56
Cwrt Isaf SA7: Birch ... 5A 62
Cwrt Ivor Sims SA6: Morr ... 4A 60
Cwrt Jiwbili SA15: Llane ... 5H 41
Cwrt Lafant SA7: L'smlt ... 2F 75
Cwrt Llwyn Fedwen
SA6: Morr ... 5B 60
Cwrt Llwynog SA6: Cwm'crw ... 2A 60
Cwrt Merlyn SA6: Cwm'crw ... 1A 60
Cwrt Myrddin SA15: Llane ... 5G 41
Cwrt Naiad SA15: Llane ... 5G 41
Cwrt Neville SA15: Llane ... 2A 52
Cwrt Newydd CF31: Bri ... 2A 126
Cwrt Olwyn Ddwr SA7: Birch ... 5H 61
Cwrt Pandora SA15: Llane ... 5G 41
Cwrt Pen y Bryn SA2: Sket ... 3G 83
Cwrt Rebecca SA4: P'dul ... 1D 46
Cwrt Rhian SA4: Gor ... 4B 56
Cwrt Rhosyn SA7: L'smlt ... 2F 75
CWRT SART ... 5H 77
Cwrt Sart SA11: Brit F ... 5H 77
Cwrt ty Gwyn SA14: L'nch ... 3D 44
Cwrt-ucha Ter. SA13: P Tal ... 5H 97
Cwrt y Cadno SA7: Birch ... 6A 62
Cwrt-y-Cadno CF31: Pen F ... 3C 120
Cwrt y Carw SA13: Coe H ... 1C 112
Cwrt y Castell SA4: Penc ... 4H 67
Cwrt-y-Clady Rd. SA10: Skew ... 6E 63
Cwrt-y-Clafdy SA10: Skew ... 6E 63
Cwrt-y-Coed CF31: Brack ... 1G 127
Cwrt y Dderwen SA15: Llane ... 2C 52
Cwrt-y-Fedw SA7: Birch ... 6A 62
Cwrt y Fedwen SA7: L'smlt ... 5E 61
Cwrt-y-Glyn SA14: C'mel ... 1H 9
Cwrt y Gollen SA10: B'och ... 4H 63
Cwrt yr Aeron SA6: Cwm'crw ... 2A 60
Cwrt yr Eos SA13: Coe H ... 1D 112
Cwrt yr Hen Ysgol
CF32: Ton ... 5B 114
Cwrt-yr-Ysgol SA11: Tonna ... 4F 65
Cwrt-y-Waun SA8: Phyd f ... 3C 36
Cwrt y Wern *SA15: Llane ... 1B 52*
*(off Lawrence Ter.)*
Cyfyng Rd. SA9: Ysta ... 3D 32
Cygnet Cl. SA2: Kill ... 4D 82
Cymdda CF32: Sarn ... 6D 114
Cyncoed Cl. SA2: Dunv ... 2B 82
Cyncoed Rd. SA13: Marg ... 3F 103
CYNFFIG ... 2A 116
Cynon Cl. SA6: Swan Ent ... 1B 74
Cynwal Ter. SA9: Cwm U ... 4C 26
Cypher Ho. SA1: Swan ... 6F 5 (5G 85)
Cypress Av. SA3: W Cro ... 4E 95
Cypress Gdns. CF36: Newt ... 4H 125
Cyprium SA1: Swan ... 3H 5 (3H 85)
Cyril Evans Way SA6: Pantl ... 2H 59
Cysgodfa SA11: Tonna ... 3G 65
Cysgod y Fro SA8: Phyd f ... 3C 36
Cysgod y Graig SA16: Burr P ... 2D 38
Cysgod y Llan SA15: Llane ... 6A 42


## D


DAFEN ... 5E 43
Dafen Felin-Foel Link
SA14: Dafen ... 3E 43
Dafen Ind. Est. SA14: Dafen ... 5E 43
Dafen Inn Row SA14: Dafen ... 5F 43
Dafen Rd. SA14: Dafen ... 4D 42
(not continuous)


A-Z Swansea 137

Dafen Row SA15: Llane ........4B 52
Daffodil Cl. SA12: Sand ....1B 96
Dahlia Cl. SA12: Sand ......2B 96
Dale Cl. SA5: Ffor F ........4G 71
Daleside CF32: Brync .....5E 115
Dale Vw. CF32: Cef C ......1D 118
Dalrymple St. SA12: A'von ...3F 97
Dalton Cl. SA12: Sand ......3C 96
Dalton Rd. SA11: Nea ......2B 78
 SA12: Sand ............4B 96
Dana Dr. SA2: Sket .........4H 83
Dan Danino Way SA6: Pantl ...2H 59
Dandorlan Rd. SA16: Graig ....1E 39
Danlan Pk. SA16: Pem .......2A 38
Danlan Rd. SA16: Pem .......2A 38
Dantwyn Rd. SA4: P'dul ......6G 35
Dan-y-Banc SA31: Carm ......4E 7
Danybanc SA14: Cross H .....2D 18
 SA15: Llane ............4B 42
Dan y Beacon SA1: St T .....2A 86
Dan y Bryn SA16: Burr P .....2C 38
Dan-y-Bryn SA11: Tonna .....3G 65
Dan-y-Bryn Rd. SA4: Gor .....5H 55
 SA13: P Tal ............3H 97
Dan y Coed CF35: P'coed ....4G 123
Dan-y-Coed SA12: C'avon .....5G 91
Dan-y-Coed Ri. CF31: Brack ...6F 121
Dan-y-Coed Rd. SA7: Birch ...6H 61
Danycwm SA14: F'oel ........4C 42
Dan y Deri SA18: Glan .......4A 14
Dan-y-Deri CF31: Bri ........1A 126
Danyffynnon SA13: P Tal .....2H 97
DAN-Y-GRAIG .............3B 86
Danygraig SA6: Cly .........4D 48
 SA9: Cwm I ............4D 26
Danygraig Av. CF36: Newt ....3G 125
Dan y Graig Cvn. Pk.
 CF33: Sth C ...........5C 116
Dan-y-Graig Rd. SA10: Nea A ..6G 63
 SA11: Nea .............2B 78
Danygraig Rd. SA1: Por T .....3B 86
 SA8: T'nos ............2B 50
Dan-y-Graig Ter.
 SA10: C'dxtn ..........3D 64
Dan-y-Lan CF31: A'knfig ......6B 114
Danylan SA14: F'oel .........2C 42
Dan-y-Parc SA6: Morr .......5H 59
Dan yr Allt SA4: Gow ........3H 69
Danyrallt SA1: F'oel ........4C 42
Daphne Cl. SA10: Nea .......4B 64
Daphne Rd. SA10: Nea .......5B 64
D'Arcy Bus. Cen. SA10: L'dcy ..3C 76
Dark Ga. SA31: Carm ........3E 7
Darran Cl. SA10: Nea A ......5E 63
Darran Pk. SA10: Nea A ......5E 63
Darren Rd. SA9: Ysta ........2E 33
 SA11: Brit F ...........5H 77
Darren Ter. SA8: T'nos ......1B 50
Darren Wen SA12: Bag .......3C 90
Dartford Cl. SA1: Bon .......5B 74
Dartford Pl. SA1: Bon .......6B 74
Dartford Rd. SA1: Bon .......5B 74
Darwin Rd. SA12: A'von ......5D 96
David Isaac Cl. SA1: L'ore ....5G 73
David's Ter. SA6: Morr .......1A 74
David St. CF31: Bri .........2B 128
 SA5: Cwmb .............6E 73
David's Way SA14: Pen g .....6H 9
David Williams Ter.
 SA1: Por T .............3C 86
Davies Arbour Rd.
 SA11: Tonna ...........5E 65
Davies Av. CF31: Bri ........4E 121
 CF36: Not ............2C 124
Davies Rd. SA8: P'dwe .....4E 37
 SA11: Nea .............1B 78
Davies Row SA5: Tre b .....3G 73
Davies Sq. SA15: Llane .....1B 52
Davies St. SA6: Morr .......6B 60
 SA9: Cae .............1H 29
Davis Av. CF32: Brync ......3F 115
Davis St. SA6: Plas ........3H 73
Dawlish Cl. SA1: Newt ......6D 94
DC Griffiths Way SA11: Nea ..2A 78
Ddol Rd. SA2: Dunv ........3A 82
De Berclos CF36: P'cwl .....3C 124
De Breos Dr. CF36: P'cwl ....3C 124
De Breos St. SA2: Brynm ....5C 84
De Clare Cl. CF36: P'cwl ....3C 124
Deeley Rd. SA9: Ysta .......2E 33
Deepdale Cl. SA3: S'gate ....2A 98
Deep Pl. SA6: Cwm'crw .....2B 60
Deepslade Cl. SA3: S'gate ...2A 98
Deer's Ter. SA10: Skew .....1E 77
De Granville Cl. SA3: P'cwl ..3C 124

De-La-Beche Rd. SA2: Sket ...4H 83
De-La-Beche St.
 SA1: Swan .......3D 4 (3F 85)
Delabeche Rd. SA15: Llane ...2A 52
De La Beche Ter. SA6: Morr ...5A 60
Delfan SA6: L'flch ..........4F 59
 SA7: L'smlt ...........3G 75
Delffordd SA8: Rhos ........2F 51
Delfryn SA14: Llwy ........6G 43
 SA18: Cap H ...........3H 19
Delhi St. SA1: St T .....2H 5 (3H 85)
Dell, The CF32: Brync ......5F 115
 CF32: Lale ............5A 126
 SA2: Kill .............4D 82
 SA4: P'liw ............6E 47
 SA12: Bag .............5A 90
 SA15: Llane ...........2H 41
De Londres Cl. CF36: P'cwl ...3C 124
Denbigh Cres.
 SA6: Yfgn, Ystwe ......1C 60
Denham Av. SA15: Llane .....3F 41
Dennis Pl. CF32: Brync .....4G 115
Denver Rd. SA5: Ffor F .....3G 71
Depot Rd. SA12: C'avon .....5H 91
Deri Av. CF35: P'coed ......2F 123
Deri Cl. CF35: P'coed ......2F 123
Deri Rd. SA9: P fawr .......5A 26
 SA18: Glan
 (shown as Heol y Deri)
Derllwyn Cl. CF32: Ton .....3B 114
Derllwyn Rd. CF32: Ton .....4A 114
Derlwyn SA2: Dunv .........2C 82
 SA10: Nea .............5H 63
Derlyn Pk. SA18: Tyc .......5C 20
 (shown as Parc Derlyn)
DERWEN ...............2F 121
Derwen Cl. CF31: Bri .......3E 121
 SA5: Wauna ...........4C 70
Derwen Deg SA8: P'dwe .....4C 36
 SA10: B'och ...........3H 63
 SA14: Cef .............5B 8
Derwen Fawr SA15: Llane ....2G 11
Derwen Fawr Rd. SA2: Sket ...1G 95
Derwen Fechan SA31: Treva ...1C 6
Derwen Las CF31: Bri .......3A 126
Derwen Rd. CF31: Bri .......1E 127
 SA8: All ..............2C 50
 SA9: Ystra ............4A 28
Derwent St. SA15: Llane .....3H 41
Derwent Vw. CF31: Brack ....5F 121
 (shown as Golwyg Derwen)
Derwlas SA4: Tir V .........1G 57
Derwydd Av. SA18: Gwaun ....3D 24
Derwydd Cvn. Site
 SA16: Burr P ...........4D 38
Derwydd Rd. SA16: Burr P ...3D 38
De Turberville Cl.
 CF36: P'cwl ...........3C 124
Devereaux Dr. SA31: Carm ....1D 6
De Villiers Dr. SA4: Gor ....6A 56
Devon Pl. SA3: T Mum ......2F 101
Devonshire Pl. SA13: P Tal ...5H 97
Devon St. SA1: Swan .......3D 84
Devon Vw. SA2: Sket .......3G 83
Devon Vw. Ter. SA1: Por T ...3C 86
Dewi Pritchard Fld.
 CF31: Brack ...........5F 121
Dewi Ter. SA1: M'hill .......1D 84
Dew Rd. SA12: Sand ........2B 96
Dewsbury Ct. SA1: Swan .....6E 5
Dickens Av. SA12: A'von .....5D 96
Dickenson Cl. SA12: Bag .....4B 90
Dickslade SA3: T Mum ......2G 101
Digby Rd. SA11: Nea ........6D 64
Dillwyn Cl. SA4: P'liw ......6E 47
Dillwyn Rd. SA2: Sket ......4H 83
 SA4: Penl .............4E 57
Dillwyn St. SA1: Swan ...4C 4 (4F 85)
 SA15: Llane ...........2A 52
Dilwyns Gdns. CF31: Bri .....3D 126
Dimpath Ter. SA15: Llane ....5B 42
Dinam Rd. SA1: Bon, Por T ...2E 87
Dinas Baglan Rd. SA12: Bag ...1E 97
Dinas St. SA6: Plas ........3G 73
Dinefwr Indoor Bowls Cen. ...1G 21
District Cen. Broadlands
 CF31: Bri .............2A 126
Dock Rd. SA13: P Tal .......4F 97
Dock St. CF36: P'cwl .......5C 124
 SA4: Lou .............6D 54
Doddridge Way CF36: P'cwl ...4B 124
Dol Afon CF35: P'coed ......4H 123

Dolafon SA14: Byn .........3H 53
Dolau Ct. SA15: Llane ......4B 52
Dolau Fach SA15: Llane .....3B 52
Dolau Fan Rd. SA16: Burr P ...1F 39
Dolau Fawr SA15: Llane .....3B 52
Dolau Rd. SA15: Llane ......3A 52
Dolawel SA9: Cwml .........1B 26
Dolcoed Pl. SA11: Tonna ....4F 65
Dolcoed Ter. SA11: Tonna ...4F 65
Dol Fach CF31: Brack .......1G 127
Dolfain SA9: Cwml .........4B 28
Dolgoy Cl. SA3: W Cro ......5F 95
Dolgoy Gdns. SA3: W Cro ....5F 95
Dolgwili Rd. SA31: Carm ....1H 7
Dol Helyg SA16: Pem .......2B 38
Dol Las SA12: Bag .........4B 90
Dol Nant Dderwen CF31: Bri ...1A 126
Dolphin Pl. SA12: Sand .....1B 96
Dolwar Fach SA14: Llwy .....1F 53
Dol Wen CF35: P'coed ......2H 123
Dol Werdd SA10: Nea .......5H 63
Dolwerdd SA14: F'oel .......4C 42
Dol-y-Coed SA2: Dunv ......2A 82
Dolycoed Av. SA16: Graig ....2E 39
Dol y Dderwen SA9: Ystra ...4B 28
 SA18: Amm ............5H 11
Dol yr Onnen SA31: Carm ....4C 6
Donnen St. SA13: Marg .....1E 103
Douglas Ct. SA3: Bishop ....1F 99
Dove Rd. SA5: Blae M ......1B 72
Downing St. SA15: Llane ....5H 41
Down Leaze SA2: C'ett ......1A 84
Downs, The SA3: Rey .......1B 110
Downs Cl. SA5: Ffor F ......5B 72
Down St. SA6: Cly .........5E 49
Draenen Ddu
 SA14: Cef, Cross H .....4A 8
Dragon 24 SA15: Llane ......5G 41
Dragon24 SA4: L'flch .......3B 58
Dring St. SA1: St T .....1H 5 (2H 85)
Drive, The SA3: S'gate .....2A 98
 SA8: T'nos ............1B 50
 SA10: Nea A ...........6G 63
Drovers Ct. SA4: Gow .......3B 70
Druce St. SA15: Llane ......6H 41
Druids Cl. SA3: T Mum ......6F 95
Druidstone Way SA4: Penl ...4G 57
Drumau Cl. SA10: Skew .....6E 63
Drumau Rd. SA10: Skew .....4A 28
 SA10: Nea A, Skew ....6C 62
Drumfields SA10: C'dxtn ....4C 64
Drummau Rd. SA10: Skew ....6F 63
Druslyn Rd. SA3: W Cro .....5E 95
Dryslwyn Cl. SA4: Penl .....4G 57
Dudley St. SA11: Nea .......1B 78
Duffryn CF35: P'coed .......3E 123
Duffryn Cl. CF35: Coyc .....1D 128
Duffryn Oaks Dr.
 CF35: P'coed ...........3E 123
Dukefield SA4: Thr X .......2E 81
Duke St. SA1: Swan ....4A 4 (4E 85)
 SA13: Marg ............1E 103
Dulais Cl. SA10: A'dul ......2F 65
Dulais Dr. SA10: A'dul ......2F 65
Dulais Fach Rd.
 SA10: A'dul ...........3F 65
 SA11: Tonna ...........3F 65
Dulais Gro. SA2: Sket ......5F 83
Dulais Rd. SA4: P'dul ......6F 35
 SA10: Cry, Sev S .......6E 29
Dulais Valley Leisure Pool ...4G 29
Dumbarton Ho. Ct.
 SA1: Swan .............4D 84
Dumfries SA9: Ystra .......2G 33
Dumfries Pl. SA9: Ystra .....1H 33
 (off William St.)
Dunlin Cl. CF36: P'cwl .....3A 124
Dunns Cl. SA3: T Mum ......1F 101
Dunns La. SA3: T Mum ......1F 101
Dunraven Bus. Pk. CF31: Bri ...2F 127
Dunraven Cl. SA4: Penc ....4H 67
Dunraven Pl. CF31: Bri .....1D 126
Dunraven Rd. SA2: Sket .....3G 83
Dunraven St. CF31: Bri .....3G 127
 CF32: A'knfig ..........5B 114
 SA12: A'von ...........3E 97
Dunster Cl. SA3: Newt ......6D 94
DUNVANT ..............3B 82
 SA1: Swan .......6D 4 (5F 85)
Dunvant RFC ............3B 82
Dunvant Rd. SA2: Dunv .....2B 82
 SA2: Dunv, Gow ........1F 81

Dunvant Rd. SA2: Kill, Sket ...3E 83
 SA4: Thr X ............1F 81
Dunvant Sq. SA2: Dunv .....2B 82
Duport Cl. SA12: Bag .......3H 89
Dupre Rd. SA1: St T .......2A 86
Durlais SA4: Crof .........5G 67
Durlais Rd. SA6: Swan Ent ...5D 60
Dwr-y-Felin Rd. SA10: B'och ...4H 63
Dwyfor SA14: Llwy .........1F 53
Dwynant SA16: Burr P ......2C 38
Dwynwen Rd. CF31: Bri .....2A 126
DYFATTY ..............2F 39
Dyfatty Pk. SA16: Burr P ....2G 39
 (shown as Parc Dyfatty)
Dyfatty St. SA1: Swan ...1E 5 (2G 85)
Dyfatty Ter. SA16: Burr P ...3F 39
Dyfed Av. SA1: Town .....1A 4 (2C 84)
Dyfed Cl. SA1: Town .......2C 84
 SA31: John ............6B 6
 (shown as Clos Dyfed)
Dyfed Rd. SA11: Nea .......6C 64
Dyfed Ter. SA1: Swan ...1A 4 (2D 84)
Dyffryn SA10: B'och .......2G 63
 SA16: Burr P ...........2G 39
Dyffryn-Aur Rd. SA7: L'smlt ...2F 75
Dyffryn Cl. SA6: Swan Ent ...6B 60
Dyffryn Ct. SA7: Swan Ent ...5C 60
 SA13: P Tal ............5H 97
Dyffryn Rd. SA4: Gor ......5A 56
 SA8: All ..............6E 37
 SA10: B'och ...........2G 63
 SA13: P Tal ............6H 97
 SA18: Amm ............1C 20
 (shown as Heol y Dyffryn)
Dyffryn Ter. SA6: Morr .....5B 60
Dyffryn Tywi SA31: Carm ....2H 7
Dyffryn Vw. SA10: B'och ....1H 63
Dyffryn Woods SA10: B'och ...4H 63
Dylan SA14: Llwy .........6H 43
Dylan Cl. SA2: Kill ........3E 83
Dylan Cres. SA12: A'von ....5D 96
Dylan Rd. SA2: Kill ........3E 83
Dylans Vw. SA2: Upl .......3C 84
Dylan Thomas Cen. ....4G 5 (4H 85)
Dylan Thomas Leisure Cen. ...6A 72
Dylan Thomas Sq. SA1: Swan ...5F 5
Dylan Thomas Theatre
 .................5F 5 (4G 85)
Dynevor Av. SA10: Nea .....5A 64
Dynevor Cl. SA10: Skew ....6E 63
Dynevor Pl.
 SA1: Swan .......3D 4 (3F 85)
 SA10: Skew ...........1C 76
Dynevor Rd. SA10: Skew ....6D 62
 SA18: Garn ............5D 14
Dynevor Ter. SA8: P'dwe ....5D 36
Dyrus Rd. SA6: Plas .......3H 73
Dysgwylfa SA2: Sket .......4H 83
Dyson Cl. SA6: Cly ........3E 49

## E

Eaglebush Cotts. SA11: Nea ...3A 78
Eagle M. SA13: P Tal .......4G 97
Eaglesbush Cl. SA11: Nea ...4A 78
Eaglesbush Valley SA11: Nea ...3A 78
Eagles Pl. SA5: Blae M .....2B 72
Eagle Vw. SA13: P Tal ......4G 97
Earl Rd. SA13: Marg .......1F 103
Earl St. SA1: Swan ........1G 85
Earlswood By-Pass
 SA10: Jer M ...........1F 89
 SA11: Brit F ...........1F 89
Earlswood Cotts. SA10: Jer M ...1F 89
East Av. CF32: Cef C ......1C 118
 CF33: Ken H ...........5F 113
East Bank Way
 SA1: St T .........2G 5 (3H 85)
Eastbourne Gro. SA2: Sket ...3H 83
E. Burrows Rd.
 SA1: Swan .......4G 5 (4H 85)
East Cliff SA3: Penn .......3B 98
East Crossways SA8: P'dwe ...4C 36
Easterfield Dr. SA3: S'gate ...2A 98
Easterly Cl. CF31: Brack ....6A 122
Eastern Prom. CF36: P'cwl ...5C 124
Eastern Slade Farm Cvn. Site
 SA3: Slade ............4B 110
Eastfield Cl. SA1: Town .....6B 72
Eastgate SA15: Llane .......1A 52
Eastland Cl. SA3: W Cro ....5D 94
Eastland Pl. SA11: Nea .....1B 78
Eastland Rd. SA11: Nea .....2B 78

**Eastlands Pk.** SA3: Bishop . . . . .5H **93**
**Eastmoor Pk. Cres.**
  SA3: W Cro . . . . . . . . . . .5D **94**
**East Rd.** SA13: P Tal . . . . . . . .3F **103**
**East St.** CF31: Bri . . . . . . . . .2B **128**
  CF32: A'knfig . . . . . . . . .5B **114**
**Eaton Cres.** SA1: Swan . . . . . . .4C **84**
**Eaton Rd.** SA5: Man . . . . . . . .4F **73**
**Ebbw Va. Row** SA12: C'avon . . .5H **91**
**Ebenezer Rd.** *SA4: Sard* . . . .*1D 34*
  *(shown as Heol Ebeneser)*
**Ebenezer St.**
  SA1: Swan . . . . . . .1E **5** (2G **85**)
**Eden Av.** SA2: Upl . . . . . . . . .3C **84**
**Edgehill Cl.** SA12: Bag . . . . . .6B **90**
**Edgemoor Cl.** SA2: Up K . . . . .5A **82**
**Edgemoor Dr.** SA2: Up K . . . . .5A **82**
**Edgeware Rd.** SA2: Upl . . . . . .3B **84**
**Edison Cres.** SA6: Cly . . . . . . .3E **49**
**Edith Mills Cl.** SA11: Brit F . . . .4H **77**
**Edward Jarvis Ct.** *SA11: Nea* . .*2B 78*
  *(off Quar Rd.)*
**Edward Rd.** SA8: All . . . . . . . .6E **37**
**Edwards St.** SA11: Nea . . . . . .2B **78**
**Edward St.** CF31: Bri . . . . . . .2E **127**
  SA13: P Tal . . . . . . . . . . .3G **97**
**EFAIL-FACH** . . . . . . . . . . . . .4H **79**
**Eglwys Nunnydd** SA13: Marg . .1A **112**
**Egypt Cen., The** . . . . . . . . . . .5B **84**
**Eiddil** SA14: Llwy . . . . . . . . . .6G **43**
**Eiddwen Rd.** SA5: P'lan . . . . . .4D **72**
**Eigen Cres.** SA1: M'hill . . .1A **4** (2D **84**)
**Eighth Av.** SA6: Clase . . . . . . .5G **59**
**Eileen Rd.** SA7: L'smlt . . . . . . .1G **75**
**Einon Cl.** SA4: Gor . . . . . . . . .4C **56**
**Eithen Pl.** CF36: P'cwl . . . . . .5B **124**
**Elan Av.** SA6: Clase . . . . . . . .5G **59**
**Elba Av.** SA13: Marg . . . . . . . .1E **103**
**Elba Cres.** SA1: Cry B . . . . . . .4G **87**
**Elba St.** SA4: Gow . . . . . . . . .2A **70**
**Elder Dr.** CF36: Newt . . . . . . . .3H **5** (3H **85**)
**Elder Rd.** SA12: Bag . . . . . . . .3A **90**
**Elder St.** CF31: Bri . . . . . . . .1E **127**
**Eleanor Cl.** CF35: P'coed . . . . .2E **123**
**Elephant St.** SA1: Swan . . . . . .2G **85**
**Elfed Av.** SA1: M'hill . . . . . . . .5C **96**
**Elfed Rd.** SA1: M'hill . . . .1A **4** (2E **85**)
**Elgar Av.** SA12: Sand . . . . . . . .1A **96**
**Elgin Rd.** SA15: Pwll . . . . . . . .2C **40**
**Elgin St.** SA5: Man . . . . . . . . .5E **73**
**Elias Dr.** SA10: B'och . . . . . . .2H **63**
**Elias Rd.** SA10: B'och . . . . . . .2H **63**
**Elias St.** SA11: Nea . . . . . . . . .1B **78**
**Elim Rd.** SA31: Carm, Ffy . . . . .1C **6**
**Eliot Cl.** SA2: Kill . . . . . . . . . .2E **83**
**Elizabeth and Rowe Harding**
  **Nature Reserve** . . . . . . . .2B **92**
**Elizabeth Cl.** SA6: Yfgn . . . . . .2C **60**
**Elizabeth Rd.** CF31: Bri . . . . .6B **120**
**Elizabeth St.** SA15: Llane . . . . .1A **52**
**Elkington Pk.** SA16: Burr P . . . .2D **38**
**Elkington Rd.** SA16: Burr P . . . .2D **38**
**Ellens Row** SA10: Skew . . . . . .6C **62**
**Ellipse** SA1: Swan . . . . . . . . .3A **86**
**Ellis Gro.** SA2: Up K . . . . . . . .4A **82**
**Elliston Ter.** *SA31: Carm* . . . . .*3E 7*
  *(off Francis Ter.)*
**Elm Cl.** SA5: Wauna . . . . . . . .4C **70**
**Elm Ct.** SA4: Gor . . . . . . . . . .3H **55**
**Elm Cres.** CF31: Bri . . .5C **126**, 6H **119**
  SA4: Penl . . . . . . . . . . . .4H **57**
**Elm Gro.** SA4: Gor . . . . . . . . .3H **55**
**Elmgrove Rd.** SA3: W Cro . . . . .4E **95**
**Elmhurst Cres.**
  SA1: St T . . . . . . . .1H **5** (2H **85**)
**Elm Ri.** CF32: Brync . . . . . . . .5E **115**
**Elm Rd.** CF36: Newt . . . . . . . .3G **125**
  SA11: Brit F . . . . . . . . . . .6G **77**
**Elmsfield Cl.** CF31: Bri . . . . . .1D **126**
**Elm Tree Rd.** SA4: Penl . . . . . .3G **57**
**Elmwood Dr.** SA11: Brit F . . . . .6H **77**
**Elmwood Rd.** SA12: Bag . . . . . .4A **90**
**Elphin Cres.** SA1: Town . . . . . .1B **84**
**Elphin Gdns.** SA1: Town . . . . . .1D **84**
**Elphin Rd.** SA1: Town . . . . . . .1B **84**
**Elwy Cres.** SA2: C'ett . . . . . . . .2B **84**
**Elwy Gdns.** SA2: C'ett . . . . . . .1C **84**
**Emanuel Pl.** SA1: Nea . . . . . . .2A **78**
**Embankment Rd.** SA15: Llane . .4B **52**
**Emily Cl.** SA1: Swan . . . . . . . .4B **86**
**Emily Flds.** SA7: Birch . . . . . . .5H **61**
**Emlyn Gdns.** SA1: M'hill . . . . . .1E **85**
**Emlyn Rd.** SA1: M'hill . . . . . . .1D **84**
**Emlyn Ter.** SA6: Plas . . . . . . . .3H **73**
  SA31: Carm . . . . . . . . . . . .5E **7**

**Emmanuel Gdns.** SA2: Sket . . . .1G **95**
**Emma St.** SA15: Llane . . . . . . .2A **52**
**Empire Wlk.** *SA11: Nea* . . . . . .*1B 78*
  *(off Ropewalk)*
**Empress Ho.** SA1: Swan . . . . . .6F **5**
**Ena Av.** SA1: Nea . . . . . . . . . .1C **78**
**Endeavour Cl.** CF31: Brack . . .5H **121**
  SA12: Sand . . . . . . . . . . .1A **96**
**Enfield Cl.** SA6: Cwm'crw . . . . .2H **59**
**Enfield St.** SA10: A'von . . . . . .4E **97**
**Engine Row** *SA4: Penc* . . . . . .*4H 67*
  *(off Banc Bach)*
**Enid Rd.** SA6: Cly . . . . . . . . . .4G **49**
**Enterprise Workshops**
  SA15: Llane . . . . . . . . . . .3D **52**
**Epona Ho.** SA7: Swan Ent . . . . .2C **74**
**Eppynt Rd.** SA5: P'lan . . . . . . .4D **72**
**Ernald Pl.** SA2: Upl . . . . . . . . .4C **84**
**Erw Deg** CF31: Bri . . . . . . . .6A **120**
**Erw Ifan** CF35: P'coed . . . . . . .3G **123**
**Erwlas** SA14: Llwy . . . . . . . . . .3G **53**
**Erwr Brenhinoedd**
  SA18: L'bie . . . . . . . . . . . .1G **11**
**Erw Rd.** SA15: Llane . . . . . . . .4H **41**
**Erw Ter.** SA16: Graig . . . . . . . .1E **39**
**Erw Wen** CF32: N Cor . . . . . . .2C **116**
**Erw Werdd** SA7: Birch . . . . . . .3G **61**
**Esgair-y-Llys** CF31: Bri . . . . . .1A **126**
**Esgair-y-Maes** CF31: Bri . . . . .2A **126**
**Esgairynys** SA18: Bry . . . . . . .3H **15**
**Espalone** SA3: Mur . . . . . . . . .6B **94**
**Esplanade, The** *SA31: Carm* . . . .*3F 7*
  *(shown as Y Llanerch)*
**Esplanade Av.** CF36: P'cwl . . . .5C **124**
**Essex Ter.** SA6: Plas . . . . . . . .2H **73**
**Esterling Dr.** CF36: P'cwl . . . . .3C **124**
**Estuary Pk.** SA14: L'nch . . . . . .5D **44**
**Ethel St.** SA11: Nea . . . . . . . . .2A **78**
**Ethos** SA1: Swan . . . . .3H **5** (3H **85**)
**Europa Way** SA5: Ffor F . . . . . .4H **71**
**Eustace Dr.** CF32: Brync . . . . .5D **114**
**Evan's Rd.** SA11: Nea . . . . . . . .3A **78**
**Evans St.** CF33: Ken H . . . . . . .4G **113**
  SA13: P Tal . . . . . . . . . . .3H **97**
**Evans Ter.** CF33: N Cor . . . . . .2C **116**
  SA1: Swan . . . . . .1D **4** (2F **85**)
  SA15: Llane . . . . . . . . . . .6C **42**
**Eva St.** SA11: Nea . . . . . . . . . .2B **78**
**Evelyn Rd.** SA10: Skew . . . . . . .1D **76**
**Evelyn Ter.** SA13: P Tal . . . . . . .4G **97**
**Eversley Rd.** SA2: Sket . . . . . . .4A **84**
**Eversley Rd. La.** SA2: Sket . . . . .4A **84**
**Evolution Fitness** . . . . . . . . . .6D **8**
**Ewart Pl.** SA5: Man . . . . . . . . .4F **73**
**EWENNI** . . . . . . . . . . . . . . . .6E **127**
**Ewenny Cl.** CF36: Not . . . . . . .1B **124**
**Ewenny Cross** CF35: Ewe . . . . .6D **126**
**Ewenny Ind. Est.** CF31: Bri . . . .3H **127**
**Ewenny Pl.** SA6: Clase . . . . . . .6F **59**
  *(not continuous)*
**Ewenny Pottery** . . . . . . . . . . .5D **126**
**Ewenny Priory** . . . . . . . . . . . .5F **127**
  CF35: Ewe . . . . . . . . . . . .5D **126**
**Excelsior** SA1: Swan . . . . . . . .4E **5**
**Exchange Ct.** *SA1: Swan* . . . . . .*4F 5*
  *(off Adelaide St.)*
**Exchange Rd.** SA11: Nea . . . . . .2A **78**
**Exchange Row** SA14: Dafen . . . .5F **43**
**Eynon St.** SA4: Gor . . . . . . . . .4C **56**

## F

**Fabian Way** SA1: Cry B . . . . . . .3H **87**
  SA1: Por T . . . . . . . .3H **5** (3H **85**)
  SA10: Cry B, Jer M, L'dcy
  . . . . . . . . . . . . . . . . . . .3H **87**
**Fabian Way (Park & Ride)** . . . . .3C **86**
**Factory La.** CF35: Coyc . . . . . .6F **123**
**Factory Rd.** SA6: Cly . . . . . . . .5E **49**
**Factory Ter.** CF32: A'knfig . . . . .6B **114**
**Fagwr Isaf** SA6: Craig-p . . . . . .2C **48**
**Fagwr Pl.** SA6: Morr . . . . . . . . .5B **60**
**Fagwr Rd.** SA6: Craig-p . . . . . .2C **48**
**FAGWYR** . . . . . . . . . . . . . . . .2C **48**
**Fairfax Cres.** CF36: P'cwl . . . . .4B **124**
**Fairfield** CF33: N Cor . . . . . . . .2C **116**
  SA12: A'von . . . . . . . . . . .3G **91**
**Fairfield Cvn. Pk.** SA3: S'gate . . .2B **98**
**Fairfield Ct.** SA7: Swan Ent . . . .6D **60**
**Fairfield Rd.** CF31: Bri . . . . . . .3E **127**

**Fairfield Ter.**
  SA1: Swan . . . . . . .2A **4** (3E **85**)
**Fairfield Way** SA11: Nea . . . . . .6B **64**
**Fairhaven Ct.** SA3: Lan . . . . . . .3E **101**
**Fairland Dr.** SA12: Bag . . . . . . .6B **90**
**Fairlawns** SA11: Brit F . . . . . . .5G **77**
**Fairlawn Ter.** CF35: P'coed . . . .3G **123**
**Fairoak** SA18: Amm . . . . . . . . .6C **12**
**Fairoak Chase** CF31: Brack . . .1H **127**
**Fair Vw.** *SA10: Nea* . . . . . . . .*4H 63*
  *(shown as Golwg Deg)*
**Fairview Av.** SA12: A'von . . . . . .3E **97**
**Fairview Cl.** SA7: L'smlt . . . . . .2G **75**
**Fairview Rd.** SA5: L'flch . . . . . .3E **59**
**Fairway** SA12: Sand . . . . . . . . .2B **96**
**Fairway Dr.** SA8: P'dwe . . . . . . .4C **36**
**Fairways** CF33: N Cor . . . . . . .1B **116**
**Fairways, The** SA7: Birch . . . . . .5G **61**
**FAIRWOOD** . . . . . . . . . . . . . .3E **81**
**Fairwood Cnr. Farm Cvn. Pk.**
  SA2: Cair . . . . . . . . . . . . .4E **81**
**Fairwood Dr.** SA12: Bag . . . . . .4B **90**
**Fairwood La.** SA2: Up K . . . . . . .4A **82**
**Fairwood Pk. Golf Course** . . . . .1A **94**
**Fairwood Rd.** SA2: Dunv . . . . . .2A **82**
  SA3: W Cro . . . . . . . . . . .3E **95**
**Fairwood Ter.** SA4: Gow . . . . . .2A **70**
**Fairy Gro.** SA2: Kill . . . . . . . . .3D **82**
**Fairy Rd.** SA2: Kill . . . . . . . . . .3D **82**
**Fairyland Rd.** SA11: Tonna . . . . .5D **64**
**Falcon Dr.** SA11: Cim . . . . . . . .4E **79**
**Falcon Pl.** SA5: Blae M . . . . . . .1B **72**
**Faraday Rd.** SA6: Cly . . . . . . . .3E **49**
**Farm Dr.** SA12: Sand . . . . . . . .3B **96**
**Farmers Rd.** SA10: B'och . . . . . .1G **63**
**Farmers Row** SA14: F'oel . . . . . .3C **42**
**Farmfield Av.** SA12: Sand . . . . . .2B **96**
**Farm Rd.** CF32: Cef C . . . . . . .1E **119**
  SA8: T'nos . . . . . . . . . . . .3A **50**
  SA11: Brit F . . . . . . . . . . .4H **77**
**Felin St.** SA6: Morr . . . . . . . . .5H **59**
**Felindre Av.** CF35: P'coed . . . . .4H **123**
**Felindre Mdws.**
  CF35: P'coed . . . . . . . . . .6H **123**
**Felindre (Park & Ride)** . . . . . . .2D **58**
**Felindre Rd.** CF35: P'coed . . . . .4G **123**
  SA5: F'dre, L'flch . . . . . . . .1D **58**
  SA9: Cwm U . . . . . . . . . . .2B **26**
**FELINFOEL** . . . . . . . . . . . . . .3C **42**
**Felinfoel Rd.** SA15: Llane . . . . .6A **42**
  *(not continuous)*
**Felin Fran** SA7: L'smlt . . . . . . .4F **61**
**Fenbrook Cl.** SA12: Bag . . . . . . .5A **90**
**Fendrod Bus. Cen.**
  SA6: Swan Ent . . . . . . . . .1B **74**
**Fendrod Way** SA7: Swan Ent . . .1C **74**
**Fenton Pl.** CF36: P'cwl . . . . . . .4C **124**
**Fenwick Dr.** CF31: Brack . . . . .6H **121**
**Fermoy Ct.** SA5: Por . . . . . . . . .2C **72**
**Ferndale Dr.** SA4: Lou . . . . . . . .6E **55**
**Fern Fld.** SA8: Rhos . . . . . . . . .1H **51**
**Fernfield** SA12: Bag . . . . . . . . .6B **90**
**Fernhill Cl.** SA3: Blk P . . . . . . .3G **95**
**Fernhill Rd.** SA4: Gor . . . . . . . .3H **55**
**Fernlea Pk.** SA10: B'och . . . . . .4H **63**
**Fernley Dr.** SA12: Bag . . . . . . . .5A **90**
**Fern St.** SA5: Cwmb . . . . . . . . .6E **73**
**Ferrara Quay**
  SA1: Swan . . . . . .5F **5** (4G **85**)
**Ferrara Sq.**
  SA1: Swan . . . . . .6F **5** (4G **85**)
**Ferrar St.** SA31: Carm . . . . . . . .3D **6**
**Ferryboat Cl.**
  SA6: Swan Ent . . . . . . . . .1B **74**
**Ferry Cl.** SA11: Brit F . . . . . . . .1H **89**
**Ferry Rd.** SA4: Lou . . . . . . . . . .5D **54**
**Ferryside** SA1: Swan . . . . .4G **5** (4H **85**)
**Ferry Vw.** SA10: Skew . . . . . . . .2E **77**
**Ffald Rd.** CF33: Pyle . . . . . . . .6E **113**
**Ffald Rd. Shop. Cen.**
  CF33: Pyle . . . . . . . . . . . .6E **113**
**Ffawydden** SA12: C'avon . . . . . .5G **91**
**Ffordd Abiah** SA6: Cly . . . . . . .4F **49**
**Ffordd Alltwen** SA4: Gow . . . . . .3H **69**
**Ffordd Amazon** SA10: Jer M . . .2A **88**
**Ffordd Aneurin Bevan**
  SA2: Sket . . . . . . . . . . . . .2G **83**
**Ffordd Antwn** CF32: Ton . . . . . .5B **114**
**Ffordd Austin** CF36: Newt . . . . .3G **125**
**Ffordd Beck** SA4: Gow . . . . . . .2H **69**
**Ffordd Bishop** SA18: Amm . . . . .2G **21**
**Ffordd Briallu** SA7: L'smlt . . . . .2E **75**
**Ffordd Bryngwyn** SA4: Gor . . . . .6B **56**

**Ffordd Brynheulog**
  SA8: P'dwe . . . . . . . . . . . .5C **36**
**Ffordd Butler** SA4: Gow . . . . . . .2A **70**
**Ffordd Cae Duke** SA4: Lou . . . . .6H **55**
**Ffordd Cambria** SA4: P'dul . . . . .6F **55**
**Ffordd Campbell** SA18: L'bie . . . .1F **11**
**Ffordd Candleston** CF31: Bri . . .2B **126**
**Ffordd Cefnllan** *SA8: P'dwe* . . . .*4C 36*
  *(shown as Cefnllan Rd.)*
**Ffordd Coed Darcy**
  SA10: L'dcy . . . . . . . . . . .4C **76**
**Ffordd Cwm Tawe**
  SA6: Yfgn, Ystwe . . . . . . . .2C **60**
**Ffordd Cwm Tawe By-Pass**
  SA6: Swan Ent . . . . . . . . .3H **73**
**Ffordd Cynghordy** SA7: L'smlt . . .1E **75**
**Ffordd Cynore** SA5: Ffor F, Por . .2H **71**
**Ffordd Dafydd** SA14: Pen g . . . . .6H **9**
**Ffordd Danygraig** SA9: Godr . . . .5D **32**
**Ffordd Dawel** SA7: L'smlt . . . . . .2F **75**
**Ffordd Ddu** CF33: Pyle . . . . . . .5E **113**
**Ffordd Derwen** SA13: Coe H . . .2D **112**
**Ffordd Dewi** SA15: L'flch . . . . . .5E **59**
**Ffordd Dillwyn-Llewellyn**
  SA4: Penl . . . . . . . . . . . . .4H **57**
**Ffordd Dinas** SA12: C'avon . . . .5G **91**
**Ffordd Donaldson**
  SA1: Swan Ent . . . . . . . . .5A **74**
**Ffordd Draenen Ddu**
  SA3: W Cro . . . . . . . . . . .6D **94**
**Ffordd Dryden** SA2: Kill . . . . . . .2D **82**
**Ffordd Eira** SA4: Gor . . . . . . . . .3B **56**
**Ffordd Ellen** SA6: Craig-p . . . . .2C **48**
**Ffordd Emlyn** SA9: Ysta . . . . . . .3E **33**
**Ffordd Florence** SA18: Amm . . . .6G **11**
**Ffordd Ganol** CF31: Bri . . . . . .1F **127**
**Ffordd Ger-y-Llyn** SA4: Tir V . . .2H **57**
**Ffordd Glandwr** SA9: Ysta . . . . .2E **33**
**Ffordd Gwyn** SA7: L'smlt . . . . . .1E **75**
**Ffordd Is-Cennen**
  SA18: Amm . . . . . . . . . . .1H **21**
**Ffordd Kilby** SA4: Lou . . . . . . . .6H **55**
**Ffordd Llundain** SA7: L'smlt . . . .1E **75**
**Ffordd Llyffant** SA7: Birch . . . . .6A **62**
**Ffordd Maendy** CF32: B'myn . . .4D **114**
**Ffordd Maescwrau**
  SA18: Amm . . . . . . . . . . .1C **22**
**Ffordd Melyn Mair**
  SA7: L'smlt . . . . . . . . . . . .2E **75**
**Ffordd Newydd** CF33: N Cor . . .1D **116**
**Ffordd Parc Ynysderw**
  SA8: P'dwe . . . . . . . . . . . .6D **36**
**Ffordd Pentwyn** SA18: Amm . . . .2A **22**
**Ffordd Priordy** CF32: Sarn . . . . .5C **114**
**Ffordd Scott** SA7: Birch . . . . . . .5G **61**
**Ffordd Silkin** SA8: P'dwe . . . . . .5D **36**
**Ffordd Stewart** SA18: Amm . . . . .6H **11**
**Ffordd Talbot** SA18: Amm . . . . .6H **11**
**Ffordd Talfan** SA4: Gor . . . . . . .6C **56**
**Ffordd Taliesin** SA2: Kill . . . . . .2E **83**
**Ffordd Tirion** CF31: Bri . . . . . .2B **126**
**Ffordd Tollborth** SA7: L'smlt . . . .1E **75**
**Ffordd Tregof** SA7: L'smlt . . . . . .4F **61**
**Ffordd Tyn-y-Coed** SA6: Cly . . . .4H **49**
**Ffordd Villiers** SA18: Amm . . . . .2G **21**
**Ffordd Walter** SA18: Amm . . . . .6A **12**
**Ffordd Watkins** SA7: Birch . . . . .3F **61**
**Ffordd Waungron**
  SA18: Amm . . . . . . . . . . .3B **22**
**Ffordd Werdd** SA14: Gors . . . . . .3D **8**
**Ffordd Wern-Ddu** SA18: Amm . . .6B **12**
**Ffordd William Walker**
  SA18: Amm . . . . . . . . . . .1H **21**
**Ffordd-y-Betws** SA18: Amm . . . .3A **22**
**Ffordd y Blodau** SA18: L'bie . . . .3G **11**
**Ffordd y Brain** SA5: Rav . . . . . .3B **72**
**Ffordd y Bryn** SA7: Birch . . . . . .6A **62**
**Ffordd y Chwarel**
  CF33: Ken H . . . . . . . . . .4G **113**
**Ffordd y Coegylfinir** SA4: Gor . . .3G **55**
**Ffordd y Coroni** SA18: Bry . . . . .3A **16**
**Ffordd y Cronlyn** SA31: Carm . . .1F **7**
**Ffordd-y-Cyrnol** SA18: Amm . . . .2A **22**
**Ffordd-y-Dderwen** CF31: Bri . . .5B **120**
**Ffordd y Deri** SA18: Tyc . . . . . . .4D **20**
**Ffordd y Draen** CF35: Coity . . . .2F **121**
**Ffordd y Faenor** SA18: Amm . . . .1G **21**
**Ffordd y Gamlas** SA4: Gow . . . . .2H **57**
**Ffordd y Glowr** SA4: P'dul . . . . .1E **46**
**Ffordd y Glowyr** SA9: Godr . . . . .5D **32**
**Ffordd y Goedwig**
  CF33: Pyle . . . . . . . . . . . .4E **113**
  SA4: Tir V . . . . . . . . . . . . .2H **57**

Ffordd y Gollen CF35: Coity . . .2G 121
Ffordd y Groes CF31: Bri . . . . .5C 126
Ffordd y Grug CF35: Coity . . . .2F 121
Ffordd y Meillion SA4: Penl . . . .3G 57
Ffordd y Morfa SA14: Cross H . . . .6F 9
Ffordd y Mynach CF33: Pyle . . . .5E 113
Ffordd y Mynydd SA7: Birch . . . .6A 62
Ffordd Ynys Tawelog
    SA18: G'llt . . . . . . . . . . . .6G 21
Ffordd y Parc SA6: Morr . . . . .5H 59
Ffordd-y-Parc CF31: Bri . . . . . .3E 121
Ffordd yr Afon CF32: B'myn . .3C 124
    SA4: Gor . . . . . . . . . . . . .5B 56
Ffordd-yr-Afon CF31: Bri . . . . .5A 120
    SA18: Amm . . . . . . . . . . . .5H 11
Ffordd yr Eglwys
    CF33: N Cor . . . . . . . . . . .6C 112
Ffordd yr Hebog CF35: Coity . .2F 121
Ffordd y Rhyd SA18: Amm . . . .2H 21
Ffordd yr Odyn SA4: P'dul . . . .1C 46
Ffordd-yr-Orsaf SA18: Amm . . . .6G 11
Ffordd Ysgol SA12: Sand . . . . .3C 96
Ffordd y Wiwer SA7: L'smlt . . . .5E 61
Ffordd y Mynach SA10: Nea A . . .1F 77
FFOREST . . . . . . . . . . . . . . .4D 34
FForest Bus. Cen. SA5: Ffor F . .4A 72
FFOREST-FACH . . . . . . . . . . . .4H 71
Fforestfach SA18: Tyc . . . . . . . .4E 21
FFOREST-GÔCH . . . . . . . . . . .4G 51
Fforest Hill SA10: A'dul . . . . . . .2F 65
Fforest Rd. SA4: Ffor . . . . . . . .5D 34
    (shown as Heol Fforest)
Fforest Villa SA14: Llane . . . . . .2E 53
Ffos Felen SA4: Gow . . . . . . . .2A 70
Ffos yr Efail Ter. SA4: P'dul . . . .6F 35
Ffridd Las CF31: Bri . . . . . . . . .1A 126
Ffrwd Va. SA10: Nea . . . . . . . . .5A 64
Ffrwdwyllt Cotts. SA13: P Tal . . .6H 97
Ffrwd-Wyllt St. SA13: P Tal . . . .5H 97
Ffrwd-y-Felin SA18: Amm . . . . . .5G 11
Ffwrn Clai SA4: P'dul . . . . . . . .1C 46
Ffwrnes Theatre . . . . . . . . . . .1A 52
Flynnon Caeconna SA5: Por . . .2B 72
Flynnon Dawel SA10: A'dul . . . .3E 65
Flynnon Groyw CF31: Bri . . . . .1A 126
Flynnon Las SA18: Amm . . . . . .2H 21
Flynnon Samlet SA7: L'smlt . . . .1E 75
Flynnon Waun SA31: Carm . . . .4B 6
Flynnon Wen CF33: N Cor . . . .6D 112
    (not continuous)
Ffynone Cl.
    SA1: Swan . . . . . . . .2A 4 (3D 84)
Ffynone Dr. SA1: Swan . . . . . . .3D 84
Ffynone Rd.
    SA1: Swan . . . . . . . .3A 4 (3D 84)
Ffynon y Maen CF33: Pyle . . . .5D 112
Field Cl. SA6: Morr . . . . . . . . .4B 60
Field St. SA1: L'ore . . . . . . . . .5G 73
Field Ter. SA13: P Tal . . . . . . . .4H 97
Fifth Av. SA6: Clase . . . . . . . . .5G 59
Finsbury Ter. SA2: Brynm . . . . .4C 84
Firm St. SA1: Swan . . . .1D 4 (2F 85)
Firs, The CF36: Newt . . . . . . . .4H 125
First Av. SA6: Clase . . . . . . . . .5F 59
Firth Rd. SA15: Llane . . . . . . . .2B 52
Firwood Cl. SA10: B'och . . . . . .1H 63
Fishermans Way
    SA1: Swan . . . . . . . .6G 5 (5H 85)
Fishmarket Quay
    SA1: Swan . . . . . . . .5G 5 (4H 85)
Fitzhamon Rd. CF36: P'cwl . . . .3C 124
Fitzroy Ho. SA1: Swan . . . . . . . .6F 5
Five Bells Rd. CF31: Bri . . . . . .2E 127
Flatholme Way CF36: Not . . . . .2B 124
Flatholm Pl. SA5: Blae M . . . . .1B 72
Fleet St. SA1: Swan . . . . .6A 4 (5E 85)
Flint Ho. SA12: Sand . . . . . . . .4C 96
    (off Moorland Rd.)
Florence Rd. SA18: Amm . . . . . .6G 11
    (shown as Ffordd Florence)
Florence St. CF36: Not . . . . . . .2C 124
    SA11: Nea . . . . . . . . . . . . .2B 78
    SA15: Llane . . . . . . . . . . . .3A 52
Foel Rd. SA8: Bry . . . . . . . . . .1F 15
Folland Ct. SA3: W Cro . . . . . . .3G 95
Folland Rd. SA18: Glan . . . . . . .4A 14
    (shown as Heol Folland)
Forbes St. SA6: Plas . . . . . . . . .3G 73
Ford Rd. SA13: P Tal . . . . . . . .3G 97
Forest Cl. CF32: Sarn . . . . . . . .6D 114
Forest Lodge La.
    SA13: C'avon . . . . . . . . . . .6H 91
Forest Vw. CF33: Pyle . . . . . . .5D 112
    SA31: Cim . . . . . . . . . . . . .4E 79

Forge Fach SA6: Cly . . . . . . . . .5E 49
Forge Rd. SA4: Crof . . . . . . . . .6E 67
    SA13: P Tal . . . . . . . . . . . .3G 97
Forge Way CF36: Not . . . . . . . .3C 124
Forster Rd. SA11: Nea . . . . . . .1C 78
Foundry Rd. SA6: Morr . . . . . . .5B 60
    SA11: Nea . . . . . . . . . . . . .3B 78
    SA18: Amm . . . . . . . . . . . .1A 22
    (shown as Heol-y-Ffowndri)
Foundry Row SA10: Skew . . . . .1C 76
    SA18: Amm . . . . . . . . . . . .1A 22
Fountain Bungalow
    CF32: A'knfig . . . . . . . . . . .6A 114
Fountain Hall Ter. SA31: Carm . .3D 6
Fourth Av. SA6: Clase . . . . . . . .5G 59
Foxfields CF31: Brack . . . . . . . .1A 128
Fox Gro. SA5: Ffor F . . . . . . . . .4F 71
Foxgrove SA4: Gor . . . . . . . . . .6A 56
FOXHOLE . . . . . . . . . . . . . . .1H 85
Foxhole Dr. SA3: S'gate . . . . . . .2A 98
Foxhole Rd. SA1: St T . . . . . . . .2H 85
Fox Hollows CF31: Brack . . . . . .6A 122
Foyer, The SA1: Swan . . . . . . . .2E 5
Frampton Ct. SA4: Gor . . . . . . .4G 55
Frampton Rd. SA4: Gor . . . . . . .4H 55
Francis Ct. SA8: Rhos . . . . . . . .6H 37
Francis Rd. SA6: Morr . . . . . . . .5H 59
Francis St. SA1: Swan . . . . . . . .5D 84
    SA8: P'dwe . . . . . . . . . . . . .6D 36
    SA10: Skew . . . . . . . . . . . .1E 77
Francis Ter. SA31: Carm . . . . . . .3E 7
Fransham St. SA15: Llane . . . . . .6B 42
Frederick Ct. SA11: Nea . . . . . . .2B 78
    (off Southgate St.)
FREDERICK PLACE . . . . . . . . . .1H 75
Frederick Pl. SA7: L'smlt . . . . . . .6G 61
Frederick St. SA5: Man . . . . . . . .5F 73
    SA12: Sand . . . . . . . . . . . .3D 96
    SA15: Llane . . . . . . . . . . . .1A 52
Freeman St. SA5: Man . . . . . . . .4F 73
Free School Ct. CF31: Bri . . . . .2E 127
Friars Cl. SA10: Nea A . . . . . . . .6G 63
Friars Pk. SA31: Carm . . . . . . . .4D 6
Friars Row SA31: Carm . . . . . . .3D 6
Frog La. SA3: L'doc . . . . . . . . . .3F 105
Frogmore Av. SA2: Sket . . . . . . .3A 84
Frogmore La. SA3: Knel . . . . . . .1H 109
Frondeg Ter. SA15: Llane . . . . . .6C 42
Fronhaul SA14: F'oel . . . . . . . . .1E 43
Fron Heulog CF31: Bri . . . . . . . .6B 120
Fron Ter. SA15: Llane . . . . . . . .3B 52
Froom Ter. SA12: A'von . . . . . . .3F 97
Fullers Row
    SA1: Swan . . . . . . .2D 4 (3F 85)
Fuller St. SA8: P'dwe . . . . . . . .5D 36
Fulmar Cl. SA3: W Cro . . . . . . .5D 94
Fulmar Rd. CF36: Not, P'cwl . . .3A 124
FURNACE
    SA15 . . . . . . . . . . . . . . . .2H 41
    SA16 . . . . . . . . . . . . . . . .3D 38
Furnace Bank SA31: Carm . . . . .2G 7
Furnace Rd. SA16: Burr P . . . . .3C 38
    SA31: Carm . . . . . . . . . . . .3E 7
Furnace Ter. SA11: Nea . . . . . . .3H 77
Furnace Way SA31: Swan . . . . .6F 73
Furze Cres. SA6: Morr . . . . . . . .4G 59
Furzeland Dr. SA2: Sket . . . . . . .4G 83
    SA10: B'och . . . . . . . . . . . .1H 63

## G

Gabalfa Rd. SA2: Sket . . . . . . . .5F 83
Gables, The SA4: Thr X . . . . . . . .2F 81
Gainsborough Cl. SA2: Sket . . . .4B 84
Gallipoli Row SA13: P Tal . . . . . .6H 97
Gallt t Ddrudwen CF31: Bri . . . .6C 126
Garbett Pl. SA10: Cry . . . . . . . . .4H 33
Gardde SA14: Llwy . . . . . . . . . .2H 53
Garden Cotts. SA11: Nea . . . . . .1B 78
Garden Cl. CF31: Brack . . . . . . .6A 122
Garden Cres. SA4: Gor . . . . . . .6C 56
Gardens, The SA4: P'dul . . . . . .1B 46
    SA9: Ysta . . . . . . . . . . . . .2E 33
Garden St. SA1: Swan . . .4D 4 (4F 85)
Garden Ter. SA6: Morr . . . . . . . .1A 74
GARDEN VILLAGE . . . . . . . . . .6C 56
Gardners La. SA11: Nea . . . . . . .3A 78
Garfield Av. CF31: Bri . . . . . . . .3E 121
Garnant SA31: Carm . . . . . . . . .5D 14
Garnant Pk. Golf Club . . . . . . . .6D 14
Garnfoel SA14: Pen g . . . . . . . . .6H 9
Garngoch Ind. Est. SA4: Gor . . .5D 56
Garngoch Ter. SA4: Gor . . . . . . .6C 56
Garnlwyd Cl. SA6: Morr . . . . . . .1F 73

Garnswllt Rd. SA4: P'dul . . . . . . .4G 35
Garreg Hollt SA14: Cross H . . . .5B 8
Garreglwyd SA16: Pem . . . . . . .1A 38
Garrod Av. SA2: Dunv . . . . . . . .6B 70
Garth Dr. CF31: Brack . . . . . . .4G 121
Garth Rd. SA6: Ystwe . . . . . . . .3D 60
    SA7: Glais . . . . . . . . . . . . .6F 49
    SA8: Phyd f . . . . . . . . . . . .1A 36
    SA18: Tair . . . . . . . . . . . . .2F 25
Garth St. CF33: Ken H . . . . . . .5F 113
Garth Vw. SA6: Yfgn . . . . . . . . .2C 60
Gas St. CF37: Ton . . . . . . . . . . .3B 4
Gasworks Ter. CF32: B'myn . . . .4C 114
GATE, THE . . . . . . . . . . . . . . .2F 9
Gate Rd. CF31: Bri . . . . . . . . . .3A 128
    SA14: Pen g . . . . . . . . . . . .2F 9
    (shown as Heol y Gât)
Gateway Bldg. SA12: Bag . . . . . .5H 89
Gateway Cvn. Pk. SA14: Byn . . .5H 53
Gathen Cl. SA15: Llane . . . . . . .2A 52
Gathen Ter. SA15: Llane . . . . . . .2A 52
Geifr Rd. SA13: Marg . . . . . . . .1F 103
Geiriol Gdns. SA1: Town . . . . . .1B 84
Geiriol Rd. SA1: Town . . . . . . . .1B 84
Gelert St. SA1: Tre b . . . . . . . . .3F 73
Gelli Aur SA5: Tre b . . . . . . . . . .2G 73
    SA10: Nea . . . . . . . . . . . . .4A 64
Gelliauar CF35: P'coed . . . . . . .2F 123
Gelli Dawel SA10: Nea . . . . . . . .4A 64
Gellidderw SA8: P'dwe . . . . . . . .4C 36
Gelli Deg SA5: Ffor F . . . . . . . . .2H 71
    SA10: Nea . . . . . . . . . . . . .4A 64
    SA14: Dafen . . . . . . . . . . . .6C 42
Gellideg SA8: P'dwe . . . . . . . . .4A 36
    SA15: Byn . . . . . . . . . . . . .2B 54
Gellifach Cres. SA6: Morr . . . . . .1F 73
Gellifawr Rd. SA6: Morr . . . . . . .1G 73
Gelli Forwyn SA18: L'bie . . . . . .2G 11
Gelli Gdns. SA7: Birch . . . . . . . .6A 62
Gelligeiros SA8: Gell . . . . . . . . .5G 37
Gelliglas Rd. SA6: Morr . . . . . . .1G 73
Gelli Grafog SA1: Por T . . . . . . .3D 86
GELLI-GRON . . . . . . . . . . . . . .4C 36
Gelligron Rd.
    SA8: P'dwe, Phyd f . . . . . . .3C 36
Gelligwyn Rd. SA6: Morr . . . . . . .1G 73
Gelli Gynore Rd. SA4: Penl . . . . .4E 57
Gelli Hir Wood Nature Reserve
    . . . . . . . . . . . . . . . . . . . .4D 80
Gelli Hyll Rd. SA4: Penl . . . . . . .4E 57
Gelli La. SA18: Tyc . . . . . . . . . .4E 21
GELLINUDD . . . . . . . . . . . . . . .5G 37
Gellionen Cl. SA6: Cly . . . . . . . .4F 49
Gellionen Rd. SA6: Cly . . . . . . .4F 49
    SA8: P'dwe . . . . . .2G 49, 6A 36
Gelli Onn SA15: Llane . . . . . . . .6A 42
Gelli Rhedyn SA5: Ffor F . . . . . .2H 71
Gelli Rd. SA14: Llane . . . . . . . . .1E 53
Gelli St. SA1: Por T . . . . . . . . . .3C 86
Gelli Wen CF31: Brack . . . . . . .2B 126
Gelli Wriddon SA18: Amm . . . . .3E 21
Gellyfowy Rd. SA8: Ynys . . . . . .1F 37
Gelly Rd. SA18: L'bie . . . . . . . . .2F 11
    (shown as Heol y Gelli)
Gemini Ct. SA12: Bag . . . . . . . .5G 89
Gem Rd. SA6: Morr . . . . . . . . . .4B 60
GENDROS . . . . . . . . . . . . . . . .5C 72
Gendros Av. E. SA5: Gen . . . . . .5C 72
Gendros Av. W. SA5: Gen . . . . .4C 72
Gendros Cl. SA5: Gen . . . . . . . .5D 72
Gendros Cres. SA5: Gen . . . . . .5D 72
Gendros Dr. SA5: Gen . . . . . . . .5C 72
GenQuip Stadium . . . . . . . . . . .4D 96
Gentle Way CF31: Bri . . . . . . . .2B 126
    (shown as Ffordd Tirion)
Genwen Rd. SA14: Llwy . . . . . . .2A 54
Geoffrey St. SA11: Nea . . . . . . .1B 78
George Bank SA3: T Mum . . . . .2G 101
George Manning Way
    SA4: Gow . . . . . . . . . . . . . .4A 70
George's Row SA11: Brit F . . . . .1F 89
George St. CF31: Bri . . . . . . . . .2H 127
    CF36: P'cwl . . . . . . . . . . . .4C 124
    SA1: Swan . . . . . . .3B 4 (3E 85)
    SA8: P'dwe . . . . . . . . . . . . .5D 36
    SA11: Nea . . . . . . . . . . . . .2B 78
    SA13: P Tal . . . . . . . . . . . .5H 97
    SA15: Llane . . . . . . . . . . . .3A 52
George St. Est. CF31: Bri . . . . . .2H 127
George Thomas Av.
    CF32: B'myn . . . . . . . . . . .3E 115
George Thomas Cl.
    CF36: Not . . . . . . . . . . . . .3C 124
Georgian Cl. CF36: P'cwl . . . . . .3D 124
Georgian Way CF31: Brack . . . . .1F 127

Geraint Jeremiah Cl.
    SA11: Brit F . . . . . . . . . . . .4A 78
Gerald St. SA1: Swan . . . . . . . .6G 73
    SA12: Sand . . . . . . . . . . . . .4E 97
Gerddi Alexander SA5: Gen . . . .5E 73
Gerddi Glasfryn Gdns.
    SA15: Llane . . . . . . . . . . . .5A 42
Gerddi Quarella CF31: Bri . . . . .6D 120
Gerddi'r Afon CF32: B'myn . . . .3E 115
Gerddi'r Briallu CF31: Coity . . . .2H 121
Gerddi ty Bryn CF35: P'coed . . .3E 123
Gerretts Cl. SA3: Bishop . . . . . .1G 99
Gery-Bont CF31: Bri . . . . . . . . .5E 121
Ger y Coed SA6: Cly . . . . . . . . .4D 48
Gery-Coed CF31: Brack . . . . . . .6H 121
    SA15: Pwll . . . . . . . . . . . . .2B 40
Ger-y-Felin SA7: L'smlt . . . . . . . .3F 75
Ger y Llan SA15: Llane . . . . . . .2A 52
    SA31: Carm . . . . . . . . . . . . .3F 7
Ger-y-Llyn CF36: P'cwl . . . . . . .3D 124
Ger-y-Maes SA14: Dafen . . . . . .5D 42
Gerymanwydd SA18: Amm . . . . .1A 22
    (off Y Stryd Fawr)
Ger y Mor SA15: Llane . . . . . . . .6H 41
Ger y Nant SA7: Birch . . . . . . . .3F 61
    SA31: L'nch . . . . . . . . . . . . .4C 44
    SA31: Carm . . . . . . . . . . . .4G 7
Gery-Pant SA4: P'dul . . . . . . . . .6G 35
Ger-y-Parc SA6: Morr . . . . . . . .5H 59
Ger yr Afon SA18: Glan . . . . . . .4A 14
Ger-yr-Afon SA9: Cwm I . . . . . .5D 26
    SA10: A'dul . . . . . . . . . . . .2F 65
    SA18: Gwaun . . . . . . . . . . .2C 24
Ger-yr-Eglwys
    SA4: Ffor, Hendy . . . . . . . . .6E 35
Ger yr Ysgol SA16: Burr P . . . . .2D 38
Gery-Sedd CF31: Brack . . . . . . .6H 121
Gethin Cl. SA5: Gen . . . . . . . . .5D 72
Gething St. SA1: Swan . . .4C 4 (4F 85)
Gethin St. SA11: Brit F . . . . . . . .6G 77
Giant's Grave Rd.
    SA11: Brit F . . . . . . . . . . . .6G 77
Giant's Wharf SA11: Brit F . . . . .6F 77
Gibbons Way CF33: N Cor . . . . .1D 116
Gilbert Cres. SA15: Llane . . . . . .6A 42
Gilbert Rd. SA15: Llane . . . . . . .6A 42
Gilbertscliffe SA3: Lan . . . . . . . .2D 100
Gilfach SA4: Penl . . . . . . . . . . .4F 57
Gilfach Rd. SA9: Cwm U . . . . . .3C 26
    SA10: Nea . . . . . . . . . . . . .3A 64
Gilfach-y-Gôg SA14: Pen g . . . . .6H 9
Gilsea Bus. Pk.
    SA6: Swan Ent . . . . . . . . . .3B 74
Girton Vs. SA2: Sket . . . . . . . . .3B 84
Glade, The CF32: Brync . . . . . . .5F 115
    CF36: Not . . . . . . . . . . . . .2C 124
    SA3: W Cro . . . . . . . . . . . .3E 95
Gladys St. SA12: A'von . . . . . . . .3E 97
GLAIS . . . . . . . . . . . . . . . . . . .1H 61
Glais Rd. SA6: Cly . . . . . . . . . . .5F 49
    SA7: Glais . . . . . . . . . . . . .4B 50
Glamorgan Grn. SA10: L'dcy . . .4C 76
Glamorgan Health & Racquets Club
    . . . . . . . . . . . . . . . . . . . .4D 76
Glamorgan St.
    SA1: Swan . . . . . . .6C 4 (4F 85)
Glanaber SA16: Burr P . . . . . . . .3B 38
Glanafon SA18: Amm . . . . . . . .2A 22
GLANAMAN . . . . . . . . . . . . . . .5A 14
Glanamman Workshops
    SA18: Glan . . . . . . . . . . . . .4A 14
Glanbran Cl. SA7: Birch . . . . . . .6H 61
Glanbran Rd. SA7: Birch . . . . . .6H 61
Glanbrydan Av. SA2: Upl . . . . . .4B 84
Glandafen Rd. SA15: Llane . . . . .4C 52
Glan Dulais SA2: Dunv . . . . . . . .3B 82
GLANDWR . . . . . . . . . . . . . . . .4G 73
Glandwr Cres. SA1: L'ore . . . . . .4G 73
Glan Dyffryn Cl. SA13: P Tal . . . .5H 97
Glanfornwg CF31: Bri . . . . . . . .4D 120
Glanffrwd Rd. SA4: P'dul . . . . . .4G 35
Glan-Ffynnon SA31: Carm . . . . .5G 7
GLANGWILI GENERAL HOSPITAL
    . . . . . . . . . . . . . . . . . . . .1H 7
Glan Hafren SA12: Bag . . . . . . .4A 90
Glanlliedi Ter. SA14: F'oel . . . . . .3G 42
Glan Llwyd SA4: P'dul . . . . . . . .5F 35
Glanllyn Rd. SA7: Glais . . . . . . .1H 61
Glanmor Ct. SA2: Upl . . . . . . . . .3C 84
Glanmor Cres. SA2: Upl . . . . . . .3C 84
Glanmorfa SA4: Gow . . . . . . . . .3A 70
Glanmor La. SA2: Upl . . . . . . . . .3C 84
Glanmôr Pk. Rd. SA2: Sket . . . . .4B 84
Glanmor Pl. SA15: Llane . . . . . .5H 41

Glanmor Rd. SA15: Llane . . . . . .6H **41**
Glanmôr Rd. SA2: Sket, Upl . . .3A **84**
Glan-Mor Ter. SA16: Burr P . . . .3E **39**
Glanmor Ter. SA4: Penc . . . . . .4H **67**
    SA15: Llane . . . . . . . . . . .5H **41**
Glannant SA31: Carm . . . . . . . .3C **6**
Glannant Ri. SA11: Cim . . . . . . .2F **79**
Glannant Rd. CF31: Bri . . . . . .6C **120**
    SA4: P'dul . . . . . . . . . . . .5H **35**
    SA31: Carm . . . . . . . . . . . .3D **6**
Glannant Ter. SA9: Ystra . . . . .2H **33**
Glannant Way SA11: Cim . . . . . .2B **78**
Glanogwr Rd. CF31: Bri . . . . . .2D **126**
Glan-Pelenna SA12: Pontr . . .5H **79**
GLAN-RHYD . . . . . . . . . . . . . . .1H **33**
GLANRHYD HOSPITAL . . . . . . . .3D **120**
Glan-Rhyd Rd. SA8: P'dwe . . .5B **36**
Glanrhyd Rd. SA9: Ystra . . . . .2H **33**
Glanrhyd Ter. SA4: Gor . . . . . .6B **56**
Glan Rd. CF36: P'cwl . . . . . . .4D **124**
Glantawelan SA31: John . . . . . .4B **6**
Glantawe Pk. SA9: Ystra . . . . .1G **33**
Glantawe St. SA6: Morr . . . . . .6A **60**
Glantowy SA31: Carm . . . . . . . .1G **7**
Glantwrch SA9: Ystra . . . . . . . .1F **33**
Glanwern SA16: Burr P . . . . . .3E **39**
Glan-y-Gors SA14: Pen g . . . . . .5F **9**
Glan y Lli SA4: Penc . . . . . . . .4B **68**
Glan-y-Llyn CF33: N Cor . . . . .2D **116**
Glan y Mor Av.
    SA13: Marg, P Tal . . . . . .2F **103**
Glan y Morfa SA4: Lou . . . . . . .4F **55**
Glanymor La. SA4: Lou . . . . . .5F **55**
Glanymor Pk. Dr. SA4: Lou . . .5E **55**
Glanymor Rd. SA4: Lou . . . . . .5F **55**
Glan y Mor Sports Cen. . . . . . .2D **38**
Glan-y-Nant CF32: Ton . . . . . .4C **114**
    CF35: Treoes . . . . . . . . .4G **123**
    CF35: Treoes . . . . . . . . .3D **128**
Glan-y-Parc CF31: Bri . . . . . .1D **126**
Glan yr Afon SA4: Gor . . . . . .5B **56**
    SA15: F'oel . . . . . . . . . . .4C **42**
    SA18: Amm . . . . . . . . . . . .5H **11**
Glan-yr-Afon SA10: Skew . . . . .2E **77**
Glanyrafon Cl. SA4: Penl . . . . .4G **57**
Glan yr Afon Ct. SA2: Sket . . . .3G **83**
Glanyrafon Gdns. SA2: Sket . . .4H **83**
Glan yr Afon Rd. CF33: Pyle . .3F **113**
    SA2: Sket . . . . . . . . . . . . .3H **83**
Glanyrafon Rd.
    CF35: P'coed . . . . . . . . .3H **123**
    SA4: P'dul . . . . . . . . . . . .6F **35**
    SA31: Carm . . . . . . . . . . . .4C **6**
Glan yr Avon SA9: Godr, Ysta . .4D **32**
Glan-yr-Ysgol SA9: Ysta . . . . .2D **32**
Glan-yr-Ystrad SA31: John . . . .6B **6**
Glan y Wern Rd. SA7: L'smlt . . .1E **75**
Glasbrook Pl. SA5: Rav . . . . . .3B **72**
Glasbury Rd. SA6: Morr . . . . . .1G **73**
Glascoed SA15: Pwll . . . . . . . .2C **40**
Glasfryn CF31: Brack . . . . . . .1A **128**
    SA14: Dafen . . . . . . . . . . .5D **42**
Glasfryn Cl. SA2: C'ett . . . . . .6A **72**
Glasfryn Rd. SA4: P'dul . . . . . .1B **46**
Glasfryn Sq. CF33: Pyle . . . . .6E **113**
Glasfryn Ter. SA4: Gor . . . . . .1E **71**
    SA15: Llane . . . . . . . . . . .5B **42**
Glaslyn Pl. SA6: Clase . . . . . .5G **59**
Glay-y-Nant SA4: Penc . . . . . .4A **68**
Glebe, The SA3: Bishop . . . . . .5H **93**
Glebeland Cl. CF35: Coyc . . . .1C **128**
Glebeland St. SA10: C'dxtn . . .4C **64**
Glebe Rd. SA4: Lou . . . . . . . . .5B **55**
Glen, The CF32: Brync . . . . . .5E **115**
Glenalla Rd. SA15: Llane . . . . .1B **52**
Glenavon Cres. CF36: P'cwl . .4A **124**
Glenavon St. SA12: A'von . . . . .4E **97**
Glendale SA10: B'och . . . . . . . .3H **63**
Glendale Ct. SA10: B'och . . . . .3H **63**
Glendower Cl. CF31: Brack . . .6F **121**
Glenfield Cl. SA2: Sket . . . . . .3F **83**
Glengower Cl. SA3: T Mum . . .1E **101**
Glen Rd. SA3: W Cro . . . . . . . .5E **95**
    SA11: Nea . . . . . . . . . . . .6D **64**
Glenroy Av. SA1: St T . . .1H **5** (2H **85**)
Glenside Rd. SA5: Por . . . . . . .2A **72**
Glen Vw. CF31: Bri . . . . . . . . .3E **121**
Glenview CF31: Pen F . . . . . . .2B **120**
Glen Vw. Ter. SA12: A'von . . . .3F **97**
Glenview Ter. SA12: P Tal . . . .2G **97**
Glenville Rd. SA3: T Mum . . . .6E **93**
Glenwood Cl. CF35: Coyc . . . .1C **128**
Glevering St. SA15: Llane . . . .1B **52**
Glien Rd. SA31: John . . . . . . . .5A **6**

Globe Row SA14: Dafen . . . . . .4E **43**
Globe St. SA6: Morr . . . . . . . . .6A **60**
Glossop Ter. CF35: P'coed . . .4G **123**
Gloucester Ho.
    SA1: Swan . . . . . . .5G **5** (4G **85**)
Gloucester Pl.
    SA1: Swan . . . . . . .5F **5** (4G **85**)
    SA3: T Mum . . . . . . . . . . .1E **101**
Glynbridge Gdns. CF31: Bri . .5E **121**
Glyncoed SA18: Cap . . . . . . . .5D **20**
Glyncoed Ter. SA15: Llane . . .1D **52**
Glyncollen Cres. SA6: Yfgn . . .3B **60**
    (not continuous)
Glyncollen Dr. SA6: Yfgn . . . . .3C **60**
Glyn Cres. SA3: Blk P . . . . . . .2G **95**
Glyncynwal Rd. SA9: Cwm U . .3C **26**
Glynderi SA4: P'dul . . . . . . . . .3H **35**
    SA18: Glan . . . . . . . . . . . .5G **13**
    SA31: Carm . . . . . . . . . . . .1G **7**
Glynderwen Cl. SA2: Sket . . . .1G **95**
Glynderwen Cres. SA2: Sket . .1G **95**
Glynderwen Rd. SA14: Llwy . .2G **53**
Glyndwr Pl. SA1: Town . . . . . .2D **84**
Glyndwr St. SA13: P Tal . . . . . .3G **97**
Glyn Garfield Cl. SA11: Britt F . .4H **77**
Glyn Hirnant SA6: Morr . . . . . .3B **60**
Glynhir Rd. SA4: P'dul . . . . . . .5G **35**
    SA18: L'bie . . . . . . . . . . . .2G **11**
Glyn-Leiros SA10: Nea . . . . . .6A **64**
Glynleiros Gdns. SA10: Nea . .6A **64**
Glyn-Llwchwr Rd. SA4: P'dul . .6F **35**
Glyn-Meirch Rd. SA8: T'nos . . .6B **36**
Glyn Moch Cotts. SA18: Glan .5G **13**
Glyn Rhosyn SA4: Gor . . . . . . .5A **56**
Glyn Rd. SA4: Britt F . . . . . . . .4G **15**
Glynstell Rd. CF36: Not . . . . .2C **124**
Glyn St. SA1: Swan . . . . . . . . .6G **73**
    SA12: A'von . . . . . . . . . . .4E **97**
Glynteg Rd. SA4: P'dul . . . . . .5G **35**
Glyn-y-Coed Rd. SA11: Nea . . .1C **78**
Glyn-y-Mel CF35: P'coed . . . .3F **123**
Glyn y Swisdir SA14: F'oel . . .1C **42**
Gnoll, The . . . . . . . . . . . . . . . .6C **64**
Gnoll Av. SA11: Nea . . . . . . . .1C **78**
Gnoll Bank SA11: Nea . . . . . . .1C **78**
Gnoll Cres. SA11: Nea . . . . . . .1C **78**
Gnoll Dr. SA11: Nea . . . . . . . . .1C **78**
Gnoll Estate Country Pk. . . . . .6D **64**
Gnoll Estate Vis. Cen. . . . . . . .6D **64**
Gnoll Pk. Rd. SA11: Nea . . . . .1C **78**
Gnoll Rd. SA9: Godr . . . . . . . .6B **32**
Gnoll Vw. SA11: Nea . . . . . . . .1C **78**
Godre Coed SA6: Morr . . . . . . .4G **59**
Godre'r Coed SA10: C'dxtn . . .4B **64**
Godre'r Fro SA8: Phyd f . . . . . .3C **36**
GODRE'R-GRAIG . . . . . . . . . . .6A **32**
Goetre Bellaf Rd. SA2: Dunv . .3B **82**
Goetre Fach Rd. SA2: Kill . . . . .4D **82**
Goetre Fawr Rd.
    SA2: Dunv, Kill . . . . . . . . .3C **82**
Golden Av. SA12: Sand . . . . . .2A **96**
Golden Cl. SA3: W Cro . . . . . . .5E **95**
Golden Lion St. SA1: Swan . . .1H **5**
Goldsmith Cl. CF31: Bri . . . . .6B **120**
Golf Rd. SA12: Sand . . . . . . . .3C **96**
Golwg Dderi SA10: Nea . . . . . .5H **63**
Golwg Hafren SA2: Sket . . . . .6H **83**
Golwg y Bryn SA3: T Mum . . . .1E **101**
Golwg y Bryn SA4: Sev S . . . . .4H **29**
    SA10: Skew . . . . . . . . . . .6D **62**
Golwg y Coed SA7: Birch . . . .3F **61**
Golwg y Cwm SA18: C'gors . . .5C **24**
Golwg y Dre SA11: Nea . . . . . .3C **78**
Golwg y Fro CF31: Brack . . . .1G **127**
Golwg-y-Gamlas SA10: Nea . .6B **64**
Golwg y Garn SA4: Penl . . . . . .4E **57**
Golwg y Graig SA10: Cry . . . . .6H **33**
Golwg y Llanw SA4: P'dul . . . .1A **46**
Golwg y Llanw SA4: P'dul . . . .1B **46**
Golwg y Lon SA6: Cly . . . . . . . .3E **49**
Golwg y Mor SA4: Penc . . . . . .4A **68**
    SA12: Sand . . . . . . . . . . . .4B **96**
Golwg y Mynydd SA6: Craig-p . .3C **48**
    SA9: Godr . . . . . . . . . . . . .5C **32**
    SA18: Amm . . . . . . . . . . . .2B **22**
Golwg-y-Mynydd SA10: Nea . .4H **63**
Golwg-yr-Afon SA4: Ffor . . . . .5D **34**
Golwg-yr-Afon SA10: A'dul . . .2F **65**
    SA14: L'nch . . . . . . . . . . . .5C **44**
Golwg yr Eglwys SA4: P'dul . . .1C **46**
Golwg yr Ynys SA18: Lwr B . . .4H **15**
Golwg y Twr SA4: P'dul . . . . . .1C **46**
Golwg-y-Tywyn SA16: Burr P . .2D **38**

Golwg y Waun SA7: Birch . . . . .4F **61**
Golwyg Derwen
    CF31: Brack . . . . . . . . . .5F **121**
Golygfor SA15: Llane . . . . . . . .2C **52**
Gomer Gdns. SA1: Town . . . . .1D **84**
Gomer Rd. SA1: Town . . . . . . . .1B **84**
Gonhill SA3: W Cro . . . . . . . . .4D **94**
Goole Rd. SA5: Rav . . . . . . . . .3A **72**
Goose Island
    SA1: Swan . . . . . . .6F **5** (5G **85**)
Goppa Rd. SA4: P'dul . . . . . . . .1D **46**
Gordon Cres. SA12: Sand . . . . .2B **96**
Gordon Rd. CF36: P'cwl . . . . .5C **124**
    SA12: Sand . . . . . . . . . . . .2B **96**
    SA14: Dafen . . . . . . . . . . .6D **42**
    (not continuous)
Gordon Rowley Way
    SA6: Pantl . . . . . . . . . . . .2H **59**
Gordon Thomas Cl.
    SA1: Swan . . . . . . . . . . . .6F **73**
Gore Ter. SA1: Swan . . . .2D **4** (3F **85**)
Goring Rd. SA15: Llane . . . . . .6A **42**
Gorof Rd. SA9: Cwm I . . . . . . .6G **27**
Goronwy Rd. SA2: C'ett . . . . . .1B **84**
Gorsafle SA9: Ystra . . . . . . . . .6B **28**
Gors Av. SA1: M'hill, Town . . . .1B **84**
Gors Ct. SA31: Carm . . . . . . . .3D **6**
Gorsddu Rd. SA14: Pen g . . . . .6F **9**
Gorsddu Ter. SA14: Pen g . . . . .5F **9**
Gorsedd SA15: Llane . . . . . . . .2C **52**
GORSEINON . . . . . . . . . . . . . .3B **56**
Gorseinon Bus. Pk. SA4: Gor . .5B **56**
Gorseinon Bus Station . . . . . .4A **56**
GORSEINON HOSPITAL . . . . . .3H **55**
Gorseinon Rd. SA4: Gor, Penl . .4C **56**
Gorseinon Shop. Pk.
    SA4: Gor . . . . . . . . . . . . . .4B **56**
Gorse La. SA1: Swan . . . . . . . .5D **84**
Gorse Rd. CF35: P'coed . . . . .6G **123**
Gors-Fach SA14: Llane . . . . . .6F **43**
Gors Gdns. SA1: Town . . . . . . .1C **84**
Gors Goch Rd. SA18: Lwr B . . .5H **15**
Gors La. SA18: C'gors . . . . . . .3C **24**
Gorslas SA14: Llane . . . . . . . . .4D **8**
Gorslas CF33: N Cor . . . . . . .6C **112**
    (not continuous)
Gorslas Ind. Est. SA14: Llane . .3D **8**
Gorslwyn Ter. SA18: C'gors . . .4C **24**
Gors Rd. SA4: Penc . . . . . . . . .4F **57**
    (not continuous)
    SA16: Burr P . . . . . . . . . . .3D **38**
Gorsto Rd. SA9: P fawr . . . . . .4A **26**
    SA18: Gwaun . . . . . . . . . .1D **24**
Gorwydd Rd. SA4: Gow . . . . . .3B **70**
Goshen Pk. SA10: Nea A . . . . .6E **63**
Gough Av. SA9: Ystra . . . . . . . .1G **33**
Gough Rd. SA9: Ystra . . . . . . .2D **32**
    (shown as Heol Gough)
Gower Coast National Nature Reserve
    . . . . . . . . . . . . . . . . . . . . .3D **108**
Gower Cres. SA12: Bag . . . . . .3H **89**
Gower Farm Touring & Camping Pk.
    SA3: Lland . . . . . . . . . . . .1H **109**
Gower Golf Course . . . . . . . . .5F **69**
Gower Heritage Cen. . . . . . . .1H **111**
Gower Holiday Village
    SA3: Scur . . . . . . . . . . . . .3H **109**
Gower Pl. SA3: T Mum . . . . . .1E **101**
Gower Ri. SA4: Gow . . . . . . . . .4B **70**
Gower Rd. SA2: Kill, Up K . . . .4H **81**
    SA3: Sket . . . . . . . . . . . . .3F **83**
Gowers Bldgs. SA11: Britt F . . .1G **89**
Gower Sq. SA11: Cry B . . . . . .4H **87**
Gower St. SA11: Britt F . . . . . .5H **77**
    SA13: P Tal . . . . . . . . . . . .5H **97**
Gower Ter. SA14: Penc . . . . . .4A **68**
GOWERTON . . . . . . . . . . . . . . .3A **70**
Gowerton By-Pass SA4: Gow . .2H **69**
Gowerton Cvn. Pk. SA4: Gow . .2H **69**
Gowerton Golf Range . . . . . . .1A **70**
Gowerton Rd. SA4: Penc . . . . .4A **68**
    SA4: The X . . . . . . . . . . . . .1F **81**
Gowerton Station (Rail) . . . . .3B **70**
    SA15: Llane . . . . . . . . . . . .5B **42**
Gowerton Vw. SA4: Gow . . . . . .2H **69**
Goya Pl. SA12: Sand . . . . . . . .4C **96**
Grafog St. SA1: Por T . . . . . . .3C **86**
Graham Av. CF31: Pen F . . . . .1C **120**
Graham Berry Ct. SA5: P'lan . .3D **72**
Graham St. SA1: Swan . . . . . . .6G **73**
Graham Ter. SA10: Skew . . . . .6D **62**
GRAIG . . . . . . . . . . . . . . . . . . .1E **39**
Graig, The CF31: Bri . . . . . . . .1D **126**
    CF32: Cef C . . . . . . . . . . .1D **118**

Graig Av. SA10: Nea A . . . . . . .5G **63**
    SA13: Marg . . . . . . . . . . . .2F **103**
    SA15: Llane . . . . . . . . . . . .2B **52**
Graig Cotts. SA8: T'nos . . . . . .1B **50**
Graig Ct. SA7: Glais . . . . . . . . .6A **50**
Graig Gellinudd SA8: Gell . . . .5G **37**
Graig Llanguicke SA8: Ynys . . .4E **37**
Graiglwyd Rd. SA2: C'ett . . . . .1A **84**
Graiglwyd Sq. SA2: C'ett . . . . .2C **84**
Graig Newydd SA9: Godr . . . . .5C **32**
Graigola Rd. SA7: Glais . . . . . .6H **49**
Graig Parc SA10: Nea A . . . . . .6H **49**
Graig Pl. SA1: Swan . . . .1D **4** (2F **85**)
Graig Rd. SA6: Morr . . . . . . . . .1H **73**
    SA7: Glais . . . . . . . . . . . . .6H **49**
    SA8: All, Gell . . . . . . . . . . .6E **37**
    SA8: P'dwe, T'nos . . . . . . .6B **36**
    SA9: Godr . . . . . . . .1H **37**, 6A **32**
    (not continuous)
    SA10: Skew . . . . . . . . . . . .1C **76**
    SA11: Britt F . . . . . . . . . . . .1H **89**
    SA18: Gwaun . . . . . . . . . . .6F **15**
Graig St. SA1: Swan . . . .1E **5** (2G **85**)
Graig Ter. SA1: Swan . . . .1D **4** (2F **85**)
    SA5: Man . . . . . . . . . . . . . .5E **73**
    SA6: Morr . . . . . . . . . . . . . .6A **60**
    SA7: Glais . . . . . . . . . . . . .6H **49**
    SA10: Skew . . . . . . . . . . . .1C **76**
GRAIG TREWYDDFA . . . . . . . .1A **74**
Graig Twrch SA9: Cwm I . . . . .5D **26**
Graigwen SA14: Llwy . . . . . . .2H **53**
Graig y Bwldan SA2: Dunv . . .2D **82**
Graig y Coed SA4: Penc . . . . .4F **67**
Graig y Darren SA9: Godr . . . .5D **32**
Graig-y-Dderi SA7: Glais . . . . .6H **49**
Graig y Fforest SA9: Godr . . . .5C **32**
Graig y Merched SA9: Ysta . . .3D **32**
Graig y Parc SA7: Glais . . . . . .6H **49**
Grampian Way SA5: Ffor F . . . .5B **72**
Granby Cl. SA15: Llane . . . . . .4B **52**
    (shown as Clos Granby)
Grandison St. SA1: Swan . . . . .1G **85**
    SA11: Britt F . . . . . . . . . . . .6H **77**
Grand Pavilion Theatre . . . . .5C **124**
Grand Theatre . . . . . .4C **4** (4F **85**)
Grange Cres. CF35: Coyc . . . .1C **128**
    SA3: W Cro . . . . . . . . . . . .5F **95**
Grange La. SA3: W Cro . . . . . . .4F **95**
Grange Rd. SA3: W Cro . . . . . .5F **95**
Grange St. SA13: P Tal . . . . . . .4H **97**
Granogwen Rd. SA1: M'hill . . .1E **85**
Grant St. SA15: Llane . . . . . . . .3B **52**
Granville Rd.
    SA1: St T . . . . . . . . . .1H **5** (2H **85**)
Granville Ter. SA14: Llane . . . .6E **43**
Grassholm Gdns.
    SA5: Blae M . . . . . . . . . . .1B **72**
Grassholm Way CF36: Not . . .2A **124**
Grave La. SA3: Oxw . . . . . . . . .3A **110**
Great Ho. Ct. SA4: Hort . . . . . .4A **110**
Gt. Western Av. CF31: Bri . . . .4E **121**
Gt. Western Cres.
    SA15: Llane . . . . . . . . . . . .2A **52**
Gt. Western Rd. SA6: Morr . . . .3A **60**
    SA12: C'avon . . . . . . . . . . .4H **91**
    SA15: Llane . . . . . . . . . . . .3A **52**
Green, The CF32: Sarn . . . . . .6D **114**
    CF35: P'coed . . . . . . . . . .3H **123**
    SA8: T'nos . . . . . . . . . . . . .2B **50**
    SA11: Nea . . . . . . . . . . . . .1A **78**
    SA31: Carm . . . . . . . . . . . . .3E **7**
Greenacre Dr. CF35: P'coed . .3F **123**
Greenacres CF33: Sth C . . . . .4C **116**
    SA4: Penc . . . . . . . . . . . . .4G **67**
    SA13: Marg . . . . . . . . . . . .5H **103**
Green Av., The CF36: P'cwl . . .5B **124**
Green Bank Rd. SA3: W Cro . . .5E **95**
Green Circ. CF33: Pyle . . . . . .6D **112**
Green Cl. SA3: May . . . . . . . . .3F **95**
Green Ct. CF31: Bri . . . . . . . . .2F **127**
Green Dragon La.
    SA1: Swan . . . . . . .4F **5** (3G **85**)
Greenfield Av. SA13: Marg . . . .2F **103**
Greenfield Cl. SA7: L'smlt . . . .1G **75**
Greenfield Cres. SA7: L'smlt . .1F **75**
Greenfield Pl. SA4: Lou . . . . . .5G **55**
Greenfield Rd. SA18: Garn . . . .4D **14**
    (shown as Heol Maesglas)
Greenfields Av. CF31: Bri . . . .1B **126**
Greenfield Ter. CF33: N Cor . . .1C **116**
    SA1: L'ore . . . . . . . . . . . . .4G **73**
    SA3: Sket . . . . . . . . . . . . .3H **83**
    SA7: L'smlt . . . . . . . . . . . . .6E **61**
Green Gables CF36: Not . . . .1C **124**
Green Gables SA3: Cilf . . . . . .1F **65**

Green Hedges Cvn. Pk.
SA10: B'och . . . . . . . . . . . .5G 51
Greenhill SA16: Graig . . . . . . . .1E 39
Greenhill Cl. SA31: Carm . . . . . .2E 7
Greenhill St. SA1: Swan . . . . . .1G 85
Green Mdw. CF32: Cef C . . . . . .1C 118
Grn. Meadow Ct. SA12: A'von . . .3E 97
Greenmeadow Farm Cvn. Site
  SA3: Oxw . . . . . . . . . . . . .5C 110
Greenmeadows CF31: Bri . . . . . .6D 126
Green Pk. Ind. Est.
  SA12: P Tal . . . . . . . . . . . .4F 97
Green Pk. St. SA12: A'von . . . . .4F 97
Greenslade SA1: T Mum . . . . . .1D 100
*Greenspace Gallery* . . . . . . . . .3E 7
(off King St.)
Green St. CF31: Bri . . . . . . . .6E 121
  SA6: Morr . . . . . . . . . . .6B 60
  SA11: Nea . . . . . . . . . . .6B 64
  SA12: A'von . . . . . . . . . .3E 97
Greenway, The SA10: L'dcy . . . .5B 76
Greenway Rd. SA11: Nea . . . . . .1B 78
Greenways CF36: P'cwl . . . . . .3E 125
  SA5: Wauna . . . . . . . . . .5C 70
Greenways Leisure Pk.
  SA3: Oxw . . . . . . . . . . . .4C 110
Greenway St. SA15: Llane . . . . .3H 41
Greenwood Cl. CF31: Bri . . . . . .4E 121
  SA2: Sket . . . . . . . . . . .4H 83
Greenwood Dr. SA11: Cim . . . . .3F 79
Greenwood Pl. SA5: Por . . . . . .2A 72
Greenwood Rd. SA11: Nea . . . . .4A 78
  SA12: Bag . . . . . . . . . . .3A 90
Gregory Cl. CF35: P'coed . . . . .3E 123
Greig Cl. SA12: Sand . . . . . . .1A 96
Greig Ct. SA12: Sand . . . . . . .1A 96
Grenfell Av. SA4: Gor . . . . . . .3H 55
Grenfell Pk. Rd.
  SA1: St T . . . . . . . . .1H 5 (2H 85)
Grenfell Town SA1: Bon . . . . . .5A 74
Grenig Rd. SA18: Glan . . . . . .5H 13
(shown as Heol Grenig)
Greyfriars CF31: Bri . . . . . . . .6E 121
  SA31: Carm . . . . . . . . . . .4E 7
Greyfriars Ct. CF36: Newt . . . .3F 125
Greys Ter. SA7: Birch . . . . . . .5A 62
Grey St. SA1: L'ore . . . . . . . .5G 73
Griffin Pk. Ct. CF36: P'cwl . . . .4D 124
Griffith John St. SA1: Swan . . . .1G 85
Griffith's Bldgs. SA11: Nea . . . .3H 77
GROES . . . . . . . . . . . . . .4G 103
Groesffordd SA18: Bry . . . . . . .3A 16
Groesffordd Fach SA31: Carm . . .2F 7
Groes-Wen La. SA13: Marg . . . .1E 103
Groeswen Pk. SA13: Marg . . . . .1E 103
Gronow Cl. SA10: Nea A . . . . . .6H 63
Gron Rd. SA18: Gwaun . . . . . . .2C 24
Grosvenor Rd. SA2: Sket . . . . . .3A 84
Grove, The SA2: Upl . . . . . . . .4C 84
  SA3: T Mum . . . . . . . . . .2E 101
  SA8: T'nos . . . . . . . . . . .2B 50
  SA31: Carm . . . . . . . . . . .3C 6
Grove Farm Rd. SA4: Grov . . . . .5B 46
Grove Gdns. CF31: Bri . . . . . .2E 127
*Grove Golf Course, The* . . . . . . .5C 116
Grove Hill Pk. SA14: Gors . . . . .5F 9
(shown as Parc Bryngelli)
Grove Ho. SA1: Swan . . . . . . . .2D 4
Grove La. SA10: Skew . . . . . . .1D 76
  SA11: Nea . . . . . . . . . . .3H 77
Grove Pl. SA1: Swan . . .2D 4 (3F 85)
  SA13: P Tal . . . . . . . . . .4G 97
Grove Rd. CF31: Bri . . . . . . . .2D 126
  SA6: Cly . . . . . . . . . . . .3E 49
  SA8: P'dwe . . . . . . . . . . .5E 37
Groves Av. SA3: Lan . . . . . . .2D 100
GROVESEND . . . . . . . . . . . .6B 46
Groves Rd. SA11: Nea . . . . . . .3B 78
Grove St. SA4: Gor . . . . . . . .3A 56
Grove Ter. SA6: Morr . . . . . . .4B 60
Guildhall Rd. Nth. SA1: Swan . . .5D 84
Guildhall Rd. Sth.
  SA1: Swan . . . . . .6A 4 (5D 84)
Guildhall Sq. SA31: Carm . . . . .3E 7
(off Hall St.)
Gulliver's Cl. SA3: W Cro . . . . .4G 95
GURNOS . . . . . . . . . . . . . .6G 27
Gurnos Ind. Est. SA9: Cwm I . . .6F 27
Gurnos Rd. SA4: Gow . . . . . . .3A 70
  SA9: Ysta . . . . . . . . . . .1F 33
  SA9: Ystra . . . . . . . . . . .1F 33
Gwalia CF31: Bri . . . . . . . . .2E 121
  SA4: Gor . . . . . . . . . . . .4C 56
Gwalia Cl. SA1: Swan . .6A 4 (5E 85)
  SA6: Cly . . . . . . . . . . . .5E 49

Gwalia Cres. SA4: Gor . . . . . .4C 56
Gwalia Rd. CF35: P'coed . . . .3H 123
Gwalia Ter. SA4: Gor . . . . . . .4C 56
Gwar-y-Caeau SA13: P Tal . . . .4H 97
Gwaun Afan SA12: C'avon . . . .4H 91
Gwaun Henllan SA18: Amm . . . .5H 11
GWAUN-CAE-GURWEN . . . . . . .2C 24
Gwaun Coed CF31: Brack . . . . .1F 127
Gwaun Henllan SA18: Amm . . . .5H 11
GWAUN-LEISION . . . . . . . . . .6G 15
Gwelfor CF32: Cef C . . . . . . .1B 118
  SA2: Dunv . . . . . . . . . . .2C 82
  SA14: Llwy . . . . . . . . . . .2H 53
  SA16: Burr P . . . . . . . . . .3D 38
Gwendoline St. SA12: A'von . . . .3F 97
Gwendraeth Pl. SA1: Bon . . . . .6C 74
Gwenlais Rd.
  SA4: P'dul, P'liw . . . . . . . .4C 46
Gwent Gdns. SA1: Town . . . . . .1C 84
Gwent Gro. SA2: Sket . . . . . . .4F 83
Gwent Ho. SA12: Sand . . . . . .4C 96
(off Moorland Rd.)
Gwent Rd. SA1: Town . . . . . . .1C 84
Gwernant SA9: Cwml . . . . . . .6H 17
Gwern Einon Rd. SA2: Sket . . . .1G 95
Gwern Fadog Rd. SA6: Yfgn . . . .3B 60
Gwernllwynchwyth Rd.
  SA7: Birch . . . . . . . . . . .4G 61
  SA7: L'smlt . . . . . . . . . . .6G 61
Gwernos SA6: Morr . . . . . . . .4B 60
Gwili Av. SA4: C'ili . . . . . . . .3F 19
Gwili Ter. SA1: M'hill . . . . . . .1D 84
Gwilym Rd. SA9: Cwml . . . . . .5G 17
(shown as Heol Gwilym)
Gwlad-y-Gan SA6: Morr . . . . . .5G 59
Gwr Cotts. SA8: T'nos . . . . . . .1B 50
Gwrhyd Rd. SA8: Phyd f . . . . . .2B 36
  SA9: P fawr . . . . . . . . . . .4A 26
Gwscwm Pk. SA16: Burr P . . . .2D 38
Gwscwm Rd.
  SA16: Burr P, Pem . . . . . . .2A 38
Gwydr Cres. SA2: Upl . . . . . . .4C 84
Gwydr La. SA2: Upl . . . . . . . .4C 84
Gwydr M. SA2: Upl . . . . . . . .4C 84
Gwydr Pl. SA4: Lou . . . . . . . .5E 55
Gwydr Sq. SA2: Upl . . . . . . . .4C 84
Gwylfa SA14: Llwy . . . . . . . .6G 43
Gwylfa Rd. SA1: Town . . . . . . .1C 84
Gwylym St. SA5: Cwmdu . . . . . .6D 72
Gwyn Ct. SA12: A'von . . . . . . .3E 97
(off Gwyn Ter.)
Gwyndy Rd. SA1: Bon . . . . . . .6B 74
Gwynedd Av. SA1: Town . . . . . .1A 84
  SA2: C'ett . . . . . . . . . . .1A 84
Gwynedd Gdns. SA1: Town . . . .1D 84
Gwynfe Rd. SA4: Lou . . . . . . .4F 55
Gwynfi St. SA5: Tre b . . . . . . .3F 73
Gwynfor Rd. SA2: C'ett . . . . . .1B 84
Gwynfryn SA14: Gors . . . . . . .2F 9
  SA18: Amm . . . . . . . . . . .6G 11
Gwynfryn Rd. SA4: P'dul . . . . .1B 46
Gwynne Ter. SA1: St T . . . . . .2B 86
Gwyns Drift SA8: All . . . . . . . .1D 50
Gwyn's Pl. SA8: All . . . . . . . .1E 51
Gwyn St. SA8: All . . . . . . . . .1D 50
Gwyn Ter. SA10: Cry . . . . . . . .6H 33
Gwyrddgoed SA8: P'dwe . . . . . .4F 36
Gwysfa Rd. SA4: Ystwe . . . . . .1C 60
Gwysfryn SA9: Cwm U . . . . . . .2G 17
Gynol Rd. SA9: Cwml . . . . . . .5G 17
Gyrnosfa SA9: Cwm I . . . . . . .6G 27

# H

Hadland Ter. SA3: W Cro . . . . . .6F 95
Hael La. SA3: S'gate . . . . . . . .3B 98
Hafan SA15: Llane . . . . . . . . .2A 52
Hafan Brynheulog SA8: P'dwe . .5C 36
Hafan Cl. SA9: Ystra . . . . . . . .1G 33
Hafan Deg CF35: P'coed . . . . .3G 123
  SA10: Sev S . . . . . . . . . . .5F 29
Hafan Deg Flats
  CF32: A'knfig . . . . . . . . . .5B 114
Hafan Glyd SA6: Cly . . . . . . . .4F 49
Hafan Plentyn SA1: Swan . . . . .6A 4
Hafan Tywi SA31: Carm . . . . . .3F 7
Hafan-y-Bryn CF31: Bri . . . . .1B 126
Hafan-y-Morfa SA15: Llane . . . .4C 42
(off Rhes Gwaith Tyn)
Hafnant SA1: Wins . . . . . . . . .3E 75
HAFOD . . . . . . . . . . . . . . .6H 73

Hafod Bryan SA14: Llwy . . . . . .2F 53
Hafod Cwnin SA31: Carm . . . . . .1G 7
Hafod Decaf CF33: Pyle . . . . .5E 113
Hafod Elfed SA31: Carm . . . . . .2D 6
Hafod La CF35: P'coed . . . . . .4G 123
Hafod Pk. SA1: Swan . . . . . . .6G 73
Hafod Rd. SA18: Tyc . . . . . . . .3D 20
Hafod St. SA1: Swan . . . . . . .1G 85
  SA13: P Tal . . . . . . . . . . .4H 97
Hafod Wen CF31: Bri . . . . . . .2C 126
(off Careg Llwyd)
Hafod-y-Gan SA4: Penc . . . . . .4G 67
Haig Pl. SA5: Gen . . . . . . . . .4C 72
Hallbank SA3: T Mum . . . . . . .2F 101
Hallbank Ter. SA3: T Mum . . . .2F 101
Hall Cl. CF33: N Cor . . . . . . .1D 116
Hall Dr. CF33: N Cor . . . . . . .1C 116
*Halliwell Theatre* . . . . . . . . . .3B 6
Hall La. SA4: Penc . . . . . . . . .4G 67
Hall St. SA1: Swan . . . . . . . .1G 85
  SA15: Llane . . . . . . . . . .6A 42
  SA18: Amm . . . . . . . . . . .1A 22
  SA18: Bry . . . . . . . . . . .4A 16
  SA31: Carm . . . . . . . . . . .3E 7
Hamilton St. SA1: L'ore . . . . . .5G 73
Handel Av. SA12: Sand . . . . . . .1A 96
Hannants, The SA10: Nea A . . . .6H 63
Hanover Cl. SA3: T Mum . . . . . .6F 95
Hanover Ct. CF31: Bri . . . . . . .6D 120
  SA2: Sket . . . . . . . . . . .3A 84
Hanover La.
  SA1: Swan . . . . . . .3A 4 (3D 84)
Hanover Parklands SA2: Sket . . .4F 83
HANOVER SQUARE . . . . . . . . .5B 74
Hanover St.
  SA1: Swan . . . . . . .3A 4 (3E 85)
Harbour, The SA16: Burr P . . . .4D 38
Harbour Quay SA1: Swan . . . . .3A 86
Harbourside Bus. Pk.
  SA13: P Tal . . . . . . . . . . .4F 97
Harbourside Rd. SA12: P Tal . . .4F 97
Harbour Vw. SA1: St T . . . . . . .3B 86
Harbour Way SA13: P Tal . . . . .4F 97
Harbour Winds Ct.
  SA3: T Mum . . . . . . . . . .2E 101
Harcourt St.
  SA1: Swan . . . . . . .2B 4 (3E 85)
HARDDFAN . . . . . . . . . . . . .1A 54
Harding Cl. SA4: Bryn . . . . . . .6A 44
Harding Cl. SA4: Lou . . . . . . .6H 55
Hardingsdown La.
  SA3: Llang . . . . . . . . . . .5F 105
Harebell Cl. SA6: Yfgn . . . . . . .2C 60
Hareslade Av. SA3: Bishop . . . .2G 99
Harewood Rd. SA12: Bag . . . . .3H 89
Harford Cl. SA2: Sket . . . . . . .5H 83
Harlech Cl. SA2: Sket . . . . . . .3G 83
Harlech Cres. SA2: Sket . . . . . .3G 83
Harlech St. SA18: Tair . . . . . . .2F 25
Harlequin Cl. SA11: Nea . . . . . .1B 78
Harlequin Sq. SA12: A'von . . . . .3E 97
Harle St. SA11: Nea . . . . . . . .6C 64
Harleyford Rd. SA4: Hendy . . . .6D 34
Harlington Rd. SA5: Cwmdu . . .5D 72
Harold St. SA18: Amm . . . . . . .6G 11
(shown as Stryd Harold)
Harries Av. SA15: Llane . . . . . .3H 41
Harries La. SA15: Llane . . . . . .3H 41
Harries St. SA1: Swan . . .1B 4 (2E 85)
Harrington Pl. SA1: Swan . . . . .1G 85
Harrington St. SA1: Swan . . . . .1G 85
Harris M. SA4: P'dul . . . . . . . .6F 35
Harris Rd. SA6: Cwml . . . . . . .6G 18
Harris St. SA6: Morr . . . . . . . .6A 60
Harry St. SA6: Morr . . . . . . . .5H 59
Hartfield Cl. SA2: Sket . . . . . . .3F 83
Harvey Cres. SA12: A'von . . . . .4D 96
(not continuous)
Hatfield Ct. SA5: Rav . . . . . . . .3B 72
Hatherleigh Dr. SA3: Newt . . . . .6D 94
Haul Fryn CF32: B'myn . . . . . .3D 114
  SA7: Birch . . . . . . . . . . .4H 61
Haulfryn CF33: Ken H . . . . . . .4H 113
  SA8: P'dwe . . . . . . . . . . .5D 36
  SA10: Nea . . . . . . . . . . .5H 63
  SA14: Bryn . . . . . . . . . . .6A 44
  SA31: Carm . . . . . . . . . . .5F 7
Haulwen Rd. SA2: C'ett . . . . . .1A 84
Havard Jones Cl.
  SA11: Brit F . . . . . . . . . . .4H 77
Havard Rd. SA14: Dafen . . . . . .6D 42
Havelock St. SA15: Llane . . . . .4B 52
Havergal Cl. SA3: Casw . . . . .2B 100
Hawkhurst Ct. CF36: Not . . . . .2B 124

Hawkstone Cl. SA3: W Cro . . . .5D 94
Hawthorn Av. SA4: Gor . . . . . . .4H 55
  SA11: Cim . . . . . . . . . . .2C 78
  SA12: Bag . . . . . . . . . . .3A 90
Hawthorn Cl. SA2: C'avon . . . . .6H 91
Hawthorn Dr. CF33: Sth C . . . .4C 116
  CF35: Coyc . . . . . . . . . .2C 128
Hawthorne Av. SA2: Upl . . . . . .3B 84
Hawthorn Pl. CF36: Newt . . . . .3G 125
Hawthorns, The SA7: Glais . . . .6A 50
Hawthorn Vs. SA9: Ystra . . . . . .5A 28
Hawthorn Way CF31: Brack . . .1A 128
Hayes Ter. CF31: Bri . . . . . . .5D 120
Haynes Ct. SA1: Swan . . .1F 5 (2G 85)
Haywain Ct. CF31: Bri . . . . . . .2F 127
Hazel Cl. CF36: Newt . . . . . . .3G 125
Hazel Ct. SA2: Sket . . . . . . . .4G 83
Hazeldene Av. CF31: Brack . . .1H 127
Hazel Mead CF32: B'myn . . . . .3D 114
Hazelmere Rd. SA2: Sket . . . . .3A 84
Hazel Rd. SA2: Upl . . . . . . . .3B 84
Hazeltree Copse SA4: Crof . . . .6E 67
Hazel Tree Cl. SA10: B'och . . . .4H 63
(shown as Cwrt y Gollen)
Hazel Tree Way CF31: Brack . . .6A 122
Hazelwell Rd. CF36: Not . . . . . .3C 124
Hazelwood Rd. SA11: Nea . . . . .6C 64
Hazelwood Row
  SA12: C'avon . . . . . . . . . .5H 91
Hazelwood Ter. SA12: C'avon . .5H 91
Headland Cl. SA3: Bishop . . . . .1G 99
Headland Rd.
  SA1: St T . . . . . . . . .1H 5 (2A 86)
  SA3: Bishop . . . . . . . . . . .1G 99
Heaseland Pl. SA2: Kill . . . . . . .3C 82
Heath Cl. SA3: W Cro . . . . . . .6E 95
Heath Ct. SA3: W Cro . . . . . . .6E 95
Heather Cl. CF32: Sarn . . . . . .6D 114
Heather Cl. CF36: P'cwl . . . . .4C 124
Heather Cres. SA2: Sket . . . . . .4G 83
Heather Rise SA10: Jer M . . . .1B 88
(shown as Allt y Grug)
Heatherslade Cl. SA3: Lan . . . .2F 101
  SA3: S'gate . . . . . . . . . . .3A 98
Heatherslade Rd. SA3: S'gate . .2A 98
Heathfield SA1: Swan . . . .2B 4 (3E 85)
  SA4: Gor . . . . . . . . . . . .5H 55
Heathfield Ct. SA1: Swan . . . . . .2C 4
Heathfield Ind. Pk. SA14: C'ili . .3F 19
Heathfield Rd. SA8: P'dwe . . . . .4E 37
Heathland Way SA10: L'dcy . . . .4B 76
Heathwood Rd. SA3: W Cro . . . .4F 95
Hebron Cl. SA6: Cly . . . . . . . .5E 49
  SA6: Cly . . . . . . . . . . . .6E 49
Hedd Aberth SA10: Sev S . . . . .3H 29
Hedgemoor CF31: Brack . . . . .1A 128
Hedgerows, The
  SA14: Dafen . . . . . . . . . . .4E 43
Hedley Ter. SA15: Llane . . . . . .6A 42
Heilbron Way SA12: P Tal . . . . .3F 97
  SA13: P Tal . . . . . . . . . . .4F 97
Helen's Rd. SA11: Nea . . . . . . .3H 77
Helen Fach CF33: Ken H . . . . .6E 113
Helios Dr. SA12: Bag . . . . . . .5H 89
Helwick Cl. SA3: T Mum . . . . .1E 101
HENDRE . . . . . . . . . . . . . .3C 122
Hendre SA2: Dunv . . . . . . . . .2C 82
Hendre Cl. SA14: L'nch . . . . . . .5B 44
Hendre Cres. SA14: L'nch . . . . .5C 44
Hendrefoelan Student Village
  SA2: Sket . . . . . . . . . . . .2E 83
Hendrefoilan Av. SA2: Sket . . . .2F 83
Hendrefoilan Cl. SA2: Sket . . . .3F 83
Hendrefoilan Dr. SA2: Sket . . . .3F 83
Hendre-Foilan Rd.
  SA2: Kill, Sket . . . . . . . . . .2D 82
Hendre Gdns. CF35: P'coed . . .3F 123
Hendre-Isaf SA14: Llwy . . . . . .2G 53
Hendre Ladus SA9: Ystra . . . . .4C 28
Hendremawr Cl. SA2: Sket . . . .2G 83
Hendre Owain SA2: Upl . . . . . .2H 83
Hendre Pk. SA14: L'nch . . . . . .5B 44
Hendre Rd. CF35: Coity, Hen, P'coed
  . . . . . . . . . . . . . . . . . .3B 122
  SA14: L'nch . . . . . . . . . . .5B 44
  SA18: Cap H, Tyc . . . . . . .3A 20
Hendre Va. CF35: P'coed . . . . .3E 123
HENDY . . . . . . . . . . . . . . .6D 34
Hendy Cl. SA2: Sket . . . . . . . .6G 83
Hendy Ind. Est. SA4: Hendy . . .6D 34
Hendy Rd. SA4: Penc . . . . . . .4A 68
Heneage Dr. SA3: W Cro . . . . .3G 95
Henfaes Rd. SA11: Tonna . . . . .4E 65
Henfaes Ter. SA11: Tonna . . . . .4F 65
Hen Felin SA8: Gell . . . . . . . .5G 37

Henfelin SA18: Garn . . . . . . . . .5E **15**
Hengwrt Community Sports Cen.
. . . . . . . . . . . . . . . . . . . . . . .4G **77**
Hen Heol Llangynnwr
SA31: Carm . . . . . . . . . . . . . .4E **7**
(not continuous)
Hen Llys SA1: Swan . . . . . . . . . .4A **5**
Henneuadd Rd. SA9: Aber . . . .1F **29**
Hennoyadd Rd. SA9: Aber . . . .1F **29**
Hennyswell SA3: Rey . . . . . . . .6H **105**
Hen Parc Av. SA2: Up K . . . . . .5A **82**
Hen Parc La. SA2: Up K . . . . . .5B **82**
Henrietta St.
SA1: Swan . . . . . . . .4B **4** (4E **85**)
Henry St. SA11: Nea . . . . . . . . .2B **78**
Henry Thomas Gallery . . . . . . .3B **6**
Henshaw St. SA12: A'von . . . . .4E **97**
Heol Aaron SA9: Cwm I . . . . . .6G **27**
Heol Aberavon SA12: Bag . . . . .1C **96**
(shown as Aberavon Rd.)
Heol Abram SA9: Cwm I . . . . . .6G **27**
Heol Adare CF32: Ton . . . . . . .4C **114**
Heol Alltygrug SA9: Ysta . . . . . .2E **33**
Heol Amman SA18: Glan . . . . . .3H **13**
Heol Arfryn SA31: Carm . . . . . . .2A **6**
Heol Argoed SA18: Amm . . . . . .4A **22**
Heol Aur SA14: Dafen . . . . . . . .3E **43**
Heol Awstin SA5: Rav . . . . . . . .3B **72**
Heol Banc y Felin SA4: Gor . . .6B **56**
Heol Barcud SA7: Birch . . . . . .6A **62**
Heol Beca SA31: Carm . . . . . . . .4C **6**
Heol Bedwas SA7: Birch . . . . . .5H **61**
Heol Beili Glas SA14: F'oel . . . .2D **42**
Heol Blaengwastod SA31: Carm . .5G **7**
Heol Bolahaul SA31: Cwmf . . . . .6F **7**
Heol Briallu SA6: Morr . . . . . . .4A **60**
Heol Brithdir SA7: Birch . . . . . .6A **62**
Heol Broch SA7: Birch . . . . . . .6A **62**
Heol Broom
CF33: Maw, Sth C . . . . .1A **116**
Heol Brown SA18: Tyc . . . . . . .4D **20**
Heol Brynbrain SA9: Cwml . . . .5G **17**
Heol Bryn Cawr SA14: Pen g . . .5H **9**
Heol Bryncelyn SA14: Dafen . . .4F **43**
Heol Bryncethin
CF32: B'myn . . . . . . . . .4D **114**
Heol Bryncwils CF32: Sarn . . .6D **114**
Heol Bryncwtyn
CF35: P'coed . . . . . . . . .5G **123**
Heol Brynglas CF31: Brack . . .6F **121**
SA4: Gor . . . . . . . . . . . .6H **55**
Heol Bryngwili
SA14: Cross H . . . . . . . . .1A **18**
Heol Bryn-Lloi SA18: Glan . . . .4A **14**
Heol Brynna SA11: Cim . . . . . . .3F **79**
Heol Brython SA2: Dunv . . . . . .2B **82**
Heol Buckley SA15: Llane . . . . .4B **42**
Heol Byeastwood
CF35: Coity . . . . . . . . . . .3A **122**
Heol Cadifor SA5: P'lan . . . . . .2E **73**
Heol Cadnawes
SA6: Cwm'crw . . . . . . . . .2A **60**
Heol Cae Copyn SA4: Lou . . . . .5F **55**
Heol Cae Glas CF32: Sarn . . . .6D **114**
CF32: Ton . . . . . . . . . . . .4C **114**
SA7: L'smlt . . . . . . . . . . . .2G **75**
Heol Cae Globe SA4: Lou . . . . .6G **55**
Heol Cae Gurwen
SA18: Gwaun . . . . . . . . . .2C **24**
Heol Cae'r Bont SA13: Marg . .6H **103**
Heol Cae Bryn SA14: Pen g . . . .5H **9**
SA18: C'bryn . . . . . . . . . .5A **10**
Heol Cae Rhosyn SA7: Birch . . .5H **61**
Heol Caerllion SA6: Cwm'crw . .1C **60**
Heol Cae Tyla CF35: Coyc . . . .1C **128**
Heol Cae Tynewydd SA4: Lou . .5G **55**
Heol Calfin SA5: Rav . . . . . . . .4B **72**
Heol Cambrensis CF33: Pyle . .5D **112**
Heol Camlan SA7: Birch . . . . . .5H **61**
Heol Camlas SA12: C'avon . . . .4H **91**
Heol Canola
CF32: Brync, Sarn . . . . . .5D **114**
Heol Caradog SA13: P Tal . . . .5H **97**
Heol Cara Hir SA10: Cry . . . . . .5H **33**
Heol Ceredig SA11: Tonna . . . .3G **65**
Heol Castell CF32: Cef C . . . . .1B **118**
Heol Castell Coety CF31: Bri . .3E **121**
Heol Catwg SA10: Nea A . . . . .4A **64**
Heol Cefni SA6: Morr . . . . . . . .6H **59**
Heol Cefn Ydfa CF32: Coyt . . .1A **114**
Heol Ceirios SA18: L'bie . . . . . .3G **11**
Heol Celyn SA11: Cim . . . . . . . .2E **79**
Heol Ceri SA5: Wauna . . . . . . .5C **70**

Heol Cleddau SA5: Wauna . . . . .5C **70**
Heol Cledwyn SA7: Birch . . . . . .5H **61**
Heol Coch CF31: Brack . . . . . . .6A **122**
Heol Coed SA6: Ystwe . . . . . . .1D **60**
Heol Coed Leyshon
CF32: Coyt . . . . . . . . . . . .2A **114**
Heol Cowgl SA18: Garn . . . . . .6E **15**
Heol Croes Faen CF36: Not . . . .1C **124**
Heol Croesty CF35: P'coed . . . .5G **123**
Heol Cropin SA14: Dafen . . . . . .4F **43**
Heol Cross Hands SA14: Gors . . . .5D **8**
Heol Crwys SA4: Gor . . . . . . . . .2A **56**
SA12: C'avon . . . . . . . . . .5H **91**
Heol Cwmaman
SA18: Garn, Glan . . . . . . .5G **13**
Heol Cwm Felin SA18: Amm . . .4B **22**
Heol Cwmfferws SA18: Tyc . . . .1C **20**
Heol Cwm Mawr
SA12: C'avon . . . . . . . . . .4G **91**
Heol Cwper SA18: Cap H, Tyc . . .5A **20**
Heol Cwrdy CF32: Sarn . . . . . .5D **114**
Heol Cynan SA4: Gor . . . . . . . .2A **56**
Heol Dal y Coppa SA7: L'smlt . . .2F **75**
Heol Daniel SA4: P'dul . . . . . . .1C **46**
SA9: Cwml . . . . . . . . . . . .6H **17**
SA14: F'oel . . . . . . . . . . . .4C **42**
Heol Dderwen SA15: Llane . . . .2C **52**
Heol Ddu SA18: Amm . . . . . . . .4C **12**
SA18: Tyc . . . . . . . . . . . .5C **20**
Heol Ddwr SA4: P'dul . . . . . . . .3H **35**
Heol Degwm CF33: N Cor . . . .1B **116**
Heol Deri SA9: P fawr . . . . . . . .4A **26**
(shown as Deri Rd.)
Heol Derwen SA11: Cim . . . . . . .3E **79**
SA14: Cross H . . . . . . . . . .6F **9**
Heol Dewi Sant SA4: Penl . . . . .4F **57**
Heol Dinbych SA15: Llane . . . .2C **52**
Heol Dinefwr SA14: Foe . . . . . . .2A **8**
Heol Disgwylfa SA31: Carm . . . .2D **6**
Heol Dolfain SA6: Yfgn . . . . . . .2B **60**
Heol Drewi CF33: Ken . . . . . . .5B **116**
Heol Drindod SA31: John . . . . . .6B **6**
Heol Dulais SA7: Birch . . . . . . .5H **61**
Heol Dwr SA18: Amm . . . . . . . .1E **23**
Heol Dwynwen CF31: Bri . . . . . .2A **126**
Heol Dwyrain CF31: Bri . . . . . .1F **127**
Heol Dyddwr SA11: Tonna . . . .3G **65**
Heol Dyfan SA6: Morr . . . . . . . .3A **60**
Heol Dyfatty SA16: Burr P . . . . . .3F **39**
Heol Dyfed SA4: Gor . . . . . . . .2A **56**
Heol Dyfnallt SA31: Carm . . . . . .4B **6**
Heol Dylan CF33: N Cor . . . . .1C **116**
SA4: Gor . . . . . . . . . . . . .2A **56**
Heol Dynys SA5: Rav . . . . . . . .3B **72**
Heol Dywyll SA6: Cly . . . . . . . .6D **48**
Heol Ebeneser
SA4: L'edi, Sard . . . . . . . . .1D **34**
Heol Eglwys CF31: Pen F . . . . .2B **120**
SA9: Ystra . . . . . . . . . . . .5A **28**
SA10: Sev S . . . . . . . . . . .5E **29**
Heol Eifion SA4: Gor . . . . . . . .4B **56**
Heol Eifion Wyn SA7: L'smlt . . .2F **75**
Heol Eirlys SA6: Morr . . . . . . . .4A **60**
Heol Eithrim SA6: Cly . . . . . . . .4E **49**
Heol Elfed SA4: Gor . . . . . . . . .2A **56**
SA7: L'smlt . . . . . . . . . . . .2F **75**
SA14: Llwy . . . . . . . . . . . .1F **53**
SA16: Burr P . . . . . . . . . . .3D **38**
Heol Elizabeth SA16: Burr P . . .3E **39**
Heol Elli SA15: Llane . . . . . . . .1C **52**
Heol Emrys SA6: P'lan . . . . . . .3C **72**
Heol Esgyn SA10: Nea A . . . . . .5F **63**
Heol Ewenny CF35: P'coed . . . .5G **123**
Heol Fach CF32: Sarn . . . . . . .5E **115**
CF33: N Cor . . . . . . . . . . .5A **112**
CF35: P'coed . . . . . . . . . .3G **123**
SA7: Birch . . . . . . . . . . . .4F **61**
SA14: Cross H . . . . . . . . . . .5C **8**
SA5: Tre b . . . . . . . . . . . .2F **73**
SA18: C'bryn . . . . . . . . . . .4B **10**
Heol Fain CF32: Sarn . . . . . . . .6D **114**
Heol-Fair CF36: P'cwl . . . . . . .4D **124**
Heol Fawr CF33: N Cor . . . . . .2D **116**
SA18: L'bie . . . . . . . . . . . .1F **11**
Heol Fechan CF31: Bri . . . . . . .5A **120**
Heol Fedw SA6: Cwm'crw . . . . .3A **60**
Heol Felen SA18: Garn . . . . . . .4C **14**
Heol Felyn Fach CF32: Ton . . .4B **114**
Heol Ffaldau CF31: Brack . . . .5G **121**
Heol Ffion SA4: Gor . . . . . . . . .4B **56**
Heol Fforest SA4: Ffor . . . . . . .5D **34**
Heol Fforwr SA10: Skew . . . . . .2B **76**
Heol Ffynnon SA4: Lou . . . . . . .5E **55**
SA15: Llane . . . . . . . . . . . .5C **52**
Heol Ficerdi SA18: Garn . . . . . .5D **14**

Heol Folland
SA18: Garn, Glan . . . . . . . .4B **14**
Heol Frank SA5: P'lan . . . . . . . .3D **72**
Heol Gadlys CF31: Bri . . . . . . .4E **121**
Heol Gam CF31: Bri . . . . . . . . .3D **126**
Heol Ganol CF32: Sarn . . . . . . .6D **114**
Heol Gerrig SA5: Tre b . . . . . . .2F **73**
Heol Giedd SA9: C'edd . . . . . . .1A **28**
Heol Glanllechau SA8: All . . . . .1D **50**
Heol Glan-Nant SA6: Yfgn . . . .2B **60**
Heol Glantawe SA9: Ystra . . . . .6A **28**
Heol Glasnant SA2: Kill . . . . . . .3D **82**
Heol Gleien
SA9: Cwm I, Cwm U . . . . .4C **26**
Heol Glynderwen SA8: All . . . . .1D **50**
SA10: Nea . . . . . . . . . . . . .5A **64**
Heol Glyndwr CF31: Brack . . . .5A **122**
Heol Godfrey SA18: Lwr B . . . . .5H **13**
Heol Goedog CF32: Cef C . . . .1C **118**
Heol Goffa SA15: Llane . . . . . . .5B **42**
Heol Gough SA9: Ysta . . . . . . .2D **32**
Heol Graig Felen SA6: Cly . . . .4D **48**
Heol Grenig
SA18: Glan . . . . . .5A **14**, 4A **24**
Heol Gron SA9: Cwm I . . . . . . .6G **27**
Heol Gruffydd SA5: Rav . . . . . . .4C **72**
Heol Gwalia SA14: Llwy . . . . . . .1F **53**
Heol Gwanwyn SA7: L'smlt . . .1G **75**
Heol Gwell SA5: Tre b . . . . . . . .3G **73**
Heol Gwenallt SA4: Gor . . . . . . .2A **56**
Heol Gwendraeth
SA16: Burr P . . . . . . . . . . .3D **38**
Heol Gwernen SA6: Cwm'crw . .4A **60**
Heol Gwili SA4: Gor . . . . . . . . .2A **56**
SA7: L'smlt . . . . . . . . . . . .2F **75**
SA14: Llwy . . . . . . . . . . . .1F **53**
Heol Gwilym SA9: Cwml . . . . . .4F **17**
SA18: L'bie . . . . . . . . . . . .1F **11**
SA18: Rhosa . . . . . . . . . . .4F **17**
Heol Gwscwm SA16: Burr P . . .2C **38**
Heol Gwyr SA15: Llane . . . . . . .2C **52**
Heol Gwyrosydd
SA5: P'lan, Tre b . . . . . . . .3C **72**
Heol Gwys SA9: Cwm U . . . . . .2B **26**
Heol Hafdy SA7: L'smlt . . . . . . .1G **75**
Heol Haydn SA18: Amm . . . . . .6G **11**
Heol Heddwch SA10: Nea A . . . .5F **63**
SA10: Sev S . . . . . . . . . . .5F **29**
Heol Hen SA10: Sev S . . . . . . .5F **29**
SA14: Llwy . . . . . . . . . . . .2F **53**
Heol Hendre SA10: B'och . . . . .1H **63**
SA14: Llwy . . . . . . . . . . . .3G **53**
SA18: Garn . . . . . . . . . . . .4D **14**
Heol Hermas SA5: P'lan . . . . . . .2E **73**
Heol Hir SA18: Gwaun . . . . . . .3D **24**
Heol Hopcyn John
CF35: Coity . . . . . . . . . . .1F **121**
Heol Illtyd SA10: Nea . . . . . . . .5A **64**
Heol Innes SA15: Llane . . . . . . .4B **42**
Heol Iorwg SA4: Penl . . . . . . . .3G **57**
Heol Isaf SA11: Cim . . . . . . . . .3E **79**
SA12: C'avon . . . . . . . . . .5G **91**
Heol Iscoed SA4: Hendy . . . . . .6D **34**
SA5: Ffor F . . . . . . . . . . . .2H **71**
Heol Islwyn SA4: Gor . . . . . . . .2A **56**
SA5: Ffor F . . . . . . . . . . . .2G **71**
Heol Jiwbili SA12: C'avon . . . . .5H **91**
Heol Jolly SA18: Garn . . . . . . . .5E **15**
Heol Langdon
SA1: Swan . . . . . . .3H **5** (3A **86**)
HEOL-LAS . . . . . . . . . . . . . . . .4G **61**
Heol Las CF33: Maw . . . . . . . .1A **116**
CF33: N Cor . . . . . . . . . . .1B **116**
CF35: Coity . . . . . . . . . . .3A **122**
CF35: P'coed . . . . . . . . . .3G **123**
SA7: Birch . . . . . . . . . . . .4F **61**
SA14: Cross H . . . . . . . . . . .5C **8**
Heol-Las SA18: Amm . . . . . . . .2H **21**
Heol Las Cl. SA7: Birch . . . . . . .5F **61**
Heol Las Fawr SA10: Cry . . . . .5H **33**
Heol Llan CF32: B'myn . . . . . . .3F **115**
CF33: N Cor . . . . . . . . . . .1B **116**
CF35: Coity . . . . . . . . . . .1B **122**
Heol Llandeilo
SA14: C'mel, Gors . . . . . . . .4E **9**
SA14: Llandeilo SA14: Cross H . . .6C **8**
Heol Llangynnwr
SA31: Carm, Llang . . . . . . .4E **7**
Heol Llansantffraid
CF32: Sarn . . . . . . . . . . . .5C **114**
Heol Lluest yr Bryn
SA31: Carm . . . . . . . . . . . .2E **7**
Heol Llwchwr SA18: Amm . . . . .3G **21**
Heol Llwyd SA18: Garn . . . . . . .5C **14**

Heol Llwyn Bedw SA4: Hendy . .6C **34**
Heol Llwyncelyn SA10: Nea . . .4A **64**
SA18: Glan . . . . . . . . . . . .5H **13**
Heol Llwynon SA10: Nea . . . . . .4A **64**
Heol Login SA18: Cap H . . . . . . .5G **7**
Heol Lotwen SA18: Cap H . . . . .4F **19**
Heol Mabon SA2: C'avon . . . . .4G **91**
Heol Maelon CF31: Bri . . . . . . .2A **126**
Heol Maendy CF32: Sarn . . . . .6E **115**
CF33: N Cor . . . . . . . . . . .1B **116**
Heol Maes SA14: L'nch . . . . . . .4D **44**
Heol Maes Eglwys
SA6: Cwm'crw, Pantl . . . . .2G **59**
Heol Maesglas SA4: Garn . . . . .4D **14**
Heol Maesgwyn SA18: All . . . . .1D **50**
Heol Maes Pica SA9: Cwm I . . .4E **27**
Heol Maesuchel SA18: Garn . . .4E **15**
Heol Maes-y-bryn SA4: Lou . . .5G **55**
Heol Maes y Cerrig SA4: Lou . .6F **55**
Heol Maes y Dderwen
SA18: Garn . . . . . . . . . . . .4D **14**
Heol-Maes-y-Dre SA9: Ystra . .5A **28**
Heol Maesyffynnon
SA31: Carm . . . . . . . . . . . .2E **7**
Heol Maes-y-Gelynen
SA6: Morr . . . . . . . . . . . . .4A **60**
Heol Maes-yr-Haf
CF35: P'coed . . . . . . . . . .5G **123**
Heol Mair CF31: Brack . . . . . . .2E **121**
SA31: Carm . . . . . . . . . . . .2A **6**
Heol Margaret SA18: L'bie . . . . .2F **11**
Heol Marlais SA18: L'bie . . . . . .2F **11**
Heol Meurig SA9: Cwm I . . . . . .6F **27**
Heol Miaren SA6: Morr . . . . . . .4H **59**
Heol Milborough SA9: Ysta . . .2E **33**
Heol Morfa CF33: Pyle . . . . . . .1F **117**
SA15: Llane . . . . . . . . . . . .6B **42**
Heol Morfa Brenin SA31: John . .6B **6**
SA18: Amm . . . . . . . . . . . .5H **11**
Heol Mostyn CF33: Pyle . . . . . .6E **113**
Heol Mwrwg SA14: L'nch . . . . . .4B **44**
Heol Nant CF33: N Cor . . . . . . .1B **116**
SA14: F'oel . . . . . . . . . . . .2D **42**
Heol Nant Bran SA7: Birch . . . .4H **61**
Heol Nant Gelli SA5: Tre b . . . .3G **73**
Heol Nant Gwinau
SA18: Garn . . . . . . . . . . . .4F **15**
Heol Nantlais SA4: Gor . . . . . . .2A **56**
Heol Nant y Cwm SA4: Gor . . .3G **55**
Heol Nant-y-Felin
SA15: Llane . . . . . . . . . . . .5B **42**
Heol Nantyglyn SA18: Glan . . . .4F **13**
Heol Nantyreos SA14: Cross H . .6C **8**
Heol Neuadd CF33: N Cor . . . .2D **116**
SA5: P'lan . . . . . . . . . . . . .3C **72**
SA9: Cwml . . . . . . . . . . . .1A **26**
Heol Newydd CF32: Cef C . . . .1C **118**
Heol Norman SA18: Amm . . . . .6G **11**
Heol Onnen CF33: N Cor . . . . .1B **116**
Heol Panteg SA16: Burr P . . . . .3C **38**
Heol Pantglas SA10: B'och . . . .1H **63**
Heol Pantruthin
CF35: P'coed . . . . . . . . . .5G **123**
Heol Pantycelyn
SA16: Burr P . . . . . . . . . . .3D **38**
Heol Pant y Dwr SA4: Gor . . . .4G **55**
Heol Pantyffynnon
SA18: Amm . . . . . . . . . . . .4G **21**
Heol Pant-y-Lliw SA4: P'liw . . .6E **47**
Heol Parcdir SA18: Amm . . . . . .1F **21**
Heol Parc Mawr
SA14: Cross H . . . . . . . . . . .6D **8**
Heol Penar SA5: P'lan . . . . . . .2E **73**
Heol Pencastell
CF33: Ken H . . . . . . . . . . .5G **113**
Heol Penderyn CF31: Brack . . .5A **122**
SA10: Nea A . . . . . . . . . . .5F **63**
Heol Penfelyn SA6: Cwm'crw . .1A **60**
Heol Penlan SA10: Nea A . . . . .5F **63**
Heol Penlanffos SA31: Carm . . .1G **7**
Heol Pen-Nant SA6: Yfgn . . . . .2B **60**
SA14: F'oel . . . . . . . . . . . .1E **43**
Heol Penrhiwiau SA8: All . . . . .1D **50**
Heol Pen Tir Garw SA5: P'lan . .2C **72**
Heol Pentre Bach SA4: Gor . . .4G **55**
Heol Pentre Felen SA4: L'flch . .5E **59**
Heol Pentwyn SA10: Skew . . . .2B **76**
Heol Pentyla SA12: Sarn . . . . .5C **114**
SA7: L'smlt . . . . . . . . . . . .2G **75**
Heol Pen-y-Beili SA4: Lou . . . . .5F **55**
Heol Penycae SA4: Gor . . . . . . .2A **56**
Heol Pen-y-Coed SA11: Cim . . .3E **79**
Heol Penygarn SA18: Tyc . . . . .6D **20**
Heol Penygroes SA14: Gors . . . .4E **9**
SA18: Blae, C'bryn . . . . . . .3B **10**

**Heol Pen-y-Scallen** SA4: Lou . . . . .5F **55**
**Heol Persondy** CF32: A'knfig . . . .5C **114**
  (not continuous)
**Heol Philip** SA9: Cwm I . . . . . . . . . .5G **27**
**Heol Phillip** SA8: All . . . . . . . . . . .1D **50**
**Heol Plas Gwyn** SA14: Pen g . . . .4H **9**
  SA18: C'bryn . . . . . . . . . . . . . . .4H **9**
**Heol Plas Isaf** SA14: L'nch . . . . . .5C **44**
**Heol Pont George**
  CF33: Pyle . . . . . . . . . . . . . .5E **113**
**Heol Rheillfordd** SA9: Cwml . . . .6H **17**
**Heol-Rhosyonbonwen**
  SA14: Cross H . . . . . . . . . . . . .4A **8**
**Heol Rhosyn** SA6: Morr . . . . . .4H **59**
  SA14: Dafen . . . . . . . . . . . . . .3E **43**
**Heol Rhuddos** SA7: L'smlt . . . . .1H **75**
**Heol Rhyd** SA6: Craig-p . . . . . . . .1C **48**
**Heol Rhydaman** SA18: Tyc . . . .4D **20**
**Heol Rhyd-Ddu-Fach**
  SA9: Cwml . . . . . . . . . . . . . . . .5G **17**
**Heol Rudd** SA31: Carm . . . . . . . . .2C **6**
**Heol Saffrwm** SA6: Morr . . . . . . . .3A **60**
**Heol Salem** SA31: John . . . . . . . . .5B **6**
**Heol Saron** SA18: Saron . . . . . . . .2A **20**
**Heol Seion** SA14: L'nch . . . . . . . . .5C **44**
**Heol Shon** CF32: Cef C . . . . . . . .1B **118**
**Heol Siloh** SA15: Llane . . . . . . . . .5H **41**
**Heol Simonston** CF35: Coity . . .4H **121**
**Heol Spencer** CF32: Brync . . . .4F **115**
  CF35: Coity . . . . . . . . . . . . . .1H **121**
**Heol Spurrell** SA31: Carm . . . . . . .2D **6**
**Heol Stanllyd** SA14: Cross H . . . . .6D **8**
**Heol Stradling** CF35: Coity . . . . .3G **121**
**Heol Tabernacle** SA18: Glan . . . .4H **13**
**Heol Tabor** SA12: C'avon . . . . . . .4H **91**
  SA14: Bryn . . . . . . . . . . . . . . . .6H **43**
**Heol Taliesin** SA12: C'avon . . . . .4H **91**
**Heol Tawe** SA9: Aber . . . . . . . . . .1G **29**
**Heol Tegfryn** CF33: Pyle . . . . . . .5E **113**
**Heol Tewgoed** SA12: C'avon . . . .4H **91**
**Heol Tircoed** SA4: Tir V . . . . . . . . .2F **57**
**Heol Tir Du** SA6: Cwm'crw . . . . . .3A **60**
**Heol Tir y Coed** SA9: Cwml . . . .1B **26**
  SA18: Glan . . . . . . . . . . . . . . . .3A **14**
**Heol Tom Handel** SA18: Tyc . . . .6A **20**
  CF33: Ken . . . . . . . . . . . . . . .2A **116**
**Heol Trallwm** SA14: Llwy . . . . . . .1G **53**
**Heol Tredeg** SA9: Cwm U . . . . . .2C **26**
**Heol Tre Dwr** CF31: Bri . . . . . . . .3F **127**
**Heol Treffynnon**
  SA6: Cwm'crw . . . . . . . . . . . . .1C **60**
**Heol Trefor** SA5: P'lan . . . . . . . . .2E **73**
**Heol Trefrhiw** SA18: Amm . . . . . .2E **21**
**Heol Tregoning** SA15: Llane . . . . .3C **52**
**Heol Treharne** CF32: Coyt . . . . .2A **114**
**Heol Trelales** CF32: Lale . . . . . . .5B **126**
**Heol Treth** CF33: Pyle . . . . . . . . .6F **113**
**Heol Treventy** SA14: Cross H . . . .4A **8**
**Heol Troeon Bach** SA4: L'edi . . . .5E **31**
**Heol Trosserch** SA14: L'nch . . . . .2C **44**
**Heol Trubshaw** SA15: Llane . . . . .4B **42**
**Heol Twrch** SA9: Cwm I . . . . . . .5E **27**
**Heol-ty-Cribbwr** CF31: Bri . . . . .5A **120**
**Heol Tycroes** SA18: Tyc . . . . . . .4D **20**
**Heol Tydraw** CF33: Pyle . . . . . . .1E **117**
**Heol ty Gwyn** SA9: Cwml . . . . . .6H **17**
  SA10: B'och . . . . . . . . . . . . . . .2H **63**
**Heol Tylluan** SA7: Birch . . . . . . . .6A **62**
**Heol ty Llwyd** SA4: L'edi . . . . . . .6D **30**
**Heol ty Maen** CF31: Bri . . . . . .5A **120**
**Heol ty Newydd**
  SA14: Cross H . . . . . . . . . . . . .1C **18**
**Heol Ty'n-y-Garn**
  CF31: Pen F . . . . . . . . . . . . . .1B **120**
**Heol Tynygarn** CF31: Pen F . . . .1C **120**
**Heol Tysant** CF31: Bri . . . . . . . . .4F **121**
**Heol Uchaf** SA31: Cim . . . . . . . . .3F **79**
  SA18: Garn . . . . . . . . . . . . . . .5D **14**
**Heol Undeb** SA12: C'avon . . . . . .5H **91**
**Heol Undeb La.** SA12: C'avon . . .5H **91**
**Heol Valentine** SA6: Cly . . . . . . . .4E **49**
**Heol Vaughan** SA16: Burr P . . . .3C **38**
**Heol Wallasey** SA18: Amm . . . . .1A **22**
**Heol Wastad Waun**
  CF35: P'coed . . . . . . . . . . . . .3F **123**
**Heol Waterloo** SA14: Pen g . . . . .5H **9**
  SA18: Cap H . . . . . . . . . . . . . .1H **19**
**Heol Waun Dwfn** SA18: Amm . . .2C **22**
**Heol Waun Wen** SA6: L'flch . . . .4E **59**
**Heol Waun-Wen**
  SA16: Burr P . . . . . . . . . . . . . .2C **38**
**Heol Westfa** CF31: Bri . . . . . . . . .3F **121**
**Heol W. Plas** CF31: Bri . . . . . . . .3F **121**
  CF35: Bri, Coity . . . . . . . . . . .4F **121**

**Heol Will George**
  SA5: Wauna . . . . . . . . . . . . . .5D **70**
**Heol Wyllt** SA4: P'dul . . . . . . . . . .6H **35**
**Heol-y-Bardd** CF31: Bri . . . . . . .1B **126**
**Heol y Barna** SA4: P'liw . . . . . . . .2E **47**
**Heol y Berllan** CF33: Pyle . . . . .5E **113**
  SA10: Cry . . . . . . . . . . . . . . . . .5H **37**
**Heol-y-Blodau** CF31: Bri . . . . . .6A **120**
**Heol-y-Bont** CF32: Ton . . . . . . .5D **114**
**Heol y Brenin**
  SA1: Swan . . . . . . . . . . . .4H **5** (4H **85**)
  SA1: L'bie . . . . . . . . . . . . . . . . .1F **11**
**Heol y Bronwen** SA12: Sand . . . .3D **96**
**Heol y Bryn** SA14: Pen g . . . . . . .5H **9**
  SA18: Bry . . . . . . . . . . . . . . . . .2A **16**
**Heol-y-Brwch** SA12: C'avon . . . .5F **91**
**Heol-y-Bwlch** SA14: Byn . . . . . . .3B **54**
**Heol y Cae** SA4: P'dul . . . . . . . . .5G **35**
  SA6: Cly . . . . . . . . . . . . . . . . . .5E **49**
**Heol-y-Capel** CF35: Coyc . . . .1C **128**
  CF36: Not . . . . . . . . . . . . . . .2C **124**
**Heol-y-Cawl** CF35: Corn . . . . . .6H **127**
**Heol y Celyn** SA7: L'smlt . . . . . .5E **61**
**Heol y Cloddiau** SA14: Dafen . . .4E **43**
**Heol y Cnap** SA5: Tre b . . . . . . . .3G **73**
**Heol-y-Coed** SA4: P'dul . . . . . . . .5H **35**
**Heol y Coedcae** SA9: Cwml . . . . .6G **17**
**Heol-y-Coed Ri.** CF31: Brack . .6F **121**
**Heol y Cwmdu** SA5: Cwmdu . . . .6C **72**
**Heol y Cyw** SA7: Birch . . . . . . . .6A **62**
**Heol y Dail** CF31: Bri . . . . . . . . .5A **120**
**Heol y Ddraig** SA4: L'flch . . . . . . .3A **58**
**Heol y Delyn** SA31: Carm . . . . . . .1E **7**
**Heol y Deri** SA6: Cwm'crw . . . . . .3A **60**
  SA18: Glan . . . . . . . . . . . . . . . .5H **13**
**Heol-y-Deri** SA14: C'ili . . . . . . . . .4E **19**
**Heol y Deryn Du** CF31: Bri . . . .6A **120**
**Heol-y-Dre** SA14: Cef . . . . . . . . . .5B **8**
**Heol y Drudwen**
  SA6: Cwm'crw . . . . . . . . . . . . .1A **60**
**Heol y Dyffryn** SA18: Amm . . . .1C **20**
**Heol y Fagwr** SA6: Cly . . . . . . . . .3G **49**
**Heol y Felin** SA4: Penl . . . . . . . . .3G **57**
  SA10: Sev S . . . . . . . . . . . . . . .4G **29**
**Heol-y-Felin** SA4: Ffor, Hendy . . .5C **34**
  SA10: Nea . . . . . . . . . . . . . . . .4A **64**
  SA16: Burr P . . . . . . . . . . . . . .3E **39**
  SA18: Amm . . . . . . . . . . . . . . .2A **22**
**Heol y Fferm** CF32: Ton . . . . . .4D **114**
**Heol y Ffin** SA18: T'nos . . . . . . . .3A **50**
**Heol-y-Ffowndri** SA18: Amm . . .1A **22**
**Heol y Ffynnon** SA31: Cim . . . . .3F **79**
**Heol y Foel** SA14: Foe . . . . . . . . .2A **8**
**Heol y Foelas** CF31: Bri . . . . . . .6B **120**
**Heol y Fran** SA6: Cwm'crw . . . . . .1A **60**
**Heol y Frenhines** CF31: Bri . . . .6A **120**
**Heol y Fronfraith Fawr**
  CF31: Bri . . . . . . . . . . . . . . . .5C **126**
**Heol y Garn** SA18: G'llt . . . . . . . .6H **21**
**Heol y Garreg Wen**
  SA3: W Cro . . . . . . . . . . . . . .6D **94**
**Heol-y-Gât** SA14: Pen g . . . . . . .2F **9**
**Heol y Geifr** CF35: P'coed . . . . .4G **123**
  SA5: L'flch . . . . . . . . . . . . . . . .4E **59**
**Heol y Gelli** SA4: Penl . . . . . . . . .4E **57**
  SA18: L'bie . . . . . . . . . . . . . . . .1F **11**
**Heol y Gelynen** SA18: Bry . . . . . .3A **16**
**Heol-y-Gerddi** CF35: P'coed . . . .2G **123**
**Heol y Gigfran**
  SA14: Cef, Cross H . . . . . . . . .4A **8**
**Heol-y-Glo**
  CF33: Pen b, Pyle . . . . . . . . .4B **113**
  SA11: Tonna . . . . . . . . . . . . . .3H **65**
**Heol y Goedlan** SA9: P fawr . . . .4A **26**
**Heol-y-Goedwig** CF36: P'cwl . . .3D **124**
**Heol y Gog** SA4: Gow . . . . . . . . .3A **70**
**Heol y Gors** SA18: C'gors . . . . . .6C **24**
**Heol-y-Gors** SA1: Town . . . . . .1C **84**
  SA5: Cwmb . . . . . . . . . . . . . .1C **84**
**Heol y Graig** SA6: Cly . . . . . . . . .5E **49**
  SA10: Cry . . . . . . . . . . . . . . . . .6H **33**
  SA14: Llwy . . . . . . . . . . . . . . . .2H **53**
**Heol-y-Graig** CF36: Newt . . . . .3G **125**
  SA11: Tonna . . . . . . . . . . . . . .3G **65**
  SA12: C'avon . . . . . . . . . . . . . .4H **91**
**Heol-y-Groes** CF31: Bri . . . . . . .2E **121**
  CF35: P'coed . . . . . . . . . . . . .3H **123**
**Heol y Grug** SA6: Morr . . . . . . . .4H **59**
**Heol y Gwartheg** SA4: Gow . . . .3B **70**
**Heol y Gwaudd** SA9: Ystra . . . . .6B **28**
**Heol-y-Gwrgan** SA13: Marg . . . .3F **103**

**Heol y Llan** SA4: Lou . . . . . . . . . .6F **55**
**Heol-y-Llan** SA16: Burr P . . . . . .3D **38**
**Heol y Llew Du**
  SA14: Cross H, Gors . . . . . . . .4E **9**
  SA18: Cap H . . . . . . . . . . . . . .4E **9**
**Heol y Lloetrach** SA16: Pem . . . .2A **38**
**Heol-y-Llwynau** SA8: T'nos . . . . .3A **50**
**Heol y Llyfrau** CF32: A'knfig . . . .5B **114**
**Heol y Maes** SA4: P'dul . . . . . . . .6G **35**
**Heol y Mynydd** SA4: Gor . . . . . .3B **56**
  SA16: Graig, Pem . . . . . . . . . .1A **38**
  SA16: Pem . . . . . . . . . . . . . . . .1A **38**
**Heol-y-Mynydd** CF32: Sarn . . . .5E **115**
  SA14: Bryn . . . . . . . . . . . . . . . .6A **44**
**Heol y Nant** CF32: Sarn . . . . . . .5E **115**
  CF31: Bri . . . . . . . . . . . . . . . .6C **120**
  SA8: Rhos . . . . . . . . . . . . . . . . .1G **51**
  SA10: Nea . . . . . . . . . . . . . . . .4A **64**
  SA12: Bag . . . . . . . . . . . . . . . .5A **90**
**Heolynant** SA6: Cly . . . . . . . . . . . .4F **49**
**Heol Ynys** SA1: Swan . . . . . . . . .4A **86**
**Heol Ynysawdre** CF32: Sarn . . . .5D **114**
**Heol Ynysydarren** SA9: Ysta . . . .3E **33**
**Heol y Parc** SA4: P'liw . . . . . . . . .5F **47**
  SA14: L'nch . . . . . . . . . . . . . . .5D **44**
**Heol-y-Parc** CF33: N Cor . . . . . .6C **112**
  SA4: Hendy . . . . . . . . . . . . . . .5C **34**
  SA8: All . . . . . . . . . . . . . . . . . . .1E **51**
  SA12: C'avon . . . . . . . . . . . . . .5G **91**
  SA14: Cef . . . . . . . . . . . . . . . . .4A **8**
**Heol-y-Plas** SA4: Ffor . . . . . . . . .4C **34**
**Heol y Prior** SA31: Carm . . . . . . .3F **7**
**Heol-yr-Afon** CF31: Bri . . . . . . . .4C **120**
**Heol yr Afon** CF32: Ton . . . . . . .4C **114**
**Heol-yr-Eglwys** CF35: Coity . . .4H **121**
**Heol yr Eglwys** CF32: Brync . . .4F **115**
  SA4: L'edi . . . . . . . . . . . . . . . . .6E **31**
  SA14: Gors . . . . . . . . . . . . . . . .3D **8**
**Heol yr Eithen**
  SA6: Cwm'crw . . . . . . . . . . . . .3A **60**
**Heol yr Eithin** CF35: P'coed . . . .6G **123**
**Heol yr Enfys** CF31: Bri . . . . . . .5A **120**
**Heol yr Eos** SA4: Penl . . . . . . . . .4E **57**
**Heol yr Eryr** SA6: Cwm'crw . . . . .1A **60**
**Heol y Rhedyn** SA6: Morr . . . . . .4H **59**
**Heol-y-Rhos** CF31: Brack . . . . . .6F **121**
**Heol y Rhosfa** SA18: Bry . . . . . . .2C **16**
**Heol-yr-Onnen** CF31: Bri . . . . . .1A **126**
  CF35: P'coed . . . . . . . . . . . . .4H **123**
**Heol yr Orsaf** CF33: Ken H . . . .4G **113**
**Heol-yr-Orsedd** SA13: Marg . . . .1E **103**
**Heol yr Wylan** SA6: Cwm'crw . . .1A **60**
**Heol yr Ynys** CF31: Bri . . . . . . . .3E **127**
**Heol yr Ysgol** CF31: Bri . . . . . . .6B **120**
  CF35: Coity . . . . . . . . . . . . . .4H **121**
  SA9: Cwml . . . . . . . . . . . . . . . .5G **17**
  SA14: Cef . . . . . . . . . . . . . . . . .4A **8**
**Heol-yr-Ysgol** CF32: Ton . . . . .4C **114**
**Heol Ysgawen** SA2: Sket . . . . . .2H **83**
**Heol Ysgol Newydd**
  SA18: Amm . . . . . . . . . . . . . . .5C **14**
**Heol Ysgyfarnog** SA7: Birch . . . .6A **62**
**Heol-y-Sheet**
  CF33: N Cor, Pyle . . . . . . . .2D **116**
  (not continuous)
**Heol-y-Splot**
  CF33: Pyle, Sth C . . . . . . . . .5D **116**
**Heol y Twyn** SA4: P'liw . . . . . . . .5E **47**
**Heol y Waun** SA4: P'liw . . . . . . . .5E **47**
  SA14: Cross H . . . . . . . . . . . . .1E **19**
**Heol-y-Waun** SA4: P'dul . . . . . . .5G **35**
  SA10: Sev S . . . . . . . . . . . . . . .4H **29**
**Heol y Wawr** SA31: Carm . . . . . . .2A **6**
**Heol y Wern** SA4: Lou . . . . . . . . .6F **55**
  SA9: Ysta . . . . . . . . . . . . . . . . .2E **33**
**Heol-y-Wern** SA10: Nea . . . . . . .5H **63**
**Heol-y-Wyrddol** SA18: Amm . . .5H **11**
**Heol Zoar** SA9: Ysta . . . . . . . . . .2E **33**
**Herbert Rd.** SA11: Nea . . . . . . . .3A **78**
**Herbert St.** CF31: Bri . . . . . . . . .6F **121**
  SA8: P'dwe . . . . . . . . . . . . . . .6D **36**
**Herbert Thomas Way**
  SA7: Birch . . . . . . . . . . . . . . . .4F **61**
**Herne St.** SA11: Brit F . . . . . . . . .6G **77**
**HERNSTON** . . . . . . . . . . . . . . . . .4E **127**
**Hernston La.** CF31: Bri, Ewe . . .3E **127**
  (not continuous)
**Hernston Retail Pk.**
  CF31: Hern . . . . . . . . . . . . . . .4F **127**
**Heron Av.** SA15: Llane . . . . . . . . .4G **41**
**Heronstone Pk.** CF31: Hern . . . .4E **127**
**Heronstone La.** CF31: Hern . . . .5D **126**
  CF35: Ewe . . . . . . . . . . . . . . . .5D **126**
**Herons Way** SA10: Nea . . . . . . . .4B **64**
**Heron Way** SA6: Swan Ent . . . . .5C **60**

**Heulwen Ter.** SA15: Llane . . . . .5B **42**
**Hewson St.**
  SA1: Swan . . . . . . . . .1B **4** (2E **85**)
**Hibbert Rd.** SA11: Nea . . . . . . . .6C **64**
**Hick St.** SA15: Llane . . . . . . . . . .2A **52**
**Highbury Cl.** SA5: Cwmb . . . . . .6E **73**
**Highbury Ct.** SA11: Nea . . . . . . .2C **78**
**Highbury Cres.** CF31: Bri . . . . . .5B **120**
**Highcliffe Ct.** SA3: Lan . . . . . . . .2D **100**
**Higher La.** SA3: Lan . . . . . . . . . . .2E **101**
**Highfield** SA4: Gor . . . . . . . . . . . .6H **55**
  SA11: Cim . . . . . . . . . . . . . . . .2C **78**
**Highfield Av.** CF31: Bri . . . . . . . .3E **121**
  CF36: P'cwl . . . . . . . . . . . . . . .5C **124**
**Highfield Cl.** CF32: Sarn . . . . . . .6D **114**
  CF36: P'cwl . . . . . . . . . . . . . . .5B **124**
  SA10: Nea . . . . . . . . . . . . . . . .4B **64**
**Highfield Ct.** SA15: Llane . . . . . .2B **52**
**Highfield Pl.** CF32: Sarn . . . . . . .6C **114**
**Highfield Rd.** SA11: Brit F . . . . . .6G **77**
  *SA18: Garn* . . . . . . . . . . . . . . .4D **14**
  *(shown as Heol Maesuchel)*
**Highfields** CF31: Brack . . . . . . . .6F **121**
**Highfields Holiday Pk.**
  SA3: Port . . . . . . . . . . . . . . . . .5H **109**
**Highfield Ter.** SA15: Llane . . . . . .2B **52**
**Highland Av.** CF32: Brync . . . . . .3F **115**
**Highland Cl.** CF32: Sarn . . . . . . .6D **114**
  SA10: Nea A . . . . . . . . . . . . . . .6E **63**
**Highland Ct.** CF32: Brync . . . . . .3F **115**
**Highland Gdns.** SA10: Nea A . . . .5F **63**
**Highland Pl.** CF31: Bri . . . . . . . . .6E **121**
**Highlands, The**
  SA10: Nea A, Skew . . . . . . . . .5F **63**
**Highland Ter.** SA2: Dunv . . . . . . .2C **82**
  SA4: P'dul . . . . . . . . . . . . . . . .1D **46**
**Highmead Av.** SA3: Newt . . . . . .1C **100**
  SA15: Llane . . . . . . . . . . . . . . .4B **42**
**Highmead Cl.** SA3: Newt . . . . . . .6D **94**
**Highmoor** SA1: Swan . . . .6F **5** (5G **85**)
**Highpool Cl.** SA3: Newt . . . . . . . .1C **100**
**Highpool La.** SA3: Newt . . . . . . . .1C **100**
**High St.** CF32: Lale . . . . . . . . . . .5A **126**
  SA3: Ken H . . . . . . . . . . . . . . .5G **113**
  SA1: Swan . . . . . . . .2E **5** (1G **85**)
  SA4: Gor . . . . . . . . . . . . . . . . .4A **56**
  SA4: Grov . . . . . . . . . . . . . . . . .6B **46**
  SA4: P'dul . . . . . . . . . . . . . . . . .5E **35**
  SA6: Cly . . . . . . . . . . . . . . . . . .5E **49**
  SA8: All . . . . . . . . . . . . . . . . . . .1E **51**
  SA8: P'dwe . . . . . . . . . . . . . . .5D **36**
  SA10: Sev S . . . . . . . . . . . . . . .5F **29**
  SA10: Skew . . . . . . . . . . . . . . . .1E **77**
  SA11: Nea . . . . . . . . . . . . . . . .6B **64**
  (not continuous)
  SA12: C'avon . . . . . . . . . . . . . .5G **91**
  SA13: P Tal . . . . . . . . . . . . . . . .3G **97**
  SA15: Llane . . . . . . . . . . . . . . .5H **41**
  *SA18: Amm* . . . . . . . . . . . . . . .1A **22**
  *(shown as Y Stryd Fawr)*
  *SA18: Glan* . . . . . . . . . . . . . . .3B **14**
  *(shown as Stryd Fawr)*
  *SA18: L'bie* . . . . . . . . . . . . . . .1F **11**
  *(shown as Heol Fawr)*
**High Vw.** CF31: Bri . . . . . . . . . . .1E **127**
  SA1: M'hill . . . . . . . . . . . . . . . . .1F **85**
**High Vw. Gdns.** SA2: Sket . . . . .1G **95**
**Hilary Ho.** SA31: Cim . . . . . . . . . .3E **79**
**Hilary Way** CF36: Not . . . . . . . . .1B **124**
**Hilland Dr.** SA3: Bishop . . . . . . . .6A **94**
**Hillbrook Cl.** SA5: Wauna . . . . . . .5C **70**
**Hill Crest** SA3: Lan . . . . . . . . . . .2F **101**
**Hillcrest** CF31: Pen F . . . . . . . . .2B **120**
  SA2: Upl . . . . . . . . . . . . . . . . .3D **84**
**HILLEND** . . . . . . . . . . . . . . . . . . . .5C **104**
**Hillgrove** SA3: Casw . . . . . . . . . .2C **100**
**Hillrise Pk.** SA6: Cly . . . . . . . . . .5D **48**
  (not continuous)
**Hill Rd.** SA10: Nea A . . . . . . . . . .6F **63**
**Hillsboro** CF31: Bri . . . . . . . . . . .6B **120**
**Hillsboro Pl.** CF31: P'cwl . . . . . .5C **124**
**Hillside** CF31: Pen F . . . . . . . . . .2C **120**
  SA4: Lou . . . . . . . . . . . . . . . . .5F **55**
  SA11: Nea . . . . . . . . . . . . . . . .2B **78**
  SA15: Llane . . . . . . . . . . . . . . .2H **41**
**Hillside Cres.** SA2: Upl . . . . . . . .3D **84**
**Hillside Grn.** CF31: Pen F . . . . . .2C **120**
**Hillside La.** SA11: Nea . . . . . . . . .2C **78**
**Hill St.** SA1: Swan . . . . .1D **4** (2F **85**)
  SA3: T Mum . . . . . . . . . . . . . . .2G **101**
  SA4: Gow . . . . . . . . . . . . . . . . .3A **70**
  SA11: Brit F . . . . . . . . . . . . . . .1H **89**
**Hill Ter.** SA12: A'von . . . . . . . . . .3G **97**
**Hill Top** SA14: F'oel . . . . . . . . . . .2D **42**
**Hilltop Cl.** SA12: Bag . . . . . . . . .4B **90**

Hill Vw. CF31: Bri . . . . . . . . . .6H 119
CF33: Ken H . . . . . . . . . . .5F 113
CF35: P'coed . . . . . . . . .3E 123
SA4: Penc . . . . . . . . . . . .4H 67
SA6: Cly . . . . . . . . . . . . . .6D 48
SA10: Jer M . . . . . . . . . . .2A 88
Hill Vw. Cres. SA6: Clase . . . . .6G 59
Hillview Ter. SA13: P Tal . . . . .4H 97
HMP Swansea
SA1: Swan . . . . . . .5C 4 (4F 85)
Hodgson's Rd. SA9: Godr . . . . .5C 32
Hogarth Pl. SA12: Sand . . . . . .4C 96
Holland St. SA13: P Tal . . . . . .4G 97
Hollett Rd. SA5: Tre b . . . . . . .3F 73
(not continuous)
Hollies, The CF31: Brack . . . .1A 128
Hollins, The SA11: Cim . . . . . .3D 78
Hollybush Cl.
SA3: Newt, W Cro . . . . . .6D 94
Hollybush Dr. SA2: Sket . . . . . .1G 83
Hollyhock Dr. CF31: Brack . . . .5A 122
Holly Oak Rd. SA4: Penl . . . . . .3G 57
Holly Rd. SA11: Cim . . . . . . . .3D 78
Holly St. SA8: P'dwe . . . . . . . .5D 36
Holly Va. CF35: P'coed . . . . . .3F 123
Holly Wlk. CF36: Newt . . . . . . .3H 125
Hollywood Pk. SA12: Sand . . . .4B 96
Holts Fld. SA3: Mur . . . . . . . .1A 100
Holy Trinity Pl. SA12: Sand . . . .2B 96
Home Farm Way SA4: Penl . . . .4H 57
Homegower Ho.
SA1: Swan . . . . . . .5A 4 (4E 85)
Honeysuckle Dr. SA6: Clase . . .4G 59
Honeysuckle La. SA4: Gor . . . .3A 56
Honeysuckle Way
`CF31: Brack . . . . . . . . . .6A 122
Hong Kong Ter. CF32: Brync . . .5F 115
Hookland Rd. CF36: Newt . . . .4E 125
Hoo St. SA1: Por T . . . . . . . . .3C 86
SA11: Brit F . . . . . . . . . . .6H 77
Hope Av. CF32: A'knfig . . . . . .5B 114
HOPKINSTOWN . . . . . . . . . . .1D 22
Hopkin St. SA5: Man . . . . . . . .4F 73
SA8: P'dwe . . . . . . . . . . .5D 36
SA12: A'von . . . . . . . . . . .3E 97
Hopkins Way SA12: A'von . . . .4C 96
Horeb Rd. SA6: Morr . . . . . . . .5A 60
Horizon Pk. SA6: Swan Ent . . .2B 74
Horizon Way SA4: Gor . . . . . . .6H 55
Hornbeam Cl. SA11: Cim . . . . .3F 79
HORTON . . . . . . . . . . . . . . .5A 110
Horton SA2: Sket . . . . . . . . . .5A 84
Horton St. SA1: Swan . . . .3D 4 (3F 85)
Hosea Row SA1: L'ore . . . . . . .4G 73
Hosea Ter. SA1: L'ore . . . . . . .4G 73
Hospital Dr. SA6: Pantl . . . . . .2H 59
Hospital Rd. SA4: Gor . . . . . . .5D 56
SA12: Sand . . . . . . . . . . .4D 96
Howards Way SA4: Gor . . . . . .3B 56
Howell Rd. SA11: Brit F . . . . . .4H 77
Howells Rd. SA2: Dunv . . . . . .3B 82
Howells Ter. SA8: All . . . . . . . .1E 51
Hubert Dr. CF31: Bri . . . . . . . .4E 121
Humphrey La.
SA1: Swan . . . . . . .3A 4 (3E 85)
Humphrey St.
SA1: Swan . . . . . . .3B 4 (3E 85)
Hunters Ridge CF31: Brack . . .6H 121
SA11: Tonna . . . . . . . . . . .5E 65
Hunter St. SA11: Brit F . . . . . . .1H 89
Huntingdon Way SA2: Sket . . . .2G 83
Huntington Cl. SA3: W Cro . . . .4G 95
Huntington Ct. SA3: W Cro . . . .4G 95
Huntsmans Cove SA3: W Cro . .5D 94
Hutchwns Cl. CF36: P'cwl . . . .4A 124
Hutchwns Ter. CF36: P'cwl . . . .4C 124
Hyacinth Dr. CF31: Brack . . . . .5A 122

## I

Ian's Wlk. SA6: Yfgn . . . . . . . .2C 60
Ice Ho. SA1: Swan . . . . .4H 5 (4H 85)
Idle Rocks SA3: Lan . . . . . . . .3C 100
Idris Pl. CF31: Bri . . . . . . . . .4E 121
Idris Ter. SA6: Plas . . . . . . . . .3H 73
Idwal Pl. SA3: P'lan . . . . . . . . .3E 73
Idwal St. SA11: Nea . . . . . . . .6D 64
Iestyn Dr. CF35: P'coed . . . . . .3G 123
Illtyd St. SA11: Nea . . . . . . . . .6D 64
ILSTON . . . . . . . . . . . . . . . . .3C 92
Ilston SA15: Llane . . . . . . . . . .2C 52
Ilston Ho. SA1: Swan . . . . . . . .1C 4
Ilston Way SA3: W Cro . . . . . . .4F 95

Imperial Cen. SA7: Swan Ent . . .1C 74
Incline Row SA13: P Tal . . . . . .6H 97
Inco Golf Course . . . . . . . . . .6H 49
Indoor Bowls Cen. . . . . . . . . .4C 96
Inkerman St.
SA1: St T . . . . . . . .3H 5 (3H 85)
SA15: Llane . . . . . . . . . . .1A 52
Innovation Cen. CF31: Bri . . . .4D 126
Iorwerth St. SA5: Man . . . . . . .5F 73
Iris Cl. SA12: Sand . . . . . . . . .1B 96
Iron Way CF32: Ton . . . . . . . .4B 114
Isaac's Rd. CF31: A'von . . . . . .4E 97
Iscennen Rd. SA18: Amm . . . . .1H 21
(shown as Ffordd Is-Cennen)
ISCOED . . . . . . . . . . . . . . . . .3F 41
Iscoed Rd. SA4: Hendy . . . . . . .6C 34
(shown as Heol Iscoed)
Isfryn SA15: Pwll . . . . . . . . . . .2B 40
Isfryn Cl. SA16: Burr P . . . . . . .1E 39
Isgraig SA16: Graig . . . . . . . . .1E 39
Island Farm Cl. CF31: Bri . . . .4D 126
Island Farm Rd. CF31: Bri . . . .4D 126
Island M. SA13: P Tal . . . . . . . .3G 97
Islawen Mdws.
CF35: P'coed . . . . . . . . . .2H 123
Islington Rd. CF31: Bri . . . . . . .5B 120
Islwyn SA14: Llwy . . . . . . . . . .1H 53
Islwyn Rd. SA1: M'hill . . .1A 4 (2E 85)
Is-y-Bryniau SA9: Cwml . . . . . .5G 17
Is-y-Rhos SA9: C'bont . . . . . . .2D 28
Ivey Pl. SA1: Swan . . . . .1E 5 (2G 85)
Ivy Av. SA11: Nea . . . . . . . . . .6D 64
Ivy Bush Ct. SA1: St T . . .2H 5 (3H 85)

## J

Jack's Den SA1: Por T . . . . . . . .3A 86
Jackson's La. SA31: Carm . . . . .3E 7
(off King St.)
Jack-y-Ddu Rd. SA11: Brit F . . .6G 77
James Cl. CF32: Brync . . . . . .5F 115
James Ct. SA1: Wins . . . . . . . .2E 75
James Griffiths Rd.
SA8: Amm . . . . . . . . . . . .6C 12
James St. CF36: P'cwl . . . . . . .5C 124
SA4: P'dul . . . . . . . . . . . .6G 35
SA8: P'dwe . . . . . . . . . . .5C 36
SA9: Ystra . . . . . . . . . . . .2C 28
(Cwm Tawe Rd.)
SA9: Ystra . . . . . . . . . . . .6A 28
(Llanfaes)
SA11: Nea . . . . . . . . . . . .6B 64
(off Castle Vw.)
SA13: P Tal . . . . . . . . . . .4H 97
SA15: Llane . . . . . . . . . . .1B 52
Janion SA15: Llane . . . . . . . . .5A 52
Jasmine Cl. SA2: Sket . . . . . . .3G 83
SA2: Sand . . . . . . . . . . . .1B 96
Jays Fld. SA11: Cim . . . . . . . . .4E 79
Jeffreys Ct. SA5: P'lan . . . . . . .3E 73
Jenkins Rd. SA10: Skew . . . . . .1F 77
Jenkins Ter. SA13: P Tal . . . . . .5H 97
(not continuous)
Jenkin St. CF31: Bri . . . . . . . . .2E 127
Jericho Rd. SA1: St T . . . . . . . .2H 85
Jersey Marine . . . . . . . . . . . . .2B 88
Jersey Quay SA12: A'von . . . . .5C 96
Jersey Rd. SA1: Bon . . . . . . . .5C 74
SA1: Wins . . . . . . . . . . . .3D 74
(not continuous)
Jersey Row SA12: C'avon . . . . .5H 91
Jersey St. SA1: Swan . . . . . . . .1G 85
SA13: P Tal . . . . . . . . . . .3H 97
Jersey Ter. SA1: Por T . . . . . . .3B 86
SA11: Brit F . . . . . . . . . . .1G 89
SA12: C'avon . . . . . . . . . .5H 91
Jersey Vs. SA12: C'avon . . . . . .5H 91
Jessop Ct. SA6: Pantl . . . . . . . .2H 59
Job's Well Rd. SA31: Carm . . . .3B 6
Jockey St. SA1: Swan . .1F 5 (2G 85)
John Penry Cres. SA5: P'lan . . . .2E 73
John's Ter. SA14: C'mel . . . . . .1H 9
(shown as Teras John)
JOHNSTOWN . . . . . . . . . . . . .6C 6
John St. CF32: Cef C . . . . . . . .1D 118
CF36: P'cwl . . . . . . . . . . .5C 124
SA1: Swan . . . . . . . . . . . .2G 85
SA2: C'ett . . . . . . . . . . . .6A 72
SA3: T Mum . . . . . . . . . .2E 101
SA12: A'von . . . . . . . . . . .3F 97
SA15: Llane . . . . . . . . . . .1A 52
SA31: Carm . . . . . . . . . . .3E 7
John's Vs. CF32: Brync . . . . . . .4F 115

John Ter. SA6: Morr . . . . . . . . .5A 60
Joiners Rd. SA4: Thr X . . . . . . .1E 81
Jones St. SA8: P'dwe . . . . . . . .5D 36
Jones Ter. SA1: Swan . . .1D 4 (2F 85)
SA18: Glan . . . . . . . . . . . .5H 13
(shown as Teras Jones)
Jordan Ter. SA10: Nea A . . . . . .5G 63
Joseph Davies Cl. SA1: Swan . .6F 73
Joseph Row CF33: Ken H . . . . .4G 113
Joseph St. SA13: P Tal . . . . . . .2G 97
Joslin Cl. CF35: Brack . . . . . . .4F 121
Joslin Rd. CF35: Bri . . . . . . . . .4F 121
Joslin Ter. CF35: Bri . . . . . . . . .4F 121
J Shed SA1: Swan . . . .4H 5 (4H 85)
Jubilee Cl. CF35: Ffor F . . . . . . .4H 71
Jubilee Cres. CF31: Bri . . . . . . .2F 127
CF32: Sarn . . . . . . . . . . . .5D 114
Jubilee Gdns. CF36: P'cwl . . . .1D 124
Jubilee Ho. SA12: Sand . . . . . .4D 96
Jubilee La. SA4: Lou . . . . . . . . .5G 55
Jubilee Rd. CF31: Bri . . . . . . . .2F 127
Julian's Way CF33: N Cor . . . . .2D 116
Julian Ter. SA12: A'von . . . . . . .3E 97
Junction 47 Retail Pk.
SA4: Gor . . . . . . . . . . . . .4D 56
Juniper Cl. CF36: Newt . . . . . . .4H 125
SA2: Sket . . . . . . . . . . . . .2G 83

## K

Keats Cl. CF31: Bri . . . . . . . . .5C 120
Keats Gro. SA2: Kill . . . . . . . . .3E 83
Keenmoor La. SA3: P'tn . . . . . .2D 108
Keen's Pl. CF32: Brync . . . . . . .5E 115
Keepers Cl. SA4: Penl . . . . . . .4H 57
Keir Hardie SA12: Bag . . . . . . .3A 90
Kelvin Rd. SA6: Cly . . . . . . . . .3E 49
Kemble St. SA2: Brynm . . . . . .5C 84
Kempthorne St. SA11: Nea . . . .2B 78
Kemys Way SA6: Swan Ent . . . .1B 74
Kendle Dr. SA2: Sket . . . . . . . .2F 83
KENFIG . . . . . . . . . . . . . . . . .1A 116
KENFIG HILL . . . . . . . . . . . . .5G 113
Kenfig Pl. SA1: Bon . . . . . . . . .6B 74
Kenilworth Ct. SA2: Bag . . . . . .5B 90
Kenilworth Pl. SA3: W Cro . . . . .4F 95
Kennedy Dr. CF35: P'coed . . . .3F 123
Kennel Row SA11: Brit F . . . . . .1G 89
Kennington Cl. SA2: Kill . . . . . .4C 82
Kensington Dr. CF31: Bri . . . . . .4B 120
Kent Rd. CF31: Bri . . . . . . . . . .2G 127
Kenwig Rd. SA1: Cim . . . . . . . .2C 78
Kern Cl. SA12: Sand . . . . . . . . .1A 96
Kestrel Cl. CF31: Bri . . . . . . . . .2A 128
SA10: Nea . . . . . . . . . . . .4B 64
Kestrel Way SA4: Gor, Penl . . . .5E 57
Kew Gdns. SA14: Tum . . . . . . .2A 18
Kilby Ct. SA4: Lou . . . . . . . . . .5G 55
Kildare St. SA5: Man . . . . . . . .1F 85
Kilfield Rd. SA3: Bishop . . . . . . .1G 99
Killan Rd. SA2: Dunv . . . . . . . .1H 81
KILLAY . . . . . . . . . . . . . . . . . .3D 82
Kilvey Cl. SA2: Sket . . . . . . . . .6A 84
Kilvey La. SA1: St T . . . . . . . . .1H 85
Kilvey Rd. SA1: St T . . . .1G 5 (2H 85)
Kimberley Cl. SA2: Sket . . . . . .3A 84
Kimberley Ct. CF31: Brack . . . .2G 127
Kimberley Rd. SA2: Sket . . . . . .3H 83
Kingdon Owen Rd. SA11: Nea . .2C 78
King Edward Rd. SA18: Tair . . . .2G 25
(not continuous)
King Edward's Rd.
SA1: Swan . . . . . . .5A 4 (5D 84)
Kingfisher Cl. CF31: Brack . . . .1H 127
Kingfisher Ct. SA15: Llane . . . . .1D 52
(not continuous)
Kingfisher Rd. CF33: N Cor . . . .6B 112
King George Av. SA15: Llane . . .1B 52
King George Ct. SA2: Sket . . . . .6G 83
Kingrosia Pk. SA6: Cly . . . . . . .4G 49
Kingsbridge Bus. Pk.
SA4: Gor . . . . . . . . . . . . .6B 56
King's Head Av. SA5: Gen . . . . .5C 72
Kingshill CF36: P'cwl . . . . . . . .4C 124
Kings La. SA1: Swan . .2E 5 (3G 85)
Kings Rd. SA3: T Mum . . . . . . .1E 101
SA18: L'bie . . . . . . . . . . . .1F 11
(shown as Heol y Brenin)
Kingston Rd. SA2: Sket . . . . . . .3A 84
King St. SA1: Swan . . .2E 5 (3G 85)
SA11: Nea . . . . . . . . . . . .1A 78
SA13: P Tal . . . . . . . . . . .3G 97
SA31: Carm . . . . . . . . . . .3E 7

King Street Gallery . . . . . . . . . .3E 7
(off King St.)
Kingsway CF31: Bri . . . . . . . . .3G 127
SA5: Ffor F . . . . . . . . . . . .3H 71
Kingsway, The
SA1: Swan . . . . . . . .3C 4 (3F 85)
Kingsway Bus. Cen.
SA5: Ffor F . . . . . . . . . . . .4H 71
Kingswood Cl. CF35: Ewe . . . . .6D 126
Kinley St. SA1: St T . . . . . . . . .3A 86
Kipling Gdns. CF31: Bri . . . . . .5B 120
Kittiwake Cl. CF36: Not . . . . . . .3A 124
KITTLE . . . . . . . . . . . . . . . . . .5F 93
Kittle Grn. SA3: Kit . . . . . . . . . .5F 93
Kittle Hill La. SA3: Kit . . . . . . . .5F 93
KNELSTON . . . . . . . . . . . . . . .1H 109
Knelston Pl. SA5: Blae M . . . . . .1C 72
Knights Rd. SA13: Marg . . . . . .2F 103
Knight St. SA12: A'von . . . . . . . .3F 97
Knoll Av. SA2: Upl . . . . . . . . . .4B 84
Knoll Gdns. SA31: Carm . . . . . .3C 6
Knox St. SA13: Marg . . . . . . . .3F 103
Knoyle Dr. SA5: Tre b . . . . . . . .1F 73
Knoyle St. SA5: Tre b . . . . . . . .1F 73
Knoyle Ter. SA5: Tre b . . . . . . . .1F 73
Kyfts La. SA3: Bury G, Cher . . .3F 105

## L

Laburnum Av. SA12: Bag . . . . .3B 90
Laburnum Dr. SA6: Morr . . . . . .3G 125
Laburnum Pl. SA2: Sket . . . . . .4G 83
Lady Charlotte La.
SA13: Marg . . . . . . . . . . . .1E 103
Lady Housty Av. SA3: Newt . . .1B 100
Lady Jane St. SA12: Sand . . . . .4E 97
Lady Margaret Vs. SA2: Sket . . .3B 84
Ladysmith Rd. SA5: Tre b . . . . .2G 73
Laing St. CF33: Ken H . . . . . . .5F 113
Lakefield Cl. SA15: Llane . . . . . .2A 52
Lakefield Pl. SA15: Llane . . . . . .5H 41
Lakefield Rd. SA15: Llane . . . . .5H 41
Lake Rd. SA12: A'von . . . . . . . .5D 96
Lakeside Technology Pk.
SA7: Swan Ent . . . . . . . . .2C 74
Lakeview Cl. CF36: P'cwl . . . . .4D 124
SA15: Llane . . . . . . . . . . . .2H 41
Lakeview Ter. SA15: Llane . . . . .2H 41
LALESTON . . . . . . . . . . . . . . .5B 126
Laleston Cl. CF36: Not . . . . . . .1B 124
Laleston Ct. CF32: Lale . . . . . . .6F 119
Lamberts Rd. SA1: Swan . . . . .3A 86
Lamb La. SA2: Kill . . . . . . . . . .2E 83
Lambourne Dr. SA3: Newt . . . . .6D 94
Lamb Row CF33: Sth C . . . . . .4D 116
Lambs Well Cl. SA3: Lan . . . . . .2F 101
Lammas St. SA31: Carm . . . . . .3D 6
Lan Av. SA6: Morr . . . . . . . . . .6A 60
Lancaster Ct. SA5: Rav . . . . . . .3A 72
Lan Coed SA1: Wins . . . . . . . .3D 74
Landeg St. SA6: Plas . . . . . . . .3H 73
Lan Deri SA1: Wins . . . . . . . . .3D 74
LANDIMORE . . . . . . . . . . . . . .3H 105
LANDIMORE . . . . . . . . . . . . . .3H 105
Landor Av. SA2: Kill . . . . . . . . .3E 83
Landor St. SA4: Lou . . . . . . . . .5E 55
LANDORE . . . . . . . . . . . . . . . .4G 73
Landore Av. SA13: Marg . . . . . .2F 103
Landore (Park & Ride) . . . . . . .5H 73
Lando Rd. SA16: Pem . . . . . . . .2A 38
Lane, The SA4: Wern . . . . . . . .2E 107
SA14: F'oel . . . . . . . . . . . .2D 42
Langcliffe Pk. SA3: T Mum . . . .3G 101
Langdon Ho.
SA1: Swan . . . . . . .3H 5 (3H 85)
Langdon Rd.
SA1: Swan . . . . . . .3H 5 (3H 85)
Langenau Strasse CF31: Bri . . .1D 126
Langer Way SA6: Cly . . . . . . . .3F 49
LANGLAND . . . . . . . . . . . . . . .2D 100
Langland Bay Golf Course . . . .3C 100
Langland Bay Mnr.
SA3: Lan . . . . . . . . . . . . . .2D 100
Langland Bay Rd. SA3: Lan . . .2D 100
Langland Cl. SA3: T Mum . . . . .2D 100
Langland Ct. SA3: Lan . . . . . . .2C 100
Langland Ct. Rd. SA3: Lan . . . .2C 100
Langland Gro. SA3: Lan . . . . . .2D 100
Langland M. SA15: Llane . . . . . .3B 52
Langland Rd. SA3: T Mum . . . .2D 100
SA15: Llane . . . . . . . . . . . .3B 52
Langland Ter. SA2: Brynm . . . . .5B 84
Langland Vs. SA3: T Mum . . . .2E 101

LANGYNNWR . . . . . . . . . . . . .3H 7
Lan Mnr. SA6: Morr . . . . . . . .6H 59
Lansbury Av.
  SA13: Marg, P Tal . . . . .1F 103
Lansdown SA3: Lan . . . . . . . .2D 100
Lansdown Ct. SA5: Ffor F . . . .6A 72
  SA11: Nea . . . . . . . . . .4H 77
Lan St. SA6: Morr . . . . . . . . .5A 60
Lapwing Cl. CF36: P'cwl . . . . .3A 124
Lapwing Rd. SA15: Llane . . . . .4G 41
Larch Cl. CF36: Newt . . . . . .4H 125
  SA11: Cim . . . . . . . . . . .3F 79
Larch Cres. SA14: F'oel . . . . . .2D 42
Larkhill SA12: Bag . . . . . . . . .3C 90
Lark Pl. SA5: Blae M . . . . . . . .2B 72
Lark Ri. CF31: Brack . . . . . . . .5A 122
Larkspur Cl. SA10: Nea . . . . . .4B 64
Larkspur Dr. SA3: W Cro . . . . .5D 94
Latimer Ct. SA5: Rav . . . . . . . .3A 72
Latt, The SA11: Nea . . . . . . . .6B 64
Lauderdale Rd. SA18: Tair . . . . .1F 25
Laugharne Ct. SA2: Sket . . . . . .4F 83
Laurel Av. SA12: Bag . . . . . . . .4B 90
Laurel Cl. CF32: Brync . . . . . .5E 115
Laurel Dr. SA5: Wauna . . . . . .4C 70
  SA18: Amm . . . . . . . . . .6C 12
Laurel Pl. SA2: Sket . . . . . . . .4G 83
Lavender Ct. CF31: Brack . . . . .6A 122
  SA5: P'lan . . . . . . . . . . .3D 72
Law Courts
  Bridgend . . . . . . . . . . .1D 126
Lawnty Marlat SA13: Coe H . .1D 112
Lawrence Cl. CF31: Bri . . . . . .5D 120
Lawrence Ter. SA15: Llane . . . .1B 52
LEASON . . . . . . . . . . . . . . . .4B 106
Le-Breos SA3: May . . . . . . . . .3E 95
Le Breos Av. SA2: Upl . . . . . . .4B 84
Leckwith Ct. CF31: Bri . . . . . . .1B 126
Leckwith Ri. CF31: Bri . . . . . . .1B 126
Lee Cl. SA1: Town . . . . . . . . . .1B 84
Lee Crymlyn SA10: L'dcy . . . . .4B 76
Lee Emanuel SA11: Nea . . . . . .2A 78
    (shown as Emanuel Pl.)
Lee St. SA1: St T . . . . . . . . . . .3A 86
Leiros Parc Dr. SA10: Nea . . . . .4B 64
Leonard St. SA11: Nea . . . . . . .6C 64
Leslie St. SA12: A'von . . . . . . .3E 97
Leucarum Ct. SA4: Lou . . . . . . .6F 55
Level, The SA16: Burr P . . . . . .2G 39
Lewis Av. CF31: Bri . . . . . . . . .6D 120
  SA9: Cwml . . . . . . . . . . .6H 17
Lewis Cres. SA14: Llwy . . . . . .6G 43
Lewis Pl. CF36: P'cwl . . . . . . . .4C 124
Lewis Rd. SA10: Cry . . . . . . . .6H 33
  SA11: Nea . . . . . . . . . . .2B 78
Lewis St. SA1: St T . . . . .3H 5 (3A 86)
  SA2: Sket . . . . . . . . . . . .4H 83
Leyshan Wlk. SA3: W Cro . . . .4D 94
Leyshon Cl. SA10: Nea A . . . . .1F 77
Leyshon Rd. SA8: Ynys . . . . . .4E 37
  SA18: Gwaun . . . . . . . . . .1C 24
Leyshon Way CF32: Brync . . . .4E 115
Lias Cott. CF36: P'cwl . . . . . . .5C 124
Lias Rd. CF36: P'cwl . . . . . . . .5C 124
Lias St. CF31: Bri . . . . . . . . . .1E 127
Libanus Rd. SA4: Gor . . . . . . . .5A 56
Libby Way SA3: T Mum . . . . . .3G 101
Liberty Stadium . . . . . . . . . . .5H 73
Library La. SA13: P Tal . . . . . . .5H 97
Lifeboat Rd. CF36: P'cwl . . . . . .5C 124
Lilac Cl. SA3: W Cro . . . . . . . . .4E 95
Lilac Gro. SA12: Bag . . . . . . . .3B 90
Lilian St. SA12: A'von . . . . . . .3E 97
Lilliput La. SA3: W Cro . . . . . . .4F 95
Lime Ct. SA5: Man . . . . . . . . . .6F 73
  SA11: Nea . . . . . . . . . . .6B 64
Lime Gro. SA2: Kill . . . . . . . . . .3C 82
  SA11: Cim . . . . . . . . . . .3D 78
Lime Gro. Av. SA31: Carm . . . . .2C 6
Lime Kiln La. SA3: Bishop . . . . .6A 94
Limekiln Rd. SA3: T Mum . . . .1E 101
LIMESLADE . . . . . . . . . . . . . .3G 101
Limeslade Ct. SA3: T Mum . . . .3G 101
Limeslade Dr. SA3: T Mum . . . .3G 101
Lime St. SA4: Gor . . . . . . . . . .4A 56
Lime Tree Way CF36: Newt . . . .3G 125
Linden Av. SA3: W Cro . . . . . . .4F 95
Linden Cl. SA10: B'och . . . . . . .2H 63
Linden Way CF36: Newt . . . . .3H 125
Lindsay Cl. CF35: P'coed . . . . . .3F 123
Lindsay Ct. CF31: Bri . . . . . . . .2F 127
Lingfield Av. SA3: W Cro . . . . . .2G 95
    (not continuous)
Link, The SA2: Sket . . . . . . . . . .5F 83
Links, The SA16: Burr P . . . . . .3B 38

Linkside SA3: Lan . . . . . . . . . .2C 100
Linkside Dr. SA3: S'gate . . . . . .6B 92
Linnet Way CF31: Brack . . . . . .6A 122
Lion St. SA1: Swan . . . . . . . . . .1F 85
Lion Way SA7: Swan Ent . . . . . .1C 74
LISBON . . . . . . . . . . . . . . . . .3F 73
Lister Av. SA12: A'von . . . . . . .3E 97
LITCHARD . . . . . . . . . . . . . . .3E 121
Litchard Bungs. CF31: Bri . . . . .4D 120
Litchard Cross CF31: Bri . . . . . .4E 121
Litchard Hill CF31: Bri . . . . . . .3E 121
  CF35: Bri . . . . . . . . . . . .2E 121
Litchard Ind. Est.
  CF31: Brack . . . . . . . . . . .4G 121
Litchard Pk. CF31: Bri . . . . . . . .4E 121
Litchard Ri. CF31: Bri . . . . . . . .3E 121
Litchard Ter. CF31: Bri . . . . . . . .4E 121
Little Acre CF35: Corn . . . . . . . .6G 127
Little Bri. St. SA31: Carm . . . . . .4E 7
Lit. Gam St.
  SA1: Swan . . . . . .4C 4 (4F 85)
LITTLE REYNOLDSTON . . . . . .1B 110
Lit. Station Rd. CF33: Ken H . .4H 113
Lit. Water St. SA31: Carm . . . . .3E 7
Lit. Wind St.
  SA1: Swan . . . . . .4F 5 (4G 85)
Llan Coed Ct. SA10: L'dcy . . . . .3C 76
Llandafen Rd. SA14: Llane . . . . .1E 53
LLANDARCY . . . . . . . . . . . . . .5C 76
Llandarcy Academy of Sport . . .5C 76
LLANDDEWI . . . . . . . . . . . . . .1G 109
LLANDEILO FERWALLT . . . . . .6G 93
Llandeilo Rd. SA14: Cross H . . .6C 8
    (shown as Heol Llandeilo)
  SA14: Gors . . . . . . . . . . . .4E 9
    (shown as Heol Llandeilo)
  SA18: Bry, Garn, Glan . . . .1B 14
  SA18: L'bie . . . . . . . . . . .1F 11
LLANDYBIE . . . . . . . . . . . . . . .1F 11
Llandybie Rd. SA18: Amm . . . .5H 11
Llandybie Station (Rail) . . . . . .1G 11
Llandyry SA14: F'oel . . . . . . . . .2D 42
LLANEDI . . . . . . . . . . . . . . . . .5E 31
Llanedi Rd. SA4: Ffor, Sard . . .1D 34
LLANELLI . . . . . . . . . . . . . . . .1A 52
Llanelli Bus Station . . . . . . . . .1A 52
Llanelli Crematorium
  SA14: L'nch . . . . . . . . . . .3G 43
Llanelli Entertainment Cen. . . . .4H 41
Llanelli Leisure Cen. . . . . . . . . .4H 41
Llanelli Public Library Gallery
     . . . . . . . . . . . . . . . . .1A 52
    (off Church St.)
Llanelli RFC . . . . . . . . . . . . . . .2E 53
Llanelli Station (Rail) . . . . . . . .3A 52
Llanelli Town AFC . . . . . . . . . .6C 42
LLANERCH . . . . . . . . . . . . . . .5B 42
Llanerch Cotts. SA15: Llane . . . .5B 42
Llanerch Cres. SA4: Gor . . . . . .3A 56
Llanerch Pl. SA1: Bon . . . . . . . .6C 74
Llanerch Rd. SA1: Bon . . . . . . .5C 74
  SA2: Dunv . . . . . . . . . . . .3C 82
Llanerch Ter. SA15: Llane . . . . .5B 42
Llanfaes SA9: Ystra . . . . . . . . .6A 28
Llanfair Gdns. SA3: T Mum . . . .6F 95
LLANGATHWG . . . . . . . . . . . .4C 64
Llangeinor Rd.
  CF32: B'myn, L'nor . . . . .1E 115
LLANGENNECH . . . . . . . . . . . .4D 44
Llangennech Station (Rail) . . . .5D 44
LLANGENNITH . . . . . . . . . . . .5D 104
LLANGEWYDD . . . . . . . . . . . .4E 119
Llangewydd Rd.
  CF31: Bri, L'ydd . . . . . . . .4E 119
    (not continuous)
  CF32: L'ydd . . . . . . . . . . .4E 119
LLANGIWG . . . . . . . . . . . . . . .2D 36
Llangorse Rd. SA5: P'lan . . . . . .4E 73
LLANGRALLO . . . . . . . . . . . . .1C 128
Llanguicke Rd. SA8: Ynys . . . . .3F 37
LLANGUNNOR . . . . . . . . . . . .3H 7
Llangunnor Rd. SA31: Carm . . . .4E 7
    (shown as Heol Llangynnwr)
Llangwm SA5: P'lan . . . . . . . . .2C 72
Llangwydfan La. SA18: L'bie . . .2G 11
LLANGYFELACH . . . . . . . . . . .4E 59
Llangyfelach Rd. SA4: Penl . . . .3G 57
  SA5: Man, Swan . . . . . . . .4G 73
  SA5: Man, Tird, Tre b . . . . .5F 59
Llangyfelach St. SA1: Swan . . . .6G 73
LLANGYNWYD . . . . . . . . . . . .5D 104
LLANILLTUD GWYR . . . . . . . . .3C 92
Llanllienwen Cl.
  SA6: Cwm'crw . . . . . . . . .2A 60

Llanllienwen Rd.
  SA6: Cwm'crw, Yfgn . . . . .3A 60
LLANMADOC . . . . . . . . . . . . . .3F 105
LLANMADOG . . . . . . . . . . . . .3F 105
LLANMORLAIS . . . . . . . . . . . .6F 67
Llannant Rd. SA4: Gor . . . . . . .1F 55
Llannon Rd. SA14: F'oel . . . . . .1D 42
LLANRHIDIAN . . . . . . . . . . . . .5C 106
Llanrhidian Cvn. Pk.
  SA3: Llanr . . . . . . . . . . . .3E 107
Llanrhidian Hill Nature Reserve
     . . . . . . . . . . . . . . . . .4C 106
LLANSAMLET . . . . . . . . . . . . .6E 61
Llansamlet Ind. Est.
  SA6: Swan Ent . . . . . . . . .3A 74
  SA7: L'smlt . . . . . . . . . . .1D 74
  SA7: Swan Ent . . . . . . . . .2D 74
Llansamlet Station (Rail) . . . . . .6G 61
LLANSAWEL . . . . . . . . . . . . . .6H 77
Llansawel SA11: Brit F . . . . . . .1H 89
Llansawel Cres. SA11: Brit F . .5G 77
Llansteffan Rd. SA31: John . . . .4B 6
Llantwit Rd. SA11: Nea . . . . . .6C 64
Llan-yr-Newydd SA4: Blu A . . .5A 68
LLAN-Y-TIR-MAIR . . . . . . . . . .1H 109
Llechyfedach SA14: Tum . . . . .1A 18
Lledglawdd Rd. SA2: Kill . . . . .1E 83
  SA5: Kill, Wauna . . . . . . .1E 83
Lletai Av. CF35: P'coed . . . . . . .3H 123
LLETHRID . . . . . . . . . . . . . . . .5G 107
Llethri Rd. SA14: F'oel . . . . . . .3D 42
    (not continuous)
LLETTYHARRI . . . . . . . . . . . . .2H 97
Lletty Harri SA13: P Tal . . . . . .2H 97
Lletty Nedd SA11: Nea . . . . . . .6C 64
Llety Gwyn CF31: Bri . . . . . . . .4D 120
Llewellyn Av. SA10: Nea . . . . . .5A 64
Llewellyn Circ.
  SA1: M'hill . . . . . . .1A 4 (2E 85)
Llewellyn Cl. SA13: P Tal . . . . .5H 97
Llewellyn Dr. CF31: Pen F . . . .1C 120
Llewellyn Pk. Dr. SA6: Morr . . .1H 73
Llewellyn Rd. SA4: Penl . . . . . .3E 57
Llewellyns Quay SA13: P Tal . . .5F 97
Llewellyn's Rd. SA13: P Tal . . .5G 97
Llewellyn St. SA11: Nea . . . . . .2B 78
  SA12: A'von . . . . . . . . . . .3F 97
  SA15: Llane . . . . . . . . . . .2A 52
Llewelyn St. SA2: Sket . . . . . . .4H 83
Llewitha Ter. SA5: Ffor F . . . . .2G 71
Lliedi Cres. SA15: Llane . . . . . .6B 42
Lliw Valley Cl. SA4: Gow . . . . .2B 70
Llon y Dderwen SA15: Llane . . .2H 41
Llottrog SA4: Penc . . . . . . . . . .5H 67
Lloyd Rd. SA5: Tre b . . . . . . . .3F 73
Lloyd St. SA8: T'nos . . . . . . . . .2A 50
  SA15: Llane . . . . . . . . . . .4H 41
  SA18: Amm . . . . . . . . . . .1H 21
Lloyd Thomas Cl. SA1: Town . .6B 72
Lluest SA9: Ystra . . . . . . . . . . .4B 28
Llundain Fach SA15: Llane . . . .3B 42
Llundainfach SA9: C'bont . . . . .2D 28
Llws Tawel SA9: Ystra . . . . . . .5A 28
Llwyd Rd. SA18: Amm . . . . . . .5H 11
    (shown as Heol Llwyd)
Llwyn Afanc SA6: Cwm'crw . . .1A 60
Llwynant SA18: C'gors . . . . . . .6C 24
Llwyn Arian SA13: Coe H . . . . .2D 112
Llwyn Arosfa SA2: Sket . . . . . .3H 83
Llwyn Bedw CF35: P'coed . . . . .3F 123
  SA5: Ffor F . . . . . . . . . . . .4A 72
Llwyn Brwydrau SA7: L'smlt . . .1H 75
Llwyn Carw SA6: Cwm'crw . . .1A 60
Llwyn Castan CF31: Bri . . . . . .2B 126
Llwyn Derw SA5: Ffor F . . . . . .3A 72
Llwyn Derw SA5: Ffor F . . . . . .3A 72
Llwynderw SA4: Gor . . . . . . . .5A 56
  SA8: Thr X . . . . . . . . . . . .1E 81
  SA8: P'dwe . . . . . . . . . . . .6D 36
Llwynderw Cl. SA3: W Cro . . . .4B 95
Llwynderw Dr. SA3: W Cro . . . .4F 95
Llwyn Derwen CF33: N Cor . . .2C 116
Llwyndu La. SA7: Glais . . . . . . .4B 50
Llwyn Eithin SA5: Ffor F . . . . . .3A 72
Llwyn Glas CF31: Bri . . . . . . . .1A 126
Llwyn Gwern CF35: P'coed . . . .3F 123

Llwyn Helig CF33: Ken H . . . . .6H 113
Llwyn Helyg SA5: Ffor F . . . . . .3A 72
  SA10: Nea . . . . . . . . . . . .4H 63
LLWYNHENDY . . . . . . . . . . . .3G 53
Llwynhendy Rd. SA14: Llwy . . .1F 53
Llwyn Hen Rd. SA18: C'gors . . .5C 24
Llwynifan SA14: L'nch . . . . . . .2B 44
Llwyn Mawr Cl. SA2: Sket . . . .2G 83
Llwyn Mawr La. SA2: Sket . . . .1G 83
  SA4: Gow . . . . . . . . . . . . .3F 69
Llwynmawr Rd. SA2: Sket . . . .1G 83
Llwyn Meredith SA31: Carm . . .1F 7
    (shown as Llwyn Meredydd)
Llwyn Meredydd SA31: Carm . .1F 7
Llwyn On CF33: N Cor . . . . . . .1D 116
Llwynon SA6: Cly . . . . . . . . . . .3F 49
  SA10: Cry . . . . . . . . . . . . .5H 33
Llwyn Onn SA5: Ffor F . . . . . . .3A 72
Llwyn Rhedyn SA2: Sket . . . . . .2G 83
Llwyn Rhosyn SA18: C'gors . . . .4D 24
Llwyn Teg SA5: Ffor F, Por . . . .2H 71
Llwynwhilwg Ter.
  SA14: Llane . . . . . . . . . . .2C 52
Llwyn y Bioden
  SA6: Cwm'crw . . . . . . . . .1A 60
LLwyn-y-Bryn SA18: Amm . . . .4H 11
Llwyn-y-Bryn SA18: Amm . . . .4H 11
  SA10: Skew . . . . . . . . . . . .2B 76
Llwyn-y-Garth SA4: P'dul . . . . .6H 35
Llwyn y Gog SA6: Cwm'crw . . .1A 60
Llwyn-y-Golomen
  SA6: Cwm'crw . . . . . . . . .1B 60
Llwyn y Graig SA4: Gor . . . . . .5E 57
Llwyn y Groes CF31: Bri . . . . . .1A 126
Llwyn-y-Mor SA3: Casw . . . . . .2C 100
Llwyn yr Eos SA14: Llane . . . . .6E 43
  SA31: Carm . . . . . . . . . . .2C 6
Llwyn-yr-Eos SA6: Morr . . . . . .4H 59
  SA14: Cross H . . . . . . . . . .2E 19
Llwyn yr Hebog
  SA6: Cwm'crw . . . . . . . . .1B 60
Llwyn yr Iar SA6: Cwm'crw . . .1A 60
Llwyn yr Ynys SA14: Llwy . . . .2F 53
Llygad-yr-Haul SA10: Nea . . . . .4H 63
Llyn Cyan SA16: Pem . . . . . . . .2A 38
  SA31: Carm . . . . . . . . . . .5G 7
Llynfa Rd. SA4: Penc . . . . . . . .4B 68
Llynfi La. CF31: Bri . . . . . . . . . .1E 127
Llynfi St. CF31: Bri . . . . . . . . . .1E 127
  SA10: Nea . . . . . . . . . . . .4B 114
Llyn Llech Owain Country Pk.
  Vis. Cen. . . . . . . . . . . . . .1D 8
Llyn Tircoed SA4: Tir V . . . . . . .1H 57
Llys Aaron SA4: P'dul . . . . . . . .6F 35
Llys Ael y Bryn SA7: Birch . . . .4G 61
Llys Alys SA15: Llane . . . . . . . .1B 52
Llys Andrew SA10: Skew . . . . . .2E 77
Llys Aneirin SA4: Gor . . . . . . . .6C 56
Llys Ariandy SA1: Swan . . . . . .4F 5
Llys Arthur SA15: Llane . . . . . .1A 52
Llys Ashburnham
  SA16: Burr P . . . . . . . . . . .3C 38
Llys Baldwin SA4: Gow . . . . . . .2A 70
Llys Bartlett SA11: Nea . . . . . .1B 78
    (off Victoria Gdns.)
  SA11: Tonna . . . . . . . . . . .4F 65
Llys Bethel SA14: Llwy . . . . . . .1F 53
Llys Briallen CF31: Brack . . . . . .5A 122
Llys Bronallt SA4: Hendy . . . . . .6D 34
Llys Bronwydd CF31: Bri . . . . . .2C 126
Llys Bryngwyn SA14: Dafen . . .5E 43
Llys Brynheulog SA8: P'dwe . . .5C 36
Llys Brynteg SA4: Gor . . . . . . . .3A 56
Llys Cae Glas SA15: Llane . . . . .1A 52
Llys Caermedi SA31: Carm . . . .2G 7
Llys Cambrian SA9: Godr . . . . .5D 32
Llys Caradog SA14: Llwy . . . . . .1G 53
Llys Castell SA13: Coe H . . . . . .1D 112
Llys Cennech SA14: L'nch . . . . .3D 44
Llys Cilsaig SA14: Dafen . . . . . .4E 43
Llys Coed CF31: Bri . . . . . . . . .2B 126
Llys Dewi Sant SA1: Swan . . . .4E 5
  SA4: Gor . . . . . . . . . . . . . .4B 56
Llys Dol SA6: Morr . . . . . . . . . .4B 60
Llys Dulais SA10: Cry . . . . . . . .6H 33
Llys Dur SA6: Morr . . . . . . . . . .4B 60
Llys Dwrgi SA7: Birch . . . . . . . .6A 62
Llys Efail Fach SA13: P Tal . . . .4G 97
    (off Broad St.)
Llys Eglwys CF31: Bri . . . . . . . .2B 126
Llys Eithin SA14: Gors . . . . . . . .4E 9
Llys Elba SA4: Gow . . . . . . . . . .2A 70
Llys Faen CF31: Bri . . . . . . . . .6E 121
Llys Felin SA10: A'dul . . . . . . . .2F 65
Llys Felin Newydd
  SA7: Swan Ent . . . . . . . . .2D 74

Llys Ffynnon—Maesglas Rd.


**Llys Ffynnon** SA31: Carm . . . 2D **6**
**Llys Fitzhamon** CF31: Bri . . . 2B **126**
**Llys Fran** SA15: Llane . . . 5B **42**
**Llys Fredrick Jones**
SA9: Ystra . . . 1F **33**
**Llys Ger y Llan** SA4: P'dul . . . 1C **46**
**Llys Glanrafon** SA8: P'dwe . . . 6D **36**
**Llys Glanymor** SA15: Llane . . . 6H **41**
LLYS GLAS . . . 2E **5** (3G **85**)
**Llys Graig Arw** SA9: Godr . . . 4D **32**
**Llys Groeswen** SA13: P Tal . . . 6H **97**
**Llys Gwalia** SA4: Gor . . . 4C **56**
**Llys Gwenci** SA7: Birch . . . 6A **62**
**Llys Gwernen** SA6: Cwm'crw . . . 4A **60**
**Llys Gwilym** SA6: Cly . . . 3H **49**
**Llys Gwyn** CF31: Bri . . . 5E **121**
SA14: L'nch . . . 5B **44**
**Llysgwyn** SA6: L'flch . . . 4F **59**
**Llys Gwynfaen** SA4: Gor . . . 3G **55**
**Llys Gwynfryn** SA10: B'och . . . 1H **63**
**Llysgwyn Ter.** SA4: P'dul . . . 6G **35**
**Llys Gwyr** SA2: Up K . . . 4B **82**
**Llys Hafan** SA1: Swan . . . 3A **86**
**Llys Hanover** SA31: Carm . . . 2D **6**
**Llys Harry** SA9: Godr . . . 5D **32**
**Llys Hebog** SA7: Birch . . . 6A **62**
**Llys Hendre** SA14: L'nch . . . 5C **44**
**Llys Iris** SA10: Nea . . . 5H **63**
**Llys Jernegan**
SA1: Swan . . . 4G **5** (4H **85**)
**Llys John Davies** SA1: Swan . . . 1E **5**
**Llys Le Breos** SA3: May . . . 3E **95**
**Llys Llwyfen** SA7: L'smlt . . . 5E **61**
**Llys Lotwen** SA18: Cap H . . . 3H **19**
**Llys Mair** SA16: Burr P . . . 3F **39**
**Llys Mieri** SA4: Penl . . . 3G **57**
**Llys Model** SA31: Carm . . . 3D **6**
**Llys Morfa** SA4: P'dul . . . 6F **35**
**Llysmorfa** SA31: Carm . . . 4F **7**
**Llys Nant Fer** SA18: Gwaun . . . 1C **24**
**Llys Nedd** SA10: Nea . . . 4A **64**
**Llysnewydd** SA15: Llane . . . 6H **41**
(not continuous)
**Llysonen Rd.**
SA31: Carm, John . . . 5A **6**
**Llys Parc** SA14: Cef . . . 4B **8**
**Llys Penallt** *SA15: Llane . . . 6C 42*
*(off Swansea Rd.)*
**Llys Pendderi** SA14: Bryn . . . 1A **54**
**Llys Penpant** SA6: L'flch . . . 4E **59**
**Llys Pentre** CF31: Bri . . . 2B **126**
SA5: Man . . . 4G **73**
**Llys Pentrefelen** SA6: L'flch . . . 5E **59**
**Llys Picton** SA31: Carm . . . 3C **6**
**Llys Rhaedr** SA9: Godr . . . 5D **32**
**Llys Royston** SA10: Nea . . . 5H **63**
**Llys Sant Teilo** SA5: L'flch . . . 4E **59**
**Llys Tawe** SA1: Swan . . . 4H **5** (4A **86**)
**Llys Teg** CF31: Bri . . . 2A **126**
**Llys-Teg** SA2: Dunv . . . 2C **82**
**Llys Tregwyr** SA4: Gow . . . 3B **70**
**Llys Tynewydd** CF35: Coity . . . 4H **121**
**Llys Tysant** CF35: Coity . . . 3H **121**
**Llys Uchaf** SA7: Birch . . . 6A **62**
**Llys Warner** SA15: Llane . . . 5B **42**
**Llys Wen** CF31: Bri . . . 2B **126**
**Llys Wenallt** SA11: Tonna . . . 3H **65**
**Llys Wern** SA10: Nea . . . 4H **63**
**Llys Westfa** SA14: F'oel . . . 2D **42**
**Llys y Brenin** SA4: Gor . . . 6H **55**
**Llys y Bryn** CF31: Bri . . . 6C **126**
**Llys-y-Bryn** SA7: Birch . . . 6A **62**
SA14: Llane . . . 6G **43**
**Llys y Coed** SA10: Nea . . . 6A **64**
**Llys-y-Coed** SA4: Lou . . . 5E **55**
SA7: Birch . . . 5A **62**
SA16: Pem . . . 2A **38**
**Llys y Dderwen**
CF35: Coity . . . 3G **121**
SA14: L'nch . . . 5C **44**
**Llys-y-Ddraenog**
SA13: Coe H . . . 2D **112**
**Llys-y-Deri** SA18: Amm . . . 6D **12**
**Llys y Drindod** SA15: Llane . . . 3B **52**
**Llys y Farchnad** SA4: Gow . . . 3B **70**
**Llys y Fedwen** CF35: Coity . . . 2H **121**
**Llys y Felin** SA4: Ffor . . . 4C **34**
SA5: Man . . . 5E **73**
SA14: L'nch . . . 3C **44**
SA15: F'oel . . . 3C **42**
**Llys-y-Fran** CF31: Bri . . . 5A **120**
**Llys y Gof** SA15: Llane . . . 6H **41**
**Llys y Graig** SA6: Morr . . . 5A **60**
**Llys y Llyfrgell** SA16: Burr P . . . 3D **38**
**Llys y Morwr** SA15: Llane . . . 2A **52**
**Llys y Nant** SA7: Glais . . . 6H **49**
SA18: L'bie . . . 1F **11**
SA31: Carm . . . 2E **7**
**Llys Ynyscedwyn** SA9: Ystra . . . 6G **27**
**Llys Ynysgeinon** SA9: Godr . . . 5D **32**
**Llys y Pinwydd** SA14: Llane . . . 6G **43**
**Llys y Plas** CF31: Bri . . . 2C **126**
**Llys y Pobydd** *SA15: Llane . . . 1B 52*
*(off Bigyn Rd.)*
**Llys yr Afon** SA9: Godr . . . 5D **32**
**Llys yr Ardd** SA6: Morr . . . 4B **60**
**Llys yr Hen Felin** SA15: Llane . . . 6A **42**
**Llys yr Onnen** CF35: Coity . . . 2H **121**
SA14: Dafen . . . 4D **42**
**Llys yr Orsaf** SA15: Llane . . . 5H **41**
**Llys yr Ysgol** SA18: Saron . . . 1B **20**
**Llys Ystrad** SA31: John . . . 6B **6**
**Llys-y-Waun** SA7: Birch . . . 5A **62**
**Llys y Wennol** CF35: Coity . . . 2G **121**
**LLys y Werin** SA4: Gor . . . 4H **55**
**Llythrid Av.** SA2: Upl . . . 4B **84**
**Lock Hill** SA11: Tonna . . . 4E **65**
**Lock's Comn. Rd.**
CF36: P'cwl . . . 4A **124**
**Lock's Ct.** CF36: P'cwl . . . 3C **124**
**Lockside** SA1: Swan . . . 5G **5** (4H **85**)
**Lock's La.** CF36: P'cwl . . . 4A **124**
(not continuous)
**Lodge, The** SA11: Nea . . . 3A **78**
**Lodge Cl., The** SA2: Sket . . . 3F **83**
**Lodge Ct.** SA11: Brit F . . . 6H **77**
**Lodge Dr.** SA12: Bag . . . 4A **90**
**Login Rd.** SA5: Wauna . . . 5F **71**
**Lombard Cl.** CF36: Not . . . 2B **124**
**Lombard St.** SA11: Nea . . . 2A **78**
(not continuous)
**Lombardy Vs.** SA10: Nea . . . 5B **64**
**Lon Aber** SA15: Llane . . . 2C **52**
**Lon Alfa** SA2: Kill . . . 2E **83**
**Lôn Bedwen** SA2: Sket . . . 2H **83**
**Lon Beili Glas** SA18: Gwaun . . . 3D **24**
**Lon Brydwen** SA4: Gor . . . 5A **56**
**Lon Brynawel** SA7: L'smlt . . . 1G **75**
**Lon Bryngwyn** SA2: Sket . . . 2B **84**
**Lon Bryn-Mawr** SA18: Amm . . . 6H **11**
**Lon Brynteg** SA10: Nea . . . 5H **63**
**Lon Cadog** SA2: Sket . . . 3A **84**
**Lon Cae Banc** SA2: Sket . . . 3A **84**
**Lon Camlad** SA6: Morr . . . 6H **59**
**Lon Caron** SA2: Sket . . . 3B **84**
**Lon Carreg Bica** SA7: Birch . . . 6A **62**
**Lon Catwg** SA8: Gell . . . 5G **37**
**Lon Cedwyn** SA2: Sket . . . 3B **84**
**Lon Ceiriog** SA14: Llwy . . . 1G **53**
**Lon Claerwen** SA6: Morr . . . 6H **59**
**Lon Coed Bran** SA2: C'ett . . . 2B **84**
**Lon Coed Parc** SA2: C'ett . . . 2B **84**
**Lôn Conduit** *SA31: Carm . . . 3E 7*
*(off King St.)*
**Lon Cothi** SA2: C'ett . . . 1A **84**
**Lon Cwmgwyn** SA2: Sket . . . 2B **84**
**Lon Cynfor** SA2: Sket . . . 3B **84**
**Lon Cynlais** SA2: Sket . . . 3A **84**
**Lon Dan-y-Coed** SA2: C'ett . . . 2B **84**
**Londeg** SA8: P'dwe . . . 4C **36**
**Lôn Derw** SA2: Sket . . . 2H **83**
**London Cl.** SA12: C'avon . . . 6G **91**
(not continuous)
**London Rd.** SA11: Nea . . . 1B **78**
**London Row** SA12: C'avon . . . 6G **91**
**London Ter.** SA12: C'avon . . . 6G **91**
**Lôn Draenen** SA2: Sket . . . 3H **83**
**Lon Draenog** SA6: Cwm'crw . . . 1A **60**
**Lone, The** SA6: Cly . . . 2D **48**
**Lone Cotts., The** SA6: Cly . . . 2D **48**
**Lon Einon** SA4: Penl . . . 4E **57**
**Lon Eithrym** SA6: Cly . . . 4E **49**
**Lon Enfys** SA7: L'smlt . . . 2E **75**
**Lone Rd.** SA6: Cly . . . 2D **48**
**Long Acre** CF33: N Cor . . . 1B **116**
SA3: Mur . . . 6A **94**
**Longacre** CF31: Bri . . . 2H **127**
**Long Acre Ct.** CF36: Not . . . 1A **124**
SA3: Bishop . . . 6A **94**
**Long Acre Dr.** CF36: Not . . . 1B **124**
**Long Acre Gdns.** SA3: May . . . 3E **95**
**Long Acre Rd.** SA31: Carm . . . 2E **7**
**Lon Gaer** SA4: Penl . . . 4E **57**
**Lon Ger-y-Coed** SA2: C'ett . . . 2B **84**
SA18: Amm . . . 6D **12**
**Longfellow Dr.** CF31: Bri . . . 5C **120**
**Longfields** SA3: W Cro . . . 5F **95**
**Longford Ct.** SA10: Nea A . . . 4F **63**
**Longford Cres.** SA1: St T . . . 3B **86**
**Longford La.** SA10: Nea A . . . 5F **63**
**Longford Rd.**
SA10: B'och, Nea A . . . 4G **63**
**Longland La.** SA13: Marg . . . 5H **103**
**Longlands Cl.** CF33: Pyle . . . 5E **113**
**Lon Glynfelin** SA10: Nea A . . . 5G **63**
**Long Mdw.** CF33: N Cor . . . 6B **112**
**Long Oaks Av.** SA2: Upl . . . 4B **84**
**Long Oaks Ct.** SA2: Sket . . . 3B **84**
**Long Oaks M.** SA2: Sket . . . 3B **84**
**Long Ridge** SA1: M'hill . . . 1F **85**
**Long Row** SA15: F'oel . . . 3C **42**
SA15: Llane . . . 6B **42**
**Long Shepherds Dr.**
SA3: Casw . . . 1B **100**
**Long St.** SA9: Ystra . . . 3C **28**
**Longview Ct.** SA6: Clase . . . 6G **59**
**Long Vw. Rd.** SA6: Clase . . . 4G **59**
**Long Vue Rd.** SA12: Sand . . . 1B **96**
**Lon Gwendraeth** SA6: Morr . . . 6H **59**
**Lon Gwesyn** SA7: Birch . . . 5H **61**
**Lon Gwynfryn** SA2: Sket . . . 3B **84**
**Lon Hafren** SA6: Morr . . . 6H **59**
**Lon Heddwch** SA6: Craig-p . . . 2C **48**
SA7: L'smlt . . . 2F **75**
**Lon Heulog** CF32: B'myn . . . 3C **114**
SA12: Bag . . . 5A **90**
**Lon Hir** SA8: All . . . 6E **37**
SA31: Carm . . . 2D **6**
**Lon Illtyd** SA2: Sket . . . 3B **84**
**Lôn Iorwg** SA2: Sket . . . 3H **83**
**Lôn Irfon** SA2: C'ett . . . 1A **84**
**Lon Ithon** SA6: Morr . . . 6H **59**
**Lon Killan** SA2: Dunv . . . 2B **82**
LON-LAS . . . 6H **61**
**Lonlas Av.** SA10: Skew . . . 1B **76**
**Lonlas Bus. Pk.** SA10: Skew . . . 6C **62**
**Lonlas Vs.** SA10: Skew . . . 1B **76**
**Lon Llwyd** SA18: Glan . . . 4C **14**
**Lon Llys Havard** SA18: Amm . . . 3B **22**
**Lon Mafon** SA2: Sket . . . 3A **84**
**Lôn Masarn** SA2: Sket . . . 2H **83**
**Lôn Mefus** SA2: Sket . . . 2H **83**
**Lon Menai** SA7: Birch . . . 5H **61**
**Lon Nedd** SA6: Morr . . . 6H **59**
**Lon Ogwen** SA7: Birch . . . 5H **61**
**Lon Olchfa** SA2: Sket . . . 4F **83**
**Lon Parc Henri** SA18: Amm . . . 4H **11**
**Lon Penfro** SA6: Cwm'crw . . . 2B **60**
**Lon Penpownd** SA18: Glan . . . 4H **13**
**Lon Pen y Coed** SA2: C'ett . . . 1A **84**
**Lon Sawdde** SA6: Morr . . . 6H **59**
**Lon Sutcliffe La.** SA4: Gow . . . 3A **70**
**Lon Tanyrallt** SA8: All . . . 1D **50**
**Lon Tanywen** SA9: Ysta . . . 1E **33**
**Lôn Teify** SA2: C'ett . . . 1B **84**
**Lon Tir-y-Dail** SA18: Amm . . . 6G **11**
**Lôn Towy** SA2: C'ett . . . 1A **84**
**Lon ty Cwm** SA31: John . . . 5A **6**
**Lon Ty'r Haul** SA7: L'smlt . . . 1G **75**
**Lon Waunhwyad** SA18: Glan . . . 3A **14**
**Lon-y-Bugail** CF31: Bri . . . 5A **120**
**Lon-y-Cariadon** CF33: N Cor . . . 6D **112**
**Lon y Cob** SA4: Gow . . . 2H **69**
**Lon-y-Coed** CF31: Bri . . . 5A **120**
SA8: P'dwe . . . 4C **36**
**Lon y Dail** SA1: Por T . . . 3C **86**
**Lon y Dderwen** SA15: Llane . . . 3B **42**
**Lon y Derwydd** SA18: Garn . . . 4E **15**
**Lon y Felin** SA4: Gor . . . 3B **56**
SA18: Amm . . . 5G **21**
**Lon y Grug** SA10: L'dcy . . . 4B **76**
**Lon-y-Gruglas** SA18: Amm . . . 2E **21**
**Lon y Maes** SA14: Llane . . . 6E **43**
**Lon y Plas** SA31: John . . . 6B **6**
**Lon yr Ardd** CF35: Coity . . . 2H **121**
**Lon-yr-Eglwys** SA14: F'oel . . . 2D **42**
**Lon yr Helyg** CF35: Coity . . . 3G **121**
**Lon yr Ysgol** SA8: Rhos . . . 1G **51**
SA14: L'nch . . . 5D **44**
**Lon-yr-Ysgol** SA14: Dafen . . . 5D **42**
**Lon-y-Wern** SA8: All . . . 1E **51**
**Lord Nelson Ho.** SA1: Swan . . . 1E **5**
**Lorraine Cl.** SA12: Sand . . . 3C **96**
Lougher Castle (remains of) . . . 6D **54**
**Lougher Gdns.** CF36: P'cwl . . . 5B **124**
**Lougher Pl.** CF33: N Cor . . . 2C **116**
**Lougher Row** CF36: Not . . . 2C **124**
LOUGHOR . . . 5F **55**
Loughor Boating Club . . . 5D **54**
**Loughor Comn.** SA4: Gor . . . 4A **56**
**Loughor Rd.** SA4: Gor . . . 6H **55**
**Low Brynneuadd**
SA18: Lwr B . . . 6G **15**
**Lwr. Banwell St.** SA6: Morr . . . 6A **60**
LOWER BRYNAMMAN . . . 5H **15**
**Lwr. Colbren Rd.**
SA18: Gwaun . . . 2C **24**
**Lwr. Cross Rd.** SA15: Llane . . . 1C **52**
LOWER CWM-TWRCH . . . 5F **27**
**Lwr. Dell, The** SA15: Llane . . . 2H **41**
**Lwr. Llansantffraid Rd.**
CF32: Sarn . . . 5C **114**
**Lower Pantteg** SA9: Ysta . . . 4D **32**
LOWER SKETTY . . . 1G **95**
**Lwr. Station Rd.** SA18: Garn . . . 5D **14**
**Lwr. Trostre Rd.** SA15: Llane . . . 4C **52**
**Lwr. Wern Rd.** SA9: Ysta . . . 2E **33**
**Lwr. West End** SA13: P Tal . . . 6H **97**
**Lucana Bldgs.** *SA13: P Tal . . . 5H 97*
*(off Talcennau Rd.)*
**Lucas Rd.** SA7: Glais . . . 1H **61**
**Lucy Rd.** SA10: Skew . . . 1C **76**
**Lundy Cl.** CF36: Not . . . 2B **124**
**Lundy Dr.** SA3: W Cro . . . 5E **95**
LUNNON . . . 4A **92**
**Lunnon Cl.** SA3: Park . . . 4A **92**
**Lupin Cl.** SA12: Sand . . . 1B **96**
**Luton Ter.** SA15: Llane . . . 2H **41**
**Lydbrook Ct.** SA1: Swan . . . 6F **73**
**Lydford Av.** SA1: St T . . . 1H **5** (2H **85**)
**Lye Ind. Est.** SA4: P'dul . . . 3G **35**
**Lynden** SA9: Cwm I . . . 5G **27**
**Lynn St.** SA5: Cwmb . . . 6E **73**
**Lynsdale Rd.** SA5: Man . . . 4F **73**
**Lynton Ct.** SA3: Newt . . . 6D **94**
Lyric Theatre & Cinema, The . . . 3E **7**


## M


**Mabon Cl.** SA4: Gor . . . 3G **55**
**McArthur Glen Designer Outlet**
**Village** CF32: Pen-ca . . . 1E **121**
**Macdonald Av.** CF35: P'coed . . . 4G **123**
MACHYNYS . . . 5B **52**
**Machynys Link Rd.**
SA15: Llane . . . 2D **52**
Machynys Peninsula Golf and
Country Club . . . 5C **52**
**Machynys Rd.** SA15: Llane . . . 6A **52**
**McKays** SA18: L'bie . . . 3G **11**
**Mackworth Ct.** SA1: Swan . . . 2E **5**
**Mackworth Dr.** SA11: Cim . . . 2F **79**
**Mackworth Rd.** CF36: P'cwl . . . 5D **124**
**Mackworth St.** CF31: Bri . . . 6E **121**
**Mackworth Ter.**
SA1: St T . . . 2H **5** (3H **85**)
**McRitchie Pl.** SA5: Gen . . . 5C **72**
**Maddison Ho.** SA1: Swan . . . 2E **5**
**Maddocks Pl.** CF31: Bri . . . 2E **127**
**Madoc Cl.** CF31: Brack . . . 6F **121**
**Madoc Pl.** SA1: Swan . . . 4C **4** (4F **85**)
**Madoc St.** SA1: Swan . . . 5C **4** (4F **85**)
**Maen Cotts.** SA10: B'och . . . 1G **63**
**Maen Gwyn** SA8: Cilm . . . 1H **37**
**Maenol Glasfryn** SA14: L'nch . . . 5C **44**
**Maenor Helyg** SA16: Pem . . . 2A **38**
**Maerdy Pk.** CF35: P'coed . . . 5G **123**
**Maerdy Rd.** SA18: Amm . . . 5H **21**
**Maes Alarch** SA9: Ysta . . . 1F **33**
**Maes-Ar-Ddafen Rd.**
SA14: Llane, Llwy . . . 3F **53**
(not continuous)
**Maes Briallu** SA7: L'smlt . . . 1G **75**
**Maes Bryn** CF31: Bri . . . 5A **120**
**Maes-Canner Rd.**
SA14: Dafen . . . 5E **43**
**Maes Collen** SA6: Cwm'crw . . . 3A **60**
**Maes Conwy** SA14: Llane . . . 6E **43**
**Maescynog** SA9: Ystra . . . 5A **28**
**Maes Dafydd** SA4: Gor . . . 6A **56**
**Maes De Braose** SA4: Gor . . . 6A **56**
**Maes Deri** SA1: Wins . . . 3E **75**
**Maesderi** SA4: Hendy . . . 6C **34**
**Maes Derwen** *SA14: Cross H . . . 6F 9*
*(off Heol y Llew Du)*
**Maes Dewi** SA31: Carm . . . 3A **6**
**Maes Gamage** CF35: Coity . . . 3G **121**
**Maes Gareth Edwards**
SA18: Gwaun . . . 6G **15**
**Maes Glas** CF32: Cef C . . . 1C **118**
CF32: Ton . . . 4D **114**
SA4: Gor . . . 5A **56**
**Maesglas** CF31: Bri . . . 6A **120**
CF33: Pyle . . . 5F **113**
SA12: C'avon . . . 5G **91**
SA14: Pen g . . . 6H **9**
**Maesglas Rd.** SA5: Gen . . . 5D **72**
*SA14: Pen g . . . 6H 9*
*(shown as Maesglas)*


A-Z Swansea 147

Maes Golau—Memorial Sq.


**Maes Golau** SA15: Llane . . . . . . 4C **42**
**Maesgrenig** SA18: Glan . . . . . . 5H **13**
**Maes Gwair** CF31: Bri . . . . . . 5A **120**
**Maes Gwyn** *CF31: Bri . . . . . . 2C **126***
*(off Careg Llwyd)*
SA10: A'dul . . . . . . 3E **65**
**Maesgwyn Dr.** SA4: P'dul . . . . . . 6F **35**
**Maesgwyn Rd.** SA4: P'dul . . . . . . 6F **35**
**Maesgwyn St.** SA12: Sand . . . . . . 4D **96**
**Maes Hafen** CF31: Bri . . . . . . 2C **126**
**Maes Lan** SA7: L'smlt . . . . . . 2G **75**
**Maeslan** SA8: Rhos . . . . . . 1G **51**
**Maes Lewis Morris**
SA31: Carm . . . . . . 5F **7**
**Maes Llan** CF33: Ken H . . . . . . 5G **113**
**Maes Llewelyn** SA18: Glan . . . . . . 5H **13**
**Maes-Llewelyn** SA31: Carm . . . . . . 2F **7**
**Maes Lliedi** SA15: Llane . . . . . . 4C **42**
**Maesllwyn** SA18: Amm . . . . . . 4G **11**
**Maes Llwynonn** SA10: C'dxtn . . . 5B **64**
**Maes Llysteg** CF31: Bri . . . . . . 2B **126**
**Maes Maddock** SA4: Gor . . . . . . 5A **56**
**Maes Mawr Rd.** SA10: Cry . . . . . . 6H **33**
**Maes Meillion** SA7: L'smlt . . . . . . 1G **75**
**Maesmelyn St.** SA13: Marg . . . 1E **103**
**Maes Morrison** SA4: P'dul . . . . . . 2C **46**
**Maes Penrhyn** SA14: Llane . . . . . . 6E **43**
**Maespiode** SA18: L'bie . . . . . . 1E **11**
**Maesquarre Rd.** *SA18: Amm . . . 6C **12***
*(shown as Ffordd Maescwarrau)*
**Maes Rhedyn** SA12: Bag . . . . . . 4A **90**
**Maes Rhosyn** SA8: Rhos . . . . . . 1G **51**
**Maes Rd.** *SA14: L'nch . . . . . . 4D **44***
*(shown as Heol Maes)*
**Maes Roan** SA14: Gors . . . . . . 5D **8**
**Maes Sant Teilo** SA5: L'flch . . . . . . 4E **59**
**Maes St.** SA1: St T . . . . . . 3A **86**
**Maes Talcen** CF31: Brack . . . . . . 6G **121**
**Maes Tal Coed** CF31: Bri . . . . . . 2B **126**
**Maes Teg** SA4: P'dul . . . . . . 5G **35**
**Maesteg Rd.**
CF32: Ton, Coyt . . . . . . 2B **114**
**Maesteg St.** SA1: St T . . . . . . 2H **85**
**Maesteg Ter.** CF36: P'cwl . . . . . . 4D **124**
**Maestir** SA15: Llane . . . . . . 5C **42**
**Maes Trawscoed** CF31: Bri . . . 2B **126**
**Maestref** SA15: Llane . . . . . . 4C **42**
**Maes ty Canol** SA12: Bag . . . . . . 4B **90**
(not continuous)
**Maes ty Cwrdd** SA14: Llwy . . . . . . 2G **53**
**Maes ty Gwyn** SA14: L'nch . . . . . . 3D **44**
**Maeswerdd** SA15: Llane . . . . . . 4C **42**
**Maesybedol** SA18: Garn . . . . . . 4D **14**
**Maes y Berllan**
SA18: Amm . . . . . . 3A **22**
**Maesybont** SA18: Glan . . . . . . 4H **13**
**Maes y Bont Rd.**
SA14: Gors, Maes . . . . . . 2F **9**
**Maes y Bryn** SA14: Bryn . . . . . . 6A **44**
**Maes-y-Bryn** SA6: Morr . . . . . . 4A **60**
**Maes y Cadno** CF35: Coity . . . . . . 2G **121**
**Maes y Capel** *SA31: Carm . . . . . . 3E **7***
*(off Myrddin Cres.)*
**Maes-y-Capel** SA16: Pem . . . . . . 2B **38**
**Maes-y-Celyn** SA4: Thr X . . . . . . 1E **81**
**Maes-y-Coed** SA4: Gor . . . . . . 6H **55**
SA6: Morr . . . . . . 4A **60**
SA9: Ystra . . . . . . 1F **33**
SA15: Llane . . . . . . 3G **41**
**Maesycoed** SA18: Amm . . . . . . 6D **12**
**Maesycoed Rd.** SA8: Cilm . . . . . . 1H **37**
**Maes y Cornel** SA8: Rhos . . . . . . 1F **51**
**Maes y Cwm** SA9: Ystra . . . . . . 5A **28**
**Maes-y-Cwrt Ter.** *SA13: P Tal . . . 5H **97***
*(off Talbot Rd.)*
**Maes-y-Dail** SA18: Amm . . . . . . 6E **11**
**Maes-y-Darren** SA9: Ysta . . . . . . 2F **33**
**Maes-y-Dderwen** SA6: L'flch . . . 4E **59**
SA7: L'smlt . . . . . . 2H **75**
SA31: Carm . . . . . . 4C **6**
**Maesydderwen** SA14: L'nch . . . 3E **45**
**Maes y Dderwen Gdns.**
SA9: Ystra . . . . . . 1H **33**
**Maes y Deri** SA7: L'smlt . . . . . . 5E **61**
SA18: Bry . . . . . . 4A **16**
**Maes-y-Deri** SA4: Gow . . . . . . 3H **69**
SA10: Cilf . . . . . . 1E **65**
**Maes-y-Deri Cl.**
CF35: P'coed . . . . . . 3F **123**
**Maes y Drindod** *SA12: Sand . . . 2B **96***
*(shown as Holy Trinity Pl.)*
**Maes y Fedwen** CF31: Bri . . . 3B **126**
SA6: Cwm'crw . . . . . . 3A **60**
**Maes-y-Felin** SA5: Rav . . . . . . 3A **72**
CF31: Bri . . . . . . 4D **120**
**Maes-y-Ffynnon Cl.**
SA11: Nea . . . . . . 2B **78**
**Maes y Fron** SA18: Garn . . . . . . 5C **14**
**Maes y Glenyn** SA4: Penc . . . . . . 5A **68**
**Maes y Glyn** SA18: Lwr B . . . . . . 4H **15**
**Maes-y-Glyn** SA18: Glan . . . . . . 4H **13**
**Maes y Gollen** SA2: Sket . . . . . . 4G **83**
**Maes y Gorof** SA9: Cwm I . . . . . . 6H **27**
**Maes y Gors** SA14: Pen g . . . . . . 5F **9**
SA15: Llane . . . . . . 2A **52**
**Maes y Gruffydd Rd.**
SA2: Sket . . . . . . 2H **83**
**Maes y Grug** CF31: Bri . . . . . . 2B **126**
**Maes y Gwernen Cl.**
SA6: Cwm'crw . . . . . . 2H **59**
**Maes y Gwernen Ct.**
SA6: Pantl . . . . . . 2H **59**
**Maes y Gwernen Dr.**
SA6: Cwm'crw . . . . . . 2H **59**
**Maes y Gwernen Rd.**
SA6: Cwm'crw . . . . . . 2H **59**
**Maes y Meillion** SA14: Gors . . . . . . 2F **9**
**Maes-y-Meillion** SA10: Nea . . . 4H **63**
**Maes y Parc** SA5: Rav . . . . . . 3A **72**
**Maes-y-Parc** SA12: C'avon . . . . . . 5H **91**
**Maes-yr-Afon** SA11: Nea . . . . . . 6B **64**
**Maes yr Awel** SA7: L'smlt . . . . . . 1F **75**
**Maes yr Efail** SA2: Dunv . . . . . . 2C **82**
SA4: Gor . . . . . . 5A **56**
SA14: L'nch . . . . . . 5C **44**
**Maes yr Ehedydd** SA31: Carm . . . 2C **6**
**Maes-yr-Eirlys** CF31: Bri . . . . . . 3B **126**
**Maes yr Eithin** CF35: Coity . . . 2F **121**
SA7: Birch . . . . . . 5A **62**
**Maes yr Eos** CF35: Coity . . . . . . 2F **121**
SA3: W Cro . . . . . . 6D **94**
**Maes yr Haf** SA4: Penc . . . . . . 4H **67**
SA7: L'smlt . . . . . . 1F **75**
SA15: Llane . . . . . . 5B **42**
**Maes-yr-Haf** SA18: Amm . . . . . . 6E **11**
**Maesyrhaf** SA14: Cross H . . . . . . 1B **18**
SA15: Pwll . . . . . . 2B **40**
**Maes-yr-Hafod** SA10: C'dxtn . . . 5B **64**
**Maes yr Haf Pl.** SA4: Lou . . . . . . 5H **55**
**Maes-yr-Haf Rd.** CF33: N Cor . . . 2D **116**
SA11: Nea . . . . . . 6B **64**
**Maes-yr-Haul** CF32: B'myn . . . 3D **114**
**Maes-y-Rhedyn** SA10: B'och . . . 4H **63**
(not continuous)
**Maes-yr-Helyg** SA18: L'bie . . . . . . 3G **11**
**Maesyrhendre** SA18: Garn . . . . . . 4D **14**
**Maes yr Onnen**
SA6: Cwm'crw . . . . . . 3B **60**
**Maes yr Ysgall** CF35: Coity . . . 2G **121**
**Maes yr Ysgol** CF33: Ken H . . . 6G **113**
SA8: P'dwe . . . . . . 4D **36**
SA18: Saron . . . . . . 2B **20**
**Maes-yr-ysgol** SA31: Carm . . . . . . 3D **6**
**Maes y Siglen** CF35: Coity . . . 2H **121**
**Maes y Wawr** SA7: Birch . . . . . . 3F **61**
**Maes y Wennol** SA31: Carm . . . . . . 3A **6**
**Maes-y-Werin** SA18: Gwaun . . . 1C **24**
**Maes-y-Wern** CF35: P'coed . . . 3F **123**
**Maesywern Rd.** SA18: Glan . . . 5H **13**
(not continuous)
**Magistrates' Court**
**Port Talbot . . . . . . 4F 97**
**Swansea . . . . . . 2D 4 (3F 85)**
**Maidens Gro.** *SA18: L'bie . . . . . . 2G **11***
*(shown as Gelli Forwyn)*
**Main Av.** CF31: Brack . . . . . . 4G **121**
**Main Rd.** CF35: Coyc . . . . . . 2C **128**
SA10: B'och . . . . . . 1H **63**
SA10: C'dxtn . . . . . . 4C **64**
(Church Rd.)
SA10: C'dxtn . . . . . . 5B **64**
(Maes Llwynonn)
SA10: Cilf . . . . . . 1F **65**
SA10: Cry . . . . . . 6H **33**
SA10: Nea A . . . . . . 6G **63**
**Mainwaring Ter.** SA5: Man . . . . . . 6F **73**
**Major St.** SA5: Man . . . . . . 5F **73**
**Maliphant St.** SA1: Swan . . . . . . 1G **85**
**Mallard Way** CF36: P'cwl . . . . . . 3A **124**
SA7: Swan Ent . . . . . . 4C **60**
**Malt Hall** SA3: Llanr . . . . . . 4C **106**
**Malvern Ter.** SA2: Brynm . . . . . . 5C **84**
**Mandela Av.** CF31: Brack . . . . . . 6A **122**
**Mandinam Pk.** SA2: Sket . . . . . . 3F **83**
**Mannesmann Cl.**
SA7: Swan Ent . . . . . . 1D **74**
**Mannesmann Rd.**
SA6: Swan Ent . . . . . . 3A **74**
**Mannheim Quay**
SA1: Swan . . . . . . 5G **5** (4H **85**)
**Manor Ct.** CF35: Ewe . . . . . . 6D **126**
**Manor Dr.** CF35: Coyc . . . . . . 2C **128**
**Manor Gro.** CF36: Newt . . . . . . 3G **125**
**Manor Rd.** SA5: Man . . . . . . 4E **73**
*SA18: Amm . . . . . . 1G **21***
*(shown as Ffordd y Faenor)*
**Manor St.** SA13: P Tal . . . . . . 4G **97**
**Manor Way** SA11: Brit F . . . . . . 5A **78**
SA31: Llanl . . . . . . 6A **6**
**Mansel Ct.** SA4: Gow . . . . . . 3A **70**
**Mansel Dr.** SA3: Mur . . . . . . 6B **94**
**MANSELFIELD . . . . . . 6B 94**
**Manselfield Rd.** SA3: Mur . . . . . . 5A **94**
**Mansel Rd.** SA1: Bon . . . . . . 5C **74**
**Mansel St.** SA1: Swan . . . 3B **4** (3E **85**)
SA4: Gow . . . . . . 3A **70**
SA11: Brit F . . . . . . 6H **77**
SA13: P Tal . . . . . . 3G **97**
SA15: Llane . . . . . . 2A **52**
SA16: Burr P . . . . . . 2D **38**
SA31: Carm . . . . . . 3E **7**
**Mansel Ter.** SA5: Man . . . . . . 6E **73**
**MANSELTON . . . . . . 5F 73**
**Manselton Rd.** SA5: Man . . . . . . 5E **73**
**Maple Av.** SA12: Bag . . . . . . 3B **90**
**Maple Cl.** SA4: Gor . . . . . . 3H **55**
SA11: Cim . . . . . . 2F **79**
**Maple Cres.** SA2: Upl . . . . . . 3B **84**
SA31: Carm . . . . . . 3B **6**
**Maple Dr.** CF31: Brack . . . . . . 1B **128**
SA5: Wauna . . . . . . 4C **70**
**Maple Gro.** SA2: Upl . . . . . . 4B **84**
**Maple Tree Cl.** SA6: Clase . . . . . . 5G **59**
**Maple Wlk.** CF36: Newt . . . . . . 3H **125**
**Maplewood Cl.** SA10: B'och . . . 2H **63**
**MARBLE HALL . . . . . . 1B 52**
**Marble Hall Rd.**
SA15: Llane . . . . . . 1B **52**
**March Hywel** SA8: Rhos . . . . . . 1H **51**
SA10: Cilf . . . . . . 1E **65**
**Marcroft Rd.** SA1: Por T . . . . . . 3D **86**
**Mardon Pk.** SA12: Bag . . . . . . 4G **89**
**Mardy Trad. Est.** SA4: Gor . . . . . . 6B **56**
**Margain Sq.** SA1: Cry B . . . . . . 4H **87**
**MARGAM . . . . . . 2F 103**
**Margam Av.** SA6: Morr . . . . . . 6B **60**
**Margam Crematorium**
SA13: Marg . . . . . . 6H **103**
**Margam Pk. Est.**
SA13: Coe H . . . . . . 2C **112**
**Margam Pl.** SA15: Llane . . . . . . 2A **52**
**Margam Rd.** SA13: Marg . . . . . . 1E **103**
**Margam Row** CF33: Ken H . . . 4G **113**
**Margaret Rd.** *SA18: L'bie . . . . . . 2F **11***
*(shown as Heol Margaret)*
**Margarets Cl.** SA11: Brit F . . . . . . 1G **89**
**Margaret St.** SA1: St T . . . . . . 3B **86**
SA10: B'och . . . . . . 2H **63**
SA13: P Tal . . . . . . 3H **97**
*SA18: Amm . . . . . . 1H **21***
*(shown as Stryd Marged)*
**Margaret Ter.** SA1: St T . . . . . . 3B **86**
**Marged St.** SA15: Llane . . . . . . 3A **52**
**Maria St.** SA11: Nea . . . . . . 2B **78**
**Marigold Ct.** CF31: Brack . . . . . . 6A **122**
**Marigold Pl.** SA10: Sev S . . . . . . 4G **29**
**Marina Vs.**
SA1: Swan . . . . . . 5H **5** (4H **85**)
**Marina Wlk.**
SA1: Swan . . . . . . 5G **5** (5H **85**)
**Marine Cl.** SA12: Sand . . . . . . 3B **96**
**Marine Dr.** SA12: Sand . . . . . . 2A **96**
**Mariners, The** SA15: Llane . . . . . . 6H **41**
**Mariners Ct.** SA1: Swan . . . . . . 3A **86**
**Mariners Point** SA12: A'von . . . 6D **96**
**Mariners Quay** SA12: A'von . . . 5C **96**
**Mariner St.**
SA1: Swan . . . . . . 1E **5** (2G **85**)
**Marine St.** SA15: Llane . . . . . . 6H **41**
**Marine Ter.** CF36: P'cwl . . . . . . 5C **124**
**Marine Vw.** SA12: Bag . . . . . . 3H **89**
**Marine Wlk.**
SA1: Swan . . . . . . 6E **5** (5G **85**)
**MARITIME QUARTER . . . 5G 5 (4H 85)**
**Maritime Rd.** SA13: P Tal . . . . . . 5G **97**
**Market M.** *SA6: Morr . . . . . . 6A **60***
*(off Globe St.)*
**Market Pct.** *SA15: Llane . . . . . . 1A **52***
*(off Murray St.)*
SA31: Carm . . . . . . 3E **7**
**Market St.** CF31: Bri . . . . . . 1E **127**
SA6: Morr . . . . . . 1A **74**
SA15: Llane . . . . . . 1A **52**
**Marlas Cl.** CF33: Pyle . . . . . . 6E **113**
**Marlas Rd.** CF33: Pyle . . . . . . 6D **112**
**Marlborough Rd.** SA2: Brynm . . . 5C **84**
SA4: Gor . . . . . . 6A **56**
**Marloes Ct.** SA5: P'lan . . . . . . 2C **72**
**Marlpit La.** CF36: P'cwl . . . . . . 2D **124**
**Marsden St.** SA1: Swan . . . . . . 6F **73**
**Marshfield Av.** CF33: Ken H . . . 6E **113**
**Marshfield Rd.** SA11: Nea . . . . . . 2A **78**
**Marsh Rd.** SA3: Llanr . . . . . . 4C **106**
SA4: Llanm, Wern . . . . . . 2E **107**
**Marsh St.** SA12: A'von . . . . . . 3E **97**
SA15: Llane . . . . . . 2A **52**
**Martell St.** SA5: Ffor F . . . . . . 5B **72**
**Martin Rd.** SA15: Llane . . . . . . 2B **52**
**Martin's Row** SA1: St T . . . . . . 1H **85**
**Martin St.** SA6: Cly . . . . . . 5E **49**
SA6: Morr . . . . . . 6A **60**
**Martyn's Av.** *SA10: Sev S . . . . . . 5F **29***
*(shown as Rhodfa Martyn)*
**Martyr's Reach** *SA2: Brynm . . . . 5C **84***
*(off St Alban's Rd.)*
**Mary St.** CF36: P'cwl . . . . . . 5C **124**
SA10: Cry . . . . . . 6H **33**
SA10: Sev S . . . . . . 4G **29**
SA11: Nea . . . . . . 1A **78**
**Mary Twill La.** SA3: Lan . . . . . . 2C **100**
**Masefield M.** CF31: Bri . . . . . . 5C **120**
**Masefield Way** SA2: Sket . . . . . . 4B **84**
**Matrix Pk.** SA6: Swan Ent . . . . . . 3A **74**
**Matthew St.** SA1: Swan . . . . . . 2G **85**
**MAWDLAM . . . . . . 1A 116**
**Mawdlam Way** CF33: N Cor . . . 6B **112**
**Maxime Ct.** SA2: Sket . . . . . . 4A **84**
**Maximin Rd.** SA13: Marg . . . . . . 3F **103**
**MAYALS . . . . . . 3E 95**
**Mayals Av.** SA3: Blk P . . . . . . 3F **95**
**Mayals Grn.** SA3: May . . . . . . 3E **95**
**Mayals Rd.** SA3: Blk P, May . . . 4D **94**
**Mayberry Rd.** SA12: Bag . . . . . . 3A **90**
**May Drew Way** SA11: Brit F . . . 4H **77**
**Mayfield Av.** CF32: Lale . . . . . . 5B **126**
CF36: Newt . . . . . . 4G **125**
**Mayfield St.** SA13: P Tal . . . . . . 4H **97**
**Mayfield Ter.** SA5: Gen . . . . . . 5E **73**
**Mayflower Cl.** SA2: Sket . . . . . . 4G **83**
**MAYHILL . . . . . . 1D 84**
**Mayhill Gdns.** SA1: M'hill . . . . . . 1E **85**
**Mayhill Rd.** SA1: M'hill . . . . . . 1E **85**
**May's Ct.** SA11: Nea . . . . . . 1B **78**
**Maytree Av.** SA3: W Cro . . . . . . 4E **95**
**Maytree Cl.** SA4: Lou . . . . . . 5G **55**
SA6: Clase . . . . . . 6G **59**
**Mead, The** SA2: Dunv . . . . . . 2C **82**
**Meadow Av.** CF33: Ken H . . . . . . 6F **113**
**Meadow Bank** SA10: L'dcy . . . . . . 4C **76**
**Meadow Cl.** CF35: Coyc . . . . . . 1C **128**
SA11: Nea . . . . . . 3A **78**
**Meadowcroft** SA3: S'gate . . . . . . 1A **98**
**Meadowcroft Cl.** SA5: Wauna . . . 4D **70**
**Meadow Dr.** SA4: Gor . . . . . . 4G **55**
**Meadow La.** CF36: P'cwl . . . . . . 3E **125**
**Meadow Rise** CF31: Brack . . . . . . 6F **121**
CF32: B'myn . . . . . . 2F **115**
CF32: Brync . . . . . . 5E **115**
SA1: Town . . . . . . 6B **72**
SA2: Sket . . . . . . 6H **83**
**Meadow Rd.** CF35: P'coed . . . 5G **123**
SA11: Nea . . . . . . 3A **78**
**Meadows, The** CF35: Corn . . . 6G **127**
CF36: P'cwl . . . . . . 4F **125**
SA10: Skew . . . . . . 1D **76**
SA11: Cim . . . . . . 2F **79**
**Meadows Rd.** SA14: Cross H . . . 6C **8**
**Meadow St.** CF31: Bri . . . . . . 6E **121**
CF32: A'knfig . . . . . . 5B **114**
CF33: N Cor . . . . . . 1C **116**
SA1: Town . . . . . . 6C **72**
SA12: C'avon . . . . . . 4H **91**
**Meadow Vw.** SA2: Dunv . . . . . . 2B **82**
SA7: L'smlt . . . . . . 2H **75**
**Meadow Wlk.** CF31: Brack . . . . . . 6F **121**
**Meadow Way** SA5: Wauna . . . . . . 4C **70**
**Mecca Bingo**
**Cwmdu . . . . . . 6D 72**
**Medway Workshops** SA4: Penl . . . 5E **57**
**Megabowl**
**Swansea . . . . . . 3F 5 (3G 85)**
**Megan Cl.** SA4: Gor . . . . . . 3B **56**
**Megan St.** SA5: Cwmdu . . . . . . 6D **72**
**Meini Tirion** CF31: Bri . . . . . . 4A **120**
**Melcorn Dr.** SA3: Newt . . . . . . 1C **100**
**MELINCRYDDAN . . . . . . 2A 78**
**Melrose Cl.** SA6: Swan Ent . . . . . . 1C **74**
**Melton Dr.** CF31: Bri . . . . . . 3D **126**
**Melyn Cl.** SA11: Nea . . . . . . 3H **77**
**Memorial Sq.** SA16: Burr P . . . . . . 3E **39**


148 A-Z Swansea

Mendip Cl. SA5: Ffor F . . . . .5A 72
Mercies, The CF36: P'cwl . . . . .4E 125
Merfield Cl. CF32: Sarn . . . . .5D 114
Merfield Ho. CF32: Sarn . . . . .5D 114
Merganser Cl. CF36: Not . . . . .3B 124
Meridian Bay
 SA1: Swan . . . . . .6E 5 (5G 85)
MERIDIAN QUAY . . . . . .6D 4 (5F 85)
Meridian Twr.
 SA1: Swan . . . . . .6E 5 (5F 85)
Meridian Wharf
 SA1: Swan . . . . . .6E 5 (5F 85)
Merlin Cl. CF36: P'cwl . . . . . .3B 124
Merlin Cres. CF31: Bri . . . . . .6B 120
 SA1: Town . . . . . . . . . . . .2C 84
Merlin La. SA31: Carm . . . . . .3E 7
Merlin St. SA31: Carm . . . . . .3D 6
Merlin's Wlk. Shop. Cen.
 SA31: Carm . . . . . . . . . . .3D 6
Mermaid's Retreat
 SA3: T Mum . . . . . . . . . .2G 101
Merthyr Mawr Rd. CF31: Bri . .3C 126
 CF32: Bri, M Mawr . . . . . .4B 126
 (not continuous)
Merthyr Mawr Rd. Nth.
 CF31: Bri . . . . . . . . . . . .2E 127
Mervyn Ter. SA12: C'avon . . . . .5F 91
Mervyn Way CF35: P'coed . . . .2E 123
Metropole Chambers
 SA1: Swan . . . . . . . . . . . .4F 5
Mews, The SA11: Nea . . . . . . .1B 78
 (off Windsor Dr.)
 SA12: Sand . . . . . . . . . . .4D 96
Mewslade SA1: M'hill . . . .1C 4 (2F 85)
Mewslade Av. SA3: Blae M . . . .2B 72
Meysydd y Coleg SA31: Carm . . .2C 6
Michaels Fld. SA3: T Mum . . . .2G 101
Michaelstone Ct.
 SA12: C'avon . . . . . . . . . .6G 91
Michaelstone Ter.
 SA12: C'avon . . . . . . . . . .6G 91
Michna St. SA31: A'von . . . . . .3E 97
 (not continuous)
Middlecroft La. SA3: Bishop . . .5G 93
Middle Rd.
 SA5: Cwmb, Cwmdu, Gen
 . . . . . . . . . . . . . . . . . .4C 72
 SA5: Rav . . . . . . . . . . . . .3A 72
MIDDLETON . . . . . . . . . . . . .3D 108
Middleton Ct. CF36: P'cwl . . . .5B 124
Middleton St. SA1: St T . . . . .3A 86
 SA11: Brit F . . . . . . . . . . .1E 75
Midland Ct. SA1: St T . . . .2H 5 (3H 85)
Midland Pl. SA7: L'smlt . . . . . .1E 75
Midland Ter. SA9: Ystra . . . . . .6G 27
Miers St. SA1: St T . . . . .3H 5 (3H 85)
Milborough Ct. SA9: Ysta . . . . .1E 33
 (off Heol Milborough)
Milborough Rd. SA9: Ysta . . . . .2E 33
 (shown as Heol Milborough)
Mile End Cl. SA5: Ffor F . . . . .5C 72
Mile End Row SA11: Nea . . . . .3A 78
Miles La. SA3: Mur . . . . . . . .6B 94
Miles Rd. SA5: Man . . . . . . . .4F 73
Miles St. SA15: Llane . . . . . . .2H 41
Milestone Ct. SA3: Scur . . . . .3H 109
Milford Way SA5: P'lan . . . . . .1C 72
Mill, The SA4: P'dul . . . . . . . .6H 35
Milland Rd. SA11: Nea . . . . . .2A 78
Milland Rd. Ind. Est.
 SA11: Nea . . . . . . . . . . . .2A 78
Millands Cl. SA3: Newt . . . . . .1B 100
Millbank SA10: Nea A . . . . . . .5H 63
Millbank La. SA31: John . . . . . .4A 6
Millbrook SA12: Bag . . . . . . . .5A 90
Millbrook Cres. SA31: Carm . . . .3D 6
Mill Brook Dr. SA7: Swan Ent . .4D 60
Millbrook St. SA6: Plas . . . . . .3G 73
Millbrook Trad. Est.
 SA1: L'ore . . . . . . . . . . . .4G 73
Millennium Coastal Pk.
 Discovery Cen. . . . . . . . . .6G 41
Millers Av. CF32: B'myn . . . . .3E 115
Millers Ct. SA3: Blae M . . . . . .2C 72
Millers Dr. SA4: Gor . . . . . . . .5B 56
Millfield CF31: Bri . . . . . . . . .6D 120
Millfield Cl. SA2: Sket . . . . . . .5G 83
Millfield Rd. SA14: F'oel . . . . .3C 42
Mill Gdns. Mobile Home Pk.
 SA3: Blk P . . . . . . . . . . . .2G 95
Mill La. CF31: Bri . . . . . . . . .6D 120
 SA3: Blk P . . . . . . . . . . . .2F 95
 SA3: Llanr . . . . . . . . . . . .4C 106
 SA15: Llane . . . . . . . . . . .6A 42

Mill Leat La. SA4: Gor . . . . . . .5B 56
Mill Mdw. CF33: N Cor . . . . . .6B 112
Mill Race SA10: Nea A . . . . . . .6G 63
Mill Rd. CF33: Pyle . . . . . . . .6D 112
 SA10: Nea . . . . . . . . . . . .4A 64
Mill Row SA8: All . . . . . . . . . .6E 37
Mill Stream Way
 SA7: Swan Ent . . . . . . . . .4D 60
Mill St. SA4: Gor . . . . . . . . . .4B 56
 SA4: Gow . . . . . . . . . . . .3A 70
 SA4: Penc . . . . . . . . . . . .4A 68
 SA31: Carm . . . . . . . . . . . .4D 6
 (not continuous)
Mill Ter. SA18: Amm . . . . . . . .4F 21
Millwell Vs. SA4: Gow . . . . . . .2A 70
Millwood Ct. SA1: Swan . . . . .6F 73
Millwood Forest Walks . . . . . .2B 110
Millwood Gdns. SA2: Kill . . . . .4E 83
Millwood St. SA5: Man . . . . . .5F 73
Milton Dr. CF31: Bri . . . . . . . .6B 120
Milton Ter. SA1: Swan . .1C 4 (2F 85)
Mincing La. SA15: Llane . . . . . .1A 52
Minerva St. CF31: Bri . . . . . . . .6E 121
Minffrwd Cl. CF35: P'coed . . . .1H 123
Minffrwd Rd.
 CF35: P'coed, Rhiwc . . . . .2H 123
 (not continuous)
Minotaur Way SA1: Swan Ent . . .5A 74
Minster Cl. SA6: Swan Ent . . . .1B 74
Min y Coed SA11: Cim . . . . . . .2E 79
Min-y-Coed CF31: Brack . . . . . .6H 121
Min St. Coe H . . . . . . . . . . .1D 112
Min-y-Don SA3: Marg . . . . . . . .3F 103
Minyffordd SA9: Ysta . . . . . . .2E 33
Min y Mor SA15: Llane . . . . . . .4H 41
Min-y-Nant CF35: P'coed . . . . .3G 123
Min yr Aber SA4: Gor . . . . . . . .3G 55
Min yr Afon SA9: Ysta . . . . . . .3E 33
Minyrafon Rd. SA6: Cly . . . . . .3E 49
Min yr Allt SA10: Nea . . . . . . .4B 64
Min-yr-Awel CF31: Pen F . . . . .3C 120
Min y Rhos SA9: Ystra . . . . . . .3B 28
Mirador Cres. SA2: Upl . . . . . . .4D 84
Misty Hills Cl. SA4: Thr X . . . . .1D 80
Mixen Cl. SA3: Newt . . . . . . . .1D 100
Mona Cl. SA6: Swan Ent . . . . .3B 74
Monastery Bus. Cen.
 SA10: Nea A . . . . . . . . . . .1G 77
Monastery Rd. SA10: Nea A . . . .1G 77
Monger St. SA1: Swan . . . . . . .1G 85
Monk's Cl. CF33: Pyle . . . . . . .5E 113
Monks Cl. SA10: Nea A . . . . . .6H 63
Monksland Rd. SA3: Scur . . . . .3H 109
Monkton Cruising & Sailing Club
 . . . . . . . . . . . . . . . . . .1F 89
Monmouth Ho.
 SA1: Swan . . . . . .4G 5 (4H 85)
Monmouth Pl. SA6: Yfgn . . . . .1B 60
Montana Pl. SA1: L'ore . . . . . . .5G 73
Monterey St. SA5: Man . . . . . .5F 73
Monton Ter. SA1: Por T . . . . . .3B 86
Montpelier Ter.
 SA1: Swan . . . . . . .3A 4 (3E 85)
Monument Hill SA31: Carm . . . .4C 6
MOORE TOWN . . . . . . . . . . . .6D 62
Moorhen Cl. SA7: Swan Ent . . .4C 60
Moorland Av. SA3: Newt . . . . . .6D 94
Moorland Grn. SA4: Gor . . . . . .6B 56
Moorland Rd. SA11: Cim . . . . .2C 78
 SA12: Sand . . . . . . . . . . .4C 96
Moorlands Rd. CF31: Bri . . . . . .3E 127
Moor La. CF36: Not . . . . . . . .6B 116
 SA3: Llang . . . . . . . . . . . .5D 104
Moor Rd. CF31: Bri . . . . . . . . .3B 128
 SA12: Bag, P Tal . . . . . . . .6A 90
Moorside Rd. SA3: W Cro . . . . .5E 95
Moorview Cl. SA5: Gen . . . . . . .4C 72
Moorview Rd. SA5: Gen . . . . . .4C 72
Mor-Awel SA14: Llwy . . . . . . . .1F 53
Morawel SA1: Wins . . . . . . . . .3E 75
MORFA
 SA14 . . . . . . . . . . . . . . .6F 9
 SA15 . . . . . . . . . . . . . . .4B 52
Morfa Afan SA12: Sand . . . . . . .3C 96
Morfa Av. SA13: Marg . . . . . . . .2E 103
Morfa Ind. Est.
 SA1: Swan Ent . . . . . . . . .5H 73
Morfa La. SA31: Carm . . . . . . .4C 6
Morfa Rd. SA1: Swan . . .1F 5 (2G 85)
 SA13: Marg . . . . . . . . . . .3F 103
Morfa Shop. Pk.
 SA1: Swan Ent . . . . . . . . .6E 73
Morfa St. CF31: Bri . . . . . . . . .6E 121
Morfa Ter. SA1: L'ore . . . . . . . .5G 73
Morfydd St. SA6: Morr . . . . . . .6A 60

Morgan Cl. SA4: Penl . . . . . . . .4E 57
Morgan Ct. CF33: N Cor . . . . . .1E 117
Morgan's Ct. SA10: Nea A . . . . .6A 64
Morgannwg Ho. SA12: Sand . . .4B 96
 (off Moorland Rd.)
Morgan Row SA1: Por T . . . . . .3D 86
Morgan's Pl. CF32: Brync . . . . .4F 115
Morgan's Rd. SA11: Nea . . . . . .3H 77
Morgan's Ter. SA11: Brit F . . . . .5H 77
Morgan St. SA1: Swan . . . . . . .6G 73
 SA8: T'nos . . . . . . . . . . . .2B 50
 SA9: Aber . . . . . . . . . . . .1H 29
 SA31: Carm . . . . . . . . . . . .3D 6
Moriah Pl. CF33: Ken H . . . . . .5G 113
Moriah Rd. SA5: Tre b . . . . . . .2F 73
Morlais Rd. SA5: P'lan . . . . . . .3E 73
 SA13: Marg . . . . . . . . . . .2F 103
 SA14: L'nch . . . . . . . . . . .5C 44
Morlan Ter. SA16: Burr P . . . . .3F 39
Morley St. SA31: Carm . . . . . . .3D 6
Morris La. SA1: St T . . . .2H 5 (3H 85)
 SA1: St T, Bon . . . . . . . . . .1B 86
Morrison Ct. SA12: Sand . . . . . .2C 96
Morrison Cres. SA12: Sand . . . .3C 96
Morrison Rd. SA12: Sand . . . . . .3C 96
Morris St. SA6: Morr . . . . . . . .1A 74
Morris Ter. SA5: Ffor F . . . . . . .2G 71
MORRISTON . . . . . . . . . . . . . .1H 7
Morriston Golf Course . . . . . . . .4H 59
MORRISTON HOSPITAL . . . . . .4H 59
Morriston Leisure Cen. . . . . . . .2A 60
Morriston Nth. Ind. Est.
 SA6: Swan Ent . . . . . . . . .5C 60
Morriston Pl. SA18: Tair . . . . . .2E 25
Morriston Sth. Ind. Est.
 SA6: Swan Ent . . . . . . . . .1B 74
 (not continuous)
Morse Row CF32: Brync . . . . . .5E 115
Mostyn Av. SA31: Carm . . . . . . .1H 7
Moulders, The CF32: A'knfig . . .6B 114
Mount, The SA4: Gow . . . . . . .3A 70
 SA6: Plas . . . . . . . . . . . . .2H 73
 SA31: Carm . . . . . . . . . . . .3E 7
Mountain Rd. SA4: Penl . . . . . .4E 57
 SA6: Craig-p . . . . . . . . . . .2C 48
 SA12: A'von . . . . . . . . . . .2F 97
 SA18: Bry . . . . . . . . . . . .3A 16
Mountain Side SA12: A'von . . . .1G 97
Mountain Vw. CF33: N Cor . . . .2D 116
 SA11: Brit F . . . . . . . . . . . .3A 78
Mountbatten Ct. SA5: Rav . . . . .3B 72
 (off Glasbrook Pl.)
Mount Cres. SA4: Penl . . . . . . .4E 57
 SA6: Morr . . . . . . . . . . . .5G 59
Mount Earl CF31: Bri . . . . . . . .3D 126
Mt. Earl Cl. CF31: Bri . . . . . . . .3D 126
Mount Hill Ri. SA31: Carm . . . . .5F 7
MOUNT PLEASANT
 SA1 . . . . . . . . . . .1C 4 (2F 85)
 SA11 . . . . . . . . . . . . . . .2C 78
 SA15 . . . . . . . . . . . . . . .3H 41
Mt. Pleasant CF31: Bri . . . . . . .6H 119
 CF32: A'knfig . . . . . . . . . .6B 114
 SA1: Swan . . . . . .1C 4 (2F 85)
 SA4: Gow . . . . . . . . . . . .3A 70
 SA6: Morr . . . . . . . . . . . .5H 59
 SA7: Glais . . . . . . . . . . . .1H 61
 SA8: P'dwe . . . . . . . . . . .5D 36
 SA11: Tonna . . . . . . . . . . .4F 65
 SA31: Carm . . . . . . . . . . . .5F 7
 (shown as Brynhyfryd)
Mt. Pleasant Bldgs.
 SA15: Llane . . . . . . . . . . .6A 42
Mt. Pleasant Ct. SA10: Skew . . .1D 76
Mt. Pleasant Dr.
 SA1: Swan . . . . .2D 4 (3F 85)
Mount St. SA4: Gow . . . . . . . .3A 70
 SA6: Morr . . . . . . . . . . . .5H 59
Mount Vw. Ter. SA12: A'von . . .3F 97
Mozart Cl. SA12: Sand . . . . . . .1A 96
Mozart St. SA12: Sand . . . . . . .1A 96
Muirfield Dr. SA3: May . . . . . . .3D 94
Mulberry Av. SA3: W Cro . . . . .4E 95
Mulgrave Way SA3: Blk P . . . . .3F 95
MUMBLES . . . . . . . . . . . . . . .1F 101
Mumbles Bay Ct. SA3: Blk P . . .3G 95
Mumbles Bus Station . . . . . . . .1F 101
Mumbles Head SA16: Pem . . . .1A 38
Mumbles Head Pk.
 SA16: Pem . . . . . . . . . . . .1B 38
Mumbles Reach
 SA3: T Mum . . . . . . . . . .2G 101
Mumbles Rd. SA3: Blk P . . . . . .2G 95
 SA3: T Mum . . . . . . . . . . .1F 101
 SA3: T Mum, W Cro . . . . . .6F 95

Murrayfield Cl. SA5: Ffor F . . . .5A 72
Murray St. SA15: Llane . . . . . . .1A 52
Murrays Wlk. CF32: Lale . . . . . .5B 126
MURTON . . . . . . . . . . . . . . . .5A 94
Murton La. SA3: Newt . . . . . . .1B 100
Mwrwg Rd. SA14: L'nch . . . . . .4B 44
 (shown as Heol Mwrwg)
Mydam La. SA4: Gor . . . . . . . .4G 55
Myddfai SA18: Amm . . . . . . . .5H 11
Myddynfych SA18: Amm . . . . . .5H 11
MYNYDD BACH . . . . . . . . . . . .4C 26
MYNYDD BÂCH . . . . . . . . . . . .6F 59
Mynyddbach SA18: Tyc . . . . . .5C 20
MYNYDD-BACH-Y-GLO . . . . . . .4E 71
Mynydd Garnllwyd Rd.
 SA6: Morr . . . . . . . . . . . .1F 73
MYNYDD-GARN-LWYD . . . . . . .1G 73
Mynydd Gelli Wastad Rd.
 SA6: Cly, Pantl . . . . . . . . .1H 59
Mynydd Newydd Rd.
 SA5: P'lan . . . . . . . . . . . .3C 72
Myrddin Ct. SA31: Carm . . . . . .3E 7
Myrddin Cres. SA31: Carm . . . . .2E 7
Myrddin Gdns. SA1: Bon . . . . . .5C 74
Myrddin Rd. SA1: Bon . . . . . . .5C 74
Myrtle Gro. SA2: Sket . . . . . . .3B 84
MYRTLE HILL . . . . . . . . . . . . .6D 6
Myrtle Hill SA4: P'dul . . . . . . . .5F 35
 SA4: Penc . . . . . . . . . . . .4H 67
 SA15: Pwll . . . . . . . . . . . .2D 40
Myrtle Rd. SA4: Gor . . . . . . . . .6C 56
 SA11: Cim . . . . . . . . . . . .2C 78
Myrtle Ter. SA3: T Mum . . . . . .2F 101
 SA15: Llane . . . . . . . . . . .1B 52
Mysydd Rd. SA1: L'ore . . . . . . .5G 73
Mysydd Ter. SA1: L'ore . . . . . . .5G 73

## N

Naiad Rd. SA1: Swan Ent . . . . .5A 74
Nant Arw SA18: Cap H . . . . . . .2H 19
Nant Cadle SA5: Por . . . . . . . .2B 72
Nant Canna CF35: Treoes . . . . .4D 128
Nant Celyn SA10: Cry . . . . . . .4H 33
Nant Dawel SA4: P'dul . . . . . . .5F 35
Nant-Fach SA14: F'oel . . . . . . .2E 43
Nant Ffornwg CF31: Bri . . . . . .5A 120
Nant Glas SA4: Tir V . . . . . . . .1H 57
Nant Gwineu Rd. SA18: Garn . . .5E 5
Nant Lais CF31: Bri . . . . . . . . .6C 120
Nantlais CF35: Corn . . . . . . . .6G 127
 SA9: Cwml . . . . . . . . . . . .5G 17
 SA18: Amm . . . . . . . . . . . .5G 11
Nantong Way SA1: Swan Ent . . .5A 74
 SA7: Swan Ent . . . . . . . . .5A 74
Nantwen SA14: Llwy . . . . . . . .2A 54
Nant y Bryn SA14: Dafen . . . . . .5D 42
Nantybwla SA31: Carm . . . . . . .1A 6
Nant-y-Ci Rd. SA18: Saron . . . . .1C 20
Nant y Clais Ct. SA12: C'avon . . .5F 91
Nant y Creyr SA7: L'smlt . . . . . .6E 61
Nant y Dderwen SA18: Saron . . .1C 20
Nantydd Ter. SA14: Llwy . . . . . .1F 53
Nant y Felin SA5: Ffor F . . . . . .4H 71
Nantyffin Nth. SA7: L'smlt . . . . .2D 74
Nantyffin Rd. SA4: P'dul . . . . . .1C 46
 SA7: L'smlt . . . . . . . . . . . .2D 74
Nantyffin Sth. SA7: L'smlt . . . . .2D 74
Nant-y-Ffynnon CF31: Brack . . .6G 121
Nant y Glyn SA10: Cilf . . . . . . .3E 65
Nant y Glyn Rd. SA18: Glan . . . .4F 13
 (shown as Heol Nantyglyn)
Nant-y-Gro SA14: Llane . . . . . . .6F 43
Nantygro SA14: L'nch . . . . . . . .3C 44
Nant-y-Mynydd SA10: Nea . . . .5H 63
Nant-yr-Adar CF31: Bri . . . . . . .5A 120
Nant-yr-Arian SA31: Carm . . . . .3C 6
Nant y Wennol CF31: Bri . . . . . .2B 126
Nant-y-Wiwer SA13: Coe H . . . .2D 112
Napier Cl. CF31: Bri . . . . . . . .1F 127
Napier Rd. SA4: P'dul . . . . . . . .2C 46
Nash Av. SA31: Carm . . . . . . . .1H 7
Nathan St. SA15: Llane . . . . . . .6H 41
National Waterfront Mus.
 . . . . . . . . . . . . .5F 5 (4G 85)
National Wetland Cen. Wales
 . . . . . . . . . . . . . . . . . .4E 53
National Wetland Cen. Wales
 Vis. Cen. . . . . . . . . . . . . .5F 53
Nautilus Ho. SA1: Swan . . . . . .6F 5
NEATH . . . . . . . . . . . . . . . .6B 64
NEATH ABBEY . . . . . . . . . . . .6G 63
Neath Abbey Blast Furnace . . . .6G 63

Neath Abbey Bus. Pk.—Ormond St.


**Neath Abbey Bus. Pk.**
SA10: Nea A 1F **77**
Neath Abbey (remains of) 1G **77**
**Neath Abbey Rd.**
SA10: Nea A 6G **63**
**Neath Abbey Wharf**
SA10: Skew 3E **77**
Neath Bus Station 1B **78**
Neath Castle 6B **64**
Neath FC 6C **64**
Neath Golf Course 3C **64**
Neath Leisure Cen. 6C **64**
NEATH PORT TALBOT HOSPITAL 3D **96**
NEATH PORT TALBOT HOSPITAL MINOR INJURIES UNIT (MIU) 2D **96**
**Neath Rd.** SA1: L'ore, Swan 1G **85**
SA6: Morr 6B **60** (Crown St.)
SA6: Morr 1A **74** (Morris St., not continuous)
SA6: Morr, Plas 3H **73**
SA8: Rhos 1G **51**
SA9: Ystra 6B **28**
SA10: B'och 6H **51**
SA11: Brit F 5H **77**
SA11: Nea, Tonna 5D **64**
Neath RUFC 6C **64**
Neath Sports Cen. 6H **63**
Neath Station (Rail) 1B **78**
**Neath Valley Ind. Est.**
SA10: Skew 1F **77**
**Nelson St.** SA1: Swan 4D **4** (4F **85**)
**Nelson Ter.** SA15: Llane 5H **41**
**Neon Rd.** SA14: L'nch 4D **44**
**Neptune Apartments**
SA1: Swan Ent 5H **73**
**Neptune Sq.** SA16: Burr P 3E **39**
**Neuadd Rd.**
SA18: Garn, Gwaun 5E **15**
**Neville Rd.** CF31: Bri 3D **126**
CF36: P'cwl 4D **124**
**Nevills Cl.** SA4: Gow 2B **70**
**Nevill St.** SA15: Llane 5H **41**
**Newall Rd.** SA10: Skew 6D **62**
**New Bridge** CF31: Bri 1D **126**
**Newbridge Gdns.** CF31: Bri 3C **126**
**Newbridge Rd.** SA12: A'von 4D **96**
NEWCASTLE 1D **126**
Newcastle Castle 6D **120**
**Newcastle Hill** CF31: Bri 1D **126**
**New Ceidrim Rd.**
SA18: Glan, Garn 5C **14**
**New Cut Rd.**
SA1: Swan 1F **5** (1G **85**)
**New Dock Rd.** SA15: Llane 3A **52**
**New Dock St.** SA15: Llane 4A **52**
**Newgale Cl.** SA5: P'lan 1C **72**
**New Henry St.** SA11: Nea 2A **78**
**New Hill** CF36: P'cwl 4C **124**
**New Inn Rd.** CF32: Bri 3A **126**
CF35: Bri, Ewe 5D **126**
**Newlands** SA12: Bag 5B **90**
**Newlands Av.** CF31: Brack 4F **121**
**Newlands Cl.** CF33: Pyle 5F **113**
**New Mill Rd.** SA2: Sket 4F **83**
**New Mill Ter.** SA7: Swan Ent 6D **60**
**Newnham Cres.** SA2: Sket 3B **84**
**New Orchard St.**
SA1: Swan 1E **5** (2G **85**)
**New Oxford Bldg.** SA1: Swan 4B **4**
**New Pk. Holiday Pk.**
SA3: Port 5H **109**
**New Quarr Rd.** SA5: Tre b 2F **73**
**New Rd.**
CF32: Cef C, Ton 4A **114**
CF33: Ken H 4F **113**
CF36: Newt, P'cwl 5D **124**
SA2: C'ett 1A **84**
SA3: Llanr 4D **106**
SA4: Crof, Llanm, Wern 3E **107**
SA4: Grov 6B **46**
SA4: P'dul 6E **35**
SA5: Tre b 2F **73**
SA7: Birch 4G **61**
SA8: Gell 1G **51**
SA8: T'nos 2A **50**
SA8: Ynys 4E **37**
*SA9: Cwml 1A 26*
*(shown as Heol Newydd)*
SA10: Cilf 1F **65**
SA10: Jer M 2B **88**
SA10: Nea A 1F **77**
SA10: Skew 1D **76**
**New Rd.** SA14: Dafen 5E **43**
SA15: Llane 2H **41**
SA18: Amm 2H **21**
SA18: Bry 3B **16**
SA18: Gwaun 1D **24**
SA18: Gwaun, Tair 1C **24**
**New School Rd.** *SA18: Garn 5C 14*
*(shown as Heol Ysgol Newydd)*
**New St.** CF31: Bri 3G **127**
CF32: A'knfig 5B **114**
SA1: Swan 1E **5** (2G **85**)
SA9: Godr 4D **32**
SA11: Nea 6B **64**
SA11: Tonna 3G **65**
SA12: A'von 3F **97**
SA15: Llane 4B **52**
SA16: Burr P 3E **39**
NEWTON
CF36 3H **125**
SA3 1C **100**
**Newton Av.** SA12: A'von 3E **97**
**Newton Ct.** SA3: Newt 6D **94**
**Newton Nottage Rd.**
CF36: Newt 3E **125**
CF36: Not, P'cwl 2D **124**
**Newton Rd.** SA3: Newt 1C **100**
SA3: T Mum 1E **101**
SA6: Cly 3E **49**
**Newton St.** SA1: Swan 3C **4** (3F **85**)
**Newton Vs.** SA3: Newt 1D **100**
**Newtown** SA5: Man 5F **73**
SA18: Amm 1F **21**
**Newtown Cl.** SA18: Amm 1F **21**
**New Well La.** SA3: Newt 1C **100**
**New Zealand St.** SA15: Llane 3H **41**
**Neyland Dr.** SA5: P'lan 1C **72**
**Nicander Pde.**
SA1: M'hill 1A **4** (2E **85**)
**Nicander Pl.**
SA1: M'hill 1B **4** (2E **85**)
**Nicholas Ct.** SA4: Gor 3B **56**
**Nicholas Rd.** SA7: Glais 6H **49**
NICHOLASTON 2E **111**
**Nicholaston Farm Cvn. Site**
*SA3: Nich 2F 111*
*(off Tor Vw.)*
**Nicholl Ct.** SA3: T Mum 3G **101**
**Nicholls Av.** CF36: P'cwl 4D **124**
**Nicholls Rd.** CF32: Coyt 1B **114**
**Nicholl St.** SA1: Swan 3B **4** (3E **85**)
**Nidum Cl.** SA10: Nea A 6H **63**
**Nightingale Ct.** SA15: Llane 1D **52**
**Nightingale Pk.** SA11: Cim 3D **78**
**Ninth Av.** SA6: Morr 4G **59**
**Nixon Ter.** SA6: Morr 5B **60**
**Nobel Av.** SA12: A'von 2E **97**
**Nolton Arc.** CF31: Bri 1E **127**
Nolton Art Gallery 1E **127**
**Nolton Ct.** SA5: P'lan 2C **72**
**Nolton Pl.** CF31: Bri 2E **127**
**Nolton St.** CF31: Bri 1E **127**
**Norfolk St.** SA1: Swan 2A **4** (3E **85**)
**Normandy Rd.**
SA1: Swan Ent 5H **73**
**Norman Rd.** *SA18: Amm 6G 11*
*(shown as Heol Norman)*
**Norman St.** SA12: A'von 3F **97**
**Northampton La.**
SA1: Swan 3C **4** (3F **85**)
**North Av.** CF33: Ken H 6E **113**
**Nth. Bank Rd.** SA13: P Tal 4E **97**
NORTH CORNELLY 1C **116**
**Nth. Cottage Dr.** SA4: Gor 5A **56**
**Northern Blvd.**
SA6: Swan Ent 3A **74**
**Northeron** SA3: W Cro 4D **94**
**Northgate Bus. Cen.**
SA5: Ffor F 3H **71**
**North Hill Rd.**
SA1: Swan 1C **4** (2F **85**)
**North Hills La.** SA3: Penm 2G **111**
**Northlands Pk.** SA3: Bishop 5H **93**
**North Mead** CF32: Sarn 6D **114**
**North Pde.** SA31: Carm 3F **7**
**North Rd.** CF31: Bri 2G **127**
SA4: Lou 5G **55**
**North St.** SA13: P Tal 5H **97**
**North Ter.** SA14: Dafen 5E **43**
**Northway** SA3: Bishop 5H **93**
**Northway Ct.** SA3: Bishop 5H **93**
**Northways** CF36: P'cwl 4D **124**
NORTON 6F **95**
**Norton Av.** SA3: T Mum 6F **95**
**Norton Dr.** SA3: S'gate 6B **92**
**Norton La.** SA3: S'gate 5B **92**
**Norton Rd.** SA3: T Mum 6F **95**
SA14: Gors, Pen g 4F **9**
NOTTAGE 2B **124**
**Nottage Mead** CF36: Not 1B **124**
**Nottage Mdws.** CF36: Not 1B **124**
**Nottage M.** SA3: Newt 2C **100**
**Nottage Rd.** SA3: Newt 2C **100**
**Notts Gdns.** SA2: Upl 3C **84**
**Nott Sq.** SA31: Carm 3E **7**
**Nurseries, The** SA15: Pwll 3E **41**
**Nursery Gdns.** CF31: Bri 3E **121**
**Nurses Cnr.** SA4: Penc 4A **68**
**Nyanza Ter.** SA1: Swan 4D **84**
**Nythfa** SA4: Tir V 1H **57**

## O

**Oakdene** SA2: Kill 3B **82**
**Oakdene Cl.** SA12: Bag 4B **90**
**Oak Dr.** SA5: Wauna 4C **70**
**Oakengates** CF36: Newt 3G **125**
**Oakfield Rd.** SA8: P'dwe 5D **36**
*SA18: Garn 4D 14*
*(shown as Heol Mas y Dderwen)*
**Oakfield St.** SA4: P'dul 6F **35**
**Oakfield Ter.** *SA18: Amm 6B 12*
*(shown as Teras Maes y Deri)*
**Oakford Pl.** SA5: Por 2A **72**
**Oak Gro.** SA11: Cim 3E **79**
**Oak Hill Pk.** SA10: Skew 6D **62**
**Oak Hill Way** SA8: P'dwe 4D **36**
**Oakland Cl.** SA7: Glais 1H **61**
**Oakland Dr.** SA10: B'och 3H **63**
**Oakland Rd.** SA3: T Mum 1E **101**
**Oaklands** SA13: P Tal 2H **97**
SA14: F'oel 2D **42**
**Oaklands Av.** CF31: Bri 1B **126**
**Oaklands Cl.** CF31: Bri 1C **126**
SA14: Cross H 5D **8**
SA16: Burr P 2C **38**
**Oaklands Ct.** SA3: Blk P 3F **95**
**Oaklands Dr.** CF31: Bri 1C **126**
**Oaklands Mobile Home Pk.**
SA5: Ffor F 3G **71**
**Oaklands Ri.** CF31: Bri 1B **126**
**Oaklands Rd.** CF31: Bri 1A **126**
SA4: P'liw 6F **47**
**Oaklands Ter.**
SA1: Swan 3B **4** (3E **85**)
**Oakleigh Rd.** SA4: Lou 5G **55**
**Oak Ridge** SA2: Sket 4F **83**
**Oaks, The** SA11: Cim 4E **79**
**Oak St.** CF32: A'knfig 5B **114**
SA4: Gor 6C **56**
**Oak Ter.** CF32: Coyt 1B **114**
SA31: Carm 2F **7**
**Oak Tree Av.** SA2: Sket 4H **83**
**Oak Tree Cl.** SA3: W Cro 6D **94**
*SA18: Amm 1C 22*
*(shown as Clos y Dderwen)*
**Oak Tree Ct.** CF31: Brack 6A **122**
**Oaktree Dr.** CF36: Newt 4H **125**
**Oak Tree Way** CF31: Brack 1G **127**
**Oak Way** CF32: Brync 5E **115**
SA4: Penl 4H **57**
**Oakwood Av.** SA6: Clase 5G **59**
**Oakwood Cl.** SA8: Cly 3H **49**
**Oakwood Dr.** SA4: Gow 4B **70**
SA8: Cly 3H **49**
**Oakwood La.** SA13: P Tal 4G **97**
**Oakwood Pl.** SA13: P Tal 3H **97**
**Oakwood Ri.** SA8: Cly 3H **49**
**Oakwood Rd.** SA2: Brynm 5B **84**
SA11: Nea 6C **64**
SA13: P Tal 5G **97**
**Oakwood St.** SA13: P Tal 3G **97**
**Ocean Cres.**
SA1: Swan 6F **5** (5G **85**)
**Ocean Vw.** SA10: Jer M 2B **88**
SA16: Graig 1E **39**
**Ocean Vw. Cl.** SA2: Sket 1G **95**
**Ocean Way** SA12: Sand 3A **96**
**Ochre Wood** SA3: Bishop 1G **99**
**Ochr-y-Waun** SA9: Cwml 6G **17**
**Ochr y Waun Rd.** SA9: Cwml 6F **17**
**Oddfellows St.** CF31: Bri 1E **127**
**Oddfellows' St.** SA9: Ystra 4A **28**
Odeon Cinema
Bridgend 1E **121**
Llanelli 1A **52**
Swansea 3F **5** (3G **85**)
**Odo St.** SA1: Swan 6G **73**
**Office Row** SA9: Ysta 3E **33**
**Ogmore Ct.** CF31: Bri 3C **126**
**Ogmore Cres.** CF31: Bri 2F **127**
**Ogmore Dr.** CF36: Not 1B **124**
**Ogmore Pl.** SA1: Bon 6B **74**
**Ogmore Rd.** CF35: Ewe 6D **126**
**Ogmore Ter.** CF31: Bri 1E **127**
CF32: Brync 3F **115**
**Ogwr Ent. Cen.** C
F32: A'knfig 4B **114**
OLCHFA 3F **83**
**Olchfa Cl.** SA2: Sket 4F **83**
Olchfa Community Sports Cen. 3F **83**
**Olchfa La.** SA2: Sket 4E **83**
**Old Bridge** CF31: Bri 1D **126**
**Old Castle Rd.** SA15: Llane 4H **41**
**Old Church Gdns.**
CF35: Coyc 1C **128**
**Old Colliery Rd.** SA4: Penc 4A **68**
**Old Farm Ct.** SA7: L'smlt 2G **75**
**Old Field Rd.** CF35: P'coed 6G **123**
**Old Foundary Rd.** SA8: P'dwe 5D **36**
**Old Furnace Ho.** *SA11: Nea 3H 77*
*(off Furnace Ter.)*
**Old Kittle Rd.** SA3: Bishop 5G **93**
**Old Lane, The** SA4: Thr X 1F **81**
**Old Llangunnor Rd.**
*SA31: Carm 4E 7*
*(shown as Hen Heol Llangynnwr)*
**Old Llansteffan Rd.**
SA31: John 5C **6**
**Old Lodge Est.** SA15: Llane 2A **52**
**Old Market Pl.** SA12: C'avon 5G **91**
**Old Market St.** SA11: Nea 6B **64**
**Old Oak La.** SA31: Carm 2F **7**
**Old Pk. Rd.** SA13: Marg 1A **112**
**Old Plunch La.** SA3: T Mum 3F **101**
Old Police Station, The (Mus.) 5C **124**
**Old Priory Rd.** SA31: Carm 2F **7**
**Old Prom.** SA12: A'von 5C **96**
**Old Rd.** SA8: Ynys 3F **37**
SA10: Nea A, Skew 1E **77** (not continuous)
SA11: Brit F, Nea 5H **77**
SA12: Bag, Brit F 2H **89**
SA15: Llane 2H **41**
SA18: Amm 5H **11**
**Old St Clears Rd.** SA31: John 4A **6**
**Old School Ct.** CF33: N Cor 2C **116**
**Old School Rd.** CF36: P'cwl 5C **124**
**Old Sheep La.** SA3: Oxw 4B **110**
**Old Station Rd.** CF36: P'cwl 4C **124**
SA31: Carm 4E **7**
**Old Tramway** SA16: Burr P 3E **39** (not continuous)
**Old Village La.** CF36: Not 2C **124**
OLDWALLS 5B **106**
OLDWAY 6A **94**
**Oldway** SA3: Bishop 6H **93**
**Old Wern Rd.** SA9: Ysta 2E **33**
**Olive Branch Cres.**
SA11: Brit F 5G **77**
**Olive Rd.** SA3: W Cro 4E **95**
**Olive St.** SA12: A'von 3E **97**
SA15: Llane 3C **52**
**Olympus Ct.** SA7: Swan Ent 4E **61**
**Onslow Ter.** CF32: B'myn 3C **114**
**Orange St.** SA1: Swan 4D **4** (4F **85**)
**Orchard, The** SA3: Newt 6D **94**
**Orchard Cl.** CF35: P'coed 2H **123**
SA3: Port 5H **109**
SA4: Gor 3A **56**
SA16: Burr P 2C **38**
**Orchard Ct.**
SA1: Swan 1E **5** (2G **85**)
*SA31: Carm 3E 7*
*(off Orchard St.)*
**Orchard Dr.** CF36: Newt 3G **125**
SA4: Thr X 1E **81**
**Orchard Gro.** SA4: Penl 4F **57**
**Orchard Pl.** SA10: Nea A 5G **63**
**Orchard St.**
SA1: Swan 2E **5** (3G **85**)
SA8: P'dwe 5D **36**
SA11: Nea 6B **64**
SA31: Carm 3E **7**
**Orchard Ter.** SA4: Wern 3E **107**
**Orchid Cl.** SA12: Sand 2B **96**
**Orchid Ct.** SA3: W Cro 6D **94**
Oriel Myrddin Gallery *3E 7*
*(off Church St.)*
**Orion Apartments**
SA1: Swan Ent 5H **73**
**Ormes Rd.** SA10: Skew 6C **62**
**Ormond St.** SA11: Brit F 5H **77**


150 A-Z Swansea

Ormsby Ter.—Pen-Cae-Crwn Rd.


**Ormsby Ter.** SA1: Por T . . . . . . . .3B 86
**Orpheus Rd.** SA6: Yfgn . . . . . . . .2C 60
**Osborne Cl.** CF31: Bri . . . . . . . .2E 121
**Osborne Pl.** CF32: B'myn . . . . .3D 114
SA4: Crof . . . . . . . . . . . . . .6E 67
**Osborne St.** SA11: Nea . . . . . . . .1B 78
**Osborne Ter.** SA2: Brynm . . . . . .5C 84
**Osbourne, The** SA3: Lan . . . . . .3D 100
**Oscar Chess Ho.** SA1: Swan . . . .4D 84
**Osprey Bus. Pk.** SA1: L'ore . . . . .4G 73
**Osprey Cl.** SA3: W Cro . . . . . . . .5D 94
SA10: Nea . . . . . . . . . . . . . .4B 64
**Osprey Dr.** SA11: Cim . . . . . . . . .3E 79
**Osprey Ho.** SA1: Swan . . . . . . . . .6B 4
Ospreys RUFC . . . . . . . . . . . . . .4H 73
**Osterley St.** SA1: St T . . . . . . . . .3A 86
SA11: Brit F . . . . . . . . . . . . .6H 77
**Overland Cl.** SA3: T Mum . . . . .2E 101
**Overland Rd.**
SA3: Lan, T Mum . . . . . . . .2E 101
OVERTON . . . . . . . . . . . . . . .5H 109
**Overton Cl.** CF36: Not . . . . . . . .3B 124
**Overton Ct.** SA1: Swan . . . . . . . . .1C 4
**Overton La.** SA3: Port . . . . . . . .5H 109
**Owensfield** SA3: Casw . . . . . . .1A 100
**Owen's La.** SA9: Godr . . . . . . . . .4C 32
**Owens Pl.** SA12: Sand . . . . . . . .3B 96
**Owen's Row** SA11: Brit F . . . . . . .6F 77
**Owls Lodge La.** SA3: May . . . . . .3D 94
**Oxford St.** SA1: Swan . . . .5A 4 (4E 85)
(not continuous)
OXWICH . . . . . . . . . . . . . . . .4C 110
**Oxwich** SA2: Sket . . . . . . . . . . . .5A 84
**Oxwich Camping Pk.**
SA3: Oxw . . . . . . . . . . . . . .4C 110
Oxwich Castle . . . . . . . . . . . . .4C 110
**Oxwich Ct.** SA6: Swan Ent . . . . . .1B 74
OXWICH GREEN . . . . . . . . . . .4C 110
Oxwich National Nature Reserve
. . . . . . . . . . . . . . . . . . .3D 110
OYSTERMOUTH . . . . . . . . . . .1E 101
Oystermouth Castle . . . . . . . . .1E 101
**Oystermouth Ct.** SA3: T Mum . . .6F 95
**Oystermouth Rd.**
SA1: Swan . . . . . . . .6A 4 (5E 85)
**Oystermouth Sq.**
SA3: T Mum . . . . . . . . . . . .1F 101
**Ozanam Ct.** SA5: Por . . . . . . . . . .2B 72


## P


**Paddock, The** SA3: W Cro . . . . . .4F 95
**Paddocks, The** SA11: Tonna . . . . .4E 65
**Paddock St.** SA15: Llane . . . . . . .2A 52
**Padley Rd.** SA1: Swan . . .3H 5 (3A 86)
**Page La.** SA1: Swan . . . . .4B 4 (4E 85)
**Page St.** SA1: Swan . . . . .3B 4 (3E 85)
**Pak Ho.** SA11: Nea . . . . . . . . . . .2A 78
**Palace Av.** SA15: Llane . . . . . . .1B 52
**Pale Rd.** SA10: Skew . . . . . . . . . .2E 77
**Palleg Pl.** SA9: Cwm I . . . . . . . . .6F 27
**Palleg Rd.** SA9: Cwm I . . . . . . . .5F 27
**Palmyra Ct.** SA3: W Cro . . . . . . .5F 95
**Pandy Cres.** CF33: Pyle . . . . . . .6D 112
**Pandy Pk.** CF32: A'knfig . . . . . .5C 114
**Pandy Rd.** CF32: A'knfig . . . . . .5B 114
**Pandy Vw.** SA11: Cim . . . . . . . . .4D 78
**Pangbourne Cl.** CF36: Not . . . . .2B 124
**Pant Bach** CF33: Pyle . . . . . . . .5D 112
**Pant Bryn Isaf** SA14: Llwy . . . . .1G 53
**Pant Celydd** SA13: Marg . . . . . .2F 103
PANTDU . . . . . . . . . . . . . . . . .1H 97
**Pant Glas** CF35: P'coed . . . . . . .3G 123
**Pantglas** SA4: Gor . . . . . . . . . . .5H 55
SA18: Amm . . . . . . . . . . . . .2H 21
**Pant Gwylan** CF31: Bri . . . . . . . .2C 126
**Pant Gwyn** CF31: Bri . . . . . . . . .2A 126
**Pantgwyn** SA2: Sket . . . . . . . . . .4H 83
**Pant Hirgoed** CF35: P'coed . . . .2F 123
**Panthowellddu**
SA11: Brit F, Nea . . . . . . . . .5A 78
**Pantiago Rd.** SA4: P'dul . . . . . . .6G 35
PANTLASAU . . . . . . . . . . . . . . .1H 59
**Pant Lasau Rd.** SA5: L'flch . . . . .3E 59
SA6: Pantl . . . . . . . . . . . . . .3E 59
**Pant Mawr** CF31: Bri . . . . . . . . .2A 126
**Pant Morfa** CF36: P'cwl . . . . . . .3D 124
**Pant Poeth** CF31: Bri . . . . . . . .2A 126
**Pant St.** SA1: Por T . . . . . . . . . .3C 86
PANTTEG . . . . . . . . . . . . . . . .4D 32
**Pant-Teg** SA15: F'oel . . . . . . . . .4C 42
**Pant y Barcud** SA31: Carm . . . . . .2C 6
**Pant-y-Blawd Cvn. Site**
SA7: Swan Ent . . . . . . . . . . .5C 60
**Pant-y-Blawd Rd.** SA7: L'smlt . . .6D 60
SA7: Swan Ent . . . . . . . . . . .6B 60
**Pant y Blodau** CF35: P'coed . . .3E 123
SA6: L'flch . . . . . . . . . . . . . .4E 59
**Pantyblodau Rd.** SA18: Blae . . . .5C 10
**Pant y Brwyn** SA9: Cwml . . . . . . .1B 26
**Pant y Celyn** SA14: Llwy . . . . . . .1F 53
**Pantycelyn** SA4: Gor . . . . . . . . . .5A 56
**Pant-y-Celyn Rd.**
SA1: Town . . . . . . . .1A 4 (2C 84)
**Pant y Deri** SA4: P'liw . . . . . . . . .5E 47
**Pant y Dryw** CF31: Bri . . . . . . . .2C 126
**Pant y Dwr** SA18: Bry . . . . . . . . .3H 15
**Pant-y-Dwr** SA4: Thr X . . . . . . . .1E 81
**Pant y Fedwen** CF31: Bri . . . . . .2B 126
SA18: C'gors . . . . . . . . . . . .3D 24
**Pant-y-Felin Rd.** SA4: P'dul . . . .4G 35
PANTYFFYNNON . . . . . . . . . . . .4F 21
**Pant-y-Ffynnon**
CF35: P'coed . . . . . . . . . . .2H 123
**Pantyffynnon Rd.** SA9: Ystra . . . .5A 28
*SA18: Amm . . . . . . . . . . . . .4G 21*
*(shown as Heol Pantyffynnon)*
Pantyffynnon Station (Rail) . . . .4G 21
**Pantyffynnon Ter.** SA9: Godr . . . .4D 32
**Pant-y-Gwanyd Rd.**
SA9: Ysta . . . . . . . . . . . . . . .2D 32
**Pantygwydr Ct.** SA2: Upl . . . . . . .4C 84
**Pantygwydr Rd.** SA2: Upl . . . . . .4C 84
**Pant-y-Pistyll** SA8: T'nos . . . . . .1B 50
PANT-Y-PYLLAU . . . . . . . . . . .2H 121
**Pant yr Arian La.** SA12: Bag . . . .6B 90
**Pant yr Hebog** CF31: Bri . . . . . .3B 126
**Pant-y-Rhedyn** SA13: Coe H . . .2C 112
**Pant yr Helyg** SA5: Ffor F . . . . . .3G 71
PANT-YR-HEOL . . . . . . . . . . . .4A 78
**Pant yr Heol**
SA11: Brit F, Nea . . . . . . . . .4H 77
**Pant-yr-Odyn** SA2: Sket . . . . . . . .1H 83
**Pant-y-Sais** SA10: Jer M . . . . . . .1B 88
Pant-y-Sais Fen Nature Reserve
. . . . . . . . . . . . . . . . . . . .1C 88
**Parade, The** SA11: Nea . . . . . . . .6B 64
*SA31: Carm . . . . . . . . . . . . . .3F 7*
*(shown as Y Rhodfa)*
**Parade Rd.** SA31: Carm . . . . . . . . .3F 7
**Paradise Cotts.** SA14: Llwy . . . .2G 53
**Paradise Vw.** SA1: Town . . . . . . .2D 84
**Parc, The** CF31: Bri . . . . . . . . . .4E 127
**Parc Amanwy Ind. Est.**
SA18: Amm . . . . . . . . . . . . .2H 21
**Parc Andrew** SA10: Skew . . . . . .2E 77
**Parcau Av.** CF31: Bri . . . . . . . . .1A 126
**Parcau Rd.** CF31: Bri . . . . . . . . .1B 126
**Parc Av.** SA6: Morr . . . . . . . . . . .2A 74
(not continuous)
**Parc Bagnall** SA31: Carm . . . . . . .2D 6
**Parc Berwig** SA14: Byn . . . . . . . .4A 54
**Parc Bronhaul** CF31: Bri . . . . . .6C 126
**Parc Bryn** SA10: Skew . . . . . . . .2D 76
**Parc Bryngelli** SA14: Gors . . . . . . .5F 9
**Parc Brynmawr** SA15: Llane . . . .3B 42
**Parc Bryn Rhos** SA18: Glan . . . . .5A 14
**Parc Bwtrimawr** SA18: Amm . . . .2H 21
**Parc Cilddewi** SA31: John . . . . . . .5A 6
**Parc Cres.** CF31: Bri . . . . . . . . .3C 128
**Parc Cwmdu** SA5: Cwmdu . . . . . .6C 72
**Parc Deri** CF31: Bri . . . . . . . . . .2C 126
**Parc Derllwyn** CF32: Ton . . . . . .3B 114
**Parc Derlyn** SA18: Tyc . . . . . . . . .5C 20
**Parc Derwen** SA18: G'llt . . . . . . .6H 21
Parc Dewi Sant . . . . . . . . . . . . . .3A 6
**Parc Dyfatty** SA16: Burr P . . . . . .2G 39
**Parcel Ter.** SA31: Carm . . . . . . . . .2G 7
**Parc Eynon** SA15: Llane . . . . . . .1A 52
**Parc Fferws** SA18: Amm . . . . . . .2F 21
**Parc Fforestfach** SA5: Cad . . . . .2H 71
**Parc Gilbertson** SA8: P'dwe . . . .4C 36
**Parc Gitto** SA14: Llwy . . . . . . . . .2G 53
**Parc Glanffrwd** SA18: Garn . . . . .5C 14
**Parc Glan yr Afon**
SA18: Glan . . . . . . . . . . . . . .4C 14
**Parc Glas** SA10: Skew . . . . . . . . .2E 77
**Parc Glyn** CF31: Bri . . . . . . . . . .2C 126
Parc Gwledig Llyn Llech Owain
Country Pk. . . . . . . . . . . . . . .1E 9
**Parc Hendre** SA18: Cap H . . . . . .3B 20
**Parc Hendy Cres.** SA4: Penc . . . .5A 68
**Parc Henry La.** *SA18: Amm . . . .4H 11*
*(shown as Lon Parc Henri)*
PARC HOWARD . . . . . . . . . . . . .5A 42
**Parc Howard Av.** SA15: Llane . . .5A 42
Parc Howard Mus. & Art Gallery
. . . . . . . . . . . . . . . . . . . .5A 42
**Parc Landwr** SA6: Swan Ent . . . .2B 74
Parc le Breos Burial Chamber
(Giant's Grave) . . . . . . . . .1G 111
**Parcmaen St.** SA31: Carm . . . . . .3D 6
**Parc Marian Way** SA1: Cry B . . .4H 87
Parc Mawr Bonymaen Sports Club
. . . . . . . . . . . . . . . . . . . .4D 74
**Parc Mawr Cl.** SA4: Penl . . . . . . .4G 57
**Parc Melin Mynach** SA4: Gor . . .3B 56
**Parc Menter** SA14: Cross H . . . . .1E 19
**Parc Morlais** SA14: L'nch . . . . . .3D 44
**Parc Nant-y-Felin**
SA18: Amm . . . . . . . . . . . . .1C 22
**Parc Nedd** SA10: Nea . . . . . . . . .5H 63
**Parc Newydd** CF35: Treoes . . . .4D 128
SA11: Brit F . . . . . . . . . . . . .5G 77
**Parc Onen** SA10: Skew . . . . . . . .2D 76
**Parc Pemberton Retail Pk.**
SA14: Llane . . . . . . . . . . . . .1E 53
**Parc Pencae** SA18: L'bie . . . . . . .1F 11
**Parc Penderi** SA4: Penl . . . . . . . .3G 57
**Parc Penrhiw** SA18: Amm . . . . . .3A 22
**Parc Pensarn** SA31: Carm . . . . . . .6E 7
**Parc Penscynnor** SA10: Cilf . . . . .3E 65
**Parc Richard** SA14: Llwy . . . . . .2H 53
**Parc Rd.** SA6: Morr . . . . . . . . . . .2A 74
Parc Slip Nature Reserve . . . .5A 114
**Parc Starling** SA31: John . . . . . . .4B 6
**Parc Tawe** SA1: Swan . . . .2F 5 (3G 85)
**Parc Tawe Link Rd.**
SA1: Swan . . . . . . . .2F 5 (3G 85)
**Parc Tawe Nth.**
SA1: Swan . . . . . . . .2F 5 (3G 85)
**Parc Ter.** SA6: Morr . . . . . . . . . . .1A 74
**Parc Thomas** SA31: Carm . . . . . . .2E 7
**Parc Tir-y-Coed** SA18: Amm . . . .3A 22
**Parc Trostre** SA14: Llane . . . . . . .2D 52
**Parc Tyisha** SA16: Burr P . . . . . .2E 39
**Parc Wern** SA10: Skew . . . . . . . .2D 76
**Parc Wern Rd.** SA2: Sket . . . . . .3B 84
**Parc-y-Berllan** CF36: P'cwl . . . .4D 124
**Parc-y-Bont** CF32: B'myn . . . . . .3E 115
**Parc y Ddraig** SA4: L'flch . . . . . .3B 58
**Parc y Delyn** SA31: Carm . . . . . . .2E 7
**Parc-y-Delyn** SA6: L'flch . . . . . . .5F 59
**Parc-y-Deri** SA10: Skew . . . . . . .2D 76
**Parc-y-Duc Ter.** SA6: Morr . . . . .1A 74
**Parc y Felin** SA2: Sket . . . . . . . . .4F 83
**Parc y Ffordd** SA31: John . . . . . . .4A 6
**Parc y Llan** SA18: L'bie . . . . . . . .1F 11
**Parc-y-Minos St.**
SA16: Burr P . . . . . . . . . . . .3E 39
**Parc yr Afon** *SA31: Carm . . . . . . .3D 6*
*(off Fountain Hall Ter.)*
**Parc-yr-Helig Rd.** SA7: Birch . . .6A 62
**Parc yr Hendre** SA18: Amm . . . .3E 21
**Parc-y-Rhos** CF35: P'coed . . . . .3G 123
**Parcyrhun** SA18: Amm . . . . . . . .2G 21
**Parc yr Odyn** SA31: John . . . . . . .5A 6
**Parc yr Onen** SA31: Carm . . . . . . .2F 7
Parc y Scarlets . . . . . . . . . . . . .2E 53
**Park, The** SA2: Sket . . . . . . . . . . .3F 83
Park & Ride
Fabian Way . . . . . . . . . . . .3C 86
Felindre . . . . . . . . . . . . . . .2D 58
Landore . . . . . . . . . . . . . . .5H 73
White City Road . . . . . . . . .4A 72
**Park Av.** CF36: P'cwl . . . . . . . . .4B 124
SA3: T Mum . . . . . . . . . . . .2F 101
SA10: Skew . . . . . . . . . . . . .1A 76
SA18: Cap H . . . . . . . . . . . .2H 19
**Park Cl.** SA1: Bon . . . . . . . . . . .5C 74
SA4: Gor . . . . . . . . . . . . . . .4A 56
SA4: P'dul . . . . . . . . . . . . . .1B 46
SA6: Morr . . . . . . . . . . . . . .5H 59
**Park Ct.** CF31: Bri . . . . . . . . . .1B 126
**Park Ct. Rd.** CF31: Bri . . . . . . .1C 126
**Park Cres.** SA10: Skew . . . . . . . .1B 76
SA15: Llane . . . . . . . . . . . . .4H 41
**Park Dr.** SA2: Upl . . . . . . . . . . . .3C 84
SA10: Skew . . . . . . . . . . . . .1B 76
**Parkes St.** SA16: Burr P . . . . . . .3E 39
**Park Fld.** SA11: Tonna . . . . . . . .3G 65
**Parkfields** CF31: Pen F . . . . . . .3C 120
(not continuous)
**Parkfields Rd.** CF31: Bri . . . . . .1C 126
**Park Hall** SA31: Carm . . . . . . . . . .2F 7
**Parkhill Rd.** SA5: Tre b . . . . . . . .3F 73
**Parkhill Ter.** SA5: Tre b . . . . . . .2F 73
**Park Howard Rd.**
SA18: C'gors . . . . . . . . . . . .3C 24
**Parklands** CF35: Corn . . . . . . . .6G 127
**Parklands Ct.** SA2: Sket . . . . . . .4G 83
SA18: Amm . . . . . . . . . . . . .2F 21
**Parklands Rd.** *SA18: Amm . . . . .1F 21*
*(shown as Heol Parcdir)*
**Parklands Vw.** SA2: Sket . . . . . .5G 83
**Park La.** SA4: Gor . . . . . . . . . . . .4A 56
SA14: L'nch . . . . . . . . . . . . .4D 44
SA18: Lwr B . . . . . . . . . . . . .5H 15
**Park Lodge Rd.** SA6: Morr . . . . .5A 60
PARKMILL . . . . . . . . . . . . . . . .5A 92
**Park Mill Rd.** SA18: Amm . . . . . .1F 21
**Park Pl.** CF32: Sarn . . . . . . . . . .6E 115
SA2: Brynm . . . . . . . . . . . . .5B 84
**Park Plaza** CF31: Hern . . . . . . .4G 127
**Park Rd.** CF32: A'knfig . . . . . . . .6A 114
SA3: S'gate . . . . . . . . . . . . .1A 98
SA4: Gor . . . . . . . . . . . . . . .4H 55
SA4: Gow . . . . . . . . . . . . . . .4A 70
SA4: Penc . . . . . . . . . . . . . .4G 67
SA6: Cly . . . . . . . . . . . . . . . .4F 49
SA6: Ystwe . . . . . . . . . . . . .2D 60
**Park Row** SA12: C'avon . . . . . . . .4H 91
**Park St.** CF31: Bri . . . . . . . . . . .1C 126
CF33: Ken H . . . . . . . . . . . .5F 113
SA1: Swan . . . . . . .3D 4 (3F 85)
SA3: T Mum . . . . . . . . . . . .1F 101
SA10: Skew . . . . . . . . . . . . .1E 77
SA11: Nea . . . . . . . . . . . . . .6C 64
SA11: Tonna . . . . . . . . . . . . .3G 65
SA13: P Tal . . . . . . . . . . . . .5H 97
SA15: Llane . . . . . . . . . . . . .1A 52
SA18: Lwr B . . . . . . . . . . . . .5H 15
**Park Ter.** CF32: Ton . . . . . . . . .4A 114
SA1: Swan . . . . . . . . . . . . . .1F 85
SA4: P'dul . . . . . . . . . . . . . .2C 46
SA15: Llane . . . . . . . . . . . . .2A 52
SA16: Burr P . . . . . . . . . . . .2D 38
SA31: Carm . . . . . . . . . . . . . .4D 6
**Park Vw.** CF31: Bri . . . . . . . . . .6A 120
CF35: Coyc . . . . . . . . . . . .1B 128
SA1: Swan . . . . . . . . . . . . . .5D 84
SA4: Lou . . . . . . . . . . . . . . .5E 55
SA13: P Tal . . . . . . . . . . . . .5H 97
SA14: F'oel . . . . . . . . . . . . .3C 42
**Park Vw. Cl.** SA11: Brit F . . . . . .6G 77
**Park Vw. Ter.** SA2: Sket . . . . . . .4H 83
**Parkview Ter.** SA15: Llane . . . . .4H 41
**Parkway** SA2: Sket . . . . . . . . . . .3F 83
**Parkwood** SA4: Gow . . . . . . . . . .4B 70
**Parkwood Hgts.** CF31: Bri . . . . .2B 126
**Parr Av.** SA11: Nea . . . . . . . . . . .6B 64
**Parry Cl.** SA10: Nea A . . . . . . . . .6G 63
**Parry Rd.** SA6: Morr . . . . . . . . . .5H 59
SA12: Sand . . . . . . . . . . . . .1A 96
**Parsons La.** SA11: Tonna . . . . . .4F 65
**Pascoes Av.** CF31: Bri . . . . . . . .6D 120
**Pastoral Way** SA2: Sket . . . . . . .2G 83
**Patagonia Wlk.** SA1: Swan . . . . . .6F 5
**Pat Chown Ct.** SA8: P'dwe . . . . .6D 36
**Paviland Pl.** SA5: Por . . . . . . . . .3C 72
**Pavilion Ct.** CF36: P'cwl . . . . . .5C 124
**Paxton Ct.** SA1: Swan . . . . . . . . . .5D 4
**Paxton Dr.** SA1: Swan . . .6D 4 (5F 85)
**Paxton St.** SA1: Swan . . . .5C 4 (4F 85)
**Payne St.** SA11: Nea . . . . . . . . . .2A 78
**Pearl Ct.** SA1: Swan . . . . . . . . . . .6B 4
SA6: Cly . . . . . . . . . . . . . . . .4G 49
**Pearl Ho.** SA1: Swan . . . . . . . . . . .3E 5
**Pearl St.** SA6: Cly . . . . . . . . . . . .4G 49
**Pearson Way** SA11: Nea . . . . . . .4A 78
**Pedrog Ter.** SA1: M'hill . . . . . . . .1D 84
**Pegler St.** SA5: Man . . . . . . . . . .5F 73
**Pelican St.** SA9: Ystra . . . . . . . . .4A 28
**Pellau Rd.** SA13: Marg . . . . . . .1F 103
**Pell St.** SA1: Swan . . . . . .3D 4 (3F 85)
PEMBERTON . . . . . . . . . . . . . .1E 53
**Pemberton Av.** SA16: Burr P . . . .3D 38
**Pemberton Pk.** SA14: Llane . . . . .6E 43
**Pemberton Rd.** SA14: Llwy . . . . .1E 53
**Pemberton St.** SA15: Llane . . . . .5H 41
PEMBREY . . . . . . . . . . . . . . . .2A 38
Pembrey & Burry Port Station (Rail)
. . . . . . . . . . . . . . . . . . . .3E 39
**Pembrey Rd.** SA15: Llane . . . . . .3G 41
**Pembroke Bldgs.** SA1: Swan . . . . .4G 5
**Pembroke Ho.** *SA12: Sand . . . . .4C 96*
*(off Moorland Rd.)*
**Pembroke Pl.** SA1: Swan . . . . . . . .4G 5
**Pembroke St.** SA5: Man . . . . . . . .5E 73
**Pembroke Ter.** SA12: A'von . . . . .4E 97
PENALLT . . . . . . . . . . . . . . . . .6C 42
**Penallt** SA2: Dunv . . . . . . . . . . .2D 82
**Penallt Rd.** SA15: Llane . . . . . . .1C 52
**Penallt Ter.** SA15: Llane . . . . . . .6C 42
PEN-BRE . . . . . . . . . . . . . . . . .2A 38
**Penbryn Av.** SA31: Carm . . . . . . . .3C 6
**Penbryn Rd.** SA10: Skew . . . . . . .1E 77
**Penbryn Ter.** SA2: Brynm . . . . . .5B 84
**Pen-Cae-Crwn Rd.** SA4: Gor . . . .3H 55

PENCAERAU . . . . . . . . . . . . .3H 77
Pencaerfenni Ct. SA4: Crof . . . . .5E 67
Pencaerfenni La. SA4: Crof . . . . .5E 67
Pencaerfenni Pk. SA4: Crof . . . . .5D 66
PEN-CAER-FENNY . . . . . . . . . .5E 67
Pencae Ter. SA15: Llane . . . . . . .1C 52
Pen-Cefn-Arda Rd. SA4: Gor . . . .2H 55
PENCEILIOGI . . . . . . . . . . . . .6F 43
PEN-CLAWDD . . . . . . . . . . . . .4H 67
Penclawdd Rd. SA4: Penc . . . . . .4C 68
PENCOED . . . . . . . . . . . . . . .3H 123
Pencoed SA2: Dunv . . . . . . . . .2D 82
Pencoed Isaf Rd. SA14: Byn . . . . .2B 54
Pencoed Rd. SA16: Burr P . . . . . .2E 39
Pencoed Station (Rail) . . . . . . . .3G 123
Pencoed Swimming Pool . . . . . . .4H 123
Pencoed Technology Pk.
    CF35: P'coed . . . . . . . . . . .5H 123
Pencoed Way CF35: P'coed . . . .6G 123
Pencoed Youth Sports Cen. . . .4G 123
Pencwmdu SA8: Cilm . . . . . . . .1G 37
Pendarren SA8: Cilm . . . . . . . . .1G 37
Pendarvis Ter. SA12: Sand . . . . .3D 96
Pendderi Cl. SA14: Bryn . . . . . . .1A 54
    (shown as Clos Pendderi)
Pendderi Rd.
    SA14: Bryn, Byn . . . . . . . . .1A 54
Penderry Rd. SA5: P'lan . . . . . . .3E 73
Penderyn Av. SA13: Marg . . . .1F 103
PENDRE . . . . . . . . . . . . . . . .4E 121
Pendre CF31: Bri . . . . . . . . . . .4E 121
Pendrill St. SA11: Nea . . . . . . . .2A 78
PENFILIA . . . . . . . . . . . . . . . .3F 73
Penfilia Rd. SA5: Man . . . . . . . .4F 73
Penfilia Ter. SA5: Man . . . . . . . .4F 73
PENGELLI . . . . . . . . . . . . . . . .6B 46
Pengors Rd. SA5: L'flch . . . . . . .4E 59
Pengry Rd. SA4: Lou . . . . . . . . .4G 55
Pen Gwern CF35: P'coed . . . . . .2F 123
Pengwern Rd. SA6: Clase . . . . . .6F 59
PENIEL GREEN . . . . . . . . . . . .6G 61
Peniel Grn. Rd. SA7: L'smlt . . . .1E 75
Peniel Rd. SA5: Tre b . . . . . . . .3G 73
Pen Isa Coed
    SA1: St T . . . . . .2H 5 (3A 86)
PENLAN . . . . . . . . . . . . . . . . .3D 72
Penlan SA14: Bryn . . . . . . . . . .6B 44
Penlan Cres. SA2: Upl . . . . . . . .3B 84
Penlan Fach SA5: P'lan . . . . . . .4E 73
Penlanffos Rd. SA31: Carm . . . .1G 7
    (shown as Heol Penlanffos)
Penlan Gro. SA5: Tre b . . . . . . .3E 73
Penlan Leisure Cen. . . . . . . . . .3D 72
Penlan Rd. SA4: Lou . . . . . . . . .5G 55
    SA5: Tre b . . . . . . . . . . . . .2E 73
    SA10: Skew . . . . . . . . . . . .2D 76
    SA31: Carm . . . . . . . . . . . .2E 7
Penlan Ter. SA5: Tre b . . . . . . . .2F 73
Penllech SA15: Pwll . . . . . . . . . .2C 40
PENLLERGAER . . . . . . . . . . . .4H 57
Penllergaer Bus. Pk.
    SA4: L'flch . . . . . . . . . . . . .3B 58
Penllergare Valley Woods . . . . .4A 58
Penllergare Valley Woods Vis. Cen.
    . . . . . . . . . . . . . . . . . . . .3H 57
Pen Llwyn CF31: Bri . . . . . . . . .2C 126
Penllwyngwyn Farm Dr.
    SA14: Bryn . . . . . . . . . . . . .6A 44
Penllwyngwyn Rd.
    SA14: Bryn . . . . . . . . . . . . .6A 44
Pen-Llwyn-March Rd.
    SA5: Gen . . . . . . . . . . . . . .5C 72
Penllwyn Pk. SA31: Carm . . . . . .4C 6
Penllwynrhodyn Rd.
    SA14: Llwy . . . . . . . . . . . . .2G 53
Penllyn SA12: C'avon . . . . . . . .5H 91
Penmachno SA6: Morr . . . . . . . .5G 59
PENMAEN . . . . . . . . . . . . . . . .2G 111
Pen Maen CF31: Bri . . . . . . . . .2C 126
    (off Careg Llwyd)
Penmaen SA2: Sket . . . . . . . . . .5A 84
Penmaen Burial Chamber . . . . .2G 111
Penmaen Ter.
    SA1: Swan . . . . . .2A 4 (3E 85)
Penmynydd SA4: Gor . . . . . . . . .5H 55
Penmynydd Rd. SA5: P'lan . . . . .3E 73
Pen-Nant SA14: F'oel . . . . . . . . .2E 43
PENNARD . . . . . . . . . . . . . . . .6E 93
Pennard Castle . . . . . . . . . . . .2H 111
Pennard Dr. SA3: S'gate . . . . . . .1A 98
Pennard Golf Course . . . . . . . . .2H 111
Pennard Rd.
    SA3: Bishop, Kit, Penn . . . .6E 93
    SA3: Penn, S'gate . . . . . . . .1A 98
Pennard St. SA5: Man . . . . . . . .4F 73

Pennine Cl. SA5: Ffor F . . . . . . .5B 72
Penny Brick Ct. SA11: Nea . . . . .2B 78
    (off Lewis Rd.)
Pen Onnen CF31: Brack . . . . . . .6H 121
Pen Pentre SA10: Cry . . . . . . . .6H 33
Penplas Rd. SA5: Blae M . . . . . .1B 72
    SA5: L'flch, P'lan . . . . . . . . .6C 58
Penpound La. SA18: Glan . . . . . .4H 13
    (shown as Lon Penpownd)
PENPRYSG . . . . . . . . . . . . . . .2H 123
Penprysg Rd. CF35: P'coed . . . .3H 123
Penprys Rd.
    SA1: Bryn, L'nch . . . . . . . . .3H 43
PEN-RHIW-FAWR . . . . . . . . . . .4A 26
Penrhiwgoch SA12: Bag . . . . . . .6H 89
Penrhiwtyn Dr. SA6: Morr . . . . . .4G 59
PENRHIWTYN . . . . . . . . . . . . .4H 77
Penrhiwtyn Dr.
    SA11: Brit F, Nea . . . . . . . . .4H 77
Penrhiwtyn St. SA11: Brit F . . . . .4H 77
PENRHOS . . . . . . . . . . . . . . . .3C 28
Penrhos SA4: Gor . . . . . . . . . . .5H 55
Penrhos Cotts. SA15: Llane . . . . .3A 52
Penrhyn Pl. SA5: Gen . . . . . . . . .4C 72
Penrhyn CF33: Ken H . . . . . . . .4G 113
Penrhyn Av. SA5: P'lan . . . . . . . .4E 73
Penrhyn Ct. SA6: Cwm'crw . . . . .3B 60
Penrhyn Gwyn SA15: Llane . . . . .5A 52
Penrhyn St. SA13: P Tal . . . . . . .1E 103
PENRICE . . . . . . . . . . . . . . . . .3C 110
Penrice Castle . . . . . . . . . . . . .2C 110
Penrice Ct. SA6: Swan Ent . . . . .2B 74
Penrice Ho. SA1: Swan . . . . . . . .1C 4
Penrice St. SA6: Morr . . . . . . . . .5A 60
Penryce Ct. SA1: Swan . . . .5E 5 (4G 85)
Penry Pl. SA15: Llane . . . . . . . . .1B 52
Pensalem Rd. SA5: P'lan . . . . . . .3E 73
PEN-SARN . . . . . . . . . . . . . . . .5E 7
Pensarn Rd. SA31: Carm . . . . . . .5E 7
Penscynor SA10: C'dxtn, Cilf . . . .3E 65
Penshannel SA10: Nea A . . . . . . .5E 63
Pentewan Cl. SA6: Cwm'crw . . . . .2B 60
Pentland Cl. SA5: Ffor F . . . . . . .4A 72
PENTRE . . . . . . . . . . . . . . . . . .6G 73
Pentre Afan SA12: Bag . . . . . . . .6H 89
Pentre Bach SA5: Gen . . . . . . . .5C 72
Pentre Banadl SA2: Kill . . . . . . . .3D 82
PENTRE-CHWYTH . . . . . . . . . .5B 74
Pentre-Chwyth Rd. SA1: St T . . .6H 73
Pentre Doc y Gogledd
    SA15: Llane . . . . . . . . . . . . .5G 41
PENTRE-DWR . . . . . . . . . . . . .3F 75
Pentre-Dwr SA7: L'smlt . . . . . . .3F 75
Pentre Fedwen SA11: Cim . . . . .2E 79
Pentrefelin St. SA31: Carm . . . . .3D 6
PENTREFFYNNON . . . . . . . . . .2E 77
Pentregethin Rd.
    SA5: Cad, Por, Rav . . . . . . .1A 72
    SA5: Gen, Man . . . . . . . . . .4C 72
Pentreguinea Rd.
    SA1: St T . . . . . .1G 5 (2H 85)
Pentrehafod Sports Hall & Pool
    . . . . . . . . . . . . . . . . . . . . .5G 73
Pentre Howell CF35: P'coed . . . .3H 123
Pentremalwed Rd. SA6: Morr . . .6A 60
Pentre-Mawr Rd. SA1: Swan . . .6G 73
Pentremeurig Rd. SA31: Carm . . .2A 6
Pentre Nicklaus Av.
    SA15: Llane . . . . . . . . . . . . .5A 52
Pentre Nicklaus Village
    SA15: Llane . . . . . . . . . . . . .5A 52
    SA15: P Tal, CF33: Ken H . . .5F 113
PENTRE-POETH . . . . . . . . . . . .
    SA6 . . . . . . . . . . . . . . . . . .5B 60
    SA15 . . . . . . . . . . . . . . . . .4B 42
Pentrepoeth Rd. SA6: Morr . . . . .4A 60
    SA15: Llane . . . . . . . . . . . .2H 41
PENTRE'R-GASEG . . . . . . . . . .4B 74
Pentre Rd. SA4: P'dul . . . . . . . . .1C 46
    SA4: P'dul, Waun . . . . . . . . .4D 46
Pentre Treharne Hill
    SA1: L'ore . . . . . . . . . . . . . .4G 73
Pentre Treharne Rd.
    SA1: L'ore . . . . . . . . . . . . . .4G 73
Pentre Wern SA13: Marg . . . . .1E 103
Pentwyn SA4: Thr X . . . . . . . . .1F 81
    SA10: B'och . . . . . . . . . . . . .2H 63
    SA11: Nea . . . . . . . . . . . . . .3B 78
Pentwyn Baglan Rd.
    SA12: Bag, P Tal . . . . . . . . .5A 90
Pentwyn Dr. SA12: Bag . . . . . . . .5B 90
Pentwyn Rd. CF35: P'coed . . . .2H 123
    SA9: Ysta . . . . . . . . . . . . . .2E 33
    SA18: Amm . . . . . . . . . . . .2A 22
    (shown as Ffordd Pentwyn)

Pentyla Baglan Rd.
    SA12: A'von . . . . . . . . . . . .2E 97
Pentyla Gdns. CF32: Sarn . . .6D 114
Pentyla Rd. SA2: C'ett . . . . . . . .2B 84
Penuel Cl. SA4: Gor . . . . . . . . . .5H 55
Penuel St. SA31: Carm . . . . . . . .3F 7
Penuel Rd. SA10: Nea A . . . . . . .6G 63
PENYBANC . . . . . . . . . . . . . . .2E 21
Pen y Banc SA10: Sev S . . . . . . .5F 29
Pen-y-banc CF31: Bri . . . . . . . . .1F 127
Penybanc SA31: Carm . . . . . . . .1G 7
    (Glynderi)
    SA31: Carm . . . . . . . . . . . . .5E 7
    (Penymorfa La.)
Penybanc La. SA4: Gor . . . . . . . .2H 55
Pen-y-Banc Rd. SA18: Amm . . . .3E 21
Pen-y-Bigyn SA15: Llane . . . . . . .2B 52
PEN-Y-BONT AR OGWAR . . . . .1E 127
Penybont Ind. Est. CF31: Bri . . . .5E 121
Penybont Rd. CF35: P'coed . . . .3H 123
PEN-Y-BRYN . . . . . . . . . . . . . .1G 113
Pen y Bryn SA9: Cwml . . . . . . . .6G 17
    SA14: F'oel . . . . . . . . . . . . .1D 42
Pen-y-Bryn CF31: Bri . . . . . . . . .1B 126
    SA10: Sev S . . . . . . . . . . . .5G 29
    SA10: Skew . . . . . . . . . . . . .2D 76
    SA11: Cim . . . . . . . . . . . . . .3C 78
    SA11: Tonna . . . . . . . . . . . .3G 65
    SA9: Ystra . . . . . . . . . . . . . .4B 28
Peny Bryn SA2: Up K . . . . . . . . .4B 82
Penybryn Av. SA16: Burr P . . . . .2E 39
Pen-y-Bryn Res. Cvn. Site
    SA10: Llwy . . . . . . . . . . . . .2H 63
Penybryn Rd. CF32: B'myn . . . . .3D 114
    SA4: Gor . . . . . . . . . . . . . . .4A 56
Penybryn Ter. CF32: B'myn . . . . .3D 114
Pen-y-Bryn Vw. CF32: Brync . . .5E 115
PEN-Y-CAE . . . . . . . . . . . . . . .
    SA13 . . . . . . . . . . . . . . . . .4H 97
    CF32 . . . . . . . . . . . . . . . . .1E 121
Pen y Cae SA31: John . . . . . . . . .5A 6
Pen-y-Cae La. SA4: Lou . . . . . . .4F 55
Pen-y-Cae Rd. SA13: P Tal . . . . .3H 97
Pen y Cwm SA2: C'ett . . . . . . . .6A 72
Pen-y-Dre SA4: Gow . . . . . . . . .4A 70
    SA11: Nea . . . . . . . . . . . . . .6C 64
Penydre SA6: Cly . . . . . . . . . . . .3F 49
PEN-Y-FAI . . . . . . . . . . . . . . . .2B 120
Pen-y-Fai La. SA15: Llane . . . . . .1G 41
Penyfai Rd.
    CF32: A'knfig, Pen F . . . . . .1B 120
PEN-Y-FAN . . . . . . . . . . . . . . .3C 52
Pen-y-Fan SA7: L'smlt . . . . . . . .2G 75
Penyfan Rd. SA15: Llane . . . . . . .3C 52
Pen-y-Ffordd CF33: N Cor . . . . .2D 116
Pen-y-Fro St. SA15: Llane . . . . . .3B 52
Pen-y-Fro CF35: P'coed . . . . . . .2F 123
    SA2: Dunv . . . . . . . . . . . . . .1A 82
Pen-y-Fro Cl. SA2: Dunv . . . . . . .1A 82
Pen y Gaer SA4: Penc . . . . . . . .4G 67
Penygaer Rd. SA14: Llane . . . . . .6C 42
    (not continuous)
Penygarn Rd. SA18: Tyc . . . . . . .6D 20
    (shown as Heol Penygarn)
Pen y Graig SA10: L'dcy . . . . . . .4B 76
Pen-y-Graig Rd. SA8: All . . . . . . .1E 51
Penygraig Rd.
    SA1: Swan, Town . . .1A 4 (2D 84)
    SA9: Cwml . . . . . . . . . . . . . .1B 26
    SA14: Llwy . . . . . . . . . . . . . .2H 53
PEN-Y-GROES . . . . . . . . . . . . .4G 9
Penygroes Rd. SA14: Gors . . . . .4E 9
    (shown as Heol Penygroes)
    SA18: C'bryn . . . . . . . . . . . .3B 10
    (shown as Heol Penygroes)
Pen y Lan SA4: Penc . . . . . . . . .4A 68
Penylan CF31: Bri . . . . . . . . . . .3E 121
Penylan Av. CF36: P'cwl . . . . . . .4B 124
Penylan Cl. CF35: P'coed . . . . . .2H 123
    SA8: P'dwe, Pdyd f . . . . . . .5A 36
Pen y Maes SA6: L'flch . . . . . . . .4F 59
Pen y Morfa SA4: Penc . . . . . . . .3B 52
Pen-y-Morfa SA15: Llane . . . . . . .3B 52
Penymorfa SA31: Carm . . . . . . . .4F 7
Penymorfa La. SA31: Carm . . . . .5E 7
Pen-y-Mor Rd. SA5: P'lan . . . . . .3F 73
Pen y Parc SA4: P'dul . . . . . . . . .1C 46
Pen-yr-Alley Av. SA10: Skew . . . .2D 76
Pen yr Allt SA9: Ysta . . . . . . . . .1D 32
Penyrallt SA18: Garn . . . . . . . . .6E 15
Penyrallt Av. CF31: Bri . . . . . . . .3E 121
Pen yr Alltwen SA8: All . . . . . . . .1E 51

Pentyla Rd. SA12: A'von . . . . . . .2E 97
Penralltwen Pk. SA8: Rhos . . . . .1F 51
Pen-yr-Grug SA9: Ysta . . . . . . . .6D 26
PEN-YR-HEOL . . . . . . . . . . . . .
    CF35 . . . . . . . . . . . . . . . . .1H 121
    SA10 . . . . . . . . . . . . . . . . .2D 76
PENYRHEOL . . . . . . . . . . . . . .
    SA2 . . . . . . . . . . . . . . . . . .3G 83
    SA4 . . . . . . . . . . . . . . . . . .3A 56
Pen-yr-Heol CF31: Pen F . . . . . .2B 120
    CF33: N Cor . . . . . . . . . . . .2D 116
    SA10: Skew . . . . . . . . . . . .2D 76
Penyrheol Dr. SA2: Sket . . . . . . .3G 83
    SA15: Llane . . . . . . . . . . . .4B 42
Penyrheol Leisure Cen. . . . . . . .3A 56
Penyrheol Rd. SA2: Sket . . . . . . .2H 55
Penyrheol Theatre . . . . . . . . . . .3A 56
Pen y Rhiw SA9: P fawr . . . . . . . .4A 26
Pen-yr-Yrfa SA6: Morr . . . . . . . . .5G 59
Penywarc Rd. SA15: Llane . . . . . .1C 52
Pen-y-Wern Rd. SA6: Cly . . . . . . .4F 49
    SA10: Nea . . . . . . . . . . . . . .4A 64
Penywern Rd. SA9: Ysta . . . . . . .1D 32
Pen y Wern Ter. SA1: L'ore . . . . .4G 73
PEOPLES PARK . . . . . . . . . . . .4H 41
Percival Ho. SA11: Nea . . . . . . . .1B 78
Peris Rd. SA5: P'lan . . . . . . . . . .3D 72
PERRISWOOD . . . . . . . . . . . . .2D 110
Peter Cash Ho. SA1: Swan . . . . .6A 4
Peter St. SA1: Swan . . . . . . . . . .1F 85
Peter Ter. SA1: Swan . . . . . . . . .1F 85
Peter Wills Ceramics, Studio
    & Art Gallery . . . . . . . . . . . .1D 126
Pheasant Rd. SA8: T'nos . . . . . . .2A 50
Pheasant Wlk. CF31: Pen F . . . . .3B 120
Philadelphia Ct. SA6: Morr . . . . . .6A 60
    (off Globe St.)
Philadelphia La. SA1: Swan . . . . .6G 73
Philadelphia Rd. CF36: P'cwl . . . .4C 124
Philip Av. CF31: Bri . . . . . . . . . .6B 120
Phillips Fld. SA3: Park . . . . . . . . .6A 92
Phillips Pde.
    SA1: Swan . . . . . . .5A 4 (4E 85)
Phillip St. SA5: Man . . . . . . . . . .5F 73
Phoebe Rd. SA1: Swan Ent . . . . .5A 74
Phoenix Av. SA13: Marg . . . . . . .1E 103
Phoenix Bus. Pk.
    SA7: Swan Ent . . . . . . . . . .1C 74
Phoenix Cen. SA7: Swan Ent . . .1D 74
Phoenix Way SA4: Gor . . . . . . . .5D 56
    SA7: Swan Ent . . . . . . . . . .3B 74
Phyllis Av. CF31: Bri . . . . . . . . . .2E 127
Phyllis St. SA5: Cwmdu . . . . . . .6D 72
Piazza, The
    SA1: Swan . . . . . . .2F 5 (3G 85)
Pibwrlwyd La. SA31: Cwmf . . . . .6F 7
Picket Mead Rd. SA3: Newt . . . .1C 100
Picton Arc. SA1: Swan . . . .4C 4 (4F 85)
Picton Av. CF31: Bri . . . . . . . . . .3D 126
    CF36: P'cwl . . . . . . . . . . . . .5C 124
Picton Cl. CF31: Bri . . . . . . . . . .3F 127
Picton Ct. SA31: Carm . . . . . . . .3C 6
Picton Gdns. CF31: Bri . . . . . . . .3E 127
Picton La. SA1: Swan . . . .4C 4 (4F 85)
    (not continuous)
Picton Pl. SA31: Carm . . . . . . . . .3C 6
Picton Rd. SA10: Skew . . . . . . . .1E 77
Picton's Monument . . . . . . . . . .4C 6
Picton St. CF33: Ken H . . . . . . . .4G 113
Picton Ter. SA1: Swan . . . .1C 4 (2F 85)
    SA10: Skew . . . . . . . . . . . . .6E 63
    SA31: Carm . . . . . . . . . . . . .4C 6
Pier Cl. SA12: Sand . . . . . . . . . .3B 96
Pier La. SA1: Swan . . . . .4G 5 (4H 85)
Pier Way SA12: Sand . . . . . . . . .3A 96
Pilgrims Cl. SA10: Nea A . . . . . . .6H 63
Pill Ter. SA11: Brit F . . . . . . . . . .6F 77
Pilot Ho. Rd.
    SA1: Swan . . . . . . .5H 5 (4H 85)
Pilot Ho. Wharf
    SA1: Swan . . . . . . .5H 5 (4H 85)
PILTON GREEN . . . . . . . . . . . .3F 109
Pil-y-Cwrdd CF33: N Cor . . . . . .1D 116
Pineacre Cl. SA2: Sket . . . . . . . .3H 83
Pine Cl. CF36: Newt . . . . . . . . . .3G 125
Pine Cres. SA6: Morr . . . . . . . . . .4H 59
Pine Gro. SA11: Cim . . . . . . . . . .3E 79
Pines, The SA10: Cilf . . . . . . . . .2E 65
Pinetree Cl. SA16: Burr P . . . . . .2F 39
Pine Tree Ct. SA2: Sket . . . . . . . .4H 83
Pine Valley SA12: C'avon . . . . . . .5F 91
Pineway SA5: Tre b . . . . . . . . . .4E 73
Pinewood SA18: Amm . . . . . . . .1C 22
Pinewood Cl. SA6: Clase . . . . . . .5G 59
Pinewood Rd. SA2: Upl . . . . . . . .4B 84

Pinewood Ter. SA12: Bag . . . . .4A 90
Pinkney St. SA1: St T . . .2H 5 (3H 85)
Pintail Cl. CF36: Not . . . . . .2A 124
Pisgah St. CF33: Ken H . . . . . .5E 113
Pitchford La. SA10: L'dcy . . . .4C 76
PITTON . . . . . . . . . . . . . . . . .2D 108
Pitton Cross Cvn. & Camping Pk.
SA3: P'tn . . . . . . . . . . . .3E 109
Pittsburgh Ct. SA5: Blae M . . .1B 72
Plantasia
Swansea . . . . . . . .3F 5 (3G 85)
Plas Cadwgan SA4: Penl . . . . .4G 57
Plas Cadwgan Rd. SA6: Ystwe . .1D 60
Plas Croeso SA4: Gor . . . . . . .5H 55
Plas Gwernfadog Dr.
SA6: Yfgn . . . . . . . . . . . .1B 60
Plas Gwyn Rd. SA14: Pen g . . . .4H 9
(shown as Heol Plas Gwyn)
Plasgwyn Rd. SA4: P'dul . . . .6G 35
Plas Heddwch CF33: N Cor . . .1D 116
Plas Ioan SA31: John . . . . . . .6B 6
Plas Kenfig CF33: N Cor . . . . .2C 116
PLASMARL . . . . . . . . . . . . . . .3H 73
Plasmarl Ind. Est.
SA6: Swan Ent . . . . . . . . .2A 74
Plasmarl Ter. SA6: Plas . . . . .3H 73
Plas Melyn SA5: Por . . . . . . . .2C 72
Plas Morlais CF33: N Cor . . . .1D 116
Plas Newydd SA2: Dunv . . . . .2A 82
SA4: Grov . . . . . . . . . . . . .1B 56
SA16: Burr P . . . . . . . . . . .2F 39
Plas Penwern SA31: John . . . . .6C 6
Plas Rd. SA4: Grov . . . . . . . . .6B 46
SA8: Rhos . . . . . . . . . . . . .1G 51
Plas Tymawr CF31: Pen F . . . .3C 120
PLASYCOED . . . . . . . . . . . . .4A 28
Plas y Coed Av. SA6: Morr . . . .6A 60
Plas y Ddol SA31: John . . . . . .5B 6
Plas-y-Fforest SA4: Ffor . . . . .4C 34
SA4: Penl . . . . . . . . . . . . .4H 57
Plas-y-mor SA16: Burr P . . . . .3E 39
Plas Ystrad SA31: John . . . . . .6B 6
Players Av. SA6: Cly . . . . . . . .4D 48
Players Ind. Est. SA6: Ystwe . . .6E 49
Play Football . . . . . . . . . . . . .6F 59
Pleasant Cl. SA4: Gor . . . . . . .3G 55
Pleasant Hill SA10: Cilf . . . . .1F 65
Pleasant Rd. SA4: Gor . . . . . . .4D 56
Pleasant Row SA5: Man . . . . . .5F 73
SA15: Llane . . . . . . . . . . .1B 52
Pleasant St.
SA1: Swan . . . . . .2E 5 (3F 85)
SA6: Morr . . . . . . . . . . . . .5A 60
Pleasant Vw. CF32: A'knfig . . .6B 114
CF32: B'myn . . . . . . . . . .3E 115
CF32: Cef C . . . . . . . . . . .1C 118
SA4: Lou . . . . . . . . . . . . .4F 55
SA15: F'oel . . . . . . . . . . . .3B 42
Pleasant Vw. Ter.
SA1: Swan . . . . . .1D 4 (2F 85)
SA5: Man . . . . . . .1A 4 (4F 73)
Pleasant Vs. SA4: P'dul . . . . . .4F 35
Florin Rd. CF33: N Cor . . . . . .6B 112
Plough Rd. SA1: L'ore . . . . . . .5G 73
Plouzane Rd. CF35: P'coed . . .5G 123
Plover Cl. SA5: Tre b . . . . . . . .1F 73
Plumley Cl. CF33: N Cor . . . . .1C 116
Plunch La. SA3: T Mum . . . . .2F 101
Plymouth St.
SA1: Swan . . . . . .4D 4 (4F 85)
Pobbles Cl. SA3: S'gate . . . . .3H 111
Pocketts Wharf
SA1: Swan . . . . . .5G 5 (4H 85)
Pod, The SA1: Swan Ent . . . . .4H 73
Pondside SA31: John . . . . . . . .4B 6
Pond St. SA31: Carm . . . . . . . .3D 6
PONT ABRAHAM SERVICE AREA
. . . . . . . . . . . . . . . . . . . . .5C 30
PONTAMMAN . . . . . . . . . . . . .6C 12
Pontamman Rd. SA18: Amm . . .6B 12
PONTARDAWE . . . . . . . . . . . . .5D 36
Pontardawe Arts Cen. . . . . . . .6D 36
Pontardawe Golf Course . . . . .4D 36
Pontardawe Ind. Est.
SA8: P'dwe . . . . . . . . . . . .5E 37
Pontardawe Leisure Cen. . . . .1C 50
Pontardawe Rd. SA6: Cly . . . . .5G 49
Pontardawe Swimming Pool . .5D 36
PONTARDDULAIS . . . . . . . . . . .5F 35
Pontarddulais Rd. SA4: Gor . . .2A 56
PONTARDULAIS . . . . . . . . . . . .5F 35
Pontardulais Community Leisure Cen.
. . . . . . . . . . . . . . . . . . . . .5G 35
Pontardulais Ind. Est.
SA4: P'dul . . . . . . . . . . . . .4F 35

Pontardulais Retail Pk.
SA5: Cad . . . . . . . . . . . . .2A 72
Pontardulais Rd. SA4: Grov . . .4B 46
SA4: Penl, P'liw . . . . . . . . .2F 57
SA5: Cad . . . . . . . . . . . . .2H 71
SA14: Cross H . . . . . . . . . .6C 8
SA14: L'nch . . . . . . . . . . . .2F 45
SA18: Tyc . . . . . . . . . . . . .6A 20
Pont Aur SA9: Ystra . . . . . . . .1H 33
Pont George Rd. CF33: Pyle . . .4E 113
PONTLLIW . . . . . . . . . . . . . . .6F 47
Pont Newydd CF35: P'coed . . .5G 123
Pont St. SA13: P Tal . . . . . . . .4H 97
Pont-y-Cob Rd. SA4: Gow . . . .2G 69
Pont-y-Cob Rd. SA4: Gow . . . .1G 69
Pontyglasdwr SA1: Swan . . . .1G 85
Poplar Av. CF36: P'cwl . . . . . .4D 124
Poplar Cl. SA2: Sket . . . . . . . .2G 83
Poplar Cl. SA14: Cross H . . . . .6C 8
Poplar Cres. CF36: P'cwl . . . .4D 124
Poplar Rd. CF36: P'cwl . . . . . .4D 124
Poplars SA12: Sand . . . . . . . .3D 96
Poplars Av. SA11: Cim . . . . . . .2C 78
Poppy Cl. SA12: Sand . . . . . . .1B 96
Poppy Ct. SA11: Nea . . . . . . . .2B 78
PORT-EYNON . . . . . . . . . . . . .5H 109
PORTHCAWL . . . . . . . . . . . . . .5C 124
Porthcawl Dual Use Sports Cen.
. . . . . . . . . . . . . . . . . . . . .4B 124
Porthcawl Rd.
CF33: N Cor, Sth C . . . . . .3C 116
Porth Nedd SA11: Nea . . . . . . .1B 78
PORTH TYWYN . . . . . . . . . . . .3E 39
Porth y Gar SA14: Byn . . . . . . .5C 54
Porth y Plas SA31: John . . . . . .5B 6
Porth y Waun SA4: Gow . . . . . .2H 69
Portia Ter. SA1: Swan . . . .1C 4 (2F 85)
Portland Ho. SA1: Swan . . . . . .3D 4
Portland St.
SA1: Swan . . . . . .3D 4 (3F 85)
PORTMEAD . . . . . . . . . . . . . . .2C 72
Portmead Av. SA5: Blae M . . . .2B 72
Portmead Pl. SA5: Blae M . . . .1B 72
PORT TALBOT . . . . . . . . . . . . .3G 97
Port Talbot Bus Station . . . . . .3F 97
Port Talbot Ind. Est.
SA13: P Tal . . . . . . . . . . . .5E 97
Port Talbot Parkway Station (Rail)
. . . . . . . . . . . . . . . . . . . . .4G 97
Port Talbot Pl. SA5: Rav . . . . . .3B 72
Port Talbot Town FC . . . . . . . . .4D 96
PORT TENNANT . . . . . . . . . . . .2D 86
Port Tennant Rd. SA1: Por T . . .3A 86
Portway SA3: Bishop . . . . . . . .5G 93
Portway, The CF36: P'cwl . . . .5C 124
Post Ho., The SA1: Swan . . . . . .3D 4
Pothouse Rd. SA31: Carm . . . . .4D 6
Potters Grn. CF32: Brync . . . .5D 114
Pottery Pl. SA5: Lou . . . . . . . .1A 56
Pottery St. SA1: Swan . . .1F 5 (2G 85)
SA15: Llane . . . . . . . . . . . .1A 52
POUNDFFALD . . . . . . . . . . . . .1E 81
Powell St. SA1: Swan . . .1E 5 (2G 85)
Powys Av. SA1: Town . . . . . . . .2C 84
Powys Gdns. SA1: Town . . . . . .2C 84
Precinct, The CF31: Bri . . . . . .4D 120
SA2: Kill . . . . . . . . . . . . . .4D 82
Prendergast St. SA15: Llane . . .1B 52
Prescelli Rd. SA5: P'lan . . . . . .4C 72
Preseli SA2: Sket . . . . . . . . . .5A 84
Preswylfa Ct. CF31: Bri . . . . . .3D 126
Preswylfa Row SA15: Llane . . .3A 52
Prettyman Dr. SA10: L'dcy . . . .5C 76
Primrose Bank SA10: B'och . . .1G 63
Primrose Cl. CF31: Brack . . . .5H 121
Primrose Ct. SA5: P'lan . . . . . .3D 72
Primrose Hill
SA1: Swan . . . . . .2B 4 (3E 85)
SA31: Carm . . . . . . . . . . . .5F 7
Primrose La. SA8: Rhos . . . . . .2G 51
Primrose Rd. SA11: Nea . . . . . .4A 78
Primrose Row SA8: P'dwe . . . .5C 36
Primrose St.
SA1: Swan . . . . . .2B 4 (3E 85)
Prince Apartments
SA1: Swan Ent . . . . . . . . . .5H 73
Prince of Wales Dr. SA31: Nea . . .6B 64
Prince of Wales Rd.
SA1: Swan . . . . . . . . . . . . .2G 85
PRINCE PHILIP HOSPITAL
(YSBYTY'R TYWYSOG PHILIP)
. . . . . . . . . . . . . . . . . . . . .5E 43

Prince Rd. CF33: Ken H . . . . . .5G 113
Princess Ct. SA15: Llane . . . . . .4H 41
Princess Dr. SA10: B'och . . . . .4H 63
Princess Ho. SA1: Swan . . . . . .4E 5
Princess Lofts SA1: Swan . . . . .4E 5
Princess Margaret Way, The
SA12: A'von, Sand . . . . . . .2A 96
Princess of Wales Ct.
SA1: Bon . . . . . . . . . . . . . .3D 74
PRINCESS OF WALES HOSPITAL
(YSBYTY TYWYSOGES CYMRU)
. . . . . . . . . . . . . . . . . . . . .5F 121
Princess Royal Theatre, The . .3G 97
Princess St. SA4: Gor . . . . . . . .3A 56
SA15: Llane . . . . . . . . . . . .4H 41
Princess Way CF31: Brack . . . .1F 127
SA1: Swan . . . . . .3E 5 (3G 85)
Prince St. SA13: Marg . . . . . . .1E 103
Princes Way CF31: Bri . . . . . . .2G 127
Principality Ho. SA1: Swan . . . .3D 4
Priors Cres. SA2: Dunv . . . . . . .2A 82
Prior St. SA13: P Tal . . . . . . . .3G 97
Priors Way SA2: Dunv . . . . . . .2A 82
Prior's Wood
& Meadow Nature Reserve
. . . . . . . . . . . . . . . . . . . . .2G 81
Priory Av. CF31: Bri . . . . . . . .4E 127
Priory Cl. CF31: Bri . . . . . . . .4E 127
SA31: Carm . . . . . . . . . . . .2G 7
Priory Ct. SA10: B'och . . . . . . .4H 63
Priory Gdns. CF31: Bri . . . . . .3E 127
Priory Oak CF31: Brack . . . . . .1F 127
Priory Rd. CF31: Bri . . . . . . . .3E 127
Priory Row SA31: Carm . . . . . .3F 7
Priory St. SA31: Carm . . . . . . .3F 7
Promenade SA3: W Cro . . . . . .4G 95
Promenade, The
SA1: Swan . . . . . .2B 4 (3E 85)
SA3: Blk P . . . . . .6A 4 (6B 84)
SA4: Penc . . . . . . . . . . . . .4F 67
Promenade Ter.
SA3: T Mum . . . . . . . . . . .2F 101
Promenade Vw. SA12: Sand . . .3B 96
Prospect Pl. SA1: Swan . . . . . .4F 5
SA2: Sket . . . . . . . . . . . . .3H 83
SA9: Cwml . . . . . . . . . . . . .6H 17
SA9: Ysta . . . . . . . . . . . . .2E 33
SA15: Llane . . . . . . . . . . . .6A 42
SA31: Carm . . . . . . . . . . . .3D 6
Prospect Ter. SA3: W Cro . . . . .6E 95
Prosser Cl. SA31: Carm . . . . . .2F 7
Protheroe Av. CF31: Pen F . . . .3B 120
Providence La. SA3: Bishop . . .6G 93
Pryce St. SA15: Llane . . . . . . . .2H 41
Pryderi Footpath SA1: M'hill . . .2E 85
Prydwen Rd. SA5: Ffor F . . . . .4G 71
Pugsley Gdns. CF32: Brync . . . .5E 115
Pumphouse Quay
SA1: Swan . . . . . .5G 5 (4G 85)
Purcell Av. SA12: Sand . . . . . .1A 96
Purcell Ind. Est. SA12: Sand . . .1A 96
Purple Cl. SA12: Sand . . . . . . .1A 96
PWLL . . . . . . . . . . . . . . . . . . .2D 40
Pwlldu La. SA3: Bishop . . . . . . .3F 99
Pwll Evan Ddu CF35: Coity . . . .3H 121
Pwll Melyn CF35: P'coed . . . . .2F 123
Pwll Rd. SA15: Pwll . . . . . . . . .2F 39
SA16: Burr P . . . . . . . . . . .2F 39
Pwll St. SA1: L'ore . . . . . . . . . .4G 73
Pwll-y-Domen Rd.
SA5: Man . . . . . . . . . . . . .5E 73
Pwllygarth St. SA31: Ken H . . . .5F 113
Pwll-yr-Hwyaid SA5: Por . . . . .2B 72
Pwll-y-Waun CF36: P'cwl . . . . .3E 125
PYE . . . . . . . . . . . . . . . . . . . . .1G 99
Pyle & Kenfig Golf Course . . . .3A 116
Pyle Cl. SA3: Bishop . . . . . . . .1G 99
Pyle Cross CF33: Pyle . . . . . . .6E 113
Pyle Ent. Cen. CF33: Pyle . . . .6G 113
Pyle Inn Way CF33: Pyle . . . . .6E 113
Pyle Life Cen. . . . . . . . . . . . . .6E 113
Pyle Rd. CF33: Pyle . . . . . . . . .4E 113
CF36: P'cwl . . . . . . . . . . . .1D 124
SA3: Bishop . . . . . . . . . . . .1G 99
Pyle Station (Rail) . . . . . . . . . .6E 113
Pyle Swimming Pool . . . . . . . .6E 113
Pyntws Ter. SA15: Llane . . . . . .2C 52

Quadrangle, The CF32: Sarn . . .5D 114
CF33: Pyle . . . . . . . . . . . . .6D 112
Quadrant, The SA2: Upl . . . . . .4B 84

Quadrant Shop. Cen.
SA1: Swan . . . . . . . .4D 4 (4F 85)
Quarella CF31: Bri . . . . . . . . .5D 120
Quarella Cres. CF31: Bri . . . . .5D 120
Quarella Rd. CF31: Bri . . . . . .4D 120
Quarr Dr. SA6: Cly . . . . . . . . . .5E 49
Quar Rd. SA11: Nea . . . . . . . . .2B 78
Quarr Rd. SA6: Cly . . . . . . . . . .5E 49
SA8: P'dwe . . . . . . . . . . . . .5D 36
Quarry Pl. SA18: Gwaun . . . . . .1C 24
Quarry Rd. SA5: Tre b . . . . . . . .3F 73
SA11: Tonna . . . . . . . . . . .4F 65
SA18: Bry . . . . . . . . . . . . .3A 16
Quarry St. SA1: Swan . . .1E 5 (2G 85)
Quay, The SA31: Carm . . . . . . .4F 5
Quay Pde.
SA1: St T, Swan . . . .4F 5 (3G 85)
Quay Rd. SA11: Nea . . . . . . . . .6A 64
Quay St. SA18: Amm . . . . . . . .1A 22
SA31: Carm . . . . . . . . . . . .4E 7
(not continuous)
Quay West SA1: Swan . . . . . . . .3F 5
Queen Mary's Wlk.
SA15: Llane . . . . . . . . . . . .2B 52
Queen's Av. CF32: Sarn . . . . . .5D 114
Queens Av. SA4: Gor . . . . . . . .5A 56
Queens Ct. CF31: Bri . . . . . . . .2H 127
SA10: Skew . . . . . . . . . . . .1E 77
(off Queens Rd.)
Queens Ct., The SA12: A'von . . .5C 96
Queen's Rd. SA3: T Mum . . . . .1E 101
SA10: Skew . . . . . . . . . . . .1E 77
Queens Rd. CF31: Bri . . . . . . . .3H 127
(not continuous)
Queen St. CF31: Bri . . . . . . . . .1E 127
CF32: B'myn . . . . . . . . . . . .3C 114
SA11: Nea . . . . . . . . . . . . .6B 64
SA31: Carm . . . . . . . . . . . .3E 7
Queen St. Bk. Rd. SA11: Nea . . .1B 78
Queensway SA5: Ffor F . . . . . . .4A 72
Queensway Bus. Cen.
SA5: Ffor F . . . . . . . . . . . . .4A 72
Queen Victoria Rd.
SA15: Llane . . . . . . . . . . . .5H 41

## R

Raby St. SA15: Llane . . . . . . . .3H 41
Radnor Dr. SA6: Yfgn . . . . . . . .2C 60
Radnor Ho.
SA1: Swan . . . . . .4G 5 (4H 85)
SA12: Sand . . . . . . . . . . . .4C 96
(off Moorland Rd.)
Radyr Av. SA3: May . . . . . . . . .2D 94
Raglan Rd. SA2: Sket . . . . . . . .3H 83
Railmill La. SA12: C'avon . . . . .5H 91
Railway Cotts.
SA6: Cwm'crw . . . . . . . . . .3A 60
Railway Pl. SA15: Llane . . . . . .5H 41
Railway Ter. CF33: Sth C . . . . .4D 116
SA1: L'ore . . . . . . . . . . . . .5B 56
SA4: Gor . . . . . . . . . . . . . .5B 56
SA5: Ffor F . . . . . . . . . . . . .5B 72
SA15: Llane . . . . . . . . . . . .5H 41
Rainbow Bus. Cen.
SA7: Swan Ent . . . . . . . . . .2C 74
Raleigh Cl. SA2: Sket . . . . . . . .4H 83
RALLT . . . . . . . . . . . . . . . . . . .3F 107
Ralph St. SA15: Llane . . . . . . . .1A 52
Ralph Ter. SA15: Llane . . . . . . .5H 41
Ramsden Rd. SA6: Cly . . . . . . .5D 48
Ramsey Cl. CF36: Not . . . . . . .2A 124
Ramsey Dr. SA6: Clase . . . . . . .5G 59
Ramsey Pl. SA5: Blae M . . . . . .1B 72
Ramsey Rd. SA6: Cly . . . . . . . .3F 49
Randell Sq. SA16: Pem . . . . . . .2A 38
Raphael Av. CF31: Brack . . . . .5A 122
Raven Cl. CF31: Bri . . . . . . . . .2G 127
Ravenhill Rd. SA5: Rav . . . . . . .4B 72
Raven Ind. Est. SA18: Garn . . . .5D 14
Ravens Cl. SA11: Cim . . . . . . . .3E 79
Ravensfield SA4: Gow . . . . . . . .5C 70
Ravens Wlk. SA3: W Cro . . . . . .6D 94
Ravenswood Cl. SA10: Nea . . . .4B 64
Rawlings Rd. SA18: L'bie . . . . .1F 11
Recorder St.
SA1: Swan . . . . . .5D 4 (4F 85)
Rectory Cl. CF32: Sarn . . . . . . .6D 114
SA4: Lou . . . . . . . . . . . . . .5F 55
Rectory Rd. SA11: Nea . . . . . . .1B 78
Redcliffe Apartments
SA3: Casw . . . . . . . . . . . . .2H 99

Redcliffe Ho.—St Christopher's Ct.


Redcliffe Ho. SA1: Swan . . . . . . . .3A 4
Redlands Cl. CF35: P'coed . . . .4G 123
Redley Cliff Nature Reserve . . .2H 99
Redman Cl. CF33: Ken H . . . . .5G 113
Red Oaks CF35: P'coed . . . . . . .3E 123
Redshank Cl. CF36: Not . . . . . .3A 124
Red St. SA31: Carm . . . . . . . . . . . .3E 7
Redwing Cl. CF31: Brack . . . . .1H 127
Redwood Cl. SA10: B'och . . . . . .1H 63
Redwood Ct. SA5: P'lan . . . . . . .3D 72
Redwood Rd. SA3: W Cro . . . . .5E 95
Rees Pl. SA11: Nea . . . . . . . . . . .1B 78
Rees Row CF32: Brync . . . . . . .5E 115
Rees St. SA12: A'von . . . . . . . . . .3E 97
Regalia Ter. SA15: Llane . . . . . . .1B 52
Regency Ho. SA1: Swan . . . . . . . .3C 4
Regent St. E. SA11: Brit F . . . . . .1H 89
Regent St. W. SA11: Brit F . . . . .1G 89
Reginald St. SA1: Por T . . . . . . .3B 86
SA13: P Tal . . . . . . . . . . . . .3G 97
Reigit La. SA3: Mur . . . . . . . . . .6B 94
Rembrandt Ct. SA2: Sket . . . . . .4B 84
Rembrandt Pl. SA12: Sand . . . . .3D 96
Reservoir Rd. *SA31: Carm . . . . . .1F 7*
*(shown as Ffordd y Cronlyn)*
Rest Bay Cl. CF36: P'cwl . . . . . .2A 124
Restway Gdns. CF31: Bri . . . . .1D 126
Restways CF36: P'cwl . . . . . . . .4B 124
Retreat, The CF31: Bri . . . . . . .3D 126
CF32: Sarn . . . . . . . . . . . . .5D 114
CF36: Not . . . . . . . . . . . . .1B 124
Reynallt Pl. CF36: P'cwl . . . . . .4C 124
Reynolds Cl. CF33: N Cor . . . . .1B 116
REYNOLDSTON . . . . . . . . . . . .6B 106
Rhanallt St. SA13: Marg . . . . . .1E 103
Rhandir SA14: Llwy . . . . . . . . . .2H 53
Rhandirfelen SA15: F'oel . . . . . . .3C 42
Rhandirfelin SA15: F'oel . . . . . . .3B 42
Rhandir Ter. SA14: L'nch . . . . . . .3C 44
Rheidol Av. SA6: Clase . . . . . . . .6F 59
Rheidol Ct. SA6: Clase . . . . . . . . .6F 59
Rhes Bricksen *SA10: Sev S . . . . .5F 29*
*(off High St.)*
Rhes Brickyard Row SA15: Llane . . . . . . . . . . . . .4C 52
Rhes Bryndulais SA10: Sev S . . .5F 29
Rhes Gwaith Tyn SA15: Llane . . .4C 52
Rhes Leith CF32: Ton . . . . . . . .5A 114
Rhester Fawr SA9: Ystra . . . . . . .5A 28
Rhianfa Gdns. SA1: Swan . . . . . . . .2A 4 (3D 84)
Rhianfa La. SA1: Swan . . . . . . . .2A 4 (3D 84)
Rhiw, The CF31: Bri . . . . . . . . . .1E 127
Rhiw Babell SA31: Carm . . . . . . . .5E 7
Rhiw Cae Mawr CF31: Brack . . .6G 121
Rhiw Cen., The CF31: Bri . . . . .1E 127
Rhiwderyn SA7: Birch . . . . . . . . .6A 62
Rhiwfawr Rd. SA9: Cwm I . . . . . .4C 26
Rhiw Las CF31: Brack . . . . . . . .6H 121
Rhiwlas SA2: Dunv . . . . . . . . . . .2C 82
SA10: Nea . . . . . . . . . . . . . .4H 63
Rhiw Rd. SA9: P fawr . . . . . . . . .4A 26
Rhiw'r Wennol Ddu CF31: Bri . . . . . . . . . . . . . .6C 126
Rhiw Tremaen CF31: Brack . . . .6G 121
Rhodes Av. SA12: A'von . . . . . . .2E 97
Rhodfa Bevan SA10: C'dxtn . . . .5B 64
Rhodfa Bryn-Mawr SA18: Amm . . . . . . . . . . . . .6H 11
Rhodfa Brynmenyn CF32: Brync . . . . . . . . . . . .4E 115
Rhodfa Bryn Rhos SA18: Glan . . . . . . . . . . . . . .5A 14
Rhodfa Canolog SA12: Bag . . . . .5H 89
Rhodfa Ceirios CF31: Pen F . . .3C 120
Rhodfa Cnocell y Coed CF31: Bri . . . . . . . . . . . . . .6C 126
Rhodfa Delme SA15: Llane . . . . .3G 41
Rhodfa Fadog SA6: Cwm'crw . . .1B 60
Rhodfa Frank SA18: Amm . . . . . .6G 11
Rhodfa Glyndwr SA31: Carm . . . . .2F 7
Rhodfa Helios SA12: Bag . . . . . .5H 89
Rhodfa Llwyneithin SA15: Llane . . . . . . . . . . . . .5A 42
Rhodfa Martyn SA10: Sev S . . . .5F 29
Rhodfa Mes CF31: Bri . . . . . . . .1A 126
Rhodfa Morgan Dr. SA31: Carm . . . . . . . . . . . . . .5F 7
Rhodfa Parc Slip CF32: Ton . . .4B 114
Rhodfa'r Brain SA5: Rav . . . . . . .3B 72
Rhodfar Capel SA16: Pem . . . . . . .2B 38
Rhodfa'r Celyn CF35: Coity . . . .2G 121
Rhodfa'r Dryw SA6: Cwm'crw . . .1A 60
Rhodfa'r Eos SA6: Cwm'crw . . . .1A 60
Rhodfa'r Wennol SA6: Cwm'crw . . . . . . . . . . .1A 60
Rhodfa'r Wiwer SA4: Ffor . . . . . .5D 34
Rhodfa Sirius SA12: Bag . . . . . . .5H 89
Rhondda St. SA1: Swan . . . . . . . .2A 4 (3E 85)
RHOS . . . . . . . . . . . . . . . . . . . .1G 51
RHOSAMAN . . . . . . . . . . . . . . .3D 16
Rhosfa Rd. *SA18: Bry . . . . . . . . .2C 16*
*(shown as Heol y Rhosfa)*
RHOSILI . . . . . . . . . . . . . . . . .2C 108
Rhos Las SA31: Carm . . . . . . . . . .5F 7
Rhos Mdw. SA8: Rhos . . . . . . . .6G 37
Rhos Rd. SA5: Gen . . . . . . . . . . .4C 72
RHOSSILI . . . . . . . . . . . . . . . .2C 108
Rhossili SA2: Sket . . . . . . . . . . .5A 84
Rhossili Activity Cen. . . . . . . . .2D 108
Rhos Ter. SA18: Tyc . . . . . . . . . .3C 20
Rhosybonwen Rd. *SA14: Cross H . . . . . . . . . . . .4A 8*
*(shown as Heol-Rhosybonwen)*
Rhosyfedwen SA18: Amm . . . . . . .3H 21
Rhos yr Abad SA12: Bag . . . . . . .2D 96
Rhych Av. CF36: P'cwl . . . . . . . .5E 125
RHYDAMAN . . . . . . . . . . . . . . .1A 22
RHYDDING . . . . . . . . . . . . . . . .4B 64
Rhyddings Pk. Rd. SA2: Brynm . . . . . . . . . . . . .4C 84
Rhyddings Ter. SA2: Brynm . . . .4C 84
Rhyddwen Pl. SA6: Craig-p . . . . .3C 48
Rhyddwen Rd. SA6: Craig-p . . . .2C 48
Rhyd-Hir SA10: Nea A . . . . . . . . .5F 63
Rhyd La. CF31: Pen F . . . . . . . .1C 120
CF32: Pen F . . . . . . . . . . . .1C 120
Rhyd Wen SA15: Llane . . . . . . . .5A 52
SA18: Rhosa . . . . . . . . . . . . .4E 17
Rhydwen SA9: Ystra . . . . . . . . . .2H 33
Rhyd-y-Coed SA7: Birch . . . . . . .6H 61
Rhyd-y-Defaid Dr. SA2: Sket . . . .5F 83
Rhyd y Felin SA7: L'smlt . . . . . . .2G 75
Rhyd-y-Fenni SA4: Crof . . . . . . . .5E 67
RHYD-Y-FRO . . . . . . . . . . . . . .3C 36
Rhyd-y-Glyn SA7: L'smlt . . . . . . .2G 75
RHYD-Y-GWIN . . . . . . . . . . . . . .1B 48
Rhydymardy SA4: Gor . . . . . . . . .4B 56
Rhyd-y-Nant CF35: P'coed . . . . .2F 123
RHYD-Y-PANDY . . . . . . . . . . . . .4A 48
Rhyd-y-Pandy Rd. SA6: Pantl, Rhyd p . . . . . . . . . . . . . . . . .1G 59, 6A 48
Rhyd-y-Pennau SA10: Nea . . . . .4H 63
Rhydypolan SA4: Gor . . . . . . . . .5A 56
Rhydyrafon SA15: Llane . . . . . . .5C 42
Rhyd yr Helyg SA2: Sket . . . . . .5G 83
Rice St. CF31: Bri . . . . . . . . . . .1D 126
SA13: P Tal . . . . . . . . . . . . .5H 97
SA15: Llane . . . . . . . . . . . . .2B 52
Richardson Rd. SA1: Swan . . . . . . . .5B 4 (4E 85)
Richardson St. SA1: Swan . . . . . . . .4B 4 (4E 85)
SA8: T'nos . . . . . . . . . . . . . .1B 50
Richard's Pl. SA1: Swan . . . . . . . .2E 5 (3G 85)
Richard St. SA5: Man . . . . . . . . .6F 73
SA15: Llane . . . . . . . . . . . . .1A 52
Richley Cl. SA12: Bag . . . . . . . . .5B 90
Richmond Cl. SA31: Carm . . . . . . .3E 7
Richmond Cotts. *SA31: Carm . . . .2F 7*
*(off Richmond Ter.)*
Richmond Ct. SA2: Upl . . . . . . . .3D 84
Richmond M. SA2: Upl . . . . . . . .3D 84
Richmond Park . . . . . . . . . . . . .3F 7
Richmond Pk. SA4: Lou . . . . . . .5G 55
SA9: Ystra . . . . . . . . . . . . . .4B 28
Richmond Pl. SA13: P Tal . . . . . .5H 97
Richmond Rd. SA2: Upl . . . . . . . .3D 84
SA4: Lou . . . . . . . . . . . . . . .5G 55
Richmond St. SA11: Nea . . . . . . .1B 78
Richmond Ter. SA2: Upl . . . . . . .3C 84
SA15: Llane . . . . . . . . . . . . .5H 41
SA31: Carm . . . . . . . . . . . . . .3E 7
Richmond Vs. SA1: Swan . . . . . .3D 84
Richmond Way SA5: Rav . . . . . . .3A 72
Rickyard, The SA10: B'och . . . . .3A 64
Ridge, The SA2: Sket . . . . . . . . .6G 83
Ridge Acre SA2: Sket . . . . . . . . .6H 83
Ridgeway SA2: Kill . . . . . . . . . . .4C 82
SA14: F'oel . . . . . . . . . . . . .2D 42
Ridgeway La. SA10: L'dcy . . . . .4B 76
Ridgewood Gdns. SA11: Cim . . .3E 79
Ridgewood Pk. SA15: Llane . . . .1D 52
Ridley Way SA3: Bishop . . . . . . .6H 93
Rifleman's Row SA1: Bon . . . . . .6A 74
Ritson St. SA11: Brit F . . . . . . . .1H 89
River Ct. CF35: Treoes . . . . . . .3D 128
Riversdale Rd. SA3: W Cro . . . . .6E 95
Riverside CF32: A'knfig . . . . . . .6C 114
SA4: Llanm . . . . . . . . . . . . . .6E 67
(not continuous)
SA10: A'dul . . . . . . . . . . . . .3F 65
*SA11: Nea . . . . . . . . . . . . . .6B 64*
*(off Brickyard Cotts.)*
SA13: P Tal . . . . . . . . . . . . .3H 97
SA16: Burr P . . . . . . . . . . . .2E 39
Riverside Bus. Pk. SA7: Swan Ent . . . . . . . . . . .5C 60
Riverside Cvn. Site SA6: Yfgn . . . . . . . . . . . . . .3D 60
Riverside Ct. SA8: P'dwe . . . . . .6D 36
Riverside Dr. SA11: Nea . . . . . . .6B 64
Riverside Ind. Pk. SA14: L'nch . . . . . . . . . . . . .4D 44
Riverside Wlk. SA13: P Tal . . . . .3F 97
River Ter. SA4: Hendy . . . . . . . . .6D 34
River Vw. SA14: Cross H . . . . . .2D 18
River Vw. Touring Pk. SA4: L'edi . . . . . . . . . . . . . .2C 30
River Way *SA18: Amm . . . . . . . .5H 11*
*(shown as Ffordd-yr-Afon)*
Road No. 2 SA12: Bag . . . . . . . . .6E 89
Road No. 3 SA12: Bag . . . . . . . . .6E 89
Robert Davies Ct. SA4: P'dul . . . .6F 35
Robert Owen Gdns. SA1: Por T . . . . . . . . . . . . . .2C 86
Robert's Rd. SA1: Swan . . . . . . .5A 86
Robert St. SA5: Man . . . . . . . . . .5F 73
Robin Rd. SA5: Blae M . . . . . . . .1B 72
Robins Hill CF31: Brack . . . . . .1H 127
Robins La. SA3: Rey . . . . . . . . .6B 106
Robinson St. SA15: Llane . . . . . .2A 52
Rock Chwyth Rd. SA8: All . . . . . .1E 51
Rockfields CF36: Not . . . . . . . . .2B 124
Rockfields Cl. CF36: Not . . . . . .2C 124
Rockfields Cres. CF36: Not . . . .2C 124
Rockfield Ter. SA11: Nea . . . . . .3A 78
Rockhill SA3: T Mum . . . . . . . . .2F 101
Rockingham Ter. SA11: Brit F . . .1H 89
Rockland Ter. SA1: Swan . . . . . .1F 85
Rock La. *SA3: Hort . . . . . . . . . .5A 110*
*(off Castle Hill)*
SA8: All . . . . . . . . . . . . . . . .1E 51
Rock St. CF32: A'knfig . . . . . . . .5B 114
Rock Ter. SA6: Morr . . . . . . . . . .5A 60
Roderick Cl. SA1: Town . . . . . . .6B 72
Rodney St. SA1: Swan . . . . . . . .6A 4 (5E 85)
Rofton Bungs. SA12: C'avon . . . .4H 91
Roger Beck Way SA2: Sket . . . . .4B 84
Roger's La. CF32: Lale . . . . . . . .5F 119
Roger St. SA5: Tre b . . . . . . . . . .1E 73
Roland Av. SA15: Llane . . . . . . . .2H 41
Roman Amphitheatre . . . . . . . . .2F 7
Roman Bri. Cl. SA3: Blk P . . . . .2G 95
Roman Ct. SA3: Blk P . . . . . . . . .2G 95
Roman Pk. SA31: Carm . . . . . . . . .5F 7
Roman Rd. SA31: Carm . . . . . . . .5E 7
Roman Way SA10: Nea . . . . . . . .6A 64
Romney Rd. SA12: Sand . . . . . . .3C 96
Rookwood Cl. SA11: Nea . . . . . .1C 78
Roper Wright Cl. SA4: Gow . . . .3H 69
Ropewalk SA11: Nea . . . . . . . . . .1B 78
*SA31: Carm . . . . . . . . . . . . . .2G 7*
*(off Priory St.)*
Ropewalk Rd. SA15: Llane . . . . .3B 52
Rope Wlk. Ter. SA11: Nea . . . . . .1B 78
Roseberry Ter. SA6: Plas . . . . . .3H 73
Rose Cross Ho. SA5: P'lan . . . . .4D 72
Rosehill SA1: Swan . . . . .2A 4 (3D 84)
Rosehill Ter. SA1: Swan . . . . . . . .2A 4 (3E 85)
Roseland Rd. SA5: Wauna . . . . .5E 71
Roseland Ter. SA1: St T . . . . . . . .2H 5 (3H 85)
Rose La. CF35: Ewe . . . . . . . . .6E 127
Rosemary Cl. SA2: Sket . . . . . . .2G 83
Rosemary Ct. SA6: Morr . . . . . . .5A 60
Rosewarne Cl. SA5: Wauna . . . .5E 71
Rosewood Av. SA12: Bag . . . . . .4B 90
Rosewood Cl. SA10: B'och . . . . .2H 63
Rosewood Ct. SA5: P'lan . . . . . . .3C 72
Ross Av. SA31: Carm . . . . . . . . . .2F 7
Rosser's Fld. SA3: T Mum . . . .3G 101
Rosser's Row SA10: Nea A . . . . .5G 63
Rosser St. SA11: Nea . . . . . . . . .6C 64
Rosser Ter. SA10: Cilf . . . . . . . . .2E 65
Rotary Intl. Way CF31: Brack, Bri . . . . . . . . .6E 121
Rotherslade Ho. SA1: Swan . . . . . . . .1B 4 (2E 85)
Rotherslade Rd. SA3: Lan . . . .2D 100
Rothwell Rd. SA1: Swan . . . . . . . .1F 5 (2G 85)
Row, The SA4: Grov . . . . . . . . . .5A 46
Rowan Av. SA2: Sket . . . . . . . . . .2G 83
Rowan Cl. CF35: P'coed . . . . . .3F 123
SA2: Kill . . . . . . . . . . . . . . . .5C 82
SA4: Gor . . . . . . . . . . . . . . .2H 55
SA6: Cly . . . . . . . . . . . . . . . .4F 49
Rowan Dr. CF36: Newt . . . . . . .3H 125
Rowan Lodge SA10: Nea . . . . . . .6H 63
Rowan's La. CF32: Brync . . . . .4F 115
Rowan Tree Av. SA12: Bag . . . . .6B 90
Rowan Tree Cl. SA10: B'och . . . . . . . . . . . . .4H 63
Rowland Ho. SA11: Cim . . . . . . .3E 79
Royal Bldgs. *SA13: P Tal . . . . . .4G 97*
*(off Talbot Rd.)*
Royal Oak Ct. SA18: L'bie . . . . . .1G 11
Royal Oak Rd. SA2: Sket . . . . . .1G 95
Royal Oak Ter. *SA31: Carm . . . . . .4B 6*
*(off Monument Hill)*
Royal Porthcawl Golf Course CF36: P'cwl . . . . . . . . . . . .1A 124
Royal Sovereign SA1: Swan Ent . . . . . . . . . . .5H 73
Royston Ct. *SA10: Nea . . . . . . . .5H 63*
*(shown as Llys Royston)*
Rufus Lewis Av. SA4: Gor . . . . . .3H 55
Rugby Av. SA11: Nea . . . . . . . . . .1B 78
Ruggles Ter. SA6: Clase . . . . . . .5G 59
Runnymede SA2: Sket . . . . . . . . .3B 84
Rural Way SA2: Sket . . . . . . . . . .2G 83
Rushfield Gdns. CF31: Bri . . . . .5F 121
Rushwind Cl. SA3: W Cro . . . . . .6D 94
Rushwind M. SA3: W Cro . . . . . .6D 94
Ruskin Av. SA12: A'von . . . . . . . .4D 96
Ruskin St. SA11: Brit F . . . . . . . .5G 77
Russell St. SA1: Swan . . .4A 4 (4E 85)
SA15: Llane . . . . . . . . . . . . .3A 52
Russell Ter. SA31: Carm . . . . . . .2C 6
Russet Cl. SA12: Sand . . . . . . . .1A 96
Rustic Cl. SA2: Sket . . . . . . . . . .2G 83
Ruston Rd. SA1: Por T . . . . . . . .3D 86
Ruthin Ct. CF35: Coyc . . . . . . . .1C 128
Rutland Pl. SA1: Swan . . . . . . . .5E 5 (4G 85)
Rutland St. SA1: Swan . . . . . . . .4E 5 (4G 85)
Ryan Cl. SA4: Penl . . . . . . . . . . .4E 57
Ryans Cl. SA10: Nea A . . . . . . . .6H 63
Ryw Blodyn SA7: L'smlt . . . . . . . .2E 75


## S


Sable Av. SA12: Sand . . . . . . . . .2A 96
Sable Cl. SA12: Sand . . . . . . . . .2A 96
Sac St. SA6: Morr . . . . . . . . . . . .6A 60
Saddler St. SA1: L'ore . . . . . . . .4G 73
St Aiden Dr. SA2: Kill . . . . . . . . .4C 82
St Alban's Rd. SA2: Brynm . . . . .5C 84
St Albans Ter. SA13: P Tal . . . . .6H 97
St Andrews Cl. SA3: May . . . . . .3D 94
St Andrew's Rd. CF31: Bri . . . . .4D 120
SA31: Carm . . . . . . . . . . . . . .3E 7
St Annes *SA3: T Mum . . . . . . . .2F 101*
*(off Western La.)*
St Anne's Cl. SA3: Lan . . . . . . .3E 101
St Anne's Cres. CF36: P'cwl . . .4E 125
St Anne's Dr. SA11: Tonna . . . . . .4F 65
St Anne's Ter. SA11: Tonna . . . . .4F 65
St Asaph Dr. SA12: Sand . . . . . . .2A 96
St Asaphs Ct. SA12: Sand . . . . . .2B 96
St Brides Cl. CF36: Not . . . . . . .2C 124
SA4: P'dul . . . . . . . . . . . . . .6G 35
St Bride's Rd. CF32: A'knfig . . .5B 114
CF35: Ewe . . . . . . . . . . . . .6D 126
St Catherines Cl. SA11: Nea . . . .2A 78
St Catherine's Ct. SA1: Swan . . . . . . . .5G 5 (4H 85)
SA12: Bag . . . . . . . . . . . . . .4B 90
St Catherine's Rd. SA12: Bag . . .5B 90
St Catherines Ter. *SA11: Nea . . .3A 78*
*(off Old Rd.)*
St Catherine St. SA31: Carm . . . .3D 6
St Catherine's Wlk. *SA31: Carm . . . . . . . . . . . . .3E 7*
*(off St Catherine St.)*
St Catherine's Wlk. Shop. Cen. SA31: Carm . . . . . . . . . . . . . .3D 6
St Catwg Wlk. SA3: May . . . . . . .2F 95
St Cenydd Rd. SA5: Por . . . . . . .2C 72
St Christopher Dr. SA2: Kill . . . . .4C 82
St Christopher's Ct. SA1: Swan . . . . . . . .6G 5 (5H 85)

**St Christophers Ct.**
  CF35: Coity . . . . . . . . . . .3G 121
**St Christopher's Rd.**
  CF31: Bri . . . . . . . . . . . . .4D 120
  CF36: Newt . . . . . . . . . . .4F 125
**St Clears Pl.** SA5: P'lan . . . . . . .1E 73
**St David Dr.** SA2: Kill . . . . . . . .3C 82
**St David's Av.** SA31: Carm . . . .3D 6
**St David's Cl.** CF31: Brack . . . .5H 121
  CF31: Bri . . . . . . . . . . . . .4D 120
  SA4: Ffor, Hendy . . . . . . .6E 35
  SA4: Lou . . . . . . . . . . . . .5F 55
  SA4: Penl . . . . . . . . . . . .4G 57
  SA15: Llane . . . . . . . . . . .6H 41
**St David's Ind. Est.**
  SA6: Swan Ent . . . . . . . .6C 60
**St Davids Pk.** . . . . . . . . . . . . .3A 6
**St David's Pk.** SA13: Marg . . .1A 112
**St David's Pl.**
  SA31: Carm . . . . . . . .4E 5 (4G 85)
  SA31: Carm . . . . . . . . . .3D 6
**St David's Rd.** CF31: Bri . . . .5C 120
  SA6: Swan Ent . . . . . . . . .1B 74
  SA9: Ysta . . . . . . . . . . . .2F 33
  SA12: Sand . . . . . . . . . . .4D 96
  SA18: Tair . . . . . . . . . . . .1F 25
**St Davids Row** SA15: Llane . . .3A 52
**St David's Shop. Cen.**
  SA1: Swan . . . . . . . . . . . .4E 5
**St David's Sq.**
  SA31: Carm . . . . . . . .4E 5 (4G 85)
  SA31: Carm . . . . . . . . . .3D 6
**St David's St.** SA11: Nea . . . .1B 78
**St David's Way** CF36: P'cwl . . .3D 124
**St Davies Arc.** SA1: Swan . . . . .4D 4
**St Donat's Av.** SA2: Sket . . . . .3G 83
**St Elli Shop. Cen.**
  SA15: Llane . . . . . . . . . . .1A 52
**St Elmo Av.** SA1: St T . . .1H 5 (2H 85)
**St Francis Rd.** CF31: Bri . . . . .4D 120
**St George** SA15: Llane . . . . . . .2D 52
**St George's Av.** CF31: Bri . . . .3D 120
**St George's Ter.** *SA3: Rey* . . . .*6B 106*
  *(off Robins La.)*
**St Govan's Pl.** SA5: Wauna . . . .5C 70
**St Helena** SA16: Graig . . . . . . .1G 39
**St Helen's** . . . . . . . . . . . . . . .5C 84
**St Helen's Av.**
  SA1: Swan . . . . . . . .5A 4 (5D 84)
**St Helen's Cres.**
  SA1: Swan . . . . . . . .6A 4 (4D 84)
**St Helen's Rd.**
  SA1: Swan . . . . . . . .6A 4 (5D 84)
**St Helier Dr.** SA12: Sand . . . . .2A 96
**St Hilary Dr.** SA2: Kill . . . . . . .3C 82
**St Illtyd Ri.** SA16: Pem . . . . . . .2B 38
**St Illtyd's Cl.** CF31: Brack . . . .5H 121
**St Illtyd's Ct.**
  SA12: Bag . . . . . . . . . . . .5B 90
**St Illtyd's Cres.** SA1: St T . . . . .3B 86
**St Illtyd's Dr.** SA12: Bag . . . . .5B 90
**St Illtyd's Rd.** CF31: Bri . . . . .6C 120
**St James' Ct.**
  SA1: Swan . . . . . . . .4A 4 (4D 84)
**St James Cres.** CF33: Pyle . . . .5E 113
  SA1: Swan . . . . . . . .4A 4 (4D 84)
**St James Gdns.** SA1: Swan . . . .3D 84
  *(not continuous)*
**St James Pk.** CF31: Brack . . . .1A 128
**St James Ri.** CF31: Bri . . . . . . .2F 127
**St Johns Ct.** SA6: Swan Ent . . . .5C 60
  *SA31: Carm* . . . . . . . . . .*3F 7*
  *(off St Peter's Ct.)*
**St John's Dr.** CF35: P'coed . . . .4G 123
  CF36: Newt . . . . . . . . . . .4F 125
**St Johns Ho.** *SA1: Swan* . . . . . .*6G 73*
  *(off Odo St.)*
**St John's Rd.** CF31: Bri . . . . . .6C 120
  SA5: Man . . . . . . . . . . . . .5E 73
  SA6: Cly . . . . . . . . . . . . .4F 49
**St John's Ter.** SA10: Nea A . . . .1F 77
**St Joseph's Ct.** SA15: Llane . . .1B 52
**St Josephs Pk.** SA12: A'von . . .2B 96
**St Judes Cl.** SA5: Tre b . . . . . .1E 73
**St Katherine Ct.** SA1: Wins . . . .2E 75
**St Kitts Pl.** SA12: Sand . . . . . . .2B 96
**St Lawrence Ct.** SA5: P'lan . . . .1E 73
**St Leger Cres.** SA1: St T . . . . . .3A 86
**St Leonard's Rd.** CF31: Bri . . .1C 126
**St Lukes Ct.** SA1: Wins . . . . . . .2E 75
**St Maddock's Cl.** CF31: Brack . .5H 121
**St Margaret's Av.**
  SA10: Jer M . . . . . . . . . . .2A 88
**St Margarets Ct.**
  SA1: Swan . . . . . . . .6H 5 (5H 85)

**St Margaret's Dr.**
  SA15: Llane . . . . . . . . . . .2G 41
**St Margaret's Flats**
  SA10: Jer M . . . . . . . . . . .1A 88
**St Marie St.** CF31: Bri . . . . . . .2D 126
**St Mary Cl.** CF35: P'coed . . . .6G 123
**St Mary Pl.** SA12: P Tal . . . . . .3F 97
**St Mary's Arc.** SA1: Swan . . . . .4D 4
**St Mary's Cl.** SA11: Brit F . . . . .1G 89
**St Mary's Ct.** CF36: Newt . . . . .3F 125
  *SA16: Burr P* . . . . . . . . . . .*3E 39*
  *(off Stepney Rd.)*
**St Mary's Ri.** SA16: Burr P . . . . .3F 39
**St Mary's Rd.** SA8: Ynys . . . . .2G 37
**St Mary's Sq.**
  SA1: Swan . . . . . . . .4E 5 (4G 85)
  *(not continuous)*
**St Marys St.** SA31: Carm . . . . . .3E 7
**St Mary St.**
  SA1: Swan . . . . . . . .4E 5 (4G 85)
  SA12: A'von . . . . . . . . . . .3F 97
**St Mary's Vw.** CF35: Coyc . . . .1D 128
**St Matthews Cl.** SA1: Swan . . . .1E 5
**St Michaels Av.** SA4: P'dul . . . .6E 35
**St Michael's Rd.** CF36: Newt . . .3F 125
**St Michael's Way**
  CF31: Brack . . . . . . . . . . .5H 121
**St Nicholas Cl.** SA5: Wauna . . .5D 70
**St Nicholas Rd.** CF31: Bri . . . .4D 120
**St Nicholas's Ct.** SA2: Kill . . . . .4E 83
**St Nicholas Sq.**
  SA1: Swan . . . . . . . .5G 5 (4G 85)
**St Non's Av.** SA31: Carm . . . . . .3C 6
**St Non's Ct.** CF31: Brack . . . . .5H 121
**St Patrick's Dr.** CF31: Bri . . . . .4D 120
**St Paul's Rd.**
  SA12: A'von, Sand . . . . . . .5C 96
**St Paul's Ter.** SA4: Gor . . . . . . .6C 56
**St Peters** *SA31: Carm* . . . . . . . .*3E 7*
  *(off St Andrews Rd.)*
**St Peter's Av.** SA5: Ffor F . . . . .5A 72
**St Peter's Ct.** SA31: Carm . . . . .3F 7
**St Peter's Rd.** SA3: Newt . . . . .1C 100
**St Peters St.** SA31: Carm . . . . .3F 7
**St Peter's Ter.** SA2: C'ett . . . . .6B 72
**St Peters Ter.** SA15: Llane . . . . .5H 41
**St Rhidian Dr.** SA2: Kill . . . . . .3C 82
**St Rhidian Rd.** SA2: Por . . . . . .2C 72
**St Stephen's Ct.**
  SA1: Swan . . . . . . . .5H 5 (4H 85)
**St Stephens Dr.**
  CF35: P'coed . . . . . . . . . .2E 123
**St Teilo's Ct.** SA3: Bishop . . . . .6G 93
**St Teilo's Rd.** CF31: Bri . . . . . .6C 120
**St Teilo St.** SA4: P'dul . . . . . . .6E 35
**St Theodore's Way**
  CF32: B'myn . . . . . . . . . . .4E 115
**ST THOMAS** . . . . . . . . . . . . . .3A 86
**St Thomas Cl.** CF31: Brack . . . .5H 121
**St Thomas Lofts** SA1: St T . . . . .1H 5
**St Thomas M.** SA1: St T . . . . . . .1H 5
**St Vincent Cres.**
  SA1: Swan . . . . . . . .6E 5 (5G 85)
**St Walls** SA4: Penc . . . . . . . . . .5H 67
**St Winifred's Rd.** CF31: Bri . . .6C 120
**Salem Rd.** SA6: Morr, Plas . . . .3G 73
  SA12: C'avon . . . . . . . . . .4H 91
  SA15: F'oel . . . . . . . . . . . .4C 42
**Salisbury Cl.** SA3: Scur . . . . . .3H 109
**Salthouse Cl.** SA4: Crof . . . . . .5D 66
**Saltoun St.** SA13: Marg . . . . . . .3F 103
**Salubrious Pas.** SA1: Swan . . . .4F 5
**Salubrious Pl.**
  SA1: Swan . . . . . . . .4E 5 (4G 85)
**Salubrius St.** SA1: Swan . . . . . . .4F 5
**Samlet Cl.** SA6: Swan Ent . . . . .6C 60
  SA7: L'smlt, Swan Ent . . . . .6C 60
**Samlet Shop. Cen.**
  SA7: Swan Ent . . . . . . . . .6D 60
**Samuel Cres.** SA5: Gen . . . . . . .5D 72
**Samuels Rd.** SA9: Cwml . . . . . . .6G 17
**SANCTA MARIA HOSPITAL** . . .3D 84
**Sanderling Cl.** CF36: P'cwl . . . .3A 124
**Sanderling Way** CF36: P'cwl . . .3A 124
**Sandfield Rd.** SA16: Burr P . . . . .2E 39
**SANDFIELDS** . . . . . . . . . . . . .2B 96
**Sandfields Rd.** CF32: A'knfig . .5B 114
  SA12: A'von . . . . . . . . . . .3E 97
**Sand La.** SA11: Brit F . . . . . . . .1H 89
**Sandown Rd.** SA12: Sand . . . . .3C 96
  *(not continuous)*
**Sandpiper Cl.** SA12: Sand . . . . .3B 96
**Sandpiper Rd.** CF36: Not . . . . .2A 124
  SA15: Llane . . . . . . . . . . .3F 41
**Sandringham Cl.** SA4: Gor . . . . .5A 56

**Sandringham Pk.**
  SA6: Swan Ent . . . . . . . . .5D 60
**SANDY** . . . . . . . . . . . . . . . . . .3G 41
**SANDYLANE** . . . . . . . . . . . . . .6B 92
**Sandy La.** CF36: P'cwl . . . . . . . .4D 124
  SA3: Park . . . . . . . . . . . . .5B 92
**Sandymeers** CF36: P'cwl . . . . . .4D 124
**Sandy Ridge** SA12: Sand . . . . .3B 96
**Sandy Rd.** SA15: Llane, Pwll . . .3E 41
**SARDIS** . . . . . . . . . . . . . . . . . .1D 34
**Sardis Cl.** SA5: Wauna . . . . . . .5D 70
**Sarlou Cl.** SA3: T Mum . . . . . . .3G 101
**Sarlou Ct.** SA2: Upl . . . . . . . . .4B 84
**SARN** . . . . . . . . . . . . . . . . . . .5D 114
**Sarnfan Baglan Rd.**
  SA12: Bag . . . . . . . . . . . .6B 90
**Sarn Hill** CF32: Sarn . . . . . . . . .6C 114
**SARN PARK SERVICE AREA** . . .6E 115
**Sarn Station (Rail)** . . . . . . . . .6C 114
**Sarn Vs.** CF32: Sarn . . . . . . . .6D 114
**SARON** . . . . . . . . . . . . . . . . . .1C 20
**Saron Cl.** SA4: Gor . . . . . . . . . .3G 55
**Saron Cotts.** SA13: P Tal . . . . . .3H 97
**Saron Rd.** SA14: Byn . . . . . . . . .2A 54
  SA18: Saron . . . . . . . . . . .6C 10
**Saunders Way** SA2: Sket . . . . . .5F 83
**Sawel Cl.** SA4: Hendy . . . . . . . .6D 34
**Sawel Ter.** SA4: Hendy . . . . . . .6D 34
**Scarlet Av.** SA12: Sand . . . . . . .2A 96
**Scarlet Ct.** SA14: Dafen . . . . . . .3F 43
**Scarlets RFC** . . . . . . . . . . . . . .2E 53
**School Ho. Cl.** CF33: N Cor . . . .1C 116
**School La.** SA8: P'dwe . . . . . . . .5D 36
  SA18: Tyc . . . . . . . . . . . . .4D 20
**School Rd.** CF32: Bryn c . . . . . .5F 115
  CF33: Ken H . . . . . . . . . . .5G 113
  SA6: Morr . . . . . . . . . . . . .5A 60
  SA7: Glais . . . . . . . . . . . .1H 61
  SA9: Cwm I . . . . . . . . . . . .6G 27
  *SA9: Cwml* . . . . . . . . . . . . .*6G 17*
  *(shown as Heol yr Ysgol)*
  SA9: Ysta . . . . . . . . . . . . .2E 33
  SA10: Cry . . . . . . . . . . . . .5H 33
  SA10: Jer M . . . . . . . . . . .1B 88
  SA11: Nea . . . . . . . . . . . .3A 78
  SA11: Tonna . . . . . . . . . . .4F 65
  SA15: Llane . . . . . . . . . . .4C 52
  SA15: Pwll . . . . . . . . . . . .2C 40
  SA18: Lwr B . . . . . . . . . . .4H 15
**School Ter.** CF33: N Cor . . . . . .2C 116
  SA12: C'avon . . . . . . . . . .5H 91
**Scott Cl.** CF31: Bri . . . . . . . . . .5C 120
**SCURLAGE** . . . . . . . . . . . . . .3H 109
**Scutari Row** SA13: P Tal . . . . . .6H 97
**Scwd-yr-Afon** SA10: A'dul . . . . .2F 65
**Seabank Cl.** CF36: P'cwl . . . . . .5B 124
**Sea Breeze** SA12: Sand . . . . . . .3B 96
**Seabrook Pl.** SA12: Sand . . . . .4D 96
**Seaforth Cl.** SA12: Sand . . . . . .1A 96
**Seagull Cl.** CF36: Not . . . . . . . .2B 124
**Sealands Dr.** SA3: T Mum . . . . .3G 101
**Sealands Farm Cvn. Pk.**
  SA3: Oxw . . . . . . . . . . . . .5C 110
**SEASIDE** . . . . . . . . . . . . . . . . .6H 41
**Seaside Cres.** SA15: Llane . . . . .5H 41
**Sea Vw.** *CF32: Cef C* . . . . . . . .*1A 118*
  *(off Cefn Rd.)*
**Seaview** SA4: Penc . . . . . . . . . .4H 67
**Sea Vw. Cotts.** SA10: Jer M . . . .2E 89
**Sea Vw. Ter.** SA1: Swan . . . . . . .2F 85
  SA12: A'von . . . . . . . . . . .2F 97
**Seaview Ter.** SA1: Bon . . . . . . .6D 74
  SA4: Penc . . . . . . . . . . . .4H 67
  SA16: Burr P . . . . . . . . . . .3D 38
**Seaward Av.** SA12: Sand . . . . . .3B 96
**Seaward Cl.** SA12: Sand . . . . . .3B 96
**Seaway Dr.** SA12: Sand . . . . . . .6G 89
**Seaway Pde.**
  SA12: Bag, Sand . . . . . . . .1A 96
**Seaway Pde. Ind. Est.**
  SA12: Bag . . . . . . . . . . . .5H 89
**Sebastopol St.**
  SA1: St T . . . . . . .3H 5 (3A 86)
**Second Av.** SA6: Clase . . . . . . .5F 59
**Sedd Goch** CF31: Brack . . . . . . .1G 127
**Seion Pl.** SA10: Sev S . . . . . . . .5G 29
**Selwyn Samuel Cen.**
  (Indoor Bowls Cen.) . . . . .4H 41
**Senny Pl.** SA6: Cwm'crw . . . . . .1B 60
**Sepia Cl.** SA12: Sand . . . . . . . .2A 96
**Serecold Av.** SA10: Skew . . . . . .2C 76
**SEVEN SISTERS** . . . . . . . . . . .5F 29
**Seven Sisters Mus.** . . . . . . . . . .5E 29
**Severn Cres.** SA12: Sand . . . . . .3B 96

**Severn Rd.** CF36: P'cwl . . . . . . .4A 124
  SA6: Clase . . . . . . . . . . . .6F 59
**Seymour Ter.** *SA31: Carm* . . . . . .*2F 7*
  *(off Park Hall)*
**SGIWEN** . . . . . . . . . . . . . . . . .1E 77
**Shakespeare Av.** CF31: Bri . . . .5B 120
**Shands Rd.** SA18: Amm . . . . . . .5F 11
**Sharpsburg Pl.** SA1: L'ore . . . . .5G 73
**Shaw's La.** *SA31: Carm* . . . . . . . .*3E 7*
  *(off Dark Ga.)*
**Shaw St.** SA4: Gow . . . . . . . . . .3A 70
**Shearwater Cl.** CF36: P'cwl . . . .3A 124
**Sheerwater Cl.** SA3: W Cro . . . .6E 95
**Shelley Dr.** CF31: Bri . . . . . . . .5B 120
**SHELONE** . . . . . . . . . . . . . . . .1G 89
**Shelone Cotts.** SA11: Brit F . . . .6G 77
**Shelone Rd.** SA11: Brit F . . . . . .1G 89
**Shelone Ter.** SA11: Brit F . . . . . .5H 77
**Shepherd's Rd.** SA6: Morr . . . . .2H 73
**Shepherd's Ter.** SA4: Gor . . . . . .3H 55
**Sherborne Wlk.**
  SA3: Blk P, W Cro . . . . . . .3F 95
**Sherringham Dr.** SA3: Newt . . . .6E 95
**Shopper's Wlk.**
  SA1: Swan . . . . . . . .4C 4 (4F 85)
**Short St.** SA1: Swan . . . . .1D 4 (2F 85)
  SA6: Cly . . . . . . . . . . . . . .3E 49
  SA11: Brit F . . . . . . . . . . . .5H 77
**Sibrwd y Dail** CF31: Pen F . . . .3C 120
**Siding Ter.** SA10: Skew . . . . . . .1B 76
**Siemens Way** SA7: Swan Ent . . .3A 74
**Siloh Cres.** SA1: L'ore . . . . . . . .4G 73
**Siloh Rd.** SA1: L'ore . . . . . . . . .4G 73
**Silurian Way** CF33: Ken H . . . .5G 113
**Silver Av.** SA12: Sand . . . . . . . .2A 96
**Silver Cl.** SA3: W Cro . . . . . . . .5D 94
  SA12: Sand . . . . . . . . . . . .1A 96
**Silverhurst** SA3: T Mum . . . . . .3F 101
**Silver Ter.** SA16: Burr P . . . . . . .3E 39
**Simpson's Way** CF33: Pyle . . . .5E 113
**SINGLETON HOSPITAL** . . . . . . .6A 84
**Singleton Park** . . . . . . . . . . . . .5A 84
**Singleton St.**
  SA1: Swan . . . . . . . .4C 4 (4F 85)
**Singlewood** SA3: Casw . . . . . . .2B 100
**Sinnatts, The** SA10: Nea A . . . . .6H 63
**Sirius Apartments**
  SA1: Swan Ent . . . . . . . . .5H 73
**Sirius Dr.** SA12: Bag . . . . . . . . .5H 89
**Sir John Morris Ho.**
  SA1: Swan . . . . . . . . . . . .1E 5
**Sitwell Way** SA12: A'von . . . . . .5D 96
**Six Mills Av.** SA4: Gor . . . . . . . .5B 56
**Sker Cl.** CF36: Not . . . . . . . . . .2B 124
  *(Sker Wlk.)*
  CF36: Not . . . . . . . . . . . . .6A 116
  *(The Courtyard)*
**Sker Wlk.** CF36: Not . . . . . . . . .2B 124
**SKETTY** . . . . . . . . . . . . . . . . . .4H 83
**Sketty Av.** SA2: Sket . . . . . . . . .4A 84
**Sketty Hall** . . . . . . . . . . . . . . . .5H 83
**Sketty La.** SA2: Sket . . . . . . . . .5H 83
**Sketty Lane Sports Cen.** . . . . . .6H 83
**Sketty Pk. Cl.** SA2: Sket . . . . . .4H 83
**Sketty Pk. Dr.** SA2: Sket . . . . . .4G 83
**Sketty Pk. Rd.** SA2: Sket . . . . . .4H 83
**Sketty Rd.** SA2: Sket, Upl . . . . .4B 84
**SKEWEN** . . . . . . . . . . . . . . . . .1E 77
**Skewen Station (Rail)** . . . . . . . .6D 62
**Skinner St.** SA1: Swan . . . . . . . .1F 85
**Skokholm Cl.** CF36: Not . . . . . .2B 124
**Skomer Cl.** CF36: Not . . . . . . . .2A 124
**Skylark Rd.** CF33: N Cor . . . . . .6C 112
**SLADE** . . . . . . . . . . . . . . . . . . .5B 110
**Slade Cl.** SA6: Swan Ent . . . . . .5D 60
**Slade Cross** SA3: Slade . . . . . . .4B 110
**Slade Gdns.** SA3: W Cro . . . . . .6E 95
**Slade Hall** SA1: Swan . . . . . . . . .1C 4
**Slade Rd.** SA3: Newt . . . . . . . . .1C 100
  SA3: Slade . . . . . . . . . . . .5B 110
**Slipway Rd.**
  SA1: Swan . . . . . . . .6G 5 (5H 85)
**Smallholdings** CF35: Coity . . . . .4B 122
**Smallwood Rd.** SA12: Bag . . . . .6B 90
**Smithfield Rd.** SA8: P'dwe . . . . .4D 36
**Smith's La.** SA13: Marg . . . . . . .5H 103
**Smith's Rd.** SA7: Birch . . . . . . . .4H 61
**Smithy's Ct.** CF31: Bri . . . . . . . .5C 126
**Smyrna Cotts.** SA13: P Tal . . . . .6H 97
**Smyrna St.** SA6: Plas . . . . . . . .3H 73
**Snowdon Dr.** SA5: Ffor F . . . . . .5A 72
**Snowdon Rd.** SA16: Burr P . . . . .3E 39
**Snow Ter.** SA9: Ystra . . . . . . . . .2H 33
**Soar Cl.** SA4: Lou . . . . . . . . . . . .5G 55

**Soar Rd.** SA14: Byn . . . . . . . . .2H **53**
**Soar Ter.** SA6: Morr . . . . . . . . .5B **60**
**Solva Rd.** SA6: Clase . . . . . . . .6F **59**
**Somerset La.** SA13: P Tal . . . . .6H **97**
**Somerset Pl.**
  SA1: Swan . . . . . . . .4F **5** (4G **85**)
  SA12: C'avon . . . . . . . . . . .5H **91**
**Somerset Rd.** SA3: Lan . . . . . .2E **101**
**Somerset St.** SA13: P Tal . . . . .6H **97**
**Somerville St.** SA2: Sket . . . . . .3B **84**
**Southall Av.** SA10: Skew . . . . . .2C **76**
**South Cl.** CF35: P'coed . . . . . .3G **123**
  CF36: P'cwl . . . . . . . . . . . .4C **124**
  SA93: Bishop . . . . . . . . . . .6H **93**
**SOUTH CORNELLY** . . . . . . . . .4D **116**
  **Sth. Cornelly Ind. Est.**
  CF33: Sth C . . . . . . . . . . . .4D **116**
**Southcross Rd.** SA12: Sand . . .2B **96**
**Southcross Way** SA12: Sand . . .2B **96**
**Southdown Ct.** SA12: Sand . . . .1B **96**
  *(off Southdown Vw.)*
**Southdown Rd.** SA12: Sand . . .3B **96**
**Southdown Vw.** SA12: Sand . . .1B **96**
**Southerndown Av.** SA3: May . . .2E **95**
**Southern Rd.** CF32: A'knfig . . . .5C **114**
**Southern Ter.** SA31: Carm . . . . . .4E **7**
**SOUTHGATE** . . . . . . . . . . . . . . .1A **98**
**Southgate Rd.** SA3: S'gate . . . .2H **111**
**Southgate St.** SA11: Nea . . . . . .2B **78**
**Southlands Dr.** SA3: W Cro . . . .5D **94**
**South Pde.** SA13: P Tal . . . . . . .3G **97**
**South Pl.** CF31: Bri . . . . . . . . .2E **127**
  CF36: P'cwl . . . . . . . . . . . .4C **124**
**South Prospect**
  SA1: Swan . . . . . . . .2F **5** (3G **85**)
**South Quay**
  SA1: Swan . . . . . . . .4H **5** (4A **86**)
**South Rd.** CF31: Bri . . . . . . . . .3G **127**
  CF36: Not, P'cwl . . . . . . . .4C **124**
**South St.** CF31: Bri . . . . . . . . .2E **127**
  SA13: P Tal . . . . . . . . . . . .5H **97**
**South Vw.** CF33: Ken H . . . . . .5G **113**
  CF35: P'coed . . . . . . . . . . .3G **123**
  SA4: Gor . . . . . . . . . . . . . .4C **56**
**Southville Rd.** SA12: Sand . . . .2B **96**
**South Wales Police Mus.** . . . .3G **127**
**Southward La.**
  SA3: Lan, Newt . . . . . . . . .1D **100**
**Spencer St.** SA5: Man . . . . . . . .4F **73**
**Spencer Ter.** SA9: Cwm I . . . . .6G **27**
**Spien Rd.** SA14: Pen g . . . . . . .6H **9**
**Spilman St.** SA31: Carm . . . . . . . .3E **7**
**Spinney, The** CF31: Brack . . . .6A **122**
  SA2: Sket . . . . . . . . . . . . . .4F **83**
**Spionkop Rd.** SA6: Ystwe . . . . .6D **48**
**Spoonbill Cl.** CF36: Not . . . . . .2B **124**
**Spowart Av.** SA15: Llane . . . . . .2H **41**
**Springbourne Cl.** SA4: Gow . . .5C **70**
**Springfield Av.** CF36: P'cwl . . . .4E **125**
  SA2: Up K . . . . . . . . . . . . . .5A **82**
**Springfield Cl.** CF31: Bri . . . . . .5E **121**
  SA4: Gow . . . . . . . . . . . . . .3A **70**
**Springfield Gdns.** CF31: Bri . . .5E **121**
**Springfield La.** CF31: Brack . . . .1H **127**
**Springfield Rd.** SA10: Skew . . .6E **63**
  SA31: Carm . . . . . . . . . . . . . .2E **7**
  *(shown as Heol Maesyffynnon)*
**Springfields** SA15: Llane . . . . .4C **52**
**Springfields St.** SA6: Morr . . . . .5A **60**
**Springfield Ter.** SA11: Nea . . . .2B **78**
  SA12: A'von . . . . . . . . . . . . .3F **97**
  SA16: Burr P . . . . . . . . . . . .3D **38**
**Spring Gdns.** SA4: Gor . . . . . . .5C **56**
  SA31: Carm . . . . . . . . . . . . . .4E **7**
**Spring Gdns. Nth.**
  SA10: Skew . . . . . . . . . . . .1E **77**
**Spring Gdns. Sth.**
  SA10: Skew . . . . . . . . . . . .1E **77**
**Spring Ter.** SA1: Swan . . . .5B **4** (4E **85**)
**Spruce Way** SA4: Penl . . . . . . .4H **57**
**Square, The** CF31: Bri . . . . . . .6D **120**
  CF32: Brync . . . . . . . . . . . .4F **115**
  CF32: Lale . . . . . . . . . . . . .6F **119**
  CF36: P'cwl . . . . . . . . . . . .5C **124**
  SA10: Cry . . . . . . . . . . . . . .6H **33**
  SA11: Nea . . . . . . . . . . . . . .6B **64**
**Square Ct.** SA31: Carm . . . . . . . .3D **6**
**Squire Cl.** SA1: Swan . . . .5E **5** (4G **85**)
**Squire Dr.** CF32: B'myn . . . . . .4E **115**
**Squirrel Wlk.** SA4: Ffor . . . . . . .5D **34**
**Stadwen Rd.** SA7: L'smlt . . . . . .1F **75**
**STAFFORD COMMON** . . . . . . .1C **70**
**Stafford Comn.** SA4: Gor . . . . .1C **70**
**Stafford St.** SA15: Llane . . . . . .3A **52**

**Stair St.** SA12: Sand . . . . . . . . .3D **96**
**Stallcourt Cl.** SA13: Marg . . . . .2F **103**
**Stallcourt St.** SA13: Marg . . . . .2F **103**
**Standert Ter.** SA10: Sev S . . . . .5G **29**
**Stanley Pl.** SA1: Swan . . .1C **4** (2F **85**)
  SA10: C'dxtn . . . . . . . . . . . .4C **64**
**Stanley Rd.** SA10: Skew . . . . . .1D **76**
  SA15: Llane . . . . . . . . . . . . .3A **52**
**Stanley St.** SA3: T Mum . . . . . .1E **101**
  SA15: Llane . . . . . . . . . . . . .4A **52**
  SA18: Gwaun . . . . . . . . . . . .2C **24**
**Stanley Ter.**
  SA1: Swan . . . . . . . .1C **4** (3F **85**)
**Stapleton Pl.** SA6: Morr . . . . . . .6A **60**
**Station App.** CF32: Ton . . . . . . .4B **114**
**Station Cl.** SA31: Carm . . . . . . . .4E **7**
**Station Cl.** CF36: P'cwl . . . . . . .4C **124**
**Station Ct.** SA1: Swan . . . . . . . .1E **5**
**Station Hill** CF31: Bri . . . . . . . .1E **127**
**Station Rd.** CF33: Ken H . . . . .4G **113**
  SA1: L'ore . . . . . . . . . . . . . .4G **73**
  SA4: Crof, Llanm . . . . . . . . .6E **67**
  SA4: Gow . . . . . . . . . . . . . .3B **70**
  SA4: Grov . . . . . . . . . . . . . .6B **46**
  SA4: Lou . . . . . . . . . . . . . . .6D **54**
  SA4: P'dul . . . . . . . . . . . . . .6E **35**
  SA4: Penc . . . . . . . . . . . . . .4A **68**
  SA5: Ffor F . . . . . . . . . . . . . .5B **72**
  SA6: Cly, Ystwe . . . . . . . . . .6E **49**
  SA7: Glais . . . . . . . . . . . . . .6G **49**
  SA7: L'smlt . . . . . . . . . . . . .1E **75**
  SA9: Aber, Cae . . . . . . . . . .1H **29**
  SA9: Ystra . . . . . . . . . . . . . .5A **28**
  SA10: A'dul . . . . . . . . . . . . .3F **65**
  SA10: Cry . . . . . . . . . . . . . .6H **33**
  SA10: Skew . . . . . . . . . . . .6D **62**
  SA11: Brit F . . . . . . . . . . . . .5H **77**
  SA13: P Tal . . . . . . . . . . . . .3G **97**
  SA14: Byn . . . . . . . . . . . . . .3A **54**
  SA14: L'nch . . . . . . . . . . . . .4D **44**
  SA15: Llane . . . . . . . . . . . . .1A **52**
  SA16: Burr P . . . . . . . . . . . .3E **39**
  SA18: Bry . . . . . . . . . . . . . .4A **16**
  SA18: Glan . . . . . . . . . . . . .4A **14**
**Station Sq.** SA4: Penc . . . . . . . .4A **68**
  *(off Blodwen Ter.)*
**Station Ter.** SA11: Nea . . . . . . .6B **64**
**Station Ter.** SA4: Penc . . . . . . .4A **68**
  *SA10: Sev S* . . . . . . . . . . . .5G **29**
  *(shown as Teras Gorsaf)*
  SA12: Sand . . . . . . . . . . . . .4D **96**
**Stebonheath Pk.** . . . . . . . . . . .1C **52**
**Stebonheath Ter.** SA15: Llane . .1C **52**
**Steele Av.** SA31: Carm . . . . . . . .3C **6**
**Steetholm Cl.** CF36: Not . . . . . .2B **124**
**Stembridge Av.** SA6: Por . . . . . .3B **72**
**Stephenson Rd.** SA2: Kill . . . . . .4E **83**
**Stephens Way** SA31: Carm . . . . .5E **7**
**Stepney La.** SA2: C'ett . . . . . . . .1A **84**
**Stepney M.** SA5: Cwmb . . . . . . .6E **73**
**Stepney Pl.** SA15: Llane . . . . . . .1A **52**
**Stepney Pct.** SA15: Llane . . . . . .1A **52**
**Stepney Rd.** SA2: C'ett . . . . . . .1A **84**
  SA5: Wauna . . . . . . . . . . . .5D **70**
  SA15: Pwll . . . . . . . . . . . . . .3E **41**
  SA16: Burr P . . . . . . . . . . . .3E **39**
  SA18: Garn . . . . . . . . . . . . .5E **15**
**Stepney St.** SA5: Cwmb . . . . . . .6E **73**
  SA15: Llane . . . . . . . . . . . . .1A **52**
**Sterry Rd.** SA4: Gow . . . . . . . . .3A **70**
**Stewart Dr.** SA18: Amm . . . . . . .6H **11**
  *(shown as Ffordd Stewart)*
**Stewart Hall** SA2: Sket . . . . . . .4A **84**
  *(off Gower Rd.)*
**Stewart St.** SA15: Llane . . . . . . .3H **41**
**Sticle Footpath** SA31: Carm . . . .4F **7**
**Stockhams Cnr.** SA11: Nea . . . .2B **78**
  *(off Briton Ferry Rd.)*
**Stonechat Cl.** CF36: Not . . . . . .2A **124**
**Stoneleigh Ct.** CF36: P'cwl . . . .4C **124**
**Stoney La.** CF35: Corn . . . . . . .6F **127**
**STORMY DOWN** . . . . . . . . . . .5B **118**
**Stormy Down** CF33: Pyle . . . . .4H **117**
**Stormy La.** CF33: N Cor . . . . . .2B **116**
**Stour Va.** SA31: Marg . . . . . . . .1E **103**
**Strade Sports Cen.** . . . . . . . . . .3F **41**
**Stradey Castle** . . . . . . . . . . . . .1F **41**
**Stradey Cl.** SA15: Llane . . . . . . .2H **41**
**Stradey Hill** SA15: Pwll . . . . . . .2D **40**
**Stradey Ho.** SA14: Llwy . . . . . . .2G **53**
**Stradey Pk. Av.** SA15: Llane . . . .3G **41**
**Stradey Rd.** SA15: Llane . . . . . . .2G **41**
**Stradling Cl.** CF32: Brync . . . . . .5D **114**
**Strand** SA1: Swan . . . .2E **5** (3G **85**)
**Strand Ct.** SA1: Swan . . .2E **5** (3G **85**)

**Strand M.** SA1: Swan . . . . . . . . .2E **5**
**Strand Row**
  SA1: Swan . . . . . . . .3E **5** (3G **85**)
**Stratford Dr.** CF36: P'cwl . . . . . .3B **124**
**Stratton Way** SA10: Nea A . . . . .6G **63**
**Strauss Rd.** SA12: Sand . . . . . . .2A **96**
**Strawberry Pl.** SA6: Morr . . . . . .5A **60**
**Stryd Arthur** SA18: Amm . . . . . .6H **11**
**Stryd Bennett** SA15: Llane . . . . .2G **41**
**Stryd Fawr** SA18: Glan . . . . . . . .5B **14**
**Stryd Harold** SA18: Amm . . . . . .6G **11**
**Stryd Marged** SA18: Amm . . . . . .6H **11**
**Stryd Masnach** SA10: Sev S . . . .5F **29**
**Stryd Masnachol** SA9: Ysta . . . .2E **33**
**Stryd Rhydychen**
  SA1: Swan . . . . . . . .4D **4** (4F **85**)
**Stryd y Bont** SA14: Pen g . . . . . .4H **9**
**Stryd-y-Coleg** SA18: Amm . . . . .6H **11**
**Stryd-y-Gwynt** SA18: Amm . . . .1H **21**
**Stryd y Parc** SA18: Amm . . . . . .1A **22**
**Stryd-yr-Eglwys** SA18: Amm . . .6H **11**
**Sturmi Way** CF33: Pyle . . . . . . .6F **113**
**Suffolk Cl.** CF36: P'cwl . . . . . . .3C **124**
**Suffolk Ct.** CF36: P'cwl . . . . . . .4C **124**
**Suffolk Pl.** CF36: P'cwl . . . . . . .4C **124**
**Suffolk St.** CF31: Bri . . . . . . . . .2E **127**
**Summercliffe Chalet Pk.**
  SA3: Casw . . . . . . . . . . . . .2B **100**
**Summerfield Dr.** CF36: Not . . . .2B **124**
**Summerfield Pl.** SA11: Nea . . . .6B **64**
**Summerland Ho.** SA3: Casw . . .2B **100**
**Summerland La.** SA3: Newt . . . .1B **100**
**Summerland Pk.** SA2: Up K . . . .5A **82**
**Summerland Ter.** SA7: L'smlt . . .1G **75**
**Sun Alliance Ho.** SA1: Swan . . .4E **85**
  *(off St Helen's Rd.)*
**Sunhill Pk.** CF31: Brynn . . . . . . .6C **126**
  *(shown as Parc Bronhaul)*
**Sunningdale Av.** SA3: May . . . . .3E **95**
**Sunningdale Dr.** SA4: Gor . . . . .2A **56**
**Sunningdale Rd.** SA12: Bag . . . .4B **90**
**Sunninghill Ter.** SA15: Llane . . . .6B **42**
**Sunnybank** CF33: Pyle . . . . . . . .5E **113**
  *SA10: Nea* . . . . . . . . . . . . .5H **63**
  *(shown as Haulfryn)*
**Sunnybank Cl.** SA3: W Cro . . . . .4E **95**
**Sunnybank Ct.** CF31: Brack . . . .6H **121**
**Sunnybank Pl.** SA12: Sand . . . . .4C **96**
**Sunnybank Rd.** SA12: Sand . . . .4C **96**
**Sunnycroft Rd.** SA12: Bag . . . . .5A **90**
**Sunny Hill** SA15: Llane . . . . . . . .5A **42**
**Sunnyland Cres.**
  SA10: Nea A . . . . . . . . . . . .6E **63**
**Sunnymead Cl.** SA1: Town . . . . .6B **72**
**Sunny Mt.** SA12: Bag . . . . . . . . .5A **90**
**Sunny Rd.** SA12: Sand . . . . . . . .4C **96**
  SA15: Llane . . . . . . . . . . . . .6A **42**
**Sunnyside Rd.** CF31: Bri . . . . . .1D **126**
**Sussex Rd.** SA16: Burr P . . . . . . .3F **39**
**Swallow Cl.** CF33: N Cor . . . . . .6C **112**
**Swallow Tree** CF33: N Cor, SA10: Nea . . . . .4B **64**
**Swan Ct.** SA2: Kill . . . . . . . . . . .4D **82**
**Swanfield** SA9: Ysta . . . . . . . . . .2F **33**
  *(shown as Maes Alarch)*
**Swanfield Pl.** SA15: Llane . . . . . .6A **42**
**Swan Gdns.** SA1: Swan . . . . . . . .4B **4**
**Swan La.** SA9: Ysta . . . . . . . . . . .1F **33**
**Swan Rd.** SA12: Bag . . . . . . . . . .5A **90**
**SWANSEA** . . . . . . . . . . . .4E **5** (4G **85**)
**SWANSEA AIRPORT** . . . . . . . . . .1E **93**
**Swansea Bay Golf Course** . . . .2C **88**
**Swansea Bus Station** . . . .4D **4** (4F **85**)
**Swansea Castle** . . . . .3E **5** (3G **85**)
**Swansea Castle**
  SA15: Llane . . . . . . . . . . . . .6B **42**
**Swansea Cathedral** . . . . . . . . . .1G **85**
**Swansea City AFC** . . . . . . . . . .4H **73**
**Swansea City AFC Academy** . . .3H **73**
**Swansea College Sports Cen.**
   . . . . . . . . . . . . . . . . . . . . . .2A **84**
**Swansea Crematorium**
  SA6: L'flch . . . . . . . . . . . . . .5F **59**
**Swansea Ent. Pk.**
  SA6: Swan Ent . . . . . . . . . .5D **60**
**Swansea Gate Bus. Pk.**
  SA1: Cry B . . . . . . . . . . . . . .3H **87**
**Swansea Ind. Est.**
  SA5: Ffor F . . . . . . . . . . . . . .4H **71**
**Swansea Leisure Cen.**
   . . . . . . . . . . . . . . .5E **5** (4G **85**)
**Swansea Mkt.**
  SA1: Swan . . . . . . . .4D **4** (4F **85**)

**Swansea Metropolitan University**
  **Architectural Stained Glass and**
  **Art & Design** . . . . . . . . . . . .3G **85**
  **Cadogan Technology Cen.**
   . . . . . . . . . . . . . . . . . . . . . .2F **85**
  **Dynevor Cen. for Art, Design**
  **& Media** . . . . . . .3D **4** (3F **85**)
  **Mount Pleasant Campus**
   . . . . . . . . . . . . . . .2D **4** (3F **85**)
**Swansea Mus.** . . . . . .5F **5** (4G **85**)
**Swansea Rd.** SA4: Gor . . . . . . . .6B **56**
  SA4: P'liw . . . . . . . . . . . . . . .6E **47**
  *(not continuous)*
  SA4: Penl . . . . . . . . . . . . . .4G **57**
  *(not continuous)*
  SA5: Cad . . . . . . . . . . . . . . .6G **57**
  SA5: Ffor F . . . . . . . . . . . . . .6B **56**
  SA5: L'flch . . . . . . . . . . . . . .4E **59**
  SA5: Wauna . . . . . . . . . . . . .4C **70**
  SA8: P'dwe . . . . . . . . . . . . . .6C **36**
  SA8: P'dwe, T'nos . . . . . . . .3A **50**
  SA15: Llane . . . . . . . . . . . . .6B **42**
**Swansea RUFC & Glamorgan CCC**
   . . . . . . . . . . . . . . . . . . . . . .5C **84**
**Swansea Station (Rail)**
   . . . . . . . . . . . . . . .1F **5** (2G **85**)
**Swansea Tennis Cen.** . . . . . . . .5A **74**
**Swansea University**
  **Science & Innovation Campus**
   . . . . . . . . . . . . . . . . . . . . . .4G **87**
**Swansea Va. Ind. Est.**
  SA6: Swan Ent . . . . . . . . . .5D **60**
**Swansea Vale Nature Reserve**
   . . . . . . . . . . . . . . . . . . . . . .5D **60**
**Swansea Vale Railway**
  **Six Pit Junction Station** . . .2D **74**
**Swansea W. Ind. Pk.**
  SA5: Ffor F . . . . . . . . . . . . . .4A **72**
**SWANSEA WEST SERVICE AREA**
   . . . . . . . . . . . . . . . . . . . . . .2H **57**
**Swansea Yacht & Sub Aqua Club**
   . . . . . . . . . . . . . . . . . . . .6G **5** (4H **85**)
**Swan St.** SA1: Swan . . . . .1E **5** (2G **85**)
  SA12: Bag . . . . . . . . . . . . . .3H **89**
**Swan Ter.** SA12: Bag . . . . . . . . .3H **89**
**Swan Wlk.** SA12: Bag . . . . . . . . .3H **89**
  SA15: Llane . . . . . . . . . . . . .4G **41**
**Sway Rd.** SA6: Morr . . . . . . . . . .5B **60**
**Sweet Briar La.** SA3: W Cro . . . .4F **95**
**Swin yr Eos** SA9: Ystra . . . . . . . .1H **33**
**SWISS VALLEY** . . . . . . . . . . . . . .2D **42**
**Swiss Valley** SA14: F'oel . . . . . . .2D **42**
**Swn y Gamlas** SA6: Cly . . . . . . . .5F **49**
**SWN-Y-GWYNT DAY HOSPITAL**
   . . . . . . . . . . . . . . . . . . . . . .1G **21**
**Swn-y-Mor** SA12: Sand . . . . . . . .3C **96**
**Swn-y-Nant** CF35: P'coed . . . . .2E **123**
  SA9: Cwm I . . . . . . . . . . . . .1E **27**
  SA10: Cry . . . . . . . . . . . . . . .4H **33**
**Swn yr Adar** CF31: Pen F . . . . . .3C **120**
**Swn yr Aderyn** CF33: Ken H . . .5G **113**
**Swn yr Afon** CF33: Ken H . . . . .4G **113**
**Swn-yr-Afon** SA10: A'dul . . . . . .1F **65**
**Sybil St.** SA6: Cly . . . . . . . . . . . .5E **49**
**Sycamore Av.** CF33: Pyle . . . . . .5F **113**
  CF36: Newt . . . . . . . . . . . . .3G **125**
  SA7: L'smlt . . . . . . . . . . . . . .5E **61**
  SA11: Cim . . . . . . . . . . . . . .2D **78**
**Sycamore Cl.** CF31: Bri . . . . . . .3E **121**
  SA2: Sket . . . . . . . . . . . . . . .3F **83**
**Sycamore Ct.** SA12: Bag . . . . . .3A **90**
**Sycamore Cres.** SA12: Bag . . . . .3A **90**
**Sycamore Rd.** SA3: W Cro . . . . .4F **95**
**Sycamore Way** SA31: Carm . . . . .3C **6**
  *(not continuous)*
**Sydney St.** SA5: Man . . . . . . . . .4F **73**
**Sylvan Way** SA2: Sket . . . . . . . .3G **83**
**Sylvia Ter.** SA5: Man . . . . . . . . . .1F **73**
**Symmons St.** SA1: Swan . . . . . . .1F **85**

## T

**Tabernacle Rd.** SA18: Glan . . . . .4H **13**
  *(shown as Heol Tabernacle)*
**Tabernacle St.** SA1: L'ore . . . . . .5G **73**
  SA10: Skew . . . . . . . . . . . . .1E **77**
**Tabernacle Ter.** SA4: Penc . . . . .4G **67**
  SA12: C'avon . . . . . . . . . . . .5G **91**
  SA31: Carm . . . . . . . . . . . . . .2E **7**
**Tai Arfryn** CF31: Bri . . . . . . . . . .2B **126**
**TAI-BACH** . . . . . . . . . . . . . . . . . .5H **97**
**Tai Bank** SA11: Tonna . . . . . . . . .3F **65**
**Tai-Canol** SA12: C'avon . . . . . . . .4H **91**

Tai Gorsaf SA15: Llane . . . . . . . .6B 42
Tai Gwalia SA9: Cwm U . . . . . .4C 26
Taillwyd Rd.
   SA10: Nea A, B'och . . . . . .5G 63
Tai'r Felin SA10: A'dul . . . . . . .2F 65
Tairfelin CF31: Bri . . . . . . . . .4D 120
TAIRGWAITH . . . . . . . . . . . . . .2F 25
Talbot Athletic Ground . . . . . . .4G 97
Talbot Grn. SA4: Gow . . . . . . .3A 70
Talbot Rd. CF33: Ken H . . . . .4G 113
   SA10: Skew . . . . . . . . . . . .2E 77
   SA11: Nea . . . . . . . . . . . . .2C 78
   SA13: P Tal . . . . . . . . . . . .4G 97
   SA18: Amm . . . . . . . . . . . .6H 11
   (shown as Ffordd Talbot)
Talbot's Rd. SA3: Penm . . . . .1E 111
Talbot St. SA4: Gow . . . . . . . .3A 70
   SA15: Llane . . . . . . . . . . . .2A 52
Talcennau Rd. SA13: P Tal . . . .5H 97
Talfan Rd. SA1: Bon . . . . . . . .5C 74
Taliesin Arts Cen. . . . . . . . . . .5B 84
Taliesin Cl. CF35: P'coed . . . . .2E 123
Taliesin Pl. SA4: Lou . . . . . . . .5E 55
Taliesyn Rd. SA1: Town . . . . . .2C 84
Talley Rd. SA5: Por . . . . . . . . .4E 73
Tall Oaks CF35: P'coed . . . . . .2E 123
Talyclun SA14: L'nch . . . . . . . .2E 45
Tal y Coed SA4: Hendy . . . . . . .6C 34
Tal-y-Wern SA13: Marg . . . . . .1E 103
Talywern SA14: L'nch . . . . . . .5C 44
TANERDY . . . . . . . . . . . . . . . . .1G 7
Tanerdy SA31: Carm . . . . . . . . .2G 7
Tank Farm Rd. SA10: L'dcy . . . .5B 76
Tan-y-Bryn CF35: P'coed . . . . .2H 123
Tan-y-Bryn SA16: Burr P . . . . . .3C 38
Tanybryn SA4: Penc . . . . . . . .4A 68
Tan-y-Bryn Ter. SA4: Penc . . . .4A 68
Tanycoed SA16: Burr P . . . . . . .2G 39
Tanycoed Rd. SA6: Cly . . . . . . .3F 49
Tanydarren SA8: Cilm . . .1H 37, 6A 32
Tanyfan SA18: Cap H . . . . . . . .3A 20
Tan y Farteg SA9: Ystra . . . . . .1F 33
Tan-y-Gelli SA18: Glan . . . . . . .4C 14
Tanygraig Rd. SA14: Byn . . . . . .2H 53
Tan-y-Groes Pl. SA13: P Tal . . .4H 97
Tan-y-Groes St. SA13: P Tal . . .4G 97
   (not continuous)
Tan y Lan SA18: L'bie . . . . . . . .2G 11
Tan-y-Lan Ter. SA6: Morr . . . . .6H 59
Tan-y-Lôn SA6: Cly . . . . . . . . . .3E 49
Tan-y-Marian Rd.
   SA1: M'hill . . . . . . . . .1A 4 (2E 85)
Tanyrallt Av. CF31: Bri . . . . . . .4E 121
Tanyrallt Rd. SA6: Cly . . . . . . . .3E 49
Tan-yr-Eglwys SA8: Cily . . . . . .4H 37
Tan-y-Rhiw SA10: Sev S . . . . . .5G 29
Tanyrhodyn SA15: F'oel . . . . . . .3C 42
Tan y Waun SA9: P'hos . . . . . . .3D 28
Tanywern La. SA9: Ysta . . . .1F 33
   (shown as Lon Tanywen)
Taplow Ter. SA1: Bon . . . . . . . .5A 74
Tavistock Cl. SA2: Sket . . . . . . .3B 84
Tavistock Rd. SA2: Sket . . . . . .3A 84
Tawe Av. SA1: Swan . . . . . . . . .6H 73
Tawe Bus. Village
   SA7: Swan Ent . . . . . . . . . .3B 74
Tawel Fan SA14: Dafen . . . . . . .6D 42
Tawelfan SA4: Tir V . . . . . . . . . .1H 57
   SA9: C'edd . . . . . . . . . . . . .2A 28
Tawe Pk. SA9: Ystra . . . . . . . . .1H 33
Tawe Pl. SA6: Cly . . . . . . . . . . .5F 49
Tawe Rd. SA1: Cry B . . . . . . . . .4H 87
   SA7: L'smlt . . . . . . . . . . . . .6F 61
Tawe St. SA6: Morr . . . . . . . . . .6B 60
Tawe Ter. SA8: P'dwe . . . . . . . .6D 36
Tawe Vw. Cres. SA6: Morr . . . .5A 60
Taylor Rd. CF31: Bri . . . . . . . . .4E 121
Taylor's Row SA11: Nea . . . . . .2A 78
Teal Cl. CF36: Not . . . . . . . . . .4B 124
Technium SA1: Swan . . .3H 5 (3H 85)
Technium 2
   SA1: Swan . . . . . . . .3H 5 (3H 85)
Technology Dr. CF31: Bri . . . .4D 126
Ted Davies Cl. CF33: N Cor . . .1C 116
Teddington Pl. SA4: P'dul . . . . . .6F 35
Tegfan SA4: Tir V . . . . . . . . . . .1H 57
   SA7: L'smlt . . . . . . . . . . . . .3G 75
   SA10: Skew . . . . . . . . . . . .2D 76
Tegfynydd SA14: F'oel . . . . . . . .2D 42
   (not continuous)
Tegid Rd. SA1: M'hill . . . . . . . . .1E 85
Teglan Pk. SA18: Tyc . . . . . . . .5C 08
Teilo Cres. SA1: M'hill . .1A 4 (2E 85)
   (not continuous)
Teilos Dr. CF31: Brack . . . . . . .6F 121

Telyn Aur SA6: Morr . . . . . . . . .4H 59
Temeraire Ct. SA1: Swan Ent . .5A 74
Temperance La. SA9: Ystra . . . .5A 28
Temple Gdns. SA31: Carm . . . . .3E 7
   (off Lammas St.)
Temple St. SA1: Swan . . .3E 5 (3G 85)
   SA15: Llane . . . . . . . . . . . .1B 52
Templeton Way SA5: P'lan . . . .1C 72
Ten Acre Wood SA13: Marg . . .5H 103
Tennant Gro. SA10: Skew . . . . .1C 76
Tennant Pl. SA1: Cry B . . . . . . .4H 87
Tennyson Dr. CF31: Bri . . . . . .5C 120
Tennyson Way SA2: Kill . . . . . . .2E 83
Tenth Av. SA6: Morr . . . . . . . . .4G 59
Tent Va. CF35: P'coed . . . . . . .3F 123
Teras Brynhyfryd
   SA10: Sev S . . . . . . . . . . .5G 29
Teras Brynteg SA18: Amm . . . .1H 21
Teras Gorsaf SA10: Sev S . . . .5G 29
Teras John SA14: C'mel . . . . . .1H 9
Teras Jones SA18: Glan . . . . . .5H 13
Teras Maes y Deri
   SA18: Amm . . . . . . . . . . .6B 12
Teras Waterloo SA18: Cap H . .2H 19
Teras yr Arced SA18: Garn . . . .5C 14
Terfyn Ynysawdre CF32: Ton . .5C 114
Tern Rd. CF36: P'cwl . . . . . . . .3A 124
Terrace Rd.
   SA1: Swan . . . . . . . .2A 4 (3D 84)
The . . . . . . .
   Names prefixed with 'The' for
   example 'The Arcade' are
   indexed under the main name
   such as 'Arcade, The'
Theodore Rd. SA13: P Tal . . . . .5H 97
Third Av. SA6: Clase . . . . . . . . .5G 59
THISTLEBOON . . . . . . . . . . . .2F 101
Thistleboon Cvn. Site
   SA3: T Mum . . . . . . . . . . .2G 101
Thistleboon Dr. SA3: T Mum . .2F 101
Thistleboon Gdns.
   SA3: T Mum . . . . . . . . . . .2F 101
Thistleboon Rd.
   SA3: T Mum . . . . . . . . . . .2F 101
Thomas Cl. SA11: Nea . . . . . . .2A 78
Thomas Cres. SA1: N Cor . . . .2C 116
Thomas Evans Ho.
   SA1: Town . . . . . . . . . . . . .1C 84
Thomas Row SA1: Swan . . . . . .2G 85
Thomas St. SA1: St T . . .2H 5 (3H 85)
   SA1: Swan . . . . . . .4E 5 (4G 85)
   SA8: P'dwe . . . . . . . . . . . .5D 36
   SA11: Brit F . . . . . . . . . . . .1H 89
   SA12: A'von . . . . . . . . . . . .3E 97
   SA15: Llane . . . . . . . . . . . .6A 42
Thomas Ter. SA6: Morr . . . . . . .1H 73
   SA15: Pwll . . . . . . . . . . . . .2B 40
Thomson Ct. SA4: Gor . . . . . . .6C 56
Thorburn Cl. SA11: Nea . . . . . . .6C 64
Thornbury Cl. SA12: Bag . . . . . .6B 90
Thorney Rd. SA12: Bag . . . . . . .3H 89
   (not continuous)
Thornhill Rd.
   SA14: Cross H, C'ili . . . . . . .4F 19
Three Cliffs Bay Camping & Cvn. Pk.
   SA3: Penm . . . . . . . . . . . .2G 111
Three Cliffs Dr. SA3: S'gate . . .6B 92
THREE CROSSES . . . . . . . . . .1F 81
Three Ships Ct.
   SA3: T Mum . . . . . . . . . . .3G 101
Tichbourne St.
   SA3: T Mum . . . . . . . . . . .2F 101
Tidal Reach SA4: P'dul . . . . . . .6E 35
Timberly SA3: Rey . . . . . . . . . .2B 110
Timbre Pl. SA12: Sand . . . . . . .2B 96
Tingle La. CF35: Ewe . . . . . . . .6F 127
Tirbach Dr. SA8: Rhos . . . . . . .1G 51
Tirbach Rd. SA9: Ysta . . . . . . . .1F 33
Tircanol Ter. SA6: Morr . . . . . . .4B 60
TIRCANOL . . . . . . . . . . . . . . .4B 60
Tir Capel SA14: Dafen . . . . . . .6D 42
Tir Celyn SA13: Coe H . . . . . .1D 112
Tir-Coed Ter. SA4: Gor . . . . . . .5H 55
TIRDEUNAW . . . . . . . . . . . . . . .1F 73
Tirdeunaw Cl. SA5: Tird . . . . . . .1F 73
Tir Einon SA14: Llwy . . . . . . . . .2F 53
Tirforgan SA14: Dafen . . . . . . .5D 42
Tirgof SA14: L'nch . . . . . . . . . .4C 44
Tir John Nth. Rd. SA1: Por T . . .2D 86
Tir Morfa Rd. SA12: Sand . . . . .2A 96
Tir Mynydd SA4: Gor . . . . . . . .4A 56
Tirmynydd Rd. SA2: Cair . . . . . .1E 81
   SA4: Thr X . . . . . . . . . . . . .1E 81
TIR-NEST . . . . . . . . . . . . . . . .5C 74

Tir Newydd CF33: N Cor . . . . . .1D 116
   (not continuous)
   SA14: Llwy . . . . . . . . . . . . .2G 53
Tir Onen SA12: Bag . . . . . . . . .4A 90
TIRPENRY . . . . . . . . . . . . . . . .5B 60
Tirpenry St. SA6: Morr . . . . . . . .5B 60
Tirprys SA18: Tyc . . . . . . . . . . .4E 21
TIR SYR WALTER . . . . . . . . . .4E 15
Tirwaun SA14: Cross H . . . . . . .6C 8
   SA16: Burr P . . . . . . . . . . . .3C 38
Tirycoed Rd. SA18: Glan . . . . . .2F 13
TIR-Y-DAIL . . . . . . . . . . . . . . . .6H 11
Tir y Dderwen SA14: Cross H . . .5B 8
Tir y Farchnad SA4: Gow . . . . . .3B 70
Tirynys SA15: F'oel . . . . . . . . . .4C 42
Tir yr Hen Ysgol SA14: Byn . . .3A 54
Tir yr Yspyty SA14: Byn . . . . . . .5C 54
Tir Ysgawen SA31: Carm . . . . . .5G 7
Tir Ysgol SA15: Llane . . . . . . . .6A 42
Tir y Waun SA9: Ystra . . . . . . . .4B 28
Toft Pl. SA15: Llane . . . . . . . . . .6B 42
Tollgate Rd. SA13: Marg . . . . . .3F 103
Tom Williams Ct. SA1: Swan . . .2G 85
TONDU . . . . . . . . . . . . . . . . . . .3B 114
Tondu Park . . . . . . . . . . . . . . .4B 114
Tondu Rd. CF31: Bri . . . . . . . . .4C 120
Tondu Station (Rail) . . . . . . . . .4C 114
Ton Glas CF31: Bri . . . . . . . . . .6A 120
   CF33: Pyle . . . . . . . . . . . . .5D 112
Ton-Mawr Rd SA12: Pontr . . . .5H 79
TONNA . . . . . . . . . . . . . . . . . . .4F 65
TONNA HOSPITAL . . . . . . . . . .3G 65
Tonnant Rd. SA1: Swan Ent . . .5A 74
TONNAU . . . . . . . . . . . . . . . . . .4F 65
Tonna Uchaf SA11: Tonna . . . . .3G 65
Ton Rhosyn CF31: Brack . . . . .6G 121
Ton Teg CF35: P'coed . . . . . . . .4G 123
Tontine St. SA1: Swan . . .1E 5 (2G 85)
Ton Tylluan CF31: Bri . . . . . . . .2C 126
Ton Vw. CF33: Ken H . . . . . . . .5G 113
Ton-y-Groes CF35: P'coed . . . .4H 123
Toronto Av. SA13: Marg . . . . . .2F 103
Torrington Rd. SA5: Gen . . . . . .5D 72
Tor Vw. SA3: Penm . . . . . . . . .2F 111
Tor-y-Mynydd SA12: Bag . . . . .2H 89
Tourist Info. Cen.
   Carmarthen . . . . . . . . . . . . .3E 7
   Llanelli . . . . . . . . . . . . . . . .6G 41
   Mumbles . . . . . . . . . . . . . .1F 101
   Swansea . . . . . .4D 4 (4F 85)
Tower Cl. CF31: Bri . . . . . . . . .2F 127
Tower Ct. SA1: Town . . . . . . . . .1C 84
   SA6: Swan Ent . . . . . . . . . .6C 60
Tower Gdns. SA1: Town . . . . . . .1C 84
Towngate Bus. Cen.
   SA13: P Tal . . . . . . . . . . . .4G 97
Town Hall Sq. SA15: Llane . . . .1A 52
TOWNHILL . . . . . . . . . . . . . . . .2C 84
Townhill Gdns. SA2: C'ett . . . . .2B 84
Townhill Rd.
   SA1: M'hill, Town . . . . . . . .1E 85
   SA2: C'ett . . . . . . . . . . . . . .2B 84
Towy Cl. SA31: John . . . . . . . . .6B 6
   (shown as Clos Tywi)
Towy Retail Pk. SA31: Carm . . . .4E 7
Towy Side SA31: Carm . . . . . . .4E 7
Towy Vw. SA31: Carm . . . . . . . .2G 7
Traeth Ffordd SA15: Llane . . . .5G 41
Traethmelyn SA12: Sand . . . . . .1A 96
Trafalgar Pl. SA2: Brynm . . . . . .5C 84
Traherne Ct. SA10: Nea A . . . . .6H 63
Trallwm Rd. SA14: Llwy . . . . . . .6G 43
TRALLWN . . . . . . . . . . . . . . . . .2F 75
Trallwn Pl. SA7: L'smlt . . . . . . .2F 75
Trallwn Rd. SA7: L'smlt . . . . . . .3F 75
Tramway SA15: Pwll . . . . . . . . .2B 40
Tramway Rd. SA8: Gell . . . . . . .4G 37
   SA15: Pwll . . . . . . . . . . . . .2B 40
Travis Way CF36: Not . . . . . . .1B 124
Trawler Rd.
   SA1: Swan . . . . . .6E 5 (5F 85)
Trawsffordd Rd. SA9: Ystra . . . .6H 27
Traws Fynydd CF31: Brack . . . .1G 127
TREBANNWS . . . . . . . . . . . . . .2B 50
TREBANOS . . . . . . . . . . . . . . . .2B 50
TRE-BOETH . . . . . . . . . . . . . . .2F 73
Trebuan SA15: F'oel . . . . . . . . .3B 42
Trecco Bay Holiday Pk.
   CF36: P'cwl . . . . . . . . . . . .4F 125
Tredegar Rd. SA4: Gor . . . . . . .5B 56
Trederwen CF33: Ken H . . . . . .4G 113
Treetops SA14: F'oel . . . . . . . . .2C 42
Trefechan Rd. SA31: Carm . . . . .2A 6
Trefelin Cres. SA13: P Tal . . . . .2H 97
Trefelin St. SA13: P Tal . . . . . . .2G 97

Trefleming Cotts. SA9: Aber . . . .1F 29
   (off Hennoyadd Rd.)
TRE-FORGAN . . . . . . . . . . . . . .4H 33
Treforgan SA10: Cry . . . . . . . . .4H 33
Treforis SA18: Amm . . . . . . . . .3A 22
TREFORRIS . . . . . . . . . . . . . . . .6H 59
Tregarne Cl. SA6: Cwm'crw . . . .2A 60
Tregaron Ho. SA13: Marg . . . . .3F 103
Tregelles Cl. SA6: Cwm'crw . . . .2A 60
Tregelles Rd. SA10: Nea A . . . .5F 63
TREGOF VILLAGE . . . . . . . . . .5E 61
TRE-GWYR . . . . . . . . . . . . . . . .3A 70
TRE-GYNWR . . . . . . . . . . . . . . .5G 7
Treharne Dr. CF31: Pen F . . . .2C 120
Treharne Rd. SA6: Morr . . . . . .5A 60
TRELALES . . . . . . . . . . . . . . . .5B 126
TREMAINS . . . . . . . . . . . . . . . .1F 127
Tremains Ct. CF31: Brack . . . .1G 127
Tremains Rd. CF31: Bri . . . . . .1E 127
Tremgarth CF31: Bri . . . . . . . . .5D 120
Trem-y-Bedol SA31: Carm . . . . .2F 7
Trem y Bryn CF31: Bri . . . . . . .4D 120
Trem y Coleg SA31: Carm . . . . .3C 6
Trem-y-Dref SA31: Carm . . . . . .2D 6
Trem-y-Dyffryn CF31: Bri . . . . .2B 126
Trem y Mor SA4: Llanm . . . . . . .6E 67
Trem-y-Mor CF31: Brack . . . . .1G 127
Trem-y-Mynydd
   SA16: Burr P . . . . . . . . . . . .2D 38
Trem y Rhedyn CF35: Coity . . .2G 121
Tre Newydd CF33: Ken H . . . . .5G 113
Trenewydd Ri. SA11: Nea . . . . .2C 78
TREOES . . . . . . . . . . . . . . . . . .4D 128
Treoes Rd. CF35: Coyc . . . . . .2C 128
Trevallen Av. SA11: Cim . . . . . .2D 78
TREVAUGHAN . . . . . . . . . . . . . .1C 6
Trevaughan Rd. SA31: Treva . . . .1C 6
Trewen Rd. SA7: Birch . . . . . . .6H 61
Trews Flds. Ind. Est.
   CF31: Bri . . . . . . . . . . . . . .5D 120
Trewyddfa Comn. SA6: Morr . . .2A 74
TREWYDDFA FACH . . . . . . . . .1H 73
Trewyddfa Gdns. SA6: Morr . . .2A 74
Trewyddfa Rd. SA6: Morr . . . . .3G 73
Trewyddfa Ter. SA6: Morr . . . . .2H 73
Triangle, The CF31: Brack . . . .1G 127
   SA8: All . . . . . . . . . . . . . . .1E 51
Trigfan Dewi SA12: C'avon . . . .4G 91
Trinity Cl. SA3: T Mum . . . . . . .1E 101
   SA4: P'dul . . . . . . . . . . . . .1B 46
Trinity College Sports Cen. . . . . .3B 6
Trinity College University of
   Wales Swimming Pool . . . . . .3B 6
Trinity Ct. SA1: Swan . . . . . . . . .2E 5
   SA12: Sand . . . . . . . . . . . .2B 96
Trinity Ho. SA13: P Tal . . . . . . .4G 97
Trinity La. SA4: Penc . . . . . . . .4G 67
Trinity Pl. SA1: Swan . . .2D 4 (3F 85)
   SA4: P'dul . . . . . . . . . . . . .1B 46
Trinity Rd. SA15: Llane . . . . . . .3A 52
Trinity St. SA4: Gor . . . . . . . . . .5B 56
Trinity Ter. SA15: Llane . . . . . . .3A 52
Trinity University College
   (Coleg Prifysol y Drindod) . . .3B 6
Trip, The CF35: Ewe . . . . . . . . .6E 127
Troed y Rhiw SA4: P'dul . . . . . .6H 35
   SA7: L'smlt . . . . . . . . . . . . .2G 75
Tros-Maen SA14: Dafen . . . . . .4C 42
Trosserch Rd. SA14: L'nch . . . .2C 44
   (shown as Heol Trosserch)
TROSTRE . . . . . . . . . . . . . . . . .3D 52
Trostre SA15: Llane . . . . . . . . . .1E 53
Trostre Bus. Village
   SA14: Llane . . . . . . . . . . . .2E 53
Trostre Ind. Pk. SA14: Llane . . .3D 52
Trostre Rd. SA14: Llane . . . . . . .3C 52
   SA14: Llane . . . . . . . . . . . .2C 52
   (not continuous)
Tro Tircoed SA4: Tir V . . . . . . . .2H 57
Tucker St. SA11: Brit F . . . . . . .5H 77
Tudno Pl. SA5: P'lan . . . . . . . . .3C 72
   (not continuous)
Tudor Bus. Pk. SA10: Nea A . . .6G 63
Tudor Ct. SA3: Mur . . . . . . . . . .6H 93
   SA4: L'edi . . . . . . . . . . . . . .6E 31
Tudor Gdns. SA10: Nea . . . . . . .5H 63
Tudor Gro. SA13: Marg . . . . . . .3G 103
Tudor Rd. SA5: Tre b . . . . . . . . .3F 73
Tudor St. SA9: Ystra . . . . . . . . .1G 33
   SA13: P Tal . . . . . . . . . . . .3G 97
Tudor Way SA3: Mur . . . . . . . . .5A 94
Tunnel Rd. SA15: Llane . . . . . . .1B 52
Turberville Cres. CF31: Bri . . . .2E 121
Turnstone Ct. SA12: Sand . . . . .3B 96
Turnstone Rd. CF36: Not . . . . .3B 124

**Twll-yn-y-Wal Rd.**
SA13: Marg . . . . . . . . . . .2F 103
**Two Stones Cres.**
CF33: Ken H . . . . . . . . .5G 113
Twyniago SA4: P'dul . . . . . . . .6G 35
Twyni Teg SA2: Kill . . . . . . . . .2D 82
Twynrefail Pl. SA18: Gwaun . . .1C 24
(not continuous)
Twyn Teg SA10: Nea . . . . . . . .5A 64
Twynybedw Rd. SA6: Cly . . . . .4E 49
Twyn yr Ysgol SA9: Ysta . . . . . .1E 33
Ty Aberdafen SA15: Llane . . . .4B 52
Ty Beck Ho. SA2: Upl . . . . . . . .4C 84
**TY BRYNGWYN LLANELLI HOSPICE**
. . . . . . . . . . . . . . . . . . .4D 42
Tybryn Ter. CF35: P'coed . . . .3E 123
Ty Caitlin SA1: Swan . . . . . . . . .3C 4
Ty Canol CF36: Not . . . . . . . .2C 124
Tycanol SA14: Cross H . . . . . . . .3D 18
Ty Canol Farm Camping Site
SA10: Nea A . . . . . . . . . . .6F 63
**TY-COCH** . . . . . . . . . . . . . . . . .2H 83
Tycoch Av. CF35: Coity . . . . . .3H 121
**Ty-Coch Maisonettes**
SA2: Sket . . . . . . . . . . . . . .3A 84
Ty-Coch Rd. SA2: Sket . . . . . . .3H 83
Tyco Ho. SA7: Swan Ent . . . . .2C 74
**Tycribwr Hill**
CF32: A'knfig, Cef C . . . . .1G 119
**TYCROES** . . . . . . . . . . . . . . . . .4D 20
Tycroes Bus. Pk. SA18: Tyc . . . .6A 20
Tycroes Rd. SA18: Tyc . . . . . . .4D 20
(shown as Heol Tycroes)
Ty Cydwel SA15: Llane . . . . . . . .2A 52
(off Paddock St.)
Tyddyn Gwaun CF32: Lale . . . .5A 126
Ty Dewi Sant SA5: Ffor F . . . . . .5B 72
**TY-DRAW** . . . . . . . . . . . . . . . . .6D 74
Ty-Draw Cres. SA1: Bon . . . . . .6C 74
Ty-Draw Hill SA13: P Tal . . . . . .3H 97
Ty Draw La. CF33: Sth C . . . . . .3C 116
Ty-Draw Pl. SA1: Bon . . . . . . . .6C 74
SA13: P Tal . . . . . . . . . . . .4G 97
Ty-Draw Rd. SA1: Bon . . . . . . . .5C 74
Ty-Draw St. SA13: P Tal . . . . . .3G 97
Tydraw Vs. CF32: B'myn . . . . .3F 115
**TY-EINON DAY HOSPITAL** . . . .4A 56
Ty Elizabeth SA15: Llane . . . . .2A 52
Ty Ffald SA13: Marg . . . . . . . .5H 103
Ty Fforest SA6: Morr . . . . . . . .5A 60
Ty Fri SA16: Graig . . . . . . . . . . .1E 39
Ty-Fry Cl. CF32: B'myn . . . . . .2E 115
Ty Fry Rd. CF32: Cef C . . . . . .2B 118
Ty-Fry Rd. SA13: Marg . . . . . . .2F 103
Ty Gnoll Newydd SA11: Nea . . .1C 78
Ty Gwyn SA4: Gow . . . . . . . . . .3B 70
Ty Gwyn Dr. CF31: Brack . . . .1A 128
Ty Gwyn Rd. SA9: Cwml . . . . . .6H 17
(shown as Heol Ty Gwyn)
Tygwyn Rd. SA6: Cly . . . . . . . .4F 49
SA7: Swan Ent . . . . . . . .4D 60
Ty-Haf SA8: P'dwe . . . . . . . . . .5E 37
Ty Heledd SA1: Swan . . . .4B 4 (4E 85)
Ty Horeb SA6: Morr . . . . . . . . .5A 60
(off Horeb Rd.)
Ty Howard SA15: Llane . . . . . . .2A 52
Ty Ilfor SA11: Nea . . . . . . . . . .1B 78
(off Alfred St.)
**TY-ISAF** . . . . . . . . . . . . . . . . . .3B 52
Ty-Isaf Rd. CF32: Cef C . . . . . .1B 118
Tyisha Rd. SA15: Llane . . . . . . .2B 52
Tyisha Ter. SA15: Llane . . . . . .4B 42
**Ty John Penri**
SA1: Swan . . . . . .4C 4 (4F 85)
Tyla Moes SA10: Nea . . . . . . . .4H 63
Tyla Rd. SA11: Brit F . . . . . . . .5H 77
Tyle Catherine SA15: Pwll . . . . .2C 40
Tyle Glas CF33: N Cor . . . . . .1D 116
SA18: Garn . . . . . . . . . . . .6E 15
**TYLE ROAD** . . . . . . . . . . . . .1A 128
Tyle Teg SA6: Cly . . . . . . . . . . .5D 48
(not continuous)
Ty Llansawel SA11: Brit F . . . . .1H 89
Ty Llew SA1: Swan . . . . . . . . . .6F 73
Ty Llwyd SA10: B'och . . . . . . . .6G 51
Tymaen Cres. SA12: C'avon . . . .4H 91
Tymaen Ter. SA12: C'avon . . . .4H 91
Ty Mawr SA1: Swan . . . . . . . . . .3B 4
Ty-Mawr SA8: P'dwe . . . . . . . . .6D 36
Tymawr St. SA1: Por T . . . . . . . .3C 86
Ty Meriel SA15: Llane . . . . . . . .2A 52
Ty Myrtwydd SA4: Lou . . . . . . .6F 55
Ty Nant CF31: Bri . . . . . . . . . .6B 120

**TYNEWYDD** . . . . . . . . . . . . . . .3H 29
Ty Newydd SA10: Sev S . . . . . .3H 29
Ty Newydd Ter. SA14: Gors . . . .5D 8
Tynton Rd. CF31: Bri . . . . . . . .6D 120
Tyn-y-bonau Rd. SA4: P'dul . . . .5F 35
Tyn-y-Cae SA8: All . . . . . . . . . . .1D 50
**TY'N-Y-CAEAU** . . . . . . . . . . . . . .6C 64
Tyn y Caeau La. CF35: Coyc . . .1B 128
Tyn-y-Caeau La. CF36: Newt . . .1E 125
Tyn-y-Cae Rd. SA7: L'smlt . . . . .1E 75
Ty'n y Coed Ter. CF32: Brync . . .5D 114
Tynycwm La. SA8: Rhos . . . . . .3H 51
Ty'n-y-Graig SA10: Cry . . . . . . .6G 33
Ty'n-y-Pant Rd. SA8: P'dwe . . . .5B 36
Ty'n-yr-Haul CF32: B'myn . . . . .3D 114
Tynyrheol Flats SA11: Cim . . . .3C 78
Tyn-y-Rheol Rd. SA10: B'och . . .3H 63
Ty'n y Twr SA12: Bag . . . . . . . . .4C 90
Tyn-y-Waun Rd. SA7: L'smlt . . . .1E 75
Ty Plas Isaf SA14: L'nch . . . . . . .5D 44
Ty'r Eglwys SA12: C'avon . . . . . .5G 91
Ty'r Felin SA5: Blae M . . . . . . . .2C 72
**TYRFRAN** . . . . . . . . . . . . . . . . .5B 42
Ty'r Fran SA7: Birch . . . . . . . . .4H 61
Ty'rfran Av. SA15: Llane . . . . . .5B 42
Ty'r Gelli SA15: Llane . . . . . . . .6G 43
Ty-r-Groes Dr. SA13: Marg . . . .3G 103
Tyr Halen Row SA12: Bag . . . . .4A 90
Tyr Rhys SA31: Carm . . . . . . . . .3F 7
Tyrisha Av. SA4: Grov . . . . . . . .6B 46
Tyrisha Ct. SA4: Grov . . . . . . . . .6B 46
Tyrisha Rd. SA4: Grov . . . . . . . .6B 46
Ty'r Maes SA5: Blae M . . . . . . . .2C 72
Tyr Newydd SA14: Llwy . . . . . . . .1F 53
Ty'r-Owen Row SA12: C'avon . . .5G 91
Ty'r Owen Ter. SA12: C'avon . . .5G 91
Ty'r Pobydd SA11: Nea . . . . . . . .2B 78
(off Eva St.)
Tyrwaun SA15: Pwll . . . . . . . . . .2B 40
Ty Segur SA11: Nea . . . . . . . . .3B 78
Ty Siversten SA1: Swan . . . . . . . .4A 4
Ty Stafford SA15: Llane . . . . . . .2A 52
Tytalwyn Av. CF33: Ken H . . . . .5F 113
Tythegston Cl. CF36: Not . . . . .1C 124
Ty Twyn Teg SA10: Nea . . . . . . .5A 64
Tywod Va. CF35: P'coed . . . . . .3F 123
Tywyn Cl. SA12: Sand . . . . . . . .4D 96
Tywyn Cres. SA12: Sand . . . . . .4C 96

**U**

Ullswater Cres. SA6: Morr . . . . .1H 73
**Ultimate Fitness Club** . . . . . . . .1E 77
Underhill SA6: Graig . . . . . . . . .1E 39
Underhill La. SA3: Nort . . . . . .5A 110
Under Pde. Rd. SA31: Carm . . . .3F 7
Underwood Pl. CF31: Brack . . .1H 127
Underwood Rd. SA10: C'dxtn . . .3D 64
Union Bldgs. SA15: Llane . . . . .6A 42
Union St. SA1: Swan . . . .3D 4 (3F 85)
SA18: Amm . . . . . . . . . .6A 12
SA31: Carm . . . . . . . . . . . .3C 6
Union Ter. SA15: Llane . . . . . . .1A 52
(off Frederick St.)
**University of Swansea**
Hendrefoelan Campus . . .2F 83
Singleton Campus . . . . . .6B 84
Upland Rd. SA11: Nea . . . . . . . .2C 78
**UPLANDS** . . . . . . . . . . . . . . . . .4D 84
Uplands SA3: Llanr . . . . . . . . .5C 106
SA4: Gow . . . . . . . . . . . . .3A 70
SA18: C'gors . . . . . . . . . . .5D 24
Uplands Cres. SA2: Upl . . . . . . .4C 84
**Uplands Cres. (Rear)**
SA2: Upl . . . . . . . . . . . . . .4C 84
Uplands SA8: P'dwe . . . . . . . . .5C 36
Uplands Ter. SA2: Upl . . . . . . . .4C 84
SA6: Morr . . . . . . . . . . . . .6A 60
**Up. Brynamman** . . . . . . . . . . . .3A 16
Up. Castle Vw. SA3: Blk P . . . . .2F 95
Up. Church Pk. SA3: T Mum . . .2F 101
**Up. Colbren Rd.**
SA18: Gwaun . . . . . . . . . .2C 24
Up. Cross Rd. SA15: Llane . . . . .1C 52
**UPPER CWM-TWRCH** . . . . . . . .3C 26
**Up. Fforest Way**
SA6: Swan Ent . . . . . . . . .6C 60
SA7: Swan Ent . . . . . . . . .6C 60
Upper Forge SA6: Cly . . . . . . . .4E 49
Up. Gendros Cres. SA5: Gen . . .5D 72
Up. Heathfield Rd. SA8: P'dwe . .4D 36
Up. Inkerman St. SA15: Llane . . .1A 52
**UPPER KILLAY** . . . . . . . . . . . . .5B 82

Up. King's Head Rd. SA5: Gen . . .5C 72
Up. Mill SA4: P'dul . . . . . . . . . . .6G 35
Upper Mill SA15: Llane . . . . . . .6B 42
Up. Park St. SA15: Llane . . . . . .1A 52
Up. Robinson St. SA15: Llane . .1A 52
(not continuous)
Up. Station Rd. SA18: Garn . . . .5D 14
Upper Strand SA1: Swan . . . . . .1G 85
Up. West End SA13: P Tal . . . . . .5H 97
Up. William St. SA15: Llane . . . .1B 52
Upton Ter. SA1: St T . . . . . . . . .3A 86
Usk Pl. SA6: Yfgn . . . . . . . . . . .1B 60
Uxilla St. CF31: Bri . . . . . . . . . .2F 127

**V**

**Vale of Neath Bus. Pk.**
SA10: Nea . . . . . . . . . . . . .5B 64
Vale of Neath Rd. SA1: Por T . . .3C 86
Vale Reach CF35: P'coed . . . . .1H 123
Vale Vw. CF31: Brack . . . . . . . .5H 121
CF32: Sarn . . . . . . . . . . . .6D 114
Valley Vw. SA2: Sket . . . . . . . . .5G 83
SA11: Cim . . . . . . . . . . . . .3D 78
Valley Way SA6: Swan Ent . . . . .2B 74
Vanewood Ct. SA3: T Mum . . . .3G 101
Vardre Rd. SA6: Cly . . . . . . . . . .4F 49
Varna Ter. SA13: P Tal . . . . . . . .5H 97
Varteg Rd. SA9: Ysta . . . . . . . . .3E 33
Vaughan Cl. SA12: A'von . . . . . .3F 97
Vaughan Cres. SA4: P'dul . . . . .2C 46
Vaughan Pl. SA4: Lou . . . . . . . . .5F 55
Vaughan St. SA15: Llane . . . . . .1A 52
Vauxhall SA15: Llane . . . . . . . . .1A 52
Vauxhall Rd. SA15: Llane . . . . . .6A 42
**VELINDRE** . . . . . . . . . . . . . . . . .2G 97
Velindre St. SA13: P Tal . . . . . . .2G 97
Venables Cl. SA5: Ffor F . . . . . . .6A 72
Vennaway La. SA3: Penn . . . . . .4E 93
Vensland SA3: Bishop . . . . . . . .6H 91
**Verandah St.**
SA1: Swan . . . . . .3C 4 (3F 85)
Vera Rd. SA6: Cly . . . . . . . . . . .4F 49
Verdi Rd. SA12: Sand . . . . . . . . .2A 96
Verig St. SA5: Man . . . . . . . . . . .5F 73
Verland Way CF35: P'coed . . . .3F 123
Vernon Cl. SA4: P'liw . . . . . . . . .1F 57
Vernon Pl. SA11: Brit F . . . . . . . .1G 89
Vernon Rd. CF36: P'cwl . . . . . .4D 124
Vernon St. CF31: Bri . . . . . . . . .6F 121
SA1: Swan . . . . . . . . . . . . .1G 85
SA11: Brit F . . . . . . . . . . . .6H 77
Versil Ter. SA4: Lou . . . . . . . . . .6G 55
Vicarage Dr. SA8: P'dwe . . . . . .4D 36
Vicarage La. SA5: Cwmdu . . . . .6D 72
Vicarage Rd. SA6: Morr . . . . . . .5H 59
SA18: Garn . . . . . . . . . . . .5D 14
(shown as Heol Ficerdi)
Vicarage Ter. SA1: St T . . . .2H 5 (3H 85)
**Vicar's Wlk.** SA10: B'och . . . . . .2H 63
Victoria Av. CF36: P'cwl . . . . . . .5B 124
SA1: Swan . . . . . .6A 4 (5D 84)
SA3: T Mum . . . . . . . . . . .1E 101
Victoria Bldgs. CF32: Coyt . . . .1B 114
Victoria Ct. SA3: Casw . . . . . . . .2B 100
Victoria Gdns. SA11: Nea . . . . . .1B 78
Victoria Ho. SA11: Nea . . . . . . . .1B 78
(off Victoria St.)
Victoria Pl. SA10: C'dxtn . . . . . .5B 64
**Victoria Quay**
SA1: Swan . . . . . .6D 4 (4G 85)
Victoria Rd. CF33: Ken H . . . . . .4G 113
SA1: Swan . . . . . .4F 5 (4G 85)
SA4: Blu A, Penc . . . . . . . .4H 67
SA4: Gow . . . . . . . . . . . . .2A 70
SA5: Wauna . . . . . . . . . . .5D 70
SA12: A'von . . . . . . . . . . .5C 96
Victoria Row SA4: Penc . . . . . . .4H 67
Victoria Sq. SA3: Casw . . . . . . . .5H 41
SA2: Upl . . . . . . . . . . . . . .3C 84
Victoria Ter. CF33: Pyle . . . . . . .6E 113
SA1: Swan . . . . . . . . . . . . .4D 84
SA12: C'avon . . . . . . . . . . .5G 91
**Victory Apartments**
SA1: Swan . . . . . . . . . . . . .5H 73
View Rd. SA6: Cly . . . . . . . . . . .5E 49
Viking Ct. SA1: Wins . . . . . . . . .2D 74
Viking Way SA1: Wins . . . . . . . .2D 74
Village Cl. SA10: B'och . . . . . . . .3H 63
Village Ct. CF33: Pyle . . . . . . . .6F 113
Village Dr. SA4: Gor . . . . . . . . . .5B 56
**Village Farm Ind. Est.**
CF33: Pyle . . . . . . . . . . . . .6F 113

Village Farm Rd. CF33: Pyle . . .1F 117
Village Gdns. SA12: Bag . . . . . .6H 89
Village La. SA3: T Mum . . . . . . .2F 101
Village Rd. SA12: Bag . . . . . . . .6H 89
Villa Ter. SA5: Tre b . . . . . . . . . .3F 73
Villiers Ct. SA11: Brit F . . . . . . . .1G 89
Villiers Rd. SA10: Skew . . . . . . .1F 77
SA18: Amm . . . . . . . . . . . .2G 21
(shown as Ffordd Villiers)
Villiers St. SA1: Swan . . . . . . . . .1G 85
SA11: Brit F . . . . . . . . . . . .1H 89
SA13: P Tal . . . . . . . . . . . .3G 97
Vincent St. SA1: Swan . . . .6A 4 (4E 85)
Vine Row SA9: Ysta . . . . . . . . . .2D 32
Vintin La. SA12: Bag . . . . . . . . .6H 89
Vintin Ter. CF36: P'cwl . . . . . . .4D 124
Viola Rd. SA12: Sand . . . . . . . . .2B 96
**Virgin Active**
Bridgend . . . . . . . . . . . . . .3B 128
**Vivian Ct.** SA2: Sket . . . . . . . . .3A 84
SA12: A'von . . . . . . . . . . .4E 97
(not continuous)
Vivian Ho. SA3: Blk P . . . . . . . . .2F 95
Vivian Mans. SA2: Sket . . . . . . . .3A 84
Vivian Pk. Dr. SA12: Sand . . . . .2C 96
(not continuous)
Vivian Rd. SA2: Sket . . . . . . . . .4A 84
(not continuous)
Vivians Row SA6: Pantl . . . . . . .2G 59
Vivian St. SA1: Swan . . . . . . . . .6G 73
Vivian Ter. SA12: A'von . . . . . . . .3E 97
Voylart Cl. SA2: Dunv . . . . . . . . .2B 82
Voylart Rd. SA2: Dunv . . . . . . . .2A 82
**Vue Cinema**
Carmarthen . . . . . . . . . . . .3E 7
Swansea . . . . . . . .4F 5 (4G 85)

**W**

Waddles Ct. SA15: Llane . . . . . .2A 52
Wade Av. SA9: Ysta . . . . . . . . . .3E 33
Wagner Rd. SA1: Sand . . . . . . . .1A 96
Waldhof Ct. SA5: Blae M . . . . . .1B 72
**Waldsassen Rd.**
CF35: P'coed . . . . . . . . . . .5G 123
**Wales National Pool** . . . . . . . . .6H 83
Wallace Rd. SA1: St T . . . . . . . . .2A 86
SA11: Nea . . . . . . . . . . . . .2B 78
Walnut Cl. SA3: W Cro . . . . . . . .5D 94
Walter Rd. SA1: Swan . . . .4A 4 (4D 84)
SA18: Amm . . . . . . . . . . . .6A 12
(shown as Ffordd Walter)
Walters Cres. SA3: T Mum . . . . .1E 101
Walters La. SA3: Llang . . . . . . .5D 104
Walter's Rd. SA11: Nea . . . . . . .3A 78
SA15: Llane . . . . . . . . . . . .2B 52
Walters Rd. CF31: Bri . . . . . . . .1C 126
SA7: L'smlt . . . . . . . . . . . . .6E 61
SA9: Cwml . . . . . . . . . . . . .6H 17
Walters Row SA2: Dunv . . . . . . .2B 82
Walters Ter. SA5: Man . . . . . . . .5E 73
Walters Ter. SA6: Morr . . . . . . . .1A 74
Waltham Cl. SA6: Morr . . . . . . . .1G 73
Warborough Cl. SA15: Llane . . .3H 41
Warborough Rd. SA15: Llane . . .2H 41
Warner Pl. SA15: Llane . . . . . . .4B 42
Warren Cl. CF31: Brack . . . . . . .1H 127
**WARREN HILL** . . . . . . . . . . . . . .1G 89
Warren Hill SA11: Brit F . . . . . . .1G 89
Warwick Cres. CF36: P'cwl . . . . .3B 124
Warwick Pl. SA3: W Cro . . . . . . .4F 95
Warwick Rd. SA2: Sket . . . . . . . .6G 83
Washington St. SA1: L'ore . . . . .5G 73
Washington Ter. SA1: L'ore . . . . .5G 73
Wassail Sq. SA1: Swan . . . . . . . .4D 4
Waterfall Courts SA13: P Tal . . . .6H 97
Waterhall Rd. CF33: Ken H . . . . .4F 113
Water La. SA6: Morr . . . . . . . . . .1B 74
Waterloo Pl. SA2: Brynm . . . . . . .5B 84
Waterloo Rd. SA14: Pen g . . . . . .1H 53
(shown as Heol Waterloo)
Waterloo St. SA15: Llane . . . . . .5H 41
Waterloo Ter. SA18: Cap H . . . . .2H 19
(shown as Teras Waterloo)
SA31: Carm . . . . . . . . . . . . .3E 7
**Waterside Bus. Pk.**
SA6: Swan Ent . . . . . . . . .2B 74
Water St. CF31: Bri . . . . . . . . . .1D 126
SA4: P'dul . . . . . . . . . . . . .6E 35
(not continuous)
SA11: Nea . . . . . . . . . . . . .6B 64
(not continuous)
SA12: A'von . . . . . . . . . . .4E 97
SA13: Marg . . . . . . . . . . .1A 112

Water St. SA15: Llane . . . . . . . .6A 42
SA18: Gwaun . . . . . . . . . . . .2C 24
SA31: Carm . . . . . . . . . . . . .3D 6
WATERTON . . . . . . . . . . . . . .3H 127
Waterton Cl. CF31: Bri . . . . . .3B 128
WATERTON CROSS . . . . . . . . .3G 127
Waterton Ind. Est. CF31: Bri . . .3C 128
Waterton La. CF31: Bri . . . . . . .3B 128
Waterton Pk. CF31: Bri . . . . . . .4A 128
Waterton Retail Pk.
CF31: Bri . . . . . . . . . . . . . .3B 128
Waterton Rd. CF31: Bri . . . . . .3G 127
CF35: Coyc . . . . . . . . . . . . .2C 128
Water Wheel Dr.
SA7: Swan Ent . . . . . . . . . .4D 60
Watkins Ter. SA9: C'bont . . . . . .2D 28
Watkin St. SA1: Swan . . .1D 4 (2F 85)
WAUNARLWYDD . . . . . . . . . . . .4C 70
Waunarlwydd Rd. SA2: C'ett . . . .5F 71
SA5: Sket, Wauna . . . . . . . . .5F 71
Waunbant Rd. CF33: Ken H . . .5G 113
Waun Burgess SA31: Carm . . . . .3B 6
Waun Cl. SA4: Lou . . . . . . . . .6G 55
Waun Daniel SA8: Rhos . . . . . .2G 51
Waun Deri SA16: Pem . . . . . . . .2B 38
Wauneos Rd. SA15: Pwll . . . . . .2D 40
Waunfarlais Rd.
SA18: Amm, L'bie . . . . . . . . .4F 11
Waunfawr SA18: Amm . . . . . . . .1F 21
WAUNGRON . . . . . . . . . . . . . .4B 46
Waun Gron SA8: Phyd f . . . . . . .4B 36
Waun-Gron Cl. SA5: Tre b . . . . .2F 73
Waun-Gron Rd. SA5: Tre b . . . . .2F 73
Waungron Rd. SA6: Cly . . . . . . .4E 49
SA18: Amm . . . . . . . . . . . . .3B 22
(shown as Ffordd Waungron)
Waun Gyrlais SA9: Ystra . . . . . .3C 28
Waunhafog Rd. SA18: Amm . . . . .4E 11
Waunhwyad La. SA18: Glan . . . .3A 14
(shown as Lon Waunhwyad)
Waun Lago SA31: Carm . . . . . . .3C 6
Waunlanyrafon SA15: Llane . . . .4H 41
Waun Las SA10: Nea . . . . . . . .5H 63
Waun Leision SA8: Gwaun . . . . .6G 15
(not continuous)
Waunlon CF36: Newt . . . . . . . .3F 125
Waun Penlan SA8: Phyd f . . . . .3C 36
Waun Rd. SA4: Lou . . . . . . . . .6G 55
SA6: Morr . . . . . . . . . . . . . .4A 60
SA15: Llane . . . . . . . . . . . . .5B 42
Waunscil Av. CF31: Bri . . . . . . .1E 127
Waun Sidan SA16: Pem . . . . . . .2A 38
Waun Sterw SA8: Phyd f . . . . . .3C 36
Waun Wen SA12: C'avon . . . . . .4H 91
Waun Wen Rd.
SA1: M'hill, Swan . . . . . . . . .2E 85
Waunwen Ter. SA1: Swan . . . . . .1F 85
Waun y Felin SA4: Penc . . . . . . .4B 68
Waun y Lan Ind. Est.
SA4: P'liw . . . . . . . . . . . . . .6E 47
Waun-y-Pistyll SA5: Tre b . . . . .3F 73
(off Gwynfi St.)
Waverley Cl. SA6: Cly . . . . . . . .4F 49
Waverley Dr. SA3: T Mum . . . .1D 100
Waverley Pk. SA6: Cly . . . . . . .4G 49
Waverley St. SA6: Cly . . . . . . . .5E 49
WDA Ind. Est. SA16: Burr P . . . .3E 39
Weavers Ho. SA1: Swan . . . . . . .5G 5
Weavers Mill SA5: Man . . . . . . .4F 73
Webbons Way SA1: Town . . . . . .6C 72
Webb Pl. SA12: A'von . . . . . . . .5D 96
Weig Fach La. SA5: Ffor F . . . . .5A 72
Weig Gdns. SA5: Gen . . . . . . . .4D 72
Weig La. SA5: Gen . . . . . . . . . .5C 72
Weig Rd. SA5: Gen . . . . . . . . . .5C 72
Welcome La.
SA1: Swan . . . . . . .3E 5 (3G 85)
Well, The CF32: Lale . . . . . . . .5A 126
Wellfield SA2: Dunv . . . . . . . . .2D 82
SA3: Bishop . . . . . . . . . . . . .6G 93
SA15: Llane . . . . . . . . . . . . .4A 42
Wellfield Av. CF36: P'cwl . . . . .4D 124
SA11: Nea . . . . . . . . . . . . . .2B 78
Wellfield Cl. SA4: Gor . . . . . . . .5A 56
Wellfield Cres. CF36: P'cwl . . . .4D 124
Wellfield Rd. SA12: A'von . . . . .2F 97
SA31: Carm . . . . . . . . . . . . . .2E 7
Wellfield Sq. SA11: Nea . . . . . . .2B 78
(not continuous)
Wellington Pl. SA12: A'von . . . . .4E 97
Wellington St.
SA1: Swan . . . . . . .5D 4 (4E 85)
Wellpark SA3: Llang . . . . . . . .5D 104
Wells Cl. SA12: Bag . . . . . . . . .5B 90
Wells Rd. SA12: Bag . . . . . . . . .5B 90

Well St. CF32: Lale . . . . . . . . .5A 126
CF36: P'cwl . . . . . . . . . . . .5C 124
Welsh Ter. SA14: Dafen . . . . . . .4E 43
Wembley SA11: Nea . . . . . . . . .4A 78
Wembley Rd. SA9: Ysta . . . . . . .2D 32
Wenallt Rd. SA11: Tonna . . . . . .4F 65
Wenham Pl. SA11: Nea . . . . . . .1C 78
Wentworth Cres. SA3: May . . . .3D 94
Wern Bank SA11: Brit F . . . . . . .6G 77
Wern Cres. SA10: Skew . . . . . . .3D 76
Wernddu CF32: Sarn . . . . . . . .6C 114
Wern-Ddu Rd. SA18: Amm . . . . .6B 12
(shown as Ffordd Wern-Ddu)
Wernddu Rd. SA8: All . . . . . . . .3D 50
Wern Deg CF35: P'coed . . . . . .5D 123
Werndew CF32: A'knfig . . . . . . .6C 114
Wern Fawr Rd. SA1: Por T . . . . .3C 86
Wern Fraith SA10: Nea . . . . . . .5H 63
Wernlys Rd. CF31: Pen F . . . . .2C 120
Wernsheaf Rd. SA2: May . . . . . .2E 95
WERN-OLAU . . . . . . . . . . . . . .4E 69
Wernoleu Rd. SA18: Amm . . . . .1C 22
Wern Rd. SA1: L'ore . . . . . . . . .4G 73
SA4: Llanm . . . . . . . . . . . . .2G 107
SA9: Ysta . . . . . . . . . . . . . . .2E 33
(shown as Heol y Wern)
SA10: Skew . . . . . . . . . . . . .1D 76
SA13: Marg . . . . . . . . . . . . .2F 103
SA15: Llane . . . . . . . . . . . . .1B 52
SA16: Burr P . . . . . . . . . . . . .2E 39
SA18: Garn . . . . . . . . . . . . .5C 14
Wern Ter. SA1: Por T . . . . . . . .3D 86
SA18: Amm . . . . . . . . . . . . .3C 22
Wern Vw. SA4: Llanm . . . . . . .3G 107
Wern Vs. SA9: Ysta . . . . . . . . . .2E 33
(off Old Wern Rd.)
Wernwood Rd. SA9: Ysta . . . . . .2E 33
Wesley Cl. SA10: Nea A . . . . . . .1F 77
Wesley Pl. SA11: Nea . . . . . . . . .1B 78
(off London Rd.)
SA13: P Tal . . . . . . . . . . . . . .6H 97
Wesley Ter. SA8: P'dwe . . . . . . .5C 36
Wesstfield Ind. Pk.
SA5: Wauna . . . . . . . . . . . . .3E 71
West Av. CF32: Cef C . . . . . . . .1C 118
Westbourne Ct. CF36: P'cwl . . . .4B 124
Westbourne Gro. SA2: Sket . . . . .3H 83
Westbourne Pl. CF36: P'cwl . . . .4C 124
SA3: T Mum . . . . . . . . . . . . .2F 101
Westbourne Rd. SA2: Sket . . . . .3H 83
SA11: Nea . . . . . . . . . . . . . .4H 77
Westbury Bungs. SA15: Llane . . .3B 52
Westbury La.
SA1: Swan . . . . . . .4A 4 (4D 84)
Westbury St.
SA1: Swan . . . . . . .5A 4 (4D 84)
SA15: Llane . . . . . . . . . . . . .3B 52
West Cliff SA3: S'gate . . . . . . . .3H 111
Westcliff SA3: T Mum . . . . . . . .3G 101
Westcliff M. SA3: T Mum . . . . . .3G 101
WEST CROSS . . . . . . . . . . . . . .5F 95
W. Cross Av. SA3: W Cro . . . . . .5F 95
W. Cross La. SA3: W Cro . . . . . .5D 94
West Crossways SA8: P'dwe . . . .4C 36
Westdale Rd. SA5: Blae M . . . . .2A 72
West Dr. CF36: P'cwl . . . . . . . .2A 124
(not continuous)
West End SA4: Penc . . . . . . . . .4G 67
SA13: P Tal . . . . . . . . . . . . . .5H 97
SA15: Llane . . . . . . . . . . . . .3H 41
West End Av.
CF36: Not, P'cwl . . . . . . . . .2B 124
Western Av. CF31: Bri . . . . . . . .2G 127
SA12: Sand . . . . . . . . . . . . . .2A 96
Western Cl. SA3: T Mum . . . . . .2F 101
Western Ct. CF31: Bri . . . . . . . .1C 126
Western La. SA3: T Mum . . . . . .2F 101
Westernmoor Cotts.
SA11: Cim . . . . . . . . . . . . . .3C 78
Westernmoor Rd. SA11: Nea . . . .1C 78
Western Residences
SA2: Sket . . . . . . . . . . . . . . .6H 83
Western Rd. SA6: Cly . . . . . . . .6D 48
SA8: P'dwe . . . . . . . . . . . . .6C 36
Western St.
SA1: Swan . . . . . . .5A 4 (4E 85)
Westfa Rd. SA2: Upl . . . . . . . . .3C 84
Westfield Av. CF31: Bri . . . . . . .6C 120
Westfield Cres. CF36: Not . . . . .1C 124
Westfield Rd. SA5: Wauna . . . . .4C 70
Westgate Cl. CF36: Not . . . . . . .2C 124

Westgrove Ct. SA4: Gor . . . . . . .2A 56
West Ho. Rd. CF31: Bri . . . . . . .6C 120
Westland Av. SA3: W Cro . . . . . .5D 94
Westland Cl. SA4: Lou . . . . . . . .5F 55
Westland SA12: Bag . . . . . . . . .6A 90
Westminster Way CF31: Bri . . . .5B 120
West Pk. Dr. CF36: Not, P'cwl . . .2B 124
Westport Av. SA3: May . . . . . . . .2E 95
West Rd. CF31: Bri . . . . . . . . . .1C 126
SA10: Nea . . . . . . . . . . . . . .6A 116
West St. CF32: A'knfig . . . . . . . .5B 114
SA4: Gor . . . . . . . . . . . . . . .4A 56
Westview Ter. SA15: Llane . . . . . .2A 52
Westward Cl. CF31: Bri . . . . . . .5A 120
SA3: May . . . . . . . . . . . . . . .3F 95
Westward Pl. CF31: Bri . . . . . . .5A 120
West Way SA1: Swan . . . .4C 4 (4F 85)
Westwinds SA3: Lan . . . . . . . . .3C 100
Westwoods Cl. SA5: Wauna . . . .5D 70
Wheatfield Ter. SA1: Swan . . . . .1F 85
Wheatley Av. SA12: Sand . . . . . .4D 96
Wheatley Rd. SA11: Nea . . . . . . .4A 78
Wheatsheaf Dr. SA2: Yfgn . . . . .2B 60
Whimbrels, The CF36: P'cwl . . . .3A 124
White City Rd. SA5: Ffor F . . . . .4A 72
White City Road (Park & Ride)
. . . . . . . . . . . . . . . . . . . .4A 72
White Cl. SA12: Sand . . . . . . . . .1A 96
Whiteford M. SA3: Llanr . . . . . .5C 106
Whiteford National Nature Reserve
. . . . . . . . . . . . . . . . . . . .1F 105
Whitehall Rd. SA5: Por . . . . . . .2C 72
Whitestone Av. SA3: Bishop . . . .1G 99
Whitestone Cl. SA3: May . . . . . .4E 95
Whitestone La. SA3: Newt . . . .1C 100
Whitestone Rd. SA3: Bishop . . . .1G 99
White St. SA1: Swan . . . .3A 4 (3E 85)
Whitethorn Ct. SA5: P'lan . . . . . .3C 72
Whitethorn Dr. CF31: Brack . . . .1G 127
Whitethorn Pl. SA2: Sket . . . . . .4G 83
White Walls
SA1: Swan . . . . . . .3D 4 (3F 85)
White Wheat Cvn. Site, The
CF36: P'cwl . . . . . . . . . . . .2E 125
Whitland Cl. SA5: P'lan . . . . . . .2C 72
Whitley Rd. SA4: Lou . . . . . . . . .5G 55
Whittington Cotts.
SA11: Tonna . . . . . . . . . . . .1G 65
Whittington St. SA11: Nea . . . . . .2A 78
SA11: Tonna . . . . . . . . . . . .3G 65
Whittington Ter. SA4: Gor . . . . . .4C 56
Wick Cotts. CF36: P'cwl . . . . . .4D 124
Wick Rd. CF35: Ewe . . . . . . . . .6D 126
Widegate SA3: S'gate . . . . . . . . .1D 98
Widgeon Cl. CF36: Not . . . . . . .2B 124
Wigan Ter. CF32: Brync . . . . . . .4F 115
Wildbrook SA13: P Tal . . . . . . . .4H 97
Wilden Av. SA13: Marg . . . . . . .1E 103
WILD MILL . . . . . . . . . . . . . . .4D 120
Wild Mill La. CF31: Bri . . . . . . .4D 120
Wild Mill Station (Rail) . . . . . .4D 120
Wilks Row SA1: Swan . . .1D 4 (2F 85)
Willesden Rd. CF31: Bri . . . . . . .5B 120
Willet Cl. SA11: Nea . . . . . . . . .6B 64
William Bowen Cl. SA4: Gow . . .3H 69
William Cl. SA1: Swan . . .4C 4 (4F 85)
William Dennis Av. SA4: Lou . . . .6H 55
William Gammon Dr.
SA3: T Mum . . . . . . . . . . . . .3G 101
William Morris Gdns.
SA1: Por T . . . . . . . . . . . . . .3C 86
Williams Cres. CF32: Brync . . . .5E 115
Williams St. SA4: P'dul . . . . . . . .6F 35
William Ter. CF32: B'myn . . . . . .3D 114
SA16: Burr P . . . . . . . . . . . . .2E 39
William St. SA1: Swan . . .4C 4 (4F 85)
SA3: T Mum . . . . . . . . . . . . .1E 101
SA8: T'nos . . . . . . . . . . . . . .3A 50
SA9: Ystra . . . . . . . . . . . . . .5F 29
William Ter. SA4: Gow . . . . . . . .4E 69
Willowbank SA4: Gow . . . . . . . .5C 70
Willowbrook Gdns. SA3: May . . .3E 95
Willow Cl. CF33: N Cor . . . . . . .6B 112
CF35: Coyc . . . . . . . . . . . . .2C 128
CF36: Newt . . . . . . . . . . . . .3H 125
Willow Ct. SA3: Cly C . . . . . . . .5B 94

Willow Gro. SA12: Bag . . . . . . .4B 90
Willows, The CF31: Brack . . . . .1F 127
CF32: Lale . . . . . . . . . . . . .5A 126
SA15: Llane . . . . . . . . . . . . .2H 41
Willows Pl.
SA1: Swan . . . . . . .2D 4 (3F 85)
Willowturf Ct. CF32: Brync . . . .5D 114
Willow Wlk. SA11: Cim . . . . . . .2F 79
Willow Way SA12: Bag . . . . . . .4A 90
Wilmot St. SA11: Nea . . . . . . . .2B 78
Wimblewood Cl. SA3: W Cro . . . .5F 95
Wimborne Rd. CF35: P'coed . . . .3H 123
Wimbourne Cres.
CF35: P'coed . . . . . . . . . . .2G 123
Wimmerfield Av. SA2: Kill . . . . .3D 82
Wimmerfield Cl. SA2: Kill . . . . .3D 82
Wimmerfield Cres. SA2: Kill . . . .3D 82
Wimmerfield Dr. SA2: Kill . . . . .3E 83
Winch Wen Ind. Est.
SA1: Wins . . . . . . . . . . . . . .2E 75
Windermere Rd. SA6: Morr . . . .6H 59
Windmill Ter.
SA1: St T . . . . . . .1G 5 (2H 85)
Wind Rd. SA9: Ystra . . . . . . . . .1G 33
Windsberry Cl. SA18: Amm . . . . .2F 21
Windsor Cl. SA1: Swan . . . . . . . .2D 4
Windsor Pl. SA3: T Mum . . . . . .1F 101
Windsor Rd. CF36: P'cwl . . . . . .4B 124
SA11: Nea . . . . . . . . . . . . . .1B 78
Windsor St. SA2: Upl . . . . . . . . .3C 84
Windsor Ter. SA4: Gor . . . . . . . .4C 56
Windsor Village
SA12: Bag, P Tal . . . . . . . . .1B 96
Wind St. CF32: Lale . . . . . . . . .6F 119
SA1: Swan . . . . . . .4E 5 (4G 85)
SA11: Nea . . . . . . . . . . . . . .6B 64
SA18: Amm . . . . . . . . . . . . .1H 21
(shown as Stryd-y-Gwynt)
Winifred Rd. SA10: Skew . . . . . .1D 76
WINSH-WEN . . . . . . . . . . . . . .4D 74
Winston St.
SA1: Swan . . . . . . .1D 4 (2F 85)
Withy Pk. SA3: Bishop . . . . . . . .6H 93
Woodbrook Ter. SA16: Burr P . . .3F 39
Woodburn Dr. SA3: W Cro . . . . .6F 95
Wood Cl. SA11: Nea . . . . . . . . .4A 78
Woodcote Cl. SA2: Kill . . . . . . . .4C 82
Woodcote Grn. SA4: Grov . . . . .5B 46
Woodend La. SA3: Lan . . . . . . .2D 100
Woodend Rd. SA15: Llane . . . . . .6B 42
Woodfield Av. SA4: P'liw . . . . . .1F 57
SA18: L'bie . . . . . . . . . . . . . .1F 11
Woodfield Rd. SA18: L'bie . . . . .2F 11
Woodfield St. SA6: Morr . . . . . . .5A 60
SA13: P Tal . . . . . . . . . . . . . .6H 97
Woodfield Ter. SA18: Amm . . . .6D 12
Woodford Rd. SA5: Blae M . . . . .2A 72
Wood Grn. CF31: Bri . . . . . . . .4B 120
Woodland Av. CF35: P'coed . . . .4G 123
CF36: P'cwl . . . . . . . . . . . .4D 124
SA3: W Cro . . . . . . . . . . . . .5E 95
SA13: Marg . . . . . . . . . . . . .2F 103
Woodland Cl. SA10: Skew . . . . .6D 62
SA11: Brit F . . . . . . . . . . . . .5G 77
Woodland Ct. SA2: Sket . . . . . . .4F 83
SA8: P'dwe . . . . . . . . . . . . .5E 37
Woodland Pk. SA6: Ystwe . . . . .1C 60
Woodland Pk. Cvn. Site
SA4: Gow . . . . . . . . . . . . . . .4C 70
Woodland Pl. CF33: N Cor . . . .2D 116
Woodland Ri. CF33: Pen F . . . . .1C 120
Woodland Rd. SA8: P'dwe . . . . .5E 37
SA9: Cwml . . . . . . . . . . . . . .2B 26
(shown as Heol Tir y Coed)
SA10: Cry . . . . . . . . . . . . . . .6H 33
SA10: Skew . . . . . . . . . . . . .6D 62
SA11: Nea . . . . . . . . . . . . . .1C 78
Woodland Row SA12: C'avon . . .4G 91
Woodlands SA4: Gow . . . . . . . .3B 70
SA14: Llwy . . . . . . . . . . . . . .1F 53
Woodlands, The
CF31: Brack . . . . . . . . . . . .6H 121
Woodlands Av. SA6: Cly . . . . . . .4F 49
Woodlands Bus. Pk.
SA9: Ystra . . . . . . . . . . . . . .6G 27
Woodlands Dr. SA11: Cim . . . . . .3E 79
Woodlands La. SA18: Amm . . . . .3B 22
Woodlands Pk. CF33: Ken H . . .6G 113
CF35: P'coed . . . . . . . . . . .3F 123
SA18: Amm . . . . . . . . . . . . .3A 22
(shown as Parc Tir-y-Coed)
Woodlands Pk. Dr. SA10: Nea . . .5B 64
Woodlands Ri. CF31: Bri . . . . . .1B 126
Woodlands Rd. SA4: Lou . . . . . .5G 55
SA4: P'liw . . . . . . . . . . . . . . .1F 57

**Woodlands Ter.**
SA1: Swan . . . . . . . .3A **4** (3E **85**)
SA14: Cross H . . . . . . . . .6C **8**
**Woodland Ter.** SA9: Cwml . . . . .2B **26**
SA10: C'dxtn . . . . . . . . . .4C **64**
**Woodland Way** CF32: Sarn . . . .6D **114**
**Woodmans Ter.** SA9: Ysta . . . . .2E **33**
**Woodmill** SA10: Nea . . . . . . . .5H **63**
(shown as Allt y Felin)
**Woodridge** CF31: Bri . . . . . . .5C **120**
**Woodridge Ct.** SA3: Lan . . . . .2D **100**
**Woodside** SA10: C'dxtn . . . . . .3D **64**
**Woodside Av.** CF31: Bri . . . . . .3E **121**
SA2: Kill . . . . . . . . . . . . .4D **82**
SA11: Nea . . . . . . . . . . . . .1C **78**
**Woodside Cl.** SA2: Kill . . . . . .4D **82**
SA3: Bishop . . . . . . . . . . .6H **93**
**Woodside Cres.** SA6: Cly . . . .4D **48**
**Wood's Row** SA31: Carm . . . . . .3E **7**
**Woodstock Gdns.**
CF35: P'coed . . . . . . . . . .2G **123**
**Wood St.** SA13: Marg . . . . . . .1E **103**
**Woodview** SA4: Gow . . . . . . . .4C **70**
SA11: Cim . . . . . . . . . . . .2E **79**
(not continuous)
**Wood Vw.** SA11: Brit F . . . . .1G **89**
**Woodview Pl.** SA5: Por . . . . . .2B **72**
**Woodview Ter.** SA10: B'och . . .2H **63**
**Woodville Rd.**
SA3: T Mum . . . . . . . . . . .1E **101**
**Woodville St.** SA4: P'dul . . . .5F **35**
**Woolacott M.** SA3: Newt . . . . .1B **100**
**Woollacott Dr.**
SA3: Newt . . . . . . .4B **4** (1B **100**)
**Worcester Ct.** SA7: Swan Ent . . .1D **74**
**Worcester Dr.** SA3: Lan . . . . . .2F **101**
**Worcester Pl.**
SA1: Swan . . . . . . .3E **5** (3G **85**)
SA5: Ffor F . . . . . . . . . . . .4A **72**
(off White City Rd.)
**Worcester Rd.** SA3: Lan . . . . . .2F **101**
**Wordsworth Av.** CF31: Bri . . .5B **120**
**Wordsworth St.**
SA1: Swan . . . . . . .1C **4** (2F **85**)
**Works Rd.** SA8: P'dwe . . . . . .6D **36**
**Wren Av.** SA11: Cim . . . . . . . .3E **79**
**Wren Cl.** CF31: Brack . . . . . .1H **127**
**Wrenwood** SA10: Nea . . . . . . . .5H **63**
(shown as Coed y Dryw)
**Wychtree St.** SA6: Morr . . . . . .1B **74**
**Wychwood Cl.** SA3: Lan . . . . .2E **101**
**Wye Cl.** SA1: Bon . . . . . . . . .5C **74**
**Wyndham Cl.** CF31: Brack . . .5H **121**
SA4: P'dul . . . . . . . . . . . .1B **46**
**Wyndham Ct.**
SA6: Swan Ent . . . . . . . . .6D **60**
**Wyndham Cres.** CF31: Bri . . . .3E **127**

**Wyndham St.** CF31: Bri . . . . . .1E **127**
SA1: Swan . . . . . . . . . . . .4E **85**
SA13: P Tal . . . . . . . . . . .5H **97**
**Wyngarth** SA1: Wins . . . . . . . .3E **75**
**Wynter Ct.** SA5: Tre b . . . . . . .2F **73**
**Wyvern Av.** SA12: Sand . . . . . .2B **96**

# Y

**Yalton** SA3: W Cro . . . . . . . . .5D **94**
**Y Berllan** CF31: Bri . . . . . . . .2A **126**
SA2: Dunv . . . . . . . . . . . .3C **82**
SA9: Ystra . . . . . . . . . . . .1G **33**
SA11: Cim . . . . . . . . . . . .2E **79**
SA13: Llane . . . . . . . . . . .5H **41**
**Y-Berllan** SA6: L'flch . . . . . .4F **59**
**Y Bracty** CF32: Brync . . . . . . .4F **115**
**Y Bwthyn** SA15: Llane . . . . . .2B **52**
(not continuous)
**Y BYNIE** . . . . . . . . . . . . . .3A **54**
**Y Clos** SA9: Cwml . . . . . . . . .6G **17**
**Y Corsydd** SA15: Llane . . . . . .4C **52**
**Y CREUNANT** . . . . . . . . . . . .5H **33**
**Y Cwm** SA16: Burr P . . . . . . .2C **38**
(shown as The Cwm)
**Y Cyswllt** SA4: Tir V . . . . . . .1H **57**
**Y Ddol** SA10: Nea . . . . . . . . .5H **63**
**Y Ddwyberth** SA16: Burr P . . .2E **39**
**Y Deri** SA2: Sket . . . . . . . . . .2G **95**
**Y Derwydd** SA16: Burr P . . . .3D **38**
**Y Dolau** SA6: L'flch . . . . . . . .4F **59**
**Y Drenewydd** SA18: Amm . . . .1F **21**
**Yew Tree Cl.** SA3: W Cro . . . .4E **95**
**Yew Tree Gdns.** SA6: Cly . . . .5E **49**
**Y-Fan** SA14: Llwy . . . . . . . . . .1F **53**
**Y Felin** SA18: Amm . . . . . . . .2A **22**
SA31: Carm . . . . . . . . . . . .3D **6**
(off Glannant Rd.)
**Y Ffowndri** SA15: Llane . . . . .4C **52**
**Y Fron** SA14: Cef . . . . . . . . . .4B **8**
SA15: F'oel . . . . . . . . . . . .3C **42**
**Y-Gaer** SA14: Dafen . . . . . . . .4D **42**
**Y Garn** SA4: Penl . . . . . . . . . .4F **57**
**Y Garreg Filltir** SA31: Carm . . . .2G **7**
(off Priory Cl.)
**Y Garreg Lwyd** SA4: L'edi . . . .6E **31**
**Y Gefnen** SA7: L'smlt . . . . . . .2G **75**
**Y Geibren**
SA4: Ffor, Hendy . . . . . . . .3B **34**
**Y Gelli** SA7: Birch . . . . . . . . .5A **62**
**Y Gilfach** SA9: Ysta . . . . . . . .1E **33**
SA10: L'dcy . . . . . . . . . . . .4B **76**
**Y Gilwern** SA9: Ysta . . . . . . . .2E **33**
**Y Glyn** SA2: Dunv . . . . . . . . .2C **82**
SA14: Cef . . . . . . . . . . . . .4A **8**
**Y Goedlan** SA9: Cwml . . . . . . .2B **26**
**Y GOETRE-HEN** . . . . . . . . . .1A **114**

**Y Gorlan** CF31: Bri . . . . . . . .4D **120**
SA2: Dunv . . . . . . . . . . . .3C **82**
**Y Gorsedd** SA18: Amm . . . . . .6H **11**
**Y Groes** CF32: Sarn . . . . . . . .6E **115**
**Y Gwernydd** SA7: Glais . . . . . .6G **49**
**Y Lan** CF35: P'coed . . . . . . . .2H **123**
**Y Llanerch** SA4: P'liw . . . . . .5F **47**
SA31: Carm . . . . . . . . . . . .3F **7**
**Y Llest** CF31: Pen F . . . . . . . .2B **120**
**Y Llwyn** SA15: Llane . . . . . . .1D **52**
**Y Llwyni** SA6: L'flch . . . . . . . .4E **59**
**Ymyl-yr-Afon** SA10: A'dul . . . .2F **65**
**Ynysafan Ter.** SA12: C'avon . . .5H **91**
**Ynysallan Rd.**
SA7: Birch, Ystwe . . . . . . . .3E **61**
**Ynysawdre Swimming Pool** . . .4C **114**
**Ynyscedwyn Ind. Est.**
SA9: Ystra . . . . . . . . . . . .6H **27**
**Ynyscedwyn Ironworks Pk.** . . .1H **33**
**Ynyscedwyn Rd.** SA9: Ystra . . .1H **33**
**Ynysderw Rd.** SA8: P'dwe . . . .6D **36**
**YNYSFORGAN** . . . . . . . . . . . .2B **60**
**Ynys-Las** SA14: Llwy . . . . . . .1F **53**
**Ynyslas** CF36: P'cwl . . . . . . . .3E **125**
**Ynys-Lee** SA12: C'avon . . . . . .6H **91**
**YNYSMEUDWY** . . . . . . . . . . .3G **37**
**Ynys-Meudwy Rd.**
SA8: Cilm, Ynys . . . . . . . . .3F **37**
**Ynys Newydd Rd.** SA2: Sket . . .6G **83**
**Ynyspenllwch Rd.** SA6: Cly . . .5G **49**
**Ynystawe Rd.** SA13: P Tal . . . .3H **97**
**YNYSTAWE** . . . . . . . . . . . . . .6D **48**
**Ynystawe Rd.** SA6: Ystwe . . . . .1D **60**
**Ynysteg** CF32: Ton . . . . . . . . .4D **114**
**Ynyswen** SA14: F'oel . . . . . . . .4C **42**
**Ynys Werdd** SA4: Penl . . . . . . .4G **57**
**Ynys-y-Bont** SA10: Cry . . . . . .4H **33**
**Ynys y Farm** Rd. SA15: Llane . .2H **41**
**Ynysygerwn Cres.**
SA10: A'dul . . . . . . . . . . . .2G **65**
**Ynysygerwyn Av.** SA10: A'dul . . .2G **65**
**Ynys y Gorod** SA13: P Tal . . . .3H **97**
**YNYSYGWAS** . . . . . . . . . . . .6H **91**
**Ynysygwas Hill** SA12: C'avon . . .6H **91**
**Ynysygwas Ter.** SA12: C'avon . . .6H **91**
**YNYSYMAERDY** . . . . . . . . . . .5A **78**
**Ynysymaerdy Rd.**
SA11: Brit F . . . . . . . . . . . .6H **77**
**Ynys-y-Mond Rd.** SA7: Glais . . .6H **49**
**Ysas** SA8: . . . . . . . . . . . . . . .2D **50**
**Ynys y Plant** SA3: W Cro . . . . . .5F **95**
(off Mumbles Rd.)
**Ynys y Wern** SA12: C'avon . . . .6H **91**
**York Ct.** SA1: Swan . . . . .5E **5** (4G **85**)
**York Pk.** CF31: Bri . . . . . . . . .3G **127**
**York Pl.** CF31: Bri . . . . . . . . .1E **127**
SA13: P Tal . . . . . . . . . . .4H **97**

**York Rd.** CF31: Bri . . . . . . . . .3G **127**
**York St.** SA1: Swan . . . . .4E **5** (4G **85**)
**Young Bus. Cen.** SA12: Sand . . .1A **96**
**Y PIL** . . . . . . . . . . . . . . . . .6E **113**
**Yr Aelwyd** SA31: Carm . . . . . . .5F **7**
**Yr Allt** SA14: L'nch . . . . . . . . .3B **44**
**Yr Aran** SA2: Dunv . . . . . . . . .1C **82**
**Yr Efail** CF35: Treoes . . . . . . .3D **128**
**Yr Elain** SA2: Dunv . . . . . . . . .2C **82**
**Yr Encil** CF31: Bri . . . . . . . . .4D **120**
**Yr Hafan** SA1: Swan . . . . . . . .4B **86**
**Yr Hafod** SA6: L'flch . . . . . . . .4F **59**
SA15: Llane . . . . . . . . . . . .5B **42**
SA18: Saron . . . . . . . . . . .6C **10**
**Yr Hendre** CF33: Ken H . . . . . .4F **113**
**Yr Hen Gorlan** SA4: Gow . . . . .3B **70**
**Yr Rhodfa** SA16: Burr P . . . . . .2F **39**
SA31: Carm . . . . . . . . . . . .3F **7**
**Yr Rhos** SA15: Llane . . . . . . . .5C **42**
**Yr Orsaf** SA18: Garn . . . . . . . .5D **14**
**Yr Ynys** CF33: N Cor . . . . . . .6D **112**
**Ysbryd-y-Coed** CF31: Pen F . . .3C **120**
**Ysgol St.** SA1: Por T . . . . . . . .3B **86**
**Ysgubor Fâch St.** SA1: Swan . . .6F **73**
**Ysguthan Rd.** SA2: A'von . . . . .4E **97**
**Yspitty Rd.** SA14: Byn . . . . . . .5C **54**
**YSTALYFERA** . . . . . . . . . . . . .2E **33**
**Ystrad Cl.** SA31: John . . . . . . .6B **6**
(shown as Clos Ystrad)
**Ystrad Dr.** SA31: John . . . . . . .6C **6**
**Ystrad Einon** SA4: Gor . . . . . .5A **56**
**YSTRAD FAWR** . . . . . . . . . . .6C **120**
**Ystrad Fawr** CF31: Bri . . . . . .1C **126**
**Ystrad-Fawr Vs.** SA9: Ystra . . .5B **28**
**YSTRADGYNLAIS** . . . . . . . . . .5A **28**
**YSTRADGYNLAIS COMMUNITY**
**HOSPITAL** . . . . . . . . . . . .1H **33**
**YSTRADOWEN** . . . . . . . . . . . .1B **26**
**Ystrad Rd.** SA5: Ffor F, Wauna . .5F **71**
**YSTRAD WAUN** . . . . . . . . . . .1E **123**
**Ystradwaun** CF35: P'coed . . . .2F **123**
**Y Stryd Fawr** SA18: Amm . . . . .1A **22**
**Ystwyth Pl.** SA6: Clase . . . . . .5G **59**
**Y Talar** SA31: Carm . . . . . . . . .5F **7**
**Y Waun** SA14: Llane . . . . . . . .6F **43**
**Y Waun Fach** SA6: L'flch . . . . .4E **59**
**Y-Wern** SA6: L'flch . . . . . . . . .4E **59**

# Z

**Zammit Cres.** SA15: Llane . . . . .1D **52**
**Zig-Zag La.** CF36: Newt, P'cwl .6E **117**
**Zion Row** SA15: Llane . . . . . . .6B **42**
**Zoar Rd.** SA9: Ysta . . . . . . . . .2E **33**
(shown as Heol Zoar)
SA11: Nea . . . . . . . . . . . .6B **64**
**Zouch St.** SA5: Man . . . . . . . . .5F **73**

Copyright of Geographers' A-Z Map Company Ltd.

No reproduction by any method whatsoever of any part of this publication is permitted without the prior consent of the copyright owners.

The representation on the maps of a road, track or footpath is no evidence of the existence of a right of way.

## SAFETY CAMERA INFORMATION

PocketGPSWorld.com's CamerAlert is a self-contained speed and red light camera warning system for SatNavs and Android or Apple iOS smartphones/tablets. Visit www.cameralert.com to download.

Safety camera locations are publicised by the Safer Roads Partnership which operates them in order to encourage drivers to comply with speed limits at these sites. It is the driver's absolute responsibility to be aware of and to adhere to speed limits at all times.

By showing this safety camera information it is the intention of Geographers' A-Z Map Company Ltd. to encourage safe driving and greater awareness of speed limits and vehicle speed. Data accurate at time of printing.

Printed and bound in the United Kingdom by Polestar Wheatons Ltd., Exeter.

Hawlfraint Geographers' A-Z Map Co. Ltd.

Ni chaniateir atgynhyrchu, trwy unrhyw gyfrwng bynnag, unrhyw ran o'r cyhoeddiad hwn heb sicrhau caniatâd ymlaen llaw gan berchnogion yr hawlfraint.

Nid yw'r ffaith bod ffordd, trac neu lwybr wedi eu nodi ar y map yn brawf bod hawl tramwyo yn bodoli.

## GWYBODAETH CAMERA DIOGELWCH

Mae CamerAlert gan PocketGPSWorld.com yn system rybuddio hunangynhwysol am gyfyngiadau cyflymder a goleuadau coch ar gyfer Llywiau Lloeren a ffonau clyfar/llechi cyfrifiadurol Android neu Apple iOS. Ewch i www.cameralert.co.uk i'w lwytho i lawr.

Cyhoeddir lleoliadau camerâu diogelwch gan y Bartneriaeth Ffyrdd Mwy Diogel sy'n eu gweithredu er mwyn annog gyrwyr i gydymffurfio â chyfyngiadau cyflymder yn y mannau hyn.
Cyfrifoldeb llwyr y gyrrwr yw bod yn ymwybodol o gyfyngiadau cyflymder, a chadw atyn nhw, bob amser.

Drwy ddangos y wybodaeth am gamerâu diogelwch, bwriad Geographers' A-Z Map Company Ltd., yw annog gyrru diogel a gwell ymwybyddiaeth o gyfyngiadau cyflymder a chyflymder cerbydau. Roedd y data'n gywir pan aed i'r wasg.

Wedi'i argraffu a'i rwymo yn y Deyrnas Unedig gan Polestar Wheatons Ltd., Exeter.